Memories
of the
Black Sea Germans

HIGHLIGHTS OF THEIR HISTORY AND HERITAGE

by

Joseph S. Height

Impendere vitae veritatem

Associated German-Russian Sponsors   USA-CAN.

Other works by the author:

Paradise on the Steppe
Homesteaders on the Steppe
Folksongs of our Forefathers
History of the Mannheim Heidt Kinship
Die Muddersproch der Kutschurganer

Translations:

The Gold of Goethe
The German Russians
The Emigration from Germany to Russia
Pioneer History of the Stang Kinship

To my dear wife *Anneliese* and
daughters *Margaret* and *Teresa*,
for their love and loyal support,
their keen interest and assistance.

Eternity past and Eternity to come
Impinge on your life.
The ancestors gave you
Your existence and striving,
The descendants carry on
Your aspirations and yearning,
And between the two you ought
To preserve and enhance
What you have inherited,
A valuable link
In the unending chain.

(O. Kröpklin)

Foreword

In two earlier works, *Paradise on the Steppe* and *Homesteaders on the Steppe,* the attempt was made to present a cultural history of both the Catholic and the Lutheran mother colonies in the three large enclaves above the Black Sea. Both books, I am pleased to note, were accorded a warm and even enthusiastic reception by our people of German-Russian background in the United States and in Canada.

Although the two complementary volumes represent the most comprehensive history ever written about the Black Sea colonies, there was still a considerable amount of historical and cultural material which the lack of space prevented me from including in either of the two books. However, rather than consign this interesting material to the limbo of oblivion, I decided to publish it in a third volume which would serve as a supplement to the other two, and thus constitute a closely related trilogy.

As was to be expected, the new book contains a rich variety of topics comprising documentaries and diaries, reports and reminiscences, historical and cultural essays, stories in dialect, poems in both German and English, and a comprehensive history of a large German-Russian settlement in western Canada.

Among the important historical documents included in this book are the complete texts, in English translations, of Catherine's famous manifesto and the rescripts of Czar Alexander I. In addition to a reprint of the fascinating diaries of the Danube journey, I decided to include the earliest report on pioneer life contained in the Mariental letter. For the benefit of the readers of the *Paradise* book, where certain materials did not appear, I have also included a reprint of three topics from the *Homesteaders* book, namely the Danube Expedition of 1817, the life of Duc de Richelieu, and Koch's visit to the German colonies in 1838. Completely new material is contained in my detailed study of the migration routes to the Black Sea, the emigration from Alsace to Russia, and the achievements of the colonists. Of special interest is the hitherto unpublished story of the "Sorrows of a refugee mother." In a subsequent chapter on Customs and Traditions, I have included a collection of German-Russian nursery rhymes, an account of a three-day wedding in Krasna, and an essay on the Origin of the *Christbaum* and the *Christkindel.* Another chapter presents brief accounts of four widely scattered German colonies in South Russia, namely Krasna and Balmas in Bessarabia, Heidelberg in the Molotchna, and Rosental in the Crimea. An entire chapter is devoted to humorous stories in the Kutschurgan dialect of Selz. A subsequent chapter contains an anthology of German poems, generally with

IV

English translations, dealing with events and experiences of the German colonists. A special chapter contains the reminiscences of early German-Russian settlers in North Dakota. In chapter fifteen I have attempted to present a comprehensive account of the large Kutschurgan settlement in Saskatchewan where I was born and raised. I think that the story of this community can, in many ways, be regarded as fairly typical of the experiences of other German-Russians settlements on the prairie of western Canada and the Dakotas.

In publishing this final volume on the history of the Black Sea Germans, I am pleased to express my gratitude to the thousands of families, from Texas to Alaska and from the Mississippi to the Pacific, who have become interested in the epic story of their forefathers. Through their generous cooperation and support they have helped to preserve that story for the present and the future generations of descendants.

Joseph S. Height

Acknowledgements

I would like to extend my sincere thanks and appreciation to all who have helped me in the preparation and production of this book. I am much indebted to Anton B. Heit, August Hoffart, Steve Brandle, John Volk, Anton J. Mitzel, Edward Weber, Lambert Schneider, and Tony Laturnus, for their dedicated help in reconstructing the map of the pioneer homesteads in the districts of Tramping Lake and Revenue. I am very grateful to Alphonse and Catherine (Gutenberg) Hoffart, Mrs. Magdalena Volk, Norman McKenzie, and Balthasar S. Heit for providing me with a number of rare historical photos of the pioneer era in western Saskatchewan.

I also wish to express my grateful appreciation to Sister Louise V. Heit, my wife Anneliese, and my daughter Margaret Ann for their painstaking help in proofreading the English and the German texts of various chapters in the book, and to my daughter Teresa Kay, who assisted me faithfully in planning the format and layout of the book.

Last but not least, I am profoundly grateful to the one hundred and one *Landsleute* listed in the "Honor Roll of Sponsors" for their contributions to the publishing fund that helped to finance the production costs of this volume.

RECOGNITION OF CO–PUBLISHERS

The publication of this book was largely made possible through the good-will and generosity of *Landsleute* who responded whole-heartedly to a pressing appeal for financial support. In doing so, they manifested a laudable interest in the ethnic history and heritage of their colonist forefathers. In grateful acknowledgement of their role in helping to establish a worthy historical memorial to those pioneering ancestors and in making it possible to preserve a valuable cultural heirloom for their descendants, the author is pleased to inscribe the names of the following donors in the book's *Honor Roll of Sponsors.*

Mr & Mrs Alex C. **Backmeyer**, Kamloops, B.C.
Mr & Mrs Melvin **Bamesberger**, Council Bluffs, IA
Norris A & Linda (Laturnus) **Berg**, Whitewater, MT
Mr. John **Bespflug**, Vancouver, B.C.
Rev. Longinus M. **Bitz**, Fargo, ND
Mr and Mrs W.A. **Bullinger**, Grand Prairie, TX
Leo & Theres (Reiter) **Burkhartsmeier**, Portland, OR
Michael & Lorna **Burkhartsmeier**, Portland, OR
Mr. Lewis H. **Christman**, Forth Worth, TX
Hildegard Neu **Danburg**, Baton Rouge, LA
William H. & Lucile H. **Deis**, Belmont, CA
Dr. and Mrs Charles **Eckroth**, St. Joseph, MO
Dr. Arthur **Engel**, Aberdeen, SD
Dr. Clifford **Felchle**, MD, San Jose, CA
Mr & Mrs M.N. **Ferderer**, St. Paul, MN
Mr. Val B. **Fischer**, Portland, OR
Egidius & Elli **Fitterer**, Victoria, B.C.
Mr. John F. **Fitterer**, Victoria, B.C.
Fred & Edith **Fleck**, Rugby, ND
Lucas & Myrtle **Folk**, Osburn, ID
Mr & Mrs Vincent **Folk**, Regina, SASK.
Mr. Raynard **Freidig**, Center, ND
Edmund A. and Olive M. **Gress**, Tacoma, WA
Mrs Madeline (Volk) **Grosser**, Edmonton, ALTA.
Agnes Leibham **Haney**, Houston, TX
John & Maria **Heidt**, Regina, SASK.
Adam J. & Blanche **Heintz**, Arvada, Colo.
Balthasar L. **Heit**, Dundas, ONT.
Sr. Louise V. **Heit**, Saskatoon, SASK.
Albert & Elizabeth **Herrmann**, Woodland, CA
John & Margaret **Hirsch**, Medicine Hat, ALTA.
Alphonse & Katie **Hoffart**, Tramping Lake, SASK.
Mr & Mrs Mike **IBACH**, West Fargo, ND
Mr. Hal **Kaiser**, Denver, Colo.
Elmer & Doris **Ketterling**, Yakima, WA
Gerald A. **Klein**, Tustin, CA
Gerald J. & Florence **Klein**, San Juan Capistrano
Leo & Anna **Koehler**, Wichita Falls, TX
Mr and Mrs Herbert **Lehr**, Lodi, CA

Mr. Raymond H. **Leibbrandt**, Baltimore, MD
Valentine & Ann Marie (Dukart) **Leible**, St. Louis
Henry M. & Virginia **Leopoldus**, Aurora, Colo.
Dr. and Mrs. George T. **Mastio**, MD, Wichita, KS
Rockus & Stella **Makelki**, Weyburn, SASK.
Henry & Brita **Makelky**, Beach, ND
Mr. Arlo C. **Mehlhaff**, Eureka, S.D.
Mr & Mrs Carl B. **Mettler**, Lodi, CA
Elizabeth **Mettler**, Sacramento, CA
Lyle & Edith L. **Miller**, Amarillo, TX
Mr & Mrs George **Mosbrucker**, Pomona, CA
Josef & Monika **Pfeifer**, Hartland, WI
George H. **Reinschmidt**, Dallas, TX
Everett & Peggy **Renner**, Bell, WN
Miss Julie **Renner**, Tacoma, WA
John J. & Rose **Renner**, Tacoma, WA
Mr and Mrs Len **Renner**, Tacoma, WA
Mr & Mrs Anthony T. **Schlachter**, Bow Island, ALT.
Mr. Gottlieb **Schlepp**, St. Francis, KS
Chris. M. **Schmaltz**, Rosell, N.M.
Martin & Ingeborg **Schneider**, Tacoma, WA
Peter & Mary **Schroh**, Manning, ALTA.
Mr & Mrs W.H. **Senger**, Gully, MN
Dann A. **Sinema**, Tucson, Ariz.
Dr. and Mrs Arthur W. **Spiry**, MD, Mobridge, SD
Edwin A. & Esther H. **Stebner**, Sacramento, CA
Mr. James P. **Stein**, Inglewood, CA
Mr & Mrs Richard H. **Stoller**, Columbus, GA
Willard & Theresa **Struck**, Leader, SASK.
Helen A. **Thurmond**, Orlando, FLA
Mr & Mrs Frank **Usselman**, Brantford, ONT.
Mr. J. Floyd **Weber**, Yakima, WN
Mr & Mrs Anton **Weisgerber**, Bremerton, WN
Mr. Herman D. **Wildermuth**, Yucca Valley, CA
Mr. John W. **Wirtz**, Port Huron, MI
Dr. & Mrs Robert J. **Wolf**, MD, Denver, Colo.
Mr. Richard **Zender**, Vallejo, CA
Mr. Lawrence H. **Zerr**, Salt Lake City, UT
Mr. Bernard Scherr, Collyer, KS

IN MEMORIAM CONTRIBUTIONS

In Memory of   *Donated by*

In Memory of	Donated by
Ralph & Rose **Bespflug**, Oyen, ALTA.	John **Bespflug**, Vancouver, B.C.
Mr & Mrs Theodore **Bullinger**, Henrietta, TX	Ted F. **Bullinger**, Tulsa, OK
Friedrich & Rosine **Burkhardt**, Blumenfeld, ND	John & Emma **Burkhardt**, Myrtle Creek, OR
Michael **Burkhartsmeier**, Sr.	Mich. **Burkhartsmeier**, Portland, OR
Peter **Decker**, Rose **Froehlich**, and	Bernadette (Decker) **Pluomen**, Eden Prairie, N.M.
Philip & Regina (Brinster) **Urlacher**	
John V. **Eckroth**, Fort Rice, ND	Mrs Ethel (John J.) **Eckroth**, Mandan, ND
Paul & Elizabeth (Zerr) **Ferderer**, St. Paul	Mr & Mrs M.N. **Ferderer**, St. Paul, MN
Helen **Frison**	Frank **Frison**, St. Paul, MN
Joseph & Elizabeth **Hartman**, Toppenish, WN	Mr & Mrs E.A. **Stebner**, Sacramento, CA
Mr & Mrs John **Hauck**; Mr. Leonard **Sali**	Mr & Mrs Henry **Hauck**, Yakima, WN
Friedr. & Lydia (Jahraus) **Holzwarth**, Greenway, SD	Milbert & Charlene **Holzwarth**, Portland, OR
Mrs Caroline **Herauf**, Kronau, SASK., and	Mr & Mrs Peter P. **Herauf**, Lethbridge, ALTA.
Mrs Maria **Schmidt**, Camrose, ALTA.	
Michael **Hopfinger**, Bison, S.D.	Anton **Hopfinger**, Aberdeen, SD
Fred **Job**, Tappen, ND	Miss Emma **Job**, Oroville, WN
Mr & Mrs Christian J. **Kaiser**	Rose **MacCharles**, Great Falls, MT
Mrs Peter **Kary**	Peter **Kary**, Allan, SASK.
Lorenz & Katherina (Leier) **Klein**	Mr & Mrs Ray **Fletcher**, Oregon City, OR
Jakob & Elizabeth (Liebig) **Kranzler**, Lodi, CA	Mrs Wm. **Kranzler**, Flagstaff, AR
Anton & Melonia **Leboldus**, Qu'Appelle, SASK.	Col. Michael J. **Leboldus**, Dunrobin, ONT.
Joseph **Leibham** & Anna Feth, Houston TX	Mrs J. W. **Haney**, Jr., Houston, TX
Frances (Reichert) **Mastio**	Dr. Geo. J. **Mastio**, Wichita, KS
Remigus & Marie Eva **Martian**, Allan, SASK.	Mr. Jack **Martian**, Burlington, ONT.
Lawrence W. **Mitzel** & son Joseph	Marge **Mitzel**, Foremost, ALTA.
John & Francis (Boehm) **Mook**, Mandan, ND	Elizabeth **Mettler**, Sacramento, CA
Ferdinand & Katherina (Volk) **Mueller**, Selz/Od.	Georgianna **Hansen**, Mount Angel, OR
Arthur G. **Sayler**, Portland, OR	Cordelia M. **Sayler**, Portland, OR
Peter & Magdalen **Scherr**	Arthur A. **Scherr**, Omaha, NE
Peter **Schlepp** of Rohrbach/Od. St. Francis, KS	Keith & Edna **Reichert**, Boise, ID
John & Elizabeth (Däffe) **Schmidt**, Peterstal/Od.	Violet H. **Delagasse**, Vancouver, WN
Harry J. & Johanna (Tschetter) **Schmidt**, Odessa	Rose Marie **Harshman**, Vancouver, WN
Julius & Agnes **Schmidt**, Portland, OR	Mary Anna **Welch**, Port Angeles, WN
Peter J. & William **Schmidt**, Odessa/Russia	Martha A. **Brohman**, Vancouver, WN
Mrs Maria **Schmidt**, Camrose, ALTA.	Mr & Mrs Peter **Herauf**, Lethbridge, ALTA.
Martin **Schurr**, Oakley, KS	George **Schurr**, Oakley, KS
Philip & Veronica (Heck) **Stark**	Gary K. **Stark**, La Palma, CA
Joseph & Anna **Thomas**, Killdeer, ND	Stella **Hartmann**, Killdeer, ND
Leo **Torscher**, Bow Island, ALTA.	Ed **Torscher**, Bow Island, ALTA.
Paul & Catherine (Fast) **Tschetter**, Huttersdorf	Bertha L. **Krause**, Ridgefield, WN
Joh. **Walz**, Jr., Freeman, SD; Jakob **Neu**, Menno, SD	Mrs Dwight S. **Danburg**, Greenwell Springs, LA
John & Ann **Weisgerber**, Watson, SASK.	Elizabeth **Weisgerber**, Las Vegas, NEV
Mr & Mrs Anton **Wolf**, Windthorst, TX	Mike **Wolf** & brothers, Windthorst, TX
George A. **Zimmerman**, Rapid City, SD	Miss Mary E. **Zimmerman**, Rapid City, SD

Contents

I.   Czarist Plans of Colonization

1. The Manifesto of Catherine the Great

Catharine II, Czarina of Russia 1762-1796

Alexander I, Czar of Russia 1801-1825

By the Grace of God!

We, Catherine the second, Empress and Autocrat of all the Russians at Moscow, Kiev, Vladimir, Novgorod, Czarina of Kasan, Czarina of Astrachan, Czarina of Siberia, Lady of Pleskow and Grand Duchess of Smolensko, Duchess of Esthonia and Livland, Carelia, Twer, Yugoria, Permia, Viatka and Bulgaria and others; Lady and Grand Duchess of Novgorod in the Netherland of Chernigov, Resan, Rostov, Yaroslav, Belooseria, Udoria, Obdoria, Condinia, and Ruler of the entire North region and Lady of the Yurish, of the Cartalinian and Grusinian czars and the Cabardinian land, of the Cherkessian and Gorisian princes and the lady of the manor and sovereign of many others.

As We are sufficiently aware of the vast extent of the lands within Our Empire, We perceive, among other things, that a considerable number of regions are still uncultivated which could easily and advantageously be made available for productive use of population and settlement. Most of the lands hold hidden in their depth an inexhaustible wealth of all kinds of precious ores and metals, and because they are well-provided with forests, rivers and lakes, and located close to the sea for purpose of trade, they are

---

✱ This first authoritative English translation was made from the official German text by Dr. Jos. S. Height and published in 1972 in Karl Stumpp, "The Emigration from Germany to Russia in the Years 1763 to 1862," Tübingen.

also most convenient for the development and growth of many kinds of manufacturing, plants, and various installations. This induced Us to issue the manifesto which was published last Dec. 4, 1762, for the benefit of all Our loyal subjects. However, inasmuch as We made only a summary announcement of Our pleasure to the foreigners who would like to settle in Our Empire, we now issue for a better understanding of Our intention the following decree which We hereby solemnly establish and order to be carried out to the full.

1.

We permit all foreigners to come into Our Empire, in order to settle in all the gouvernements, just as each one may desire.

2.

After arrival, such foreigners can report for this purpose not only to the Guardianship Chancellery established for foreigners in Our residence, but also, if more convenient, to the governor or commanding officer in one of the border-towns of the Empire.

3.

Since those foreigners who would like to settle in Russia will also include some who do not have sufficient means to pay the required travel costs, they can report to our ministers in foreign courts, who will not only transport them to Russia at Our expense, but also provide them with travel money.

4.

As soon as these foreigners arrive in Our residence and report at the Guardianship Chancellery or in a border-town, they shall be required to state their true decision, whether their real desire is to be enrolled in the guild of merchants or artisans, and become citizens, and in what city; or if they wish to settle on free, productive land in colonies and rural areas, to take up agriculture or some other useful occupation. Without delay, these people will be assigned to their destination, according to their own wishes and desires. From the following register it can be seen in which regions of Our Empire free and suitable lands are still available. However, besides those listed, there are many more regions and all kinds of land where We will likewise permit people to settle, just as each one chooses for his best advantage.

5.

Upon arrival in Our Empire, each foreigner who intends to become a settler and has reported to the Guardianship Chancellery or in other border-towns of Our Empire and, as already prescribed in § 4, has declared his decision, must take the oath of allegiance in accordance with his religious rite.

6.

In order that the foreigners who desire to settle in Our Empire may realize the extent of Our benevolence to their benefit and advantage, this is Our will —:

1. We grant to all foreigners coming into Our Empire the free and unrestricted practice of their religion according to the precepts and usage of their Church. To those, however, who intend to settle not in cities but in colonies and villages on uninhabited lands we grant the freedom to build churches and belltowers, and to maintain the necessary number of priests and church servants, but not the construction of monaster-

ies. On the other hand, everyone is hereby warned not to persuade or induce any of the Christian co-religionists living in Russia to accept or even assent to his faith or join his religious community, under pain of incurring the severest punishment of Our laws. This prohibition does not apply to the various nationalities on the borders of Our Empire who are attached to the Mahometan faith. We permit and allow everyone to win them over and make them subject to the Christian religion in a decent way.

2. None of the foreigners who have come to settle in Russia shall be required to pay the slightest taxes to Our treasury, nor be forced to render regular or extraordinary services, nor to billet troops. Indeed, everybody shall be exempt from all taxes and tribute in the following manner: those who have been settled as colonists with their families in hitherto uninhabited regions will enjoy 30 years of exemption; those who have established themselves, at their own expense, in cities as merchants and tradesmen in Our Residence St. Petersburg or in the neighboring cities of Livland, Esthonia, Ingermanland, Carelia and Finland, as well as in the Residential city of Moscow, shall enjoy 5 years of tax-exemption. Moreover, each one who comes to Russia, not just for a short while but to establish permanent domicile, shall be granted free living quarters for half a year.

3. All foreigners who settle in Russia either to engage in agriculture and some trade, or to undertake to build factories and plants will be offered a helping hand and the necessary loans required for the construction of factories useful for the future, especially of such as have not yet been built in Russia.

4. For the building of dwellings, the purchase of livestock needed for the farmstead, the necessary equipment, materials, and tools for agriculture and industry, each settler will receive the necessary money from Our treasury in the form of an advance loan without any interest. The capital sum has to be repaid only after ten years, in equal annual instalments in the following three years.

5. We leave to the discretion of the established colonies and village the internal constitution and jurisdiction, in such a way that the persons placed in authority by Us will not interfere with the internal affairs and institutions. In other respects the colonists will be liable to Our civil laws. However, in the event that the people would wish to have a special guardian or even an officer with a detachment of disciplined soldiers for the sake of security and defense, this wish would also be granted.

6. To every foreigner who wants to settle in Russia We grant complete duty-free import of his property, no matter what it is, provided, however, that such property is for personal use and need, and not intended for sale. However, any family that also brings in unneeded goods for sale will be granted free import on goods valued up to 300 rubles, provided that the family remains in Russia for at least 10 years. Failing which, it will be required, upon its departure, to pay the duty both on the incoming and outgoing goods.

7. The foreigners who have settled in Russia shall not be drafted against their will into the military or the civil service during their entire stay here. Only after the lapse of the years of tax-exemption can they be required to provide labor service for the country. Whoever wishes to enter military service will receive, besides his regular pay, a gratuity of 30 rubles at the time he enrolls in the regiment.

8. As soon as the foreigners have reported to the Guardianship Chancellery or to our border towns and declared their decision to travel to the interior of the Empire and establish domicile there, they will forthwith receive food rations and free transportation to their destination.

9. Those among the foreigners in Russia who establish factories, plants, or firms, and produce goods never before manufactured in Russia, will be permitted to sell and export freely for ten years, without paying export duty or excise tax.

10. Foreign capitalists who build factories, plants, and concerns in Russia at their own expense are permitted to purchase serfs and peasants needed for the operation of the factories.

11. We also permit all foreigners who have settled in colonies or villages to establish market days and annual market fairs as they see fit, without having to pay any dues or taxes to Our treasury.

7.

All the afore-mentioned privileges shall be enjoyed not only by those who have come into our country to settle there, but also their children and descendants, even though these are born in Russia, with the provision that their years of exemption will be reckoned from the day their forebears arrived in Russia.

8.

After the lapse of the stipulated years of exemption, all the foreigners who have settled in Russia are required to pay the ordinary moderate contributions and, like our other subjects, provide labor-service for their country. Finally, in the event that any foreigner who has settled in Our Empire and has become subject to Our authority should desire to leave the country, We shall grant him the liberty to do so, provided, however, that he is obligated to remit to Our treasury a portion of the assets he has gained in this country; that is, those who have been here from one to five years will pay one-fifth, while those who have been here for five or more years will pay one-tenth. Thereafter each one will be permitted to depart unhindered anywhere he pleases to go.

10.

If any foreigner desiring to settle in Russia wishes for certain reasons to secure other privileges or conditions besides those already stated, he can apply in writing or in person to our Guardianship Chancellery, which will report the petition to Us. After examining the circumstances, We shall not hesitate to resolve the matter in such a way that the petitioner's confidence in Our love of justice will not be disappointed.

Given at the Court of Peter, July 22, 1763
in the Second Year of Our Reign.

The original was signed by Her Imperial Supreme Majesty's own hand in the following manner:

Printed by the Senate, July 25, 1763

2. Vorontzov's Volga Paradise

A broadsheet signed by Count Alexander Voronzov, Russian ambassador to the Hague, giving a description of the benefits and advantages
which her Imperial Russian Majesty, Catherine II, is pleased to grant
to the colonists to be settled in the Volga River region.

Her Imperial Majesty and Autocrat of all the Russians has been pleased to
graciously permit German foreigners to be settled in one of the most fruitful
and advantageous regions on both sides of the great Volga River. The region
lies between 50 and 52 degrees of north latitude, not far from the city of
Saratov and has a climate like that of Lyons in France and is better than that
of the Upper Rhine. This region, which is very healthful and extremely fertile, lies in a beautiful flat plain where the soil consists of black humus to a
depth of two or three feet. Since the land has never been plowed, it is most
suitable for agriculture and the production of all kinds of grain. All seed
grain, without the use of any fertilizer, can produce a fifteen or sixteen-fold
crop.

For the raising of cattle there are incomparably good meadowlands and
the grass, which grows as high as a man, is already four feet high at the end
of April. All kinds of grain and vegetables thrive well here, namely wheat,
rye, barley, buckwheat, oats, peas, lentils, and the like. Also flax and hemp
do well, and also tobacco, rice, and cotton, and the finest of silk. The mulberry trees grow wild on the islands of the Volga, and in the forests you can
find cherry and almond trees.

The forests and fields are full of all kinds of fowl and wildgame such as
rabbits, wood grouse, moorhens, partridges, wild doves, ducks, geese, and the
like, as well as all kinds of precious fur-bearing animals. The Volga river
abounds in fish of various kinds, so that the inhabitants of that region can
eat as much of these as they like every day. Among the flowers that grow in
the open fields of this region, we find tulips and hyacinths, and in the
meadows there grows a wild asparagus of such good quality that it can
scarcely be achieved by the most expert gardeners in other countries. This
flower-rich region is most favorable for bees, and one can hardly find a
region where so much honey and wax can be gathered.

Everyone can therefore easily imagine what splendid opportunities this
country offers to the industry and enterprise of new immigrants, for by
means of boats that move on the Volga the goods and products can be
shipped not only to the North Sea and the Baltic, but also to the Caspian
Sea and thence to Persia, and via the Don River to the Black Sea and into the

Mediterranean. Consequently, there is the big advantage of trade and commerce all around Europe. And with all this, people live in the most beautiful climate, where winter is scarcely noticed during the four months.

To each and every foreigner who settles in these colonies, and to their children, including those born in Russia, we shall grant a 30-year period of exemption from all imperial taxes, and thereafter we grant them status equal to that of the old inhabitants of the country.

The happiness of complete and unrestricted freedom of religion and of conscience, so that each one may practice his religious rites according to the tenets and customs of his church. Similarly, they are permitted to have the necessary pastors and schoolmasters.

In addition, the new colonists will not only receive an adequate advance loan for their daily provisions and their transportation from Petersburg to their determined place of settlement, at the cost of the Imperial government; after their arrival in the colonies, they will continue to receive the necessary loan for their daily livelihood for an entire year after the construction of suitable houses has been completed, for which the necessary loans will also be graciously granted. The same applies to the construction of barns and sheds, the purchase of the necessary horses, cows, sheep, goats, pigs, and chickens, the acquisition of wagons and plows, and also the various kinds of seed-grain for summer and winter sowing, and the seeds for various kinds of vegetables.

To every family will be granted the usufruct of the apportioned land in hereditary possession.

Every married man or adult above 20 years of age will receive from the day of his acceptance as a colonist, 4 good *Groschen* or 16 *Kreuzer* for his daily food money; every married woman or girl above 16 years of age will receive 2 *Groschen,* and each child one half a *Groschen.*

Similarly, the immigrant travellers will be granted free transportation for themselves and their belongings to Lübeck and to Petersburg, and from there to the colony on the Volga.

At the place of settlement each family will be apportioned a sufficient number of *dessiatines* of land, as well as loans for the purchase of the needed seed and the necessary household utensils and farm implements.

Finally, the colonists will never be required to repay the costs of their transportation to Russia.

3. Letter of the Minister of the Interior

Letter of Count W. Kotschubei, Minister of the Interior, to S. A. Bekleschov, Military Governor of Kherson. July 24, 1803.

"The foreigners Ziegler and Schurter have undertaken to conduct a number of families from Alsace and other German provinces to New Russia. In their letter of July 3, they report from Ulm that the first Transport of settlers, consisting of 27 families numbering 110 souls, has been dispatched to Odessa, and they hope to send several more transports.

After I had made all necessary arrangements to facilitate their journey through foreign countries, I also informed the governor of the city of Odessa that it is His Majesty's supreme wish that all necessary care be accorded to the immigrants after they arrive in Russia. Meanwhile the New Russian Welfare Office has received detailed instructions regarding their settlement, together with a sum of money that will be needed for that purpose at the present time. In accordance with those instructions the Office will turn to you, your Excellency, in all the cases where its own resources are insufficient. You, honored sir, will of course not only strengthen its measures by your cooperation, but will also grant the settlers every support within your power.

There are two considerations that make this necessary. First, the fact that, according to the reports received, these colonists are for the most part good winegrowers, farmers, and craftsmen. For this reason, each of them must be provided with suitable equipment, according to his occupation. The winegrowers are to be brought into the Crimea, the farmers will be established on good land in the *gubernie** of Kherson and Ekaterinoslav, and the craftsmen are to be offered the possibility of remaining in the cities. Secondly, on the ways and means that are employed to settle these first immigrants, will depend the successful settlement of those who will come later, for they will, naturally, be informed about everything.

I therefore authorize you to cooperate with all the resources at your disposal in the task of establishing these colonists safely and suitably, according to the provisions that have been submitted to the New Russian Welfare Office. Among the colonists are many winegrowers. In order to make their skill and knowledge available for viticulture, we must enable them to get settled on the Crimean peninsula. If it should prove impossible to give them suitable land for winegrowing in the mountainous areas of the Crimea, I empower you to purchase such land, without delay, from private individuals, and to authorize the civil governor of Taurida to devote his special care to the colonists in the Crimea and to grant them every means to establish regular vineyards.

*gubernie, from Fr. gouvernement. In Czarist Russia the word meant *province*.

7

4. Rescript of Czar Alexander I

Rescript concerning the Settlement and the Rights of the Colonists. Composed by Count Kotschubei, Minister of the Interior, and endorsed by Czar Alexander I with the words: "SO BE IT." February 20, 1804.

"The foreigner Ziegler, who has conducted a certain number of colonists into the country last year (1803), visited me here to offer his services again in recruiting colonists this year. After having examined his proposals and carefully studied the whole matter, I venture, in all humility and obedience, to present to Your Imperial Majesty the following statement:

The recruiting of colonists has been undertaken and is being continued at the present time on the basis of the Manifesto of 1763.[1] This document contains no restriction on the type of people that are to be accepted, but refers in a general way to all classes and professions. Consequently, at the very beginning many worthless and, for the most part, greatly impoverished heads of households arrived, who were of little benefit to the state. The colonies of Saratov and some of the existing colonies in New Russia[2] confirm the truth of this statement.

As far as one can judge, the present invitations extended by Ziegler and Schurter[3] have also been made indiscriminately. From the description given me by Ziegler regarding the colonists he has brought in, it is evident that they included many unneeded craftsmen who were unmarried, sickly or feeble, and even afflicted with chronic ailments, and it should be mentioned that the majority of them were also extremely poor.

Since the Czarina Catherina II wished to populate the uninhabited steppes, she decided to call in foreigners. However, the continuing increase of our population and the resultant overcrowding in the *gubernias* (provinces) of the interior may necessitate the scattered resettlement of our own subjects, and since there will not be such a surplus of land suitable for settlement available in the South, we must now diminish the effort to settle those areas with foreigners, and must strive to settle only a limited number of immigrants who are capable of serving as *models in agricultural occupations and crafts*. If, therefore, the admission of people from foreign countries is to be

---

[1] The Manifesto of Catherine II was published July 25, 1763.

[2] The reference is to the German colonies that were established on the Lower Volga between 1763 and 1769 and to the colonies which Catherine II also established in the regions of Chortitza and Ekaterinoslav in "New Russia" between 1789 and 1792.

[3] Ziegler and Schurter appear to have been Austrian who were hired by the Russian government to organize and conduct emigrant wagon-trains from Vienna to the Russian bordertown of Radzivilov.

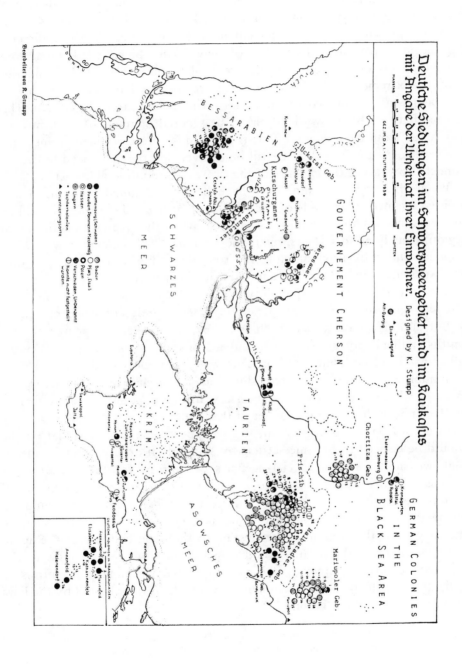

Deutsche Siedlungen im Schwarzmeergebiet und im Kaukasus
mit Angabe der Urheimat ihrer Einwohner.

Designed by K. Stumpp

GERMAN COLONIES
IN THE
BLACK SEA AREA

Bearbeitet von K. Stumpp

9

continued, it will be necessary to limit them to the most needed occupations, and exclusively to competent and well-to-do heads of households.

At the present time the settlement of these immigrants has been directed for the most part into the regions of New Russia. Since it is known, however, that few suitable crown lands are available even here, and considering that it is extremely difficult to find them, we need to determine—even before the people are permitted to immigrate—where they are to be settled. This means that suitable crown land has to be secured or tracts of land must be purchased from landowners.[4] For, if the land is not determined in due time, the settlement of the colonists will be delayed and they will need to live for almost two years at the expense of the Crown at a considerable cost.

When the available land areas have been determined beforehand and secured against other kinds of use, the settlement on these lands should be reserved only for those foreigners who can be of the greatest benefit in that region, namely good farmers, men who are fairly well acquainted with wine-growing, the cultivation of mulberry trees and other useful plants, or who are experienced in animal husbandry, particularly in the raising and handling of sheep, and, in general, people who have all the necessary knowledge of efficient agriculture. These people are to be given preferential acceptance.

But also village craftsmen, such as tailors, shoemakers, carpenters, black-smiths, millers, potters, weavers, and masons are to be accepted. On the other hand, all craftsmen and artisans who are useless in the life of rural communities will not be granted admission to the class of colonists, except in cases where it is considered necessary to accept a moderate number of craftsmen into the developing cities of the South.

In accord with this regulation, it also appears inappropriate that people should be enticed to become settlers by solicitation or any other means, or that we should utilize special agencies or persons for the recruiting of colonists. Instead, the people who want to settle in Russia could be directed to report to our resident foreign ministers or other agents who would examine the presented passports, testimonials, or other documents issued by the mayors or the communities attesting to the good conduct of the applicants, whereupon the agents would provide them with travel visas to the (Russian) frontier. Moreover, it is necessary that the immigrant fulfills all obligations to the present government to which he is duty-bound by the laws of the country and the Empire.[5]

---

[4] Already in 1804 Duc de Richelieu, governor of Odessa, obtained Crown land and purchased additional tracts from Russian and Polish noblemen to establish the German colonies in the Gross-liebental *volost* near Odessa.

[5] Soon after their arrival at the place of settlement, the colonists were required to take the oath of allegiance to the Russian Crown.

In view of the fact that the journey undertaken by only one or two families is fraught with difficulties, the Resident Minister in the city of Regensburg can be authorized to divide the accepted immigrants into parties numbering between 20 and 30 families, and to make the necessary arrangements for their transportation on water or on land, whatever appears more feasible. For this purpose he would lease boats and wagons at the expense of the Russian government and appoint one of the emigrants to serve as the leader to whom all members of the party owe obedience during the journey. Because of his competence and mobility, the foreigner Ziegler can be appointed assistant to the Resident Minister and entrusted with the task of organizing the respective groups of families, hiring the teamsters and boatmen for each expedition, and checking the colonists' travel documents and even their physical condition. On the basis of the instructions to be issued to him, a salary commensurate with his task would be paid. A party of immigrants who have agreed to settle in a certain colony can choose one or more men and send them ahead to inspect the designated land and determine its qualities.[6]

The annual emigration of colonists from Germany must not exceed 200 families. For this reason the Resident Minister must be instructed to accept and expedite only from 100 to 150 families, with the understanding that other families may emigrate on their own from localities that lie close to the (Russian) frontier.

The ministers at the foreign courts who may be concerned with these matters are to be sent the following instructions:

1. They may not make any advance payments, except for the lease of the wagons and the boats in which the people are to be transported.
2. Those who present themselves as would-be immigrants must produce testimonials or truthful witnesses indicating that the colonists possess assets in ready cash of at least 300 *Gulden,* or goods not exceeding 300 *Gulden* in value. Those who cannot furnish proof of this are not to be accepted, for experience has shown that the settlement of indigent people proceeds very slowly and fares badly.
3. It is understood that the immigrants must be people with families. Unmarried persons are by no means to be accepted, except when a colonist takes them into his family.
4. Families consisting of only husband and wife should not, if possible, be brought in, for experience has shown that it is very difficult for them to operate a farm and to prosper, since they cannot afford to employ hired labor.

---

[6]Such a scouting party was sent to the Crimea in the winter of 1804/5 to inspect the land that was to be allotted to the immigrant wine-growers.

Furthermore, these colonists can be accorded all the rights and privileges that have, in general, been determined for the colonists who are being settled in New Russia at the present time. These rights consist of the following:

1. Freedom of religion.
2. Exemption from taxes and all burdens[7] for ten years.
3. After the expiration of these ten years, the colonists will pay a land-tax to the Crown, namely 15-20 kopecks per dessiatine[8] in the ensuing ten years. After the expiration of this period, the tax will be equal to the amount that is ordinarily paid by the Crown settlers in that district. However, as soon as the years of exemption are over, the settlers will have to perform the statutory regional services, just like the Russian subjects among whom they are settled, with the exception that they will not have to provide recruits; nor will they need to billet any soldiers, except in cases where troops are marching through the district.
4. Freedom from military and civil service. Everyone, however, is permitted to enter the service, if he chooses to do so. But this will not exempt him from paying his debt to the Crown.
5. The repayment of the money that was advanced by the Crown is to be made in annual instalments during the ten years following the years of exemption.
6. All colonists will be granted free land, namely 60 dessiatines for each family, except in the mountainous region of the Crimea, where special regulations for land allotment will need to be established.
7. From the day of arrival at the frontier, subsistence money will be paid, namely 10 kopecks a day for every adult and 6 kopecks for every child, until they have arrived at their determined place of settlement. This money constitutes a part of the government's expenditure which does not have to be repaid, except in the event that a person wants to leave Russia, in which case he is obligated to refund whatever he has received.
8. After arriving at the destination, every person will receive from 5 to 10 kopecks daily, depending on the food prices, and the accumulated amount of this loan must be repaid, together with the other advanced loans.

---

[7]The "burdens" (Beschwerden) referred to here were the so-called "Landdienste" or "Landesbeschwerden" which the Russian citizens were required to perform for their country in time of war or serious disasters. These services included, besides the billeting of troops on the march, mentioned in art. 3, the hauling of provisions to the front, the transportation of the wounded soldiers to the lazarets, the hauling of timber for the construction of bridges, the baking of biscuits and the making of shirts for the troops.

[8]A dessiatine of land was equal to 2.7 acres.

9. The money advanced for the construction of houses, the purchase of livestock, and in general for farm and household equipment is established at 300 rubles per family. However, this amount can be increased for people who have come with considerable financial means if they need a larger amount for some kind of useful enterprise.
10. All settlers are permitted to bring in their personal possessions duty-free, no matter what these might be. Moreover, every family[9] will be allowed to bring in goods for sale, valued at 300 rubles. But these goods must be their own property, not goods that have been loaned or entrusted to them.
11. If anyone, at any time, wishes to depart from the Empire, he is free to do so, provided he pays not only the entire amount of his debt to the Crown, but also the taxes for three years.
12. Everyone is permitted to establish factories, to engage in any kind of trade, to become a member of a guild or corporation, and to sell his products anywhere within the imperial realm.

It is absolutely necessary to add that whenever an immigrant colonist proves to be disobedient and insubordinate to the constituted authorities, or leads a dissolute life, he will be summarily deported from the country, after he has paid his debt to the Crown. This regulation is also extended to those colonists who have already been established in their settlement. In this way it will be an easier task to inculcate good morality in the colonies and to spare the local authorities the troubles to which they might be exposed by the disorderly conduct or other irregularities of the colonists.

In submitting these proposals to your Imperial Majesty for your gracious perusal, I most submissively solicit your supreme confirmation of the same, so that I can properly implement the measures that must now be taken in regard to the future recruiting of colonists.

(Signed)   Count Viktor Kotschubei
Carl Hablitz, director
Nikolai Shulkovski, department head

---

[9] In an appendix, the term "family" was defined in this context as, a. the husband, wife, and young children; b. two adult laborers; and c. four adult women.

5. Richelieu's Directive of Settlement

Drawn up by Duc de Richelieu, Governor of Odessa. February 23, 1804.

1. For the founding of the first colonies in the *gubernie* of Kherson, Ekaterinoslav, and Taurida, land areas will be apportioned in the vicinity of seaports.
2. Odessa and Theodosia are recognized as such seaports.
3. In the vicinity of Theodosia and the mountain region of Taurida, wine-growers and people experienced in horticulture are to be settled. For this purpose existing Crown lands must be considered, or the needed tracts of land must be acquired by purchase.
4. Since viticulture and horticulture are the chief objectives of settlement in these regions, and inasmuch as only comparatively few areas of suitable land are available, and these at high prices, the government considers that an apportionment of 20 dessiatines per family will be quite sufficient.
5. If there are also grain farmers who would like to settle in the Crimea, they are to be settled chiefly in the Molotchna, a region that is not very far from the Mennonites who have been settled in the *gubernie* of Ekaterinoslav. In the event that the number of immigrants should greatly increase, they are to be settled on the lands that were formerly the steppes of the nomad Kalmucks, who have now been located on the lands of the Don Cossacks. In accord with their own wish, the Mennonites are also to be settled on the Molotchna River, where two large tracts of land have been placed at their disposal by the Nogaitza. The resettlement of the Mennonites will have the advantage of bringing them closer to Taganrog, where they can dispose of their products.
6. The settlements near Odessa are intended chiefly for grain farmers.
7. For this purpose the colonists who have arrived from Germany are to be settled on the land which has been purchased from Count Pototzky. As the number of immigrants increases, they will be settled more towards the interior, in the direction of Olviopol in the district of Tiraspol.
8. Henceforth the Bulgarian homesteaders will be settled on the lands that are adjacent to the existing Bulgarian colonies. As the number of these colonists increases, they will likewise be settled in the direction of Olviopol in the district of Tiraspol.
9. Craftsmen of all kinds are to be established in the cities, according to the choice of each immigrant. But those who are now arriving from Germany are to be located in Odessa.

6. Prospectus of Privileges of the Colonists

Translator's note. A synopsis which was circulated in Germany to gain settlers for the proposed colonies in South Russia.

1. Freedom of religion in all respects.
2. Exemption from taxes and other burdens for ten years.
3. After ten years of exemption, the colonists will be treated just like the other subjects of the Empire, with the exception that they will not be required to billet troops, save those who are marching through the villages.
4. The colonists are exempt from military and from civil service. Each one, however, is free to enter the service of the Imperial Crown, but this will not exempt him from paying all his Crown debts.
5. To get established, every settler will receive an advance loan which must be repaid in the ten years following the decade of exemption.
6. Every family is permitted to bring along its movable property duty-free, plus commodities for sale not exceeding 300 rubles in value.
7. Craftsmen are permitted to join guilds and associations. Each one may carry on trade and commerce throughout the Empire, without any restrictions.
8. Through the magnanimity of His Imperial Majesty all serfdom has been abolished in the provinces of the Russian Empire.
9. Every family will receive from the Crown a grant of from 30 to 60 dessiatines of productive land for its use. In addition to the police dues, each family will pay an annual ground tax of 15-20 kopecks per dessiatine, but this tax will not be payable until after the ten years of exemption have expired.
10. Any settler who desires to leave the imperial realm of Russia and return to his native land, must first pay his Crown debts, plus the taxes of three years for the use of the land.

Lauingen, March 20, 1804   Imp. Russian Transport of Colonists
                                       Carl von Otto

7. Request for Testimonials of Character

Letter of the mayor of Seltz to the sub-prefect in Weissenburg.

"The mayor of Seltz has the honor of informing you that he has received a petition today from thirty citizens and their families who require testimonials of status and character for the purpose of taking their departure from here and going to South Russia. The petitioners claim that there exists an Imperial decree which permits every French citizen to depart within the next ten years. I have no knowledge of such a decree, nor do I believe I am authorized to issue the requested testimonials. However, in order to preclude further demands, I request that you, Mr. Sub-Prefect, give me definite instructions and the authority to issue such testimonials. Your written decision will inform the petitioners what I am permitted to do and what are the obligations of the citizens who are presenting this petition to you."

(signed) Mast

Seltz, March 20, 1808.

The following day, the sub-prefect gave a cold, peremptory reply: "The mayor is strictly forbidden to issue either passports or testimonials of character to the people who are proposing to emigrate to Russia, until such a time when the government will have given its permission for such emigration." Name of sub-prefect is illegible.

8. A Testimonial of Character

Issued by the Mayor of Eschelbach/Sinsheim-Baden. March 20, 1809.

"Mathias Hermes, citizen of Eschelbach, near Kislau, in the Grand Duchy of Baden, has appeared before the mayor and the court to state his intention of emigrating from here to Russia with his wife Franziska, nee Schilling, and requests that an official testimonial regarding his assets, character, health, and family be submitted to the commissioner H. Thierry in Bruchsal.

We accordingly testify to the following:

1. Neither the parents nor the children are afflicted with any kind of sickness.
2. The family is of praiseworthy conduct and morals, and well experienced in agriculture.
3. The family consists of a son and daughter, namely Mathias, age 13, and Magdalena, age 10 years.
4. The assets of the applicant consist of goods and chattels, house and fields, which, after the payment of all liabilities, should yield the sum of 250 florins.
5. The husband and wife are not subject to any kind of servitude or serfdom.

The court dutifully submits these findings, without any reservations, to the appropriate office of the Grand Duchy for the purpose of obtaining an emigration permit and a passport for the above-named applicant.

9. A Russian Visa of Admission

"At the request of Michael Schafër, a citizen of Bietigheim near Rastatt in Baden has expressed his intention of migrating to Russia to become a colonist, it is hereby made known and certified that the undersigned, by virtue of an order of the Imperial Russian Court, promises and guarantees that the said petitioner will be granted entry into Russia and will receive the necessary passports. These papers, however, will only be issued on condition that he has been granted his freedom by his government, and provided that he has a family who will accompany him, for under no circumstances will unmarried men be accepted as colonists in Russia."

In witness whereof, my signature and seal

Vienna, Feb. 24, 1809

State Councilor of His Imperial Majesty and Knight of the Order of Anna, II Class

THE MOTHER COLONIES OF "NEW RUSSIA"

est. in the period 1804–1825

1. *The Liebental Enclave*

   a) Seven Lutheran:
   Großliebental (1804)
   Neuburg (1804)
   Alexanderhilf (1805)
   Lustdorf (1805)
   Peterstal (1805)
   Freudental (1805)
   Güldendorf (1817)

   b) Four Catholic:
   Kleinliebental (1804)
   Josephstal (1804)
   Mariental (1804)
   Franzfeld (1805)

2. *Prischib-Molotschna Area*

   a) Sixteen Lutheran: b) Five Catholic:

a) Sixteen Lutheran:	b) Five Catholic:
Prischib (1804)	Kostheim 1804)
Durlach (1804)	Walldorf (1808)
Altnassau (1804)	Heidelberg (1809)
Hoffental (1804)	Leitershausen (1810)
Weinau (1804)	Hochheim (1818)
Altmontal (1805)	Blumental (1828)
Wasserau (1807)	
Hochstädt (1808)	
Rosental (1808)	
Karlsruhe (1816) et. al.	

3. *Halbstadt-Molotschna Area*

   a) Mennonite enclave: 33 colonies

4. *Crimean Enclave*

Five Lutheran:	b) Two Catholic:
Friedental (1804)	Rosental (1805)
Neusatz (1804)	Kronental (1810)
Sudak (1805)	
Heilbrunn (1805)	
Zürichtal (1805)	

5. *Swedish District*

a) Three Lutheran:	b) One Catholic:
Schwedendorf	Klosterdorf (1804)
Schlangendorf (1804)	
Mühlhausendorf (1804)	

6. *Glückstal Enclave (All Lutheran)*

   Glückstal (1808)
   Kassel (1808)
   Bergdorf (1809)
   Neudorf (1809)

7. *Kutschurgan Enclave* (All Catholic)

Selz (1808)	Baden (1808)
Kandel (1808)	Elsass (1808)
Strassburg (1808)	Mannheim (1809)

8. *Beresan Enclave*

a) Seven Catholic:	b) Four Lutheran:
Speier (1808)	Rohrbach (1808)
Landau (1809)	Worms (1808)
Sulz (1809)	Johannestal (1810)
Rastadt (1809)	Waterloo (1819)
München (1809)	
Karlsruhe (1810)	
Katharinental (1817)	

9. *The Bessarabian Colonies*

   a) Twenty-three Lutheran (1814–22)
   b) One Catholic: Krasna (1814)

10. *Mariupol Enclave* (1823/24)

    a) Nine Lutheran:
    Grunau (1823)
    Kronsdorf (1824) et. al.

    b) Six Catholic (1823)

Göttland	Neuhof
Kaisersdorf	Tiegenort
Eichwald	Tiergart

11. *South Caucasus Area*

    a) Two Lutheran:
    Annenfeld (1818)
    Helenendorf (1818)

12. *Georgian Area*

    a) Four Lutheran:
    Alexanderdorf (1817)
    Elisabethtal (1817)
    Marienfeld (1817)
    Katharinenfeld (1818)

13. *Jekaterinoslav Area*

    Old colonies est. by Catherine II
    a) Luth.; Josefstal and Rübalsk (1779)
    b) Catholic: Jamburg (1792)
    c) Mennonite: Chortitza (1789)
    and nine others

II. The Migration Routes to the Black Sea

1. The Route over Land and over Water

In 1838 the German scholar J. G. Koch, who was traveling through South Russia on an extensive tour of research, had occasion to visit the German colonies near Odessa, where the 90-year-old mother of Mayor Lang of Lustdorf told of the hardships which the German immigrants had experienced during their migration to the Black Sea. In her interesting and historically valuable eyewitness account[1] she stated: "There were great hardships during the first years of settlement and many people did not survive those storms. Most of the German immigrants perished even before they were able to take possession of the land that had been apportioned to them. The worst thing that confronted the immigrants was that nothing whatsoever had been prepared for them when they arrived at the places where they were to be settled. In the beginning they received nothing from the government but some wretched, drafty wattled huts (wickerwork covered with clay) in which they almost perished during the cold winter. The following year the settlers dug themselves into the earth and built *"semelankas"*—earthen huts, like those of the Russians."

"The journey to Russia," she continued, "had already been terrible; it lasted two summers and one winter. One group of emigrants travelled all the way down the Danube in boats. They fared the worst, for at the mouth of the river malignant diseases broke out, and a large number of people were stricken, some of them fatally. The other group of emigrants took the overland route via Vienna, Moravia, and Galicia where they remained during the winter, before continuing their journey to their destination. In the beginning, all of us women were quite scared of the Russians. Moreover, we lived in fear and dread of the Turks, who at that time were still in possession of the far side of the Dniester River. We suspected that every vessel that came into view might be a part of the piratical Turkish fleet."

---

[1] Koch, J. G., *Reisen in Russland*, Dresden u. Leipzig (1841), p. 139.

This remarkable account represents a trustworthy reminiscence of the two migration routes along which the first immigrants to Russia were transported in the years 1803 and 1804. It also reveals the fact that a large number of the immigrants who had survived the journey were fated to perish after their arrival in the Odessa area because of the failure of the immigration authorities to provide proper shelter.

The available sources of information regarding the recruitment of German settlers and their transportation to "New Russia" are too sparse to enable us to present a complete account. It is known, however, that Czar Alexander and his ministers established immigration agents in a number of key cities in Germany. One of the first agents was Count von Fahnenberg, who was stationed at Regensburg as Resident Minister. In Vienna there was the Imperial State Councilor von Klüpfel; in Lauingen, another riverport on the Danube, there was Carl von Otto; in Frankfurt there was the Russian consul von Bethmann, and in Bruchsal-Baden, a certain Franz Thyerie was a representative of the Frankfurt office. No doubt, there were other agents whose identity remains unknown. From a letter by Count Kotschubei, the Russian Minister of the Interior, we also learn that two Austrians, Ziegler and Schurter, were commissioned to organize and supervise the immigrant transports at Ulm, which was the collecting point for the immigrants and the chief port of embarkation for the river journey to Vienna. A certain Major Escher also organized a transport of Swiss emigrants.

It has sometimes been asserted that the German settlers who came to Russia had to pay for the transportation costs from their village of origin to the Russian port of entry at Radzivilov. For example, in an article, "Der Weg nach Russland," the Soviet German writer, L. V. Malinowski, states that "the overland journey from Ulm to Radzivilov took two full months and cost an immigrant family of five or six people the sum of 300 Gulden, which was as much as the amount of money each colonist had to possess when he arrived at the border."[2]

We shall, for the present, ignore the question of the duration of the overland journey and deal with the question of the payment of the cost of transportation. Malinowski's contention in this regard is flatly contradicted by the evidence of available documents and corroborative testimony. In the Kotschubei Rescript of Feb. 21, 1804, the Minister of the Interior expressly states that the Resident Minister at Regensburg is authorized "to make the necessary arrangements for the transportation of the immigrants on water and on land . . . *and to lease boats and wagons at the expense of the Russian*

---

[2]Malinowski, L. V., "Der Weg nach Russland," In: Neues Leben, Sept. 14, 1976, p. 7.

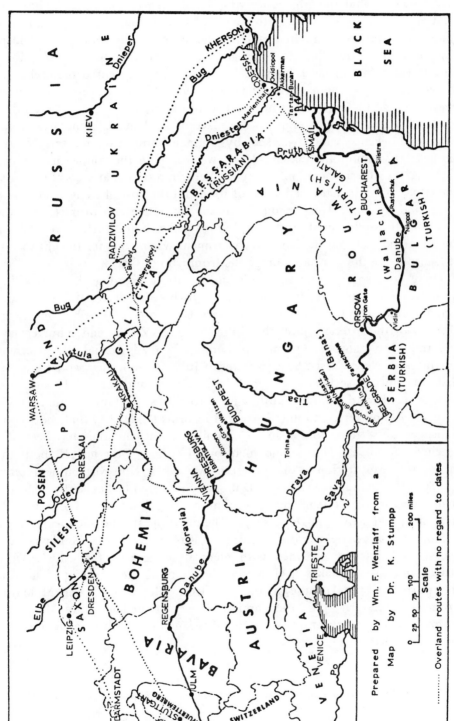

Migration Routes to Russia via the Danube waterway and the overland trek via Dresden-Lemberg-Radzivilov

government." That this procedure was already in effect in 1803, is shown in a letter written by colonist Anton Wolf of Kleinliebental to his relatives in Waldprechtsweiler-Baden. In this letter he states: "The immigrants had to pay the cost of travelling to the Danube. On the Danube (i.e. from Ulm) they traveled *free* as far as Vienna. In Vienna they presented themselves to the Russian ambassador. After they were accepted they were transported *free of charge* to the Russian border town of Radzivilov . . . and then they got further free transportation to the place of settlement." Similarly, in the letter of grievance which was sent by German immigrants quartered in the barracks at Ovidiopolis, January 1805, we read: "In the course of our long journey, the Russian commissioner Ziegler requested that we *advance him our money* to defray the daily cost of food and the cost of transportation by water and by land. This we did upon the assurance and promise that the government would reimburse us." This evidence should suffice to establish the historical fact that the Russian government was paying for the entire cost of transporting the German immigrants from Ulm to Odessa.

There are also excellent sources of information regarding the routes that were taken by the organized transports. In his first letter to Lieutenant-General Bekleschow, who was the Military Governor of the Chersonese, the Minister of the Interior states that "the foreigners Ziegler and Schurter have undertaken to transport a number of families from Alsace and other German provinces to New Russia. In their letter of July 3, 1803, they report that the first transport of settlers consisting of 27 families numbering 110 souls has been dispatched to Odessa, and they hope to send several more transports."

In his second letter, Count Kotschbei informs Bekleschev that the second transport of settlers comprising 25 families with 100 souls has been dispatched to Odessa. There is no mention in either of the letters about the means of transportation or the route that was taken. However, on September 1, 1803, the Quarantine Office at Dubossary reported to Bekleschev that the first transport of German immigrants numbering 98 persons, of whom 26 were sick, had arrived in Dubossary.[3] The mention of "the unexpected large number of "sick people" who had come to Russia "by way of Moldavia" and who "needed to be provided with medical services on the way between Galatz and Jassy" makes it clear that the route of these and the following transports was the Danube all the way from Ulm to Galatz in Moldavia. From the latter riverport the immigrants were then hauled by Moldavian wagons via Kischinev or Jassy to the Russian port of entry at Dubossary, which lay northwest of Odessa.

---

[3]Stach, J., *Die deutschen Kolonien in Südrussland,* Prischib, Verlag Gottlieb Schaad (1913), p. 6.

As we have already noted, 26 of the 96 people in the first transport were sick upon arrival and 12 persons were missing from the original party of 110. The nature of their illness is doubtless to be found in the diseases that were prevalent in the malarial environment of the mouth of the Danube, such as typhus, dysentery, and intermittent fever. In the light of these conditions, we may assume that the 12 missing persons probably became victims of one of these diseases.

But the first transport had additional tribulations after they departed from Galatz and were approaching the Russian port of entry in their Moldavian wagons. When they reached the Moldavian village of Kriulani, where they were to be ferried across the Dniester, they were detained by the riverguard Captain Alexo Slavko, because they were unable to pay the required toll of 4 rubles and 2½ kopecks.

The incident placed the Dubossary Quarantine Office in a quandary, for the feeding and sheltering of the detained immigrants at Kriulani for a number of days would have cost the government a good deal more than a few rubles. Fortunately, the arrival of the Civil Governor of Cherson, State Councilor Okulov, put an end to the senseless and costly delay. He gave orders that the amount owing the Moldavian government be paid immediately out of the fund provided for the settlement of the colonists.

But this seemingly ridiculous incident confronts us with a most curious situation. We have here 27 heads of immigrant families that have been able to provide food for their dependents during the entire two-month journey on land and on water, and suddenly, just as they are about to cross the border into Russia, they are so pitifully indigent that they are unable to raise a measly four rubles to pay for the toll across the Dniester. How could these families have arrived at the Russian border as penniless as beggars when every family was supposed to have 300 *Gulden* or rubles before it would be granted permission to enter the country! The complete lack of money has only one plausible explanation. These immigrants of the first transport not only lost 12 of their company; they also lost all their money while they were en route down the Danube to Galatz and passed through the Turkish-dominated countries of Bulgaria and Rumania. Somewhere in these waters, the floating *"Ulmer Schachtel"* of the German immigrants were boarded by a horde of Turkish river pirates and robbed of everything they possessed! As we shall see presently, in factual detail, that is precisely what happened to the *fourth* transport.

After the 12-day period in quarantine at Dubossary, the first transport arrived in Odessa on September 12, 1803, on 25 wagons under the guidance of Customs Inspector Silberharnisch. Duc de Richelieu himself undertook to find suitable winterquarters for them in the city of Odessa.

To prevent further incidents with the Moldavian ferrymen, Okulov declared that in the future the Russian government would pay all the toll fees. The next problem confronting the State Councilor was to find suitable quarters for the immigrants and to get the necessary medicaments for those who were sick. Since the Dubossary Quarantine Station had no suitable quarters for the arriving immigrants, the personnel decided to renounce their obligations and requested that the 12-day quarantine period be abolished altogether. But Okulov demonstrated his authority and practical shrewdness by giving the order that all future transports of German colonists arriving at the quarantine station would be lodged in the homes of the Dubossary residents, while the latter were to be quartered in the neighboring Moldavian villages of Luneya and Pogrebi. At the same time, Major Asezki, the commandant of the Tiraspol district, was ordered to see to it that the quarters requested by the Quarantine Office would be made available in the said villages. The Office was also ordered to provide the money needed for medicines.

The personal presence of State Councilor Okulov made it highly unlikely that his orders would be ignored, as was the case with the written order that was issued a month earlier by the Moldavian consul Gervé. He had notified the Quarantine Office in good time of the arrival of the first transport of colonists and stressed the need of making preparations for lodgings in the Quarantine compound and providing the people with food and other necessities, "so that the people would not become weary and exhausted on reaching the border."

After considerable delay which was caused by new difficulties with the Quarantine Office, the instructions of Bekleschev and the request of Gervé were carried out, and medical care was provided for the colonists who were en route from Galatz to Dubossary. A doctor, a medic, and an interpreter were engaged for the purpose. The second transport must have arrived in Dubossary near the end of September, but there is no available information on the date of arrival or the size and condition of this party.

The third transport consisting of 103 souls, of which at least 63 were sick, arrived in Dubossary, but the time of arrival is not known; it may have been late in November. The unexpected large number of sick people was a matter of much embarrassment to the officials of the Quarantine Office, for even at this late date there was not enough space in the Quarantine Compound to provide lodgings for the sick; nor were there sufficient quantities of medicine on hand to take care of their needs. Apparently, the order of the responsible authorities had again been callously ignored, and all that Bekleschev could do in the critical situation was to engage two more doctors.

The fourth transport consisted of 40 families numbering 130 people. It was therefore larger than any of the three earlier ones. On the basis of a rare document that was discovered by the Soviet German writer, L. V. Malinowski, in the State Archives of Leningrad, it is possible for us to present a most detailed account[4] of a shocking incident that happened to the fourth transport after it had reached the lower regions of the Danube which were under Turkish rule at the time. As the slow-moving *"Ulmer Schachtel"* was approaching the river-town of Silistria, thirty well-armed Turks in three boats surrounded the German barge and began firing at it. The German immigrants who had a few guns with them returned the fire, but were soon forced to surrender when one of the passengers was killed and twelve others were wounded. Brandishing their sabres, the river pirates boarded the barge and robbed the terrified passengers of all their money and valuables.

The distressed immigrants continued their journey to the next town named Harsova, where there was also a Turkish fortress. A group of men went to see the Pasha and lodged an indignant complaint, orally and in writing, about the dastardly act of Turkish piracy, and demanded restitution

AREA MAP OF MOLDAVIA

25

of their losses. The Pasha accepted their written complaint and in their presence forwarded it by messenger to Constantinople where, he assured them, the Sultan would take care of the matter. Meanwhile, the injured party had no alternative but to continue their journey to Galatz, which they reached the following day. Needless to say, this transport, like the first one, was unable to pay the Moldavian ferryman for taking them across the Dniester to Dubossary.

After the fourth transport arrived in Odessa on December 16, 1803, the leaders of the party submitted their grievance to Duc de Richelieu, who had recently been appointed military governor of Odessa. He dealt with the matter in the same way as the Pasha of Kursova had done, and forwarded the letter of grievance to the Czar in St. Petersburg, together with a list of all the heads of families and the amount of losses in money and valuables suffered by each family.

This report also enables us to obtain a synopsis of the financial status of the 40 families belonging to the fourth transport. We discover that the leader of the transport, who was generally called the *"Reiseschulz"* and who usually became the first mayor of the settlement, had lost the sum of 2,500 *Gulden* while the poorest passenger lost only 8 *Thaler* in cash, plus valuables worth 10 *Thaler*.[5] It is probable that the leader of the transport was also carrying money entrusted to him by the government to pay for the hiring of wagon

---

[4] The present account is based on Malinowski's article. See footnote 2.
[5] In 1817 the Gulden was worth 3 rubles, the Thaler (= 100 Kreuzer) was worth approx. 4 rubles. The Rhenish Florin was worth about half a Thaler or 2 rubles. The silver ruble which was not introduced until 1839 was worth about three times the paper ruble.

transportation from Galatz to the Russian border. The money lost by three widows amounted to 284 *Thaler*. Of forty families, four were quite well-to-do, for the average family had 1,153 *Thaler*. In a second group comprising 22 families, each family had assets ranging from 300 to 1,000 *Thaler*. The poorest group of 14 families had on the average lost 55 *Thaler* in cash and 67 *Thaler* in valuables per family.

It is very doubtful that the Sultan of Constantinople ever made any effort to make good the losses which the German immigrants sustained at the hands of his rapacious pirates. On the other hand, all that the Duc de Richelieu was able to achieve was that the Czar granted the indigent immigrants who had lost 20,000 *Thaler* a loan of 10,000 rubles, which had to be repaid after a period of years.

Nothing is mentioned in the available reports about the arrival of the fifth, sixth, and seventh transports. Presumably, all of them arrived in the late fall, probably in the second half of November. We can assume that they were also beset with difficulties and tribulations, including sickness and disease contracted in the Danube delta. It is also doubtful whether the accommodations and medical service at the Dubossary Quarantine Station were significantly improved.

It is known that the eighth transport reached Odessa in the early part of December. It appears to have been the first transport that received good medical aid on the way from Galatz to the Russian border, for there were only two sick people among the 118 members of this party. Since the weather had now turned frosty and cold, the immigrants were provided with warm winter clothing at Dubossary. Richelieu also reduced the quarantine period to six days. Like the preceding groups, these immigrants were placed into winter quarters in the city of Odessa, under the care of the Guardianship Office for Foreign Settlers. Two more transports were expected, but they did not reach Odessa until the spring of 1804.

On December 27, 1803, Councilor Kontenius, the chief justice of the Guardianship Office, determined that there were 87 wine-growing families among the immigrants of the eight transports and that, with the arrival of the last two transports, there would probably be about 100 families that could be settled in the Crimea. The families with a knowledge of farming would be settled in several villages near Odessa, and the craftsmen would be established in the city.

In the early spring of 1804, about the time that the ninth transport arrived in Odessa, Richelieu discovered that a large unscheduled transport of 240 immigrants had been conducted from Switzerland by a certain Escher who was a Major in the Moscow Dragoon Regiment. The Swiss wagon train departed on August 30, 1803, and travelled the route via Meersburg to Ulm and Vienna. From there Escher chose the overland route through Moravia and Galician Poland to Radzivilov, where he and his party remained for the winter, before continuing the trek to Yekaterinoslav. Although the government officials knew nothing of this transport, Escher demanded food money for his party, and this was granted to him by the Guardianship Office, upon the instructions of Duc de Richelieu. Escher then conducted his Swiss immigrants into the Crimea where they were established in the new colony of Zurichtal.

After a group of delegates, who had been sent into the Crimea in late January to select suitable available land, returned to Odessa with favorable reports, new transports were organized to take the wine-growing families into the Crimea. Accordingly, fifty Catholic families were settled in the colony of Rosental and six Catholic families in Simferopol. At the same time, fourteen Lutheran families were settled in Sudak, about fifteen families in Herzenberg, and twenty-four in Friedental.

In the course of the spring of 1804, more transports of German immigrants continued to arrive in Odessa. Count Kotschubei now instructed the Dubossary Office to relax most of the quarantine regulations, but to improve the medical services for the sick immigrants. However, by now it was fairly obvious to the immigration authorities that the attempt to bring the German immigrants by way of the Danubian port of Galatz and the ill-equipped quarantine station at Dubossary was an egregious error that had exposed the poor immigrants to the triple hazard of losing their money, their health, and even their lives.

The whole operation lacked judicious planning and proper preparation. Already in the spring of 1804, Dubossary was really no longer important as a gateway to New Russia. Almost all the transports of German immigrants were now coming through the port of entry at Radzivilov, near the Polish border of Podolia. Already in the late summer and fall of 1803, several wagon trains were rolling along the Vienna-Lemberg post road that led through Moravia and the Austro-Polish province of Galicia. However, since there was no accommodation available for these immigrants in Odessa, they were compelled to stay over the winter in Radzivilov and in the neighboring Polish border-town of Brody.

Throughout the spring until the fall of 1804, the immigrant wagon trains kept moving down from Podolia to Odessa. Besides the regularly organized transports comprising from 40 to 50 families, there were numerous smaller groups of immigrants who were travelling independently "on their own." As scores of families continued to crowd into the Odessa suburbs, Duc de Richelieu became deeply concerned about the problem of finding suitable temporary shelter and, eventually, winter quarters for these people.

By the beginning of winter, Dec. 21, 1804, the number of German immigrants who had arrived in Odessa by way of the Danube or by the overland route via Radzivilov exceeded five thousand. The ten transports that arrived via Dubossary in 1803 comprised at least 300 families, or 1,350 souls, if we estimate the average family to have had 4.5 members. State Councilor Klüpfel reported that 402 families were dispatched from Vienna via Radzivilov in organized wagon trains to Odessa in 1804, and that an additional 412 families arrived independently in small groups. These 814 families would represent about 3,700 immigrants, which added to the 1,350 who arrived in 1803, would make a total of 5,013.

The first and most pressing need was to settle the immigrants who had arrived via Dubossary in 1803 and were still in winter quarters in the city of Odessa. Since the immigration officials had provided no buildings or housing of any kind, the immigrants had to erect their own makeshift dwellings. They were hauled out to the selected site of the new settlement and the government delivered four corner posts and a few poles to each family. The construction of the dwelling was a simple matter. The four corner posts were fixed into the ground and between them the wattled walls of wickerwork and clay were erected. Over the walls a framework of staves and rafters was placed which was covered with bulrushes or hay—and the building was finished. Windows and doors were supplied later.

In these dingy, drafty hovels the first settlers on the Grossliebental steppe spent their first winter, namely 16 families in Kleinliebental, 32 in Josephstal, 11 in Mariental, and an undetermined number in Grossliebental.

As we have already noted, 150 families who had reached Odessa in 1803 were settled in the newly established villages in the Crimea in the summer of 1804. In September of that year, sixty immigrant families were sent from Odessa into the area of the Swedish Colonies near Bereslav where three groups were settled, namely 24 Lutheran families in Schlangendorf, 12 Lutheran families in Mühlhausendorf, and 24 Catholic families in Klosterdorf.

Although Duc de Richelieu succeeded fairly well in getting the immigrants of 1803 settled, he was confronted with a much more difficult problem in finding suitable winter quarters for the hundreds of families who were converging into the Odessa area in the summer and fall of 1804. Since he could no longer obtain any accommodation for the German immigrants in the city itself, he thought of placing them in the Russian villages on the outskirts of the city, but soon realized that it was most inadvisable to crowd the settlers into the small Russian homes, in view of the differences in language, religion, nationality, and way of life. It was then proposed to place the immigrants into the Army Barracks at Ovidiopol, which was not too far from Odessa.

However, after Richelieu inspected the barracks he found that those adobe structures were sadly dilapidated and quite unfit for human habitation. By chance he found that the Naval Barracks, which were also unoccupied, could be re-conditioned without great expense and be made available to house the immigrants.

Accordingly, in the beginning of August, scores of families were lodged in the barracks, and their number increased from week to week through the following autumn. After all the available quarters were packed to capacity, the remainder of the unhoused immigrants were lodged in the Armenian village of Grigoriopol on the Dniester.

The frightfully unhygienic conditions of the dingy, overcrowded, earthen barracks soon caused a virulent outbreak of diseases that led to the death of 366 persons in the period between St. Michael's Day (Sept. 29) and Christmas. Even as late as February, 1805, at least 150 people were still lying prostrate with high fever and dysentery; many succumbed in the following weeks. Finally, upon the return of Richelieu from Petersburg, the survivors were liberated from the appalling death-trap. The sick were lodged in the small lazaret in Grossliebental and those who were in a tolerable state of health were settled in the newly established villages of Alexanderhilf, Neuburg, and Lustdorf. One large group was transported into the Crimea and settled in the new colony of Neusatz. Those who had succumbed in the barracks of Ovidiopol—their number exceeded 500—were buried in mass graves on a suburban hillock which became known as the *"Pestberg"*—the Hill of Pestilence. But the epidemic of dysentery continued to decimate the families who had been settled in the primitive wattled huts that were erected in the new villages. Thus the year 1804 proved to be a year of dreadful tribulation and disaster for hundreds of immigrant families.

After the first big wave of immigration to New Russia in 1803-1804, the influx of German immigrants declined considerably in the next few years until the massive immigration movement of 1808. However, the Vienna-Lemberg post road via Moravia and Galicia to Radzivilov was to become the main route of German immigration to Russia from 1804 until the end of 1808. In comparison with the Danube waterway, this route proved to be much less hazardous to the health and life of the immigrants.

In his article, *"Der Weg nach Russland,"* Malinowski asserted that the overland route was incredibly poor and wearisome, and that the journey from Ulm to Radzivilov took all of two months. To be sure, in those days the Vienna-Lemberg post road was not a smoothly paved highway, but it was a well-travelled dirt road on which a stage coach could normally make the journey in ten days. A trek by wagon train transporting from 30 to 40 families with all their belongings would, of course, take considerably longer, especially when the weather was unfavorable. Fortunately, we do not have to resort to guesswork and conjecture about the travel time, for the extant *Passport Lists* (PL) of 1808, which were preserved in the archives at Yekaterinoslav, give us first-hand reliable information.

From these records it appears that Johann Jägel of Rastatt (PL:I,11) and Jakob Miller (PL:I,10) both of them with large families, made the first leg of the journey on the Danube River from Ulm to Vienna in the normal time of 7 days. After a stop-over of a few days, they left Vienna on October 25, 1808, and travelled by wagon via Brünn, in Moravia, which they reached on October 30, and continued through Galicia via Lemberg to the town of Brody, which they reached on November 15. Two days later they were in Radzivilov, the Russian port of entry. Thus, the duration of the journey from Ulm to Radzivilov was only 30 days, compared with the 30 or 42 days required to travel down the Danube from Ulm to Galatz. In the late fall of 1808, when the weather could be inclement and cold, Johann-Georg Lämmle (PL:111) left Ulm on October 30 and arrived in Radzivilof on December 11—a journey of 42 days. Similarly, a group of five families from Plittersdorf/Rastatt left Vienna on November 11 and reached Lemberg on December 5, covering the distance in 24 days. If we add the normal seven days for the river journey from Ulm to Vienna and 5 days for the trek from Lemberg to Radzivilov, we still get a respectable 36 days of travel-time for the entire journey—a far cry from the 60-63 days that Malinowski envisioned.

The duration of the Danube journey from Ulm to Galatz is not indicated in the available sources. However, there is ample evidence to be found in the Danube journeys that were undertaken by German immigrants in 1817, the year of the fateful Swabian Expedition. In a diary which was kept by the immigrant Joh. Chr. Bidlingsmeier, we read that a boatload of families from Württemberg left Ulm on June 2 and reached Vienna on June 9. After a four-day stop-over, they left Vienna on June 13 and reached Galatz on July 16, making the entire journey in 40 days of actual travel time.

A month later in the same year (1817), Friedrich Schwartz and his family embarked at Ulm on July 1 and reached Vienna on July 10. After a four-day stop-over they got on a larger boat that left Vienna on July 14 and reached Galatz in Moldavia on August 19. The entire travel time from Ulm to Galatz took 46 days.

We can therefore assume that the travel time from Ulm to Galatz for the transports of 1803 must have been approximately 44 days. From Galatz they would have needed another four or five days of travel by wagons to reach the Russian port of entry at Dubossary.

2. The Overland Route of 1809

Through a remarkable stroke of good fortune a large number of passports of the German-Russian pioneer settlers in the Odessa area were deposited in the archives of the Colonist Welfare Office at Ekaterinoslav, the present day Dnepropetrovsk. There they were discovered in 1943 by a German research group headed by Dr. Karl Stumpp, who had transcripts made of all the available passports and was later able to publish them in his monumental work, "The Emigration from Germany to Russia in the Years 1763-1862."

In view of their historical significance, these records deserve closer study and analysis, for they provide us with first-hand information about the identity of more than 400 immigrant colonists, as well as precise information of the itinerary and duration of the great emigration treks of 1808 and 1809.

At the outset, however, there are several points that need to be elucidated about the nature and contents of the passport records.* First of all, it should be noted that double dates are generally used to indicate the time when the passports were issued at Frankfurt am Main by the Russian consul von Bethmann. This double dating also occurs in the visa stamp entries in the city of Leipzig. The first date represents the Old Style reckoning of the Russian calendar, while the second date is the New Style reckoning of the Gregorian calendar, which was 12 days after the old. Thus 27.3./8.4.1809 means March 27 (Old Style), or April 8 (New Style), 1809.

Secondly, it should be remarked that the original passports did not, in most cases, give precise information about the names and location of the villages from which the colonists emigrated. As we shall see in our subsequent investigation, the exact determination was provided by the editor, Dr. Stumpp, on the basis of information obtained from later census records. Thirdly, the final destination of the immigrants—the places where they were actually settled—could, of course, not have appeared on the original passports, since these colonies were not in existence at the time of immigration. For that reason, the appearance of *Zielorte* like Landau, Karlsruhe, Kassel, etc. are merely editorial additions. The original passports had only general designations, such as Taurien, Russland, *Südrussland*.

1. The Villages of Origin

There are instances where the passports clearly indicate the name of the village of origin and the state or province in which it was located. For

---

*The passport list begins on p. 973 of Karl Stumpp, "The Emigration from Germany to Russia in the Years 1763-1862." 1:13 means List 1 and passenger no. 13. (Ed.)

example, Stolp in Pommern (1:13), Schwemmlingen im Trierschen (8:14), Blankenborn im Frankreich-Elsässer Gebiet (2:35), and several others. However, there are many instances where only the name of the village was given, without any further information of its location. For example, Surburg (4:31), Beinheim (4:69), Claburg, actually Cleeburg, all of which are located in Lower Alsace. There are also numerous instances where only the state or the country is indicated, for example: aus dem Elass (4:44), aus Württemberg (4:36), aus dem Französischen (4:22), von Preussen (8:12), von Lothringen (8:15), von Grosspolen (4:14), and, quite often, "aus dem Reich," i.e. from the (German) Empire."

With much painstaking effort, Dr. Stumpp was able to provide a more precise determination for most of the places of emigration by establishing the *Kreisstadt* (administrative center) or the canton in which a particular village was located. This was made possible by referring to the available census records that contained this kind of information, particularly the records published by Johannes Brendel and Conrad Keller.

However, there are numerous instances where the supplemental determinations were erroneously made or left undetermined. Thus Joh. *Hof* (1:23) came from Oberschlettenbach-Als, not from Kapsweyer-Pf; Ludwig *Schwöbel* (1:28) was from Lembach-Als, not from Winzenbach; Larl *Schirek* (3:18) was from Lembach-Als, not from Winzenbach; Georg *Kowitz* (3:39) was from Bitschhofen-Als, not from the non-existent Litschhof; Joseph *Gruber* (3:58) from Salmbach-Als, not from Lembach; Jakob *Reinhard* (4:1) from Münchweiler-Pf, not Haslach-Baden. Seb. *Martin* (4:5) from Seltz-Als, not Schwanheim-Pf; Anton *Bopp* (4:31) from Surburg, not from Gurburg; Jakob *Michael* (4:100) from Cleeburg-Als, not from the garbled Claburg; Joh. *Helbling* (5:67) from Wingen-Als, not Erlenbach-Pf; Adam *Vogel* (6:18) from Steinfeld-Pf, not from Schaidt; Michael *Nuleth* (6:29) from Altstadt-Als, not from Abstatt-Wü; Peter *Brilz* (6:67) from Ingenheim-Pf, not Ingolsheim-Als; Stefan *Mock* (6:71) from Kapsweyer-Pf, not from Schleithal-Als; Simon und Bernhard *Welder* (6:90; 6:133) from Plittersdorf-Ba, not from Eppingen; Joseph *Hoffart* (8:26) from Aspach/Weissenburg-Als, not from Aspach/Altkirch-Als; Adam *Dexheimer* (8:34) from Thalfang/Trier, not from the distorted Alsenz; Franz *Dubine* (7:21) from Weingarten-Pf, not Weingarten-Wü; Joh. *Bernhard* (5:52) from Hagenbach-Pf, not from Obersteinbach-Als.

2. The Destination of the Emigrants

On the basis of the census records of 1816 and 1840 for the colonies established in the Odessa area, Dr. Stumpp was able to determine the villages where most of the emigrants with 1809 passports were settled. However,

33

there are more than 100 passport transcripts where the original designation "nach Taurien" was not replaced by the name of the village where the particular immigrant was settled. In the course of additional research I have been able to determine the village of settlement in at least 90 instances, so that the number of immigrants who actually settled in *"Taurien"* is insignificant. The term was commonly used at the time to designate the territory of "New Russia" or South Russia.

3. *Number and Composition of the Immigrant Families*

A general survey of the religious affiliation and the place of settlement of the 550 families who emigrated in 1809, according to the available passport records, provides the following data:

a. Some 210 families were settled in the six Catholic colonies of the Beresan district (Katharinental was not established until 1817).
b. About 110 Lutheran families were settled in Rohrbach and Worms in the Beresan district, and in Kassel, Bergdorf and Neudorf in the Glückstal district.
c. About 30 Catholic families were settled in the Kutschurgan area.
d. About a dozen families, Catholic and Lutheran, were settled in the Grossliebental district.
e. Perhaps 12 families were settled in Taurida and in the Crimea.
f. For at least 70 families the place of settlement is uncertain.

Thus the total number of immigrant families for the year 1809 can be set at about 444. However, this number represents only a fraction (certainly less than half) of the families who came to South Russia that year. This is confirmed by the evidence that is based on other immigration records and census records of the colonies in the Beresan district in the year 1809. We also know from the Brendel records of 1811 that another 90 Catholic families who had come from Als/Pf/Ba in 1809 were settled in the Kutschurgan district. The Lutheran colonies likewise had a large number of immigrant families from Pf/Ba/Als that year, namely 89 for Rohrbach and 50 for Worms. Similarly, about 150 families were settled in Kassel, Bergdorf and Neudorf. This means that some 830 families emigrated from S.W. Germany in 1809, compared with the 444 families represented in the extant passport records.[1]

---

[1]It should be noted that only two or three emigrant families from Württemberg are represented in 550 passport records of 1808/1809. This is not surprising when we consider that King Friedrich of Württemberg prohibited all emigration from his country by a decree that was published May 29, 1807. The prohibition remained in force until March 15, 1815.

But the colonies in the Odessa area are not the only ones that come under consideration. We must also take into account the colonies in the Taurida and the Crimea which were established in 1809 and 1810. In the region of Taurida there were the following: Hochstädt, a Lutheran settlement, which had 26 families who came from Ba/Pf/Als in 1809. Waldorf, which had 25 Catholic families from Baden; Heidelberg, with 89 Catholic families from Baden; Leitershausen, with 28 Catholic families from Baden; Kostheim, with at least 20 from Baden. In the Crimea there was Kronental with 25 families from Baden and Alsace. This makes a total of some 200 families who came from Ba/Pf/Alsace in 1809 and settled in the Taurida and Crimea. Added to the total for the Odessa area, this makes a grand total of 1,100 families who immigrated to "New Russia" in 1809.

In solid confirmation of the fact that the extant passport records represent only a minority of the families who immigrated to South Russia in 1809, we need only review the emigration records of Baden which were published by Joseph Hässler in 1939.[2] According to his research some 477 families emigrated from north and central Baden in 1809. However, only about half of these families are represented in the passport records found at Ekaterinoslav. For example, it is known that 14 families emigrated that year from Eppingen, 11 from Odenbach, 7 from Jöhlingen and 9 from Hilsbach, but the passports contain only 6 families from Hilsbach and one from Odenbach. Similarly, of the 30 families from Baden who settled in 1809 in the district of Kutschurgan, only 3 occur in the passports. Or to take another example: it is known that 8 Schneider families emigrated in 1809, but only one occurs in the passports.

To sum up our findings, it appears that only about 200 of the 477 families who emigrated from Baden in 1809 were settled in the Odessa area, namely 144 in the Beresan district, 30 in the Kutschurgan, and 20 in the Glückstal district. A majority of 277 families were established in the Molotchna district[3] in the Taurida and in the Crimea. Accordingly, if we add the 277 families who were settled in the Taurida and the Crimea (of whom only a

---

[2]Hässler, Joseph, Zur Auswanderung aus Baden nach Russland. In: *Der Wanderweg der Russland-deutschen.* Kohlhammer, Stuttgart (1939) pp. 16-35.

[3]The suggestion made by Dr. K. Stumpp in his article, "Die Urheimat der deutschen Kolonisten in Russland" (Der Wanderweg der Russlanddeutschen, Stuttgart, p. 15) that the emigration route of 1809 passed through Silesia and Warsaw to Grodno and continued from there via Ekaterinoslav to the Molotchna is far-fetched and implausible. There is no reason why the emigrants would have taken a circuitous route that brought them almost to the border of Lithuania, involving a detour of more than 300 miles. That the immigrants to the Molotchna district entered Russia via Lemberg in Austrian Poland is confirmed by the evidence of the passports of Ludwig Lutz (6:13) and Joseph Zander (4:17), who travelled to the Molotchna via Brody/Radzivilov and settled in Hochstädt/Taurien.

few appear in the passport records) to the 830 families who are known to have been settled in the colonies of the Odessa area, we obtain a grand total of at least 1,100 families for the great emigration of 1809.

4. The Overland Route of 1809

From the beginning of the emigration movement of 1803 until 1808, the passports for the emigrants were generally issued at Karlsruhe, Regensburg, and Vienna. In examining the passports of 1809, we are struck by the fact that they were all issued by von Bethmann, the Russian consul at Frankfurt am Main, and that the immigration route to Russia was no longer that of the earlier years. The question now arises why the emigrants of 1809 took the circuitous route through Saxony and Silesia, instead of taking the well-established route through Austria via the Danube, and the road through eastern Bohemia and the province of Galicia in Austrian Poland. The answer is to be found in the fact that in 1809 Napoleon was conducting a military campaign against Austria on the upper Danube. On April 17 his main army was stationed at Donauwörth and the first engagements took place at Abensberg (April 9) and at Landshut (April 20). On July 5 and 6, the fateful Battle of Wagram was fought, in which Napoleon was defeated, but it was not until mid-October that he departed from Vienna. It would, obviously, have been a most hazardous undertaking for the emigrants to pass through Austria during the spring and summer of the year 1809.

As we have already indicated, the overland emigration route of 1809 passed through the German states of Saxony and Silesia, and the Polish province of Galicia, which was under Austrian sovereignty at that time. A detailed examination of the visa stamp entries on the passports enables us not only to determine the towns and villages through which the emigrants passed, but also to set up a model timetable of the journey.

In my book, *Paradise on the Steppe,* I published a report made by a certain Johann Lösch, who had immigrated to Russia in 1809 but was so disillusioned by the prevailing conditions in the newly established colonies that he found it necessary to return to his native village of Leimersheim in the Palatinate. His report, which was published in 1811, has considerable historical value for our investigation of the migration route, for he states that he "set out from Leimersheim on May 17, 1809, and reached Odessa on August 24." This means that the journey took 99 days! He also indicates that the route he travelled took him "through Saxony, Prussia, and Galicia to Radzivilov, the first Russian town in Podolia," and that the "road from there to Odessa passed through Yampol, Old and New Konstantinov, Bratslav and Balta."

These statements are excellently confirmed in one of the extant passports (7:24), where we read that Johann Georg Lösch "travelled with his wife and three children, plus a young man named Johann Philipp Marthaler." His passport also contained visa stamp entries for seven towns through which he passed. Furthermore, from the census records of 1811 for the colony of Kandel/Odessa, where he was briefly settled, we obtain the information that he was at that time 37 years old; his wife Maria, 25; and of his three sons, Peter was 7, Philipp, 5, and Adam 2 years. From other passport records we also discover that 15 other families from Leimersheim and neighboring villages travelled in the same wagon train as the Lösch family.

Since the passport records of 1809 also contain the names of more than 250 families who emigrated from the Palatinate throughout the spring, summer, and autumn of that year, we are able by means of a comparative analysis of the visa stamp entries to determine precisely the names of the towns and villages through which they passed and the average timetable of their journey.

Taking the Lösch passport entries as a working model and supplementing it from the data given in the other passports, we obtain the following composite travel schedule for the journey from Leimersheim/Germersheim-Pf to Radzivilov on the Russian border. The principal towns and villages are indicated on the accompanying map.

Leimersheim	May 17	Breslau	June 10	Rzeszov	June 23
Erfurt	May 20	Brieg	June 11	Jaroslav	June 25
Leipzig	May 20	Oppeln	June 12	Lemberg	June 27
Dresden	May 29	Gleiwitz	June 13	Zloczov	June 29
Görlitz	June 1	Babice	June 15	Podhace	June 30
Bunzlau	June 4	Myslenice	June 18	Brody	June 30
Hainau	June 5	Bochnia	June 19	Radzivilov	July 1
Liegnitz	June 7	Tarnov	June 21		

Thus the journey to the Russian frontier would have taken 45 days. To this must be added the period of quarantine in Radzivilov which would have lasted from 24 to 28 days; and the final long lap through Podolia and across the Dniester steppe, which would have required between three and four weeks. The duration of the entire journey would, therefore, have been anywhere between 93 and 99 days. This is also confirmed by Lösch's fellow countryman, Anton Marius, who reported that the journey to Odessa took three months.

There were two main routes that led from Radzivilov to Odessa: a. the western road that passed through the Podolian towns of Kamenenz and

Mogilev, and continued along the left bank of the Dniester via Dubossary to Odessa, a distance of some 360 miles; and b. the eastern road which passed through the towns of Yampol and Staro (old) Konstantinon, and continued via Bratslov and Balta to Odessa—a distance of about 375 miles. The latter road was taken by the Lösch party and probably by most of the immigrants of 1809. It may have been the better road. In 1822 Jakob Mayr needed 30 days to travel from Radzivilov to Odessa via the western road, whereas he made the return trip on the eastern road in only 21 days. Perhaps the average time for either road was about 24 days.

5. *The Means of Transportation*

In the earlier years (1803-1808) the emigrants had to provide their own transportation to the riverport of Ulm or Donauwörth. From there the

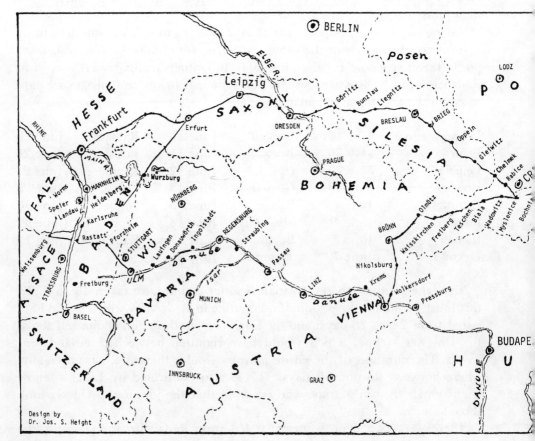

Russian government provided free transportation on the river barges known as *"Ulmer Schachteln"* as far as Vienna. For the overland route from Vienna to Radzivilov the government also provided the transportation by leasing wagons from the post road stations. In 1809, however, they had to provide their own transportation all the way to the Russian border.

They travelled in covered wagons drawn by two horses, though sometimes only one horse was used. Ordinarily, a wagon transported only one family consisting of four or five persons, but there were also instances where a family with eight or nine children travelled in one wagon (6:109). Sometimes as many as 15 or 20 families organized a large wagon train; at other times three or four families formed a travel group. Thus, Mathias Asperger, with his wife and five children, joined three other families numbering 11 souls to make the journey from Flehingen/Karlsruhe and arrived at Radzivilov

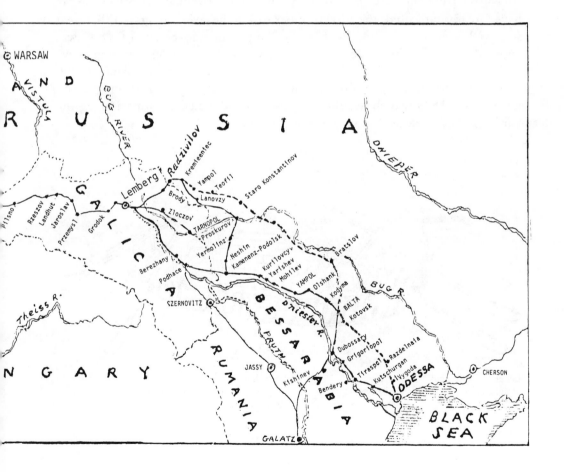

with three wagons and seven horses on July 21, 1809 (4:33).

The fact that some wagons were capable of transporting six to eight persons, with all their baggage, a distance of some 1,600 miles makes it fairly obvious that the vehicles had nothing in common with the rickety wooden wagonettes of the Russian peasants, but must have been large sturdy wagons produced by the village craftsmen of Baden and the Palatinate. They may well have been similar to the so-called "Hungarian wagons" which the German settlers in Hungary used when they migrated to the Grossliebental district in 1807. Indeed, they may well be compared with the famed Conestoga wagons which the Palatinate wainwrights of Pennsylvania produced for the American pioneers who migrated to the West.

According to the evidence available in the extant passports of 1809 more than 380 wagons were moving slowly but steadily along the overland route to Russia from the early part of May until late November. However, as we have already indicated, the total number of families who emigrated that year was well over a thousand, so that the emigration movement of 1809 was larger than any in the preceding years. It was only exceeded by the massive Swabian expedition of 1817 which is said to have involved over 10,000 people. Unfortunately, we do not have a diary travelogue of the emigration journey of 1809 which would give us some detailed information of the hardships and hazards that were encountered.

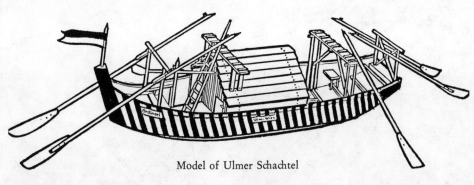

Model of Ulmer Schachtel

Length of ship's side	92 feet	After-deck	3–7 feet
Height of ship's side	5–5½ feet	Length of cabin	15–18 feet
Width of ship	24 feet	Height of gable	12 feet

From the East the sun is shining.
We Christians are hastening
To yonder haven of refuge
Where happiness and joy await us.

Jakob Fr. Koch

III.   The Swabian Expedition

As we have seen, the first great wave of emigration to Russia came in the years 1803 and 1804 when 6,775 people arrived at Odessa. Almost half of the 1,475 families had come from Württemberg; the others were from Baden, Alsace, the Palatinate, and Switzerland. In the years 1805, 1806, and 1807 emigration to Russia was almost completely interrupted by the military campaigns which the selfcrowned emperor Napoleon was waging in central Europe against the Austrians and the Russians. On May 29, 1807, King Friedrich of Württemberg, eager to supply Napoleon with conscripted troops, prohibited all further emigration, and this prohibition remained in force until March 15, 1815.

The second wave of emigration from Württemberg, which began in 1816 and reached its peak the following year, proved to be considerably larger than the first. From January 1 to July 31, 1817, according to official records, 10,298 people emigrated to Russia, including the Russian part of Poland. At least 9,000 of these emigrants (over 1,500 families) proposed to settle in the Caucasus region of New Russia.

Apart from the large number of people involved, this emigration differed from the earlier one in significant respects. Whereas the earlier emigrants took the Danube waterway from Ulm to Vienna and then travelled by wagon train through Bohemia and Austrian Poland via Radzivilov to Odessa, the emigrants of 1817 decided to go down the Danube all the way from Ulm to the Russian river port of Ismail. The motives that led to the Swabian emigration movement of 1817 also had a distinctive character. The earlier emigration had been predominantly motivated by economic and political reasons. While these factors still played an important role, the expedition of 1817 was strongly pervaded by the spirit of religious zealots and chiliast visionaries who sought "a haven of refuge" in the imminent expectation of the millenium. To properly understand the character of the Swabian emigration of 1817 we therefore need to examine more closely the pietist and religious-separatist movements that played such a decisive role in the emigration process of that period.[1]

---

[1] For most of the historical material in this chapter I am chiefly indebted to Dr. Georg Leibbrandt's comprehensive and authoritative book, *"Die Auswanderung der Schwaben nach Russland 1816—1823"*, Ausland und Heimat Verlag, Stuttgart (1928). Cf. also Karl Stumpp, *Ostwanderung der Württemberger 1816 bis 1822.* Sammlung G. Leibbrandt, p. 205 ff.

The pietist movement that began in the sixties of the 18. century in Württemberg was directed against the rationalism that had invaded the Church and the State. In the Lutheran Church this rationalistic spirit was clearly evident in the hymnbook that was issued in 1791 by the consistorial councilor Griesinger. Many people, particularly among the conservative peasant and artisan class were indignant that many time-honored hymns were replaced by new ones which they found shallow, cold, and uninspiring. The introduction of the new Lutheran liturgy in 1809 also created a wave of unrest and resentment when a purely symbolical interpretation of the sacraments and the doctrine of atonement displaced the traditional teaching. Communion became merely a commemorative meal. The ritual of baptism contained no mention of the corruption of original sin; there was no renunciation of the devil; and the godparents were reduced to the status of mere witnesses. Many people also resented the efforts of the Church to give secular subjects a larger role in the school curriculum, to the detriment of religion instruction.

Like the Puritans, the Pietists became convinced that true religion could no longer be found in the established Church, but only in the enlightened heart of the believer. They therefore refused to attend church services, and sought religion in the "warme Stunde", the congenial hour of edification and inspiration in the privacy of the home. These religious separatists, also known as *Stundenbrüder* (Stundists) held their conventicles generally twice a week, and celebrated the "agape" of the early Christians rather than the churchly sacrament. At their meetings they sang pietistic hymns which were often accompanied by a zither. One of the brethren delivered a discourse, while others freely contributed comments and discussions. The women, however, were not allowed to speak at these assemblies.

For the Pietists the criterion of truth was "the inner light", the inspiration of the Spirit. Their fundamental principle was an active brotherly love. They also had a kind of penitential discipline. Transgressors were publicly reprimanded and punished, in severe cases by partial or total excommunication. The Pietists were opposed to all military service and the taking of oath. Some of them celebrated the Sabbath instead of the Sunday.

Even in their outward appearance the Pietists stood apart from other Christians. Their clothing was plain and sombre. Like the Anabaptists, the men wore long beards, long coats, and white conical hats. The women wore long dark skirts, and large bonnets that completely concealed their hair. Both men and women wore a cocarde shaped like a large star that was covered with red satin and fringed with colored lace. Like the Quakers, the Separatists refused to doff their hats to anyone, regardless of rank or station. They also addressed all persons, including kings and nobles, by the democratic "duc," instead of the honorific "Sie."

The Separatists led well-ordered lives, and were quite often regarded as exemplary models of upright behavior. They had a good reputation for honesty and thrift, and never resorted to violence, even when they were unjustly harassed and imprisoned. They were of determined spirit, full of spiritual pride, and self-assured in their possession of the truth. Regarding themselves as "saints" and as "children of God", they kept aloof from other Christians whom they deprecated as "children of the world". The established Church was widely denounced as "Babylon the harlot."

While the peaceful Separatists were permitted by the government to hold their religious meetings, the so-called "revolutionary Separatists", who were strongly influenced by the prevailing ideas of freedom and equality, were regarded as politically dangerous to the social order and liable to punishment and imprisonment. But also the peaceful Separatists were often harassed and their outspoken leaders confined to jail for several weeks or months. However, these stringent measures tended to foment rather than to quell the fires of separatism.

The Separatist movement in Württemberg reached its apogee with the appearance of a leader named Johann Georg Rapp, a weaver from the village of Iptingen. He had read a great deal of the writings of the notable mystic Jakob Böhme, and became an eloquent, energetic protagonist. Since 1795 he held pietistic "hours" in the conventicles of friends and neighbors, preached repentance, and spoke out against the corruption of the Church. He prevailed upon his followers to refuse to have their children baptized by the clergy, to take oaths, and to refrain from marital intercourse. Because of vigorous countermeasures taken by the government, Rapp and 700 of his followers decided in 1804, to emigrate to America, where they hoped to find "an unrestricted religious way of life". He subsequently established a colony called "Harmony" near Pittsburg, Pennsylvania, and a second settlement called "New Harmony" in Indiana. Both communities were established as a theocratic state on the basis of communal property and the law of celibacy.

The Separatist movement in Württemberg received a new impetus and focus from the revival of *Chiliasm,* a doctrine which proclaimed the imminent coming of the millenium — the thousand-year kingdom of peace and prosperity (Gr. *kilia,* a thousand). Already in 1740 the Biblical scholar J. Bengel had stated in his commentary on the Book of Revelations, that the millenium would appear in the year 1836. Jung-Stilling, a court councilor in Baden, who propagated similar adventist beliefs, proclaimed that the thousand-year kingdom would be established in the East. The eschatological mood prevailing among the Separatists became stronger at the turn of the century, and reached a fever pitch when Czar Alexander I vanquished Napoleon in the disastrous defeat of 1812. The religious character of the Czar led the Swabian Chiliasts to regard him as the "white eagle" of Revelations, just as they considered Napoleon "the black angel", the incarnate Anti-Christ. Baroness von Krüdener, a travelling prophetess of Chiliasm, who had been close to Alexander in Paris, in 1815, propagated the idea that Russia would be "the haven of refuge for the faithful of the last days". In the same year she came to Württemberg where she met the Separatist leaders Johann Jakob Koch of Schluchtern and his brother Philip of Marbach. She began preaching her Chiliast message in their conventicles, and succeeded in persuading many of the believers to migrate to Russia. After being expelled from the country, the Baroness went to Switzerland where she continued her activities in 1816 and 1817. In 1824 she emigrated to the Crimea, where she died on December 25.

Apart from their millenarian beliefs, the Swabian Separatists also had sound practical reasons to emigrate. The political situation at the beginning of the century grew worse from year to year. Although Württemberg had the largest and best agricultural land in Germany, its finances were in a deplorable condition, its administration was inefficient, and law and order in a state of turmoil. In 1796 French troops had occupied the lands of Württemberg and Bavaria, and the inhabitants were afflicted with dreadful harassments, contributions, and requisitionings. In 1806 and 1807 Swabian conscripts were compelled to serve in Napoleon's campaign against the Prussians in Silesia; in 1809 they were fighting against the Austrians, and in 1812 against the Russians. Of the 15,000 who fought valiantly at Smolensk and Borodino only 150 made it back over the Beresina.

The peasants and artisans also resented the wasteful, luxurious extravagance of the royal court, and the expensive indulgence of the "noble passion" of game hunting. They also protested the abolition of the time-honored rights traditionally enjoyed by the communities, the imposition of intolerable taxes and services for the military, and the ruthless conscription of their sons into the army.

The economic situation, which threatened to reduce the peasantry to a state of chronic poverty, was one of the principal factors of emigration. The country experienced a fateful series of poor crops in 1809, 1810, and from 1812 to 1815. In 1816 the unseasonable wet weather caused a total crop failure when grain, grapes, fruit, and fodder rotted in the fields. Two-thirds of the livestock perished or had to be slaughtered because of shortage of feed. People were forced to eat wild roots, tree bark, and bran.

The Swabian emigration to Russia was initiated in the late summer of 1816 by Friedrich Fuchs, the leader of the Separatist group at Schwaikheim. His earlier imprisonment in the fortress of Hohenasperg did not cool his zeal and determination. After his release he organized an "emigration harmony" and obtained an immigration permit from the Russian embassy at Stuttgart. On September 12 he embarked with 40 families on an "Ulmer Schachtel" that brought them safely to Vienna, where Gottfried Löffler and Adam Schüle were elected as elders of the emigrant group. From Vienna the journey was continued down the Danube on a flat-bottomed river barge known as a "Zille", which brought the emigrants via Ofen, Orshua, and Galati to the Russian port of Ismail, where they were placed in quarantine for 30 days. Since the funds of the immigrants had been nearly exhausted, the local Greek merchants provided them with food during their protracted stay. They were then transported by Moldavian wagons to the colony of Grossliebental, where they arrived on December 12. The following spring the Schwaikheim party started out on the long last leg of the journey that brought them to their destination near Tiflis on the Caspian Sea.

The news of the successful journey of the Schwaikheimer harmony created a great deal of excitement among the Swabian Chiliasts back home, and their leaders lost no time in organizing a number of "fraternal emigration harmonies of the children of God". The Koch brothers issued a proclamation calling upon their followers to emigrate from Babel to the Caucasus, the land of freedom and promise. Twenty-four elders were chosen to administer the religious and mundane affairs of the emigrants. The well-to-do pledged one tenth of their capital assets to help finance the cost of the journey for the poorer members. In a short time 130 families applied for membership in the Marbacher harmony. At the same time the Esslinger "harmony of the faithful", an offshoot of the Zell-Altbach group, made preparations to emigrate. This party decided to establish community property according to the system of the early Christian church. Each member was requested to indicate his name, place of residence and cash assets, and to make a pledge to support all widows and orphans. By the beginning of December 1816 the Esslinger group already numbered 70 families under the leadership of Johann Georg Frick of Altbach and Johann Reuer of Esslingen. Ulm was designated as the gathering place, and the date for the Danube journey was set for February 1, 1817.

Several other emigration harmonies were being established, each with its own leaders. Among the principal harmonies were the following:

Schwarzwälder: led by Friedrich Koch of Bössingen
Nagold-Freudenstadt: led by Jakob Barth of Altbach
Weissach: led by Johann Leibbrandt of Unterweissach
Oetlingen: led by Johann Georg Bidlingmaier and Jakob Lutz of Plochingen
Walddorf: led by Johann Maier and Philipp Rohrer (of Grafenberg)
Plattenhardt: led by Adam Böpple
Pliezhausen: led by Stephan Schmid
Reutlingen: led by Martin Vollmer

While the emigration harmonies were being established, the leaders had to apply to the ministry, i. e. to the King of Württemberg, for emigration permits. They also sought to obtain a general exemption from the 10 percent emigration

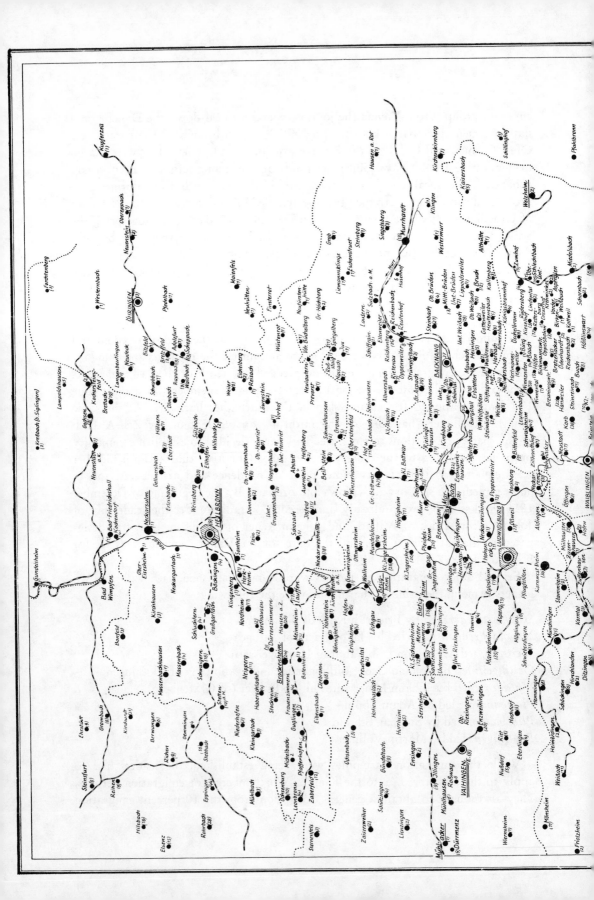

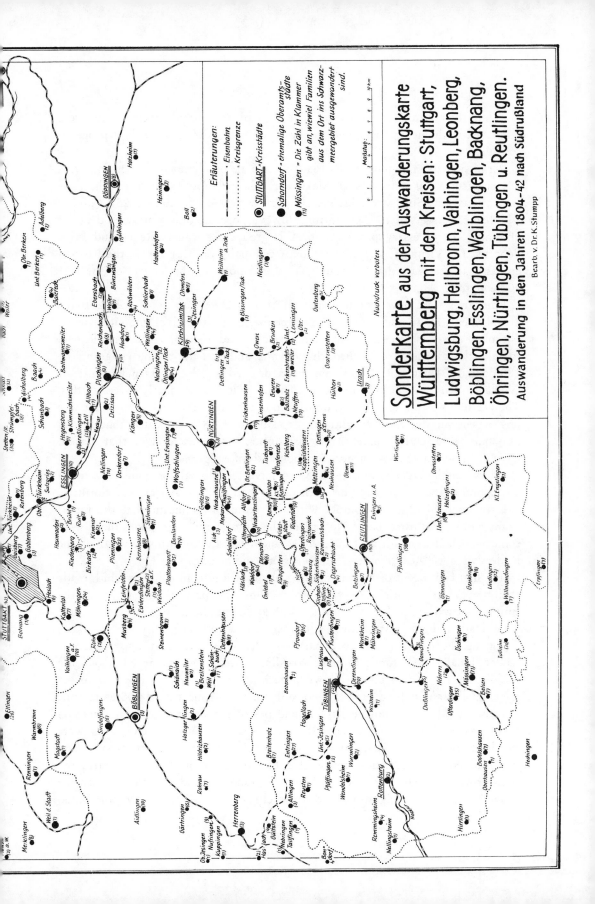

Sonderkarte aus der Auswanderungskarte Württemberg mit den Kreisen: Stuttgart, Ludwigsburg, Heilbronn, Vaihingen, Leonberg, Böblingen, Esslingen, Waiblingen, Backnang, Öhringen, Nürtingen, Tübingen u. Reutlingen.

Auswanderung in den Jahren 1804–42 nach Südrußland

Bearb. v. Dr. K. Stumpp

Erläuterungen:

⌁	Eisenbahn
⌁	Kreisgrenze
◉	STUTTGART-Kreisstädte
⦿	Schorndorf = ehemalige Oberamtsstädte
●	Mössingen = Die Zahl in Klammer (11) gibt an, wieviel Familien aus dem Ort ins Schwarzmeergebiet ausgewandert sind.

Maßstab:
0 1 2 3 4 5 6 7 8 9 10 km

Nachdruck verboten

tax, but their request was denied. The lists of the would-be emigrants were published in the newspapers, and the heads of households put up their property for sale.

Permission to immigrate to Russia also had to be obtained. A petition with 700 signatures was sent to Czar Alexander, who promptly granted it. The Russian embassy at Stuttgart subsequently agreed to issue permits to 230 families who had cash assets of 100,000 florins. However, because of a protracted delay in obtaining the necessary passports for this group, the leaders Reuer und Frick departed for Vienna to expedite the matter. Finally on May, 1817, the Russian embassy at Stuttgart granted four general passports to the leaders of the first 900 emigrants.

Emissaries were now sent to Ulm and also to Odessa to make the necessary arrangements for the departure of the expedition and its arrival in South Russia. Although the Russian embassy in Vienna strongly advised the responsible leaders to take the overland route through Bohemia and Galicia, as the emigrants of 1803 and 1804 had done, Reuer and Frick decided to take the Danube route all the way to Russian riverport of Ismail. The other leaders evidently agreed to this. The decision was no doubt based on two considerations: the journey by boat was less expensive, and the Schwaikheim expedition of 1816 indicated that it was also quite safe. Unfortunately, this assumption was a grave error that was to have the most tragic consequences for thousands of emigrants.

Every immigrant was also required to have testimonials of good citizenship and moral character. In addition, each family had to have at least 300 florins in cash or goods. Failure to comply with this requirement meant that the immigrant would be turned back. Not all of the immigrants were poor; there were some who had as much as 1,000, 2,000 and even 4,000 florins; several of the leaders were well-to-do millers, wine-growers, and artisans.

The first contingent of 900 emigrants was divided into 14 columns which made their departure at brief intervals. From Ulm, the port of embarkation, the emigrants travelled to Vienna on the so-called "Ulmer Schachteln", which carried a full load of about 200 passengers plus their trunks and baggage.

Among the first columns to depart was the Weissacher Harmony which its leader Johann Leibbrandt brought to Ulm where they embarked about the middle of May. Other boats followed, week after week. According to a report issued at Passau on June 16, 1817, not only the above mentioned 900 emigrants, but also an additional unforeseen 900 had passed through the port and were on their way to Vienna. At Obernzell in Bavaria 300 Swabian emigrants were detained because their passports were not in order; also 36 emigrants from Baden, who did not have sufficient money for the journey. The Esslinger Harmony, numbering 225 souls, embarked at Ulm on June 20, and by mid-summer the growing stream of emigration reached its climax. From Vienna a report dated

48

July 15 stated: "Almost every day groups of German emigrants are passing through, intent on seeking their good fortune on the uninhabited steppes of Russia." The emigrant movement continued until the end of summer. On August 5 the Nagold-Freudental Harmony led by Jakob Barth was still in Württemberg. On August 13 a boatload of Swiss and Alsatian emigrants, for the most part zealous followers of the Chiliast prophetess von Krüdener, departed from Vienna.

Ulmer Schachtel, with cathedral in background

In Vienna the emigrants usually had to wait a few days before they could continue their journey. The leaders had to charter the necessary boats ("Zillen"), with their crews of four or five boatmen. Baggage and provisions had to be hauled aboard. For reasons of economy the leaders packed as many people into the boats as possible. Indeed some of the boats were dreadfully overcrowded. While the "Ulmer Schachteln" that had brought the emigrants to Vienna usually had about 200 passengers, the "Zillen" that were to transport them to the mouth

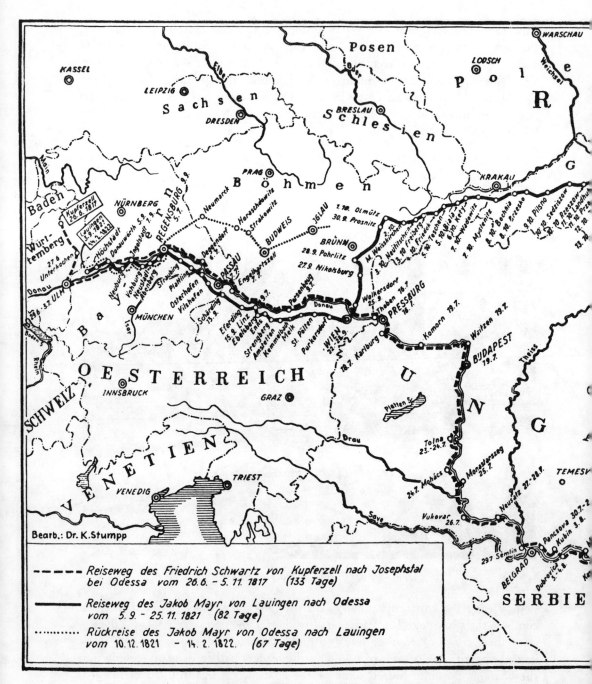

─ ─ ─ Reiseweg des Friedrich Schwartz von Kupferzell nach Josephstal
bei Odessa vom 26.6. – 5. 11. 1817 (133 Tage)

──────── Reiseweg des Jakob Mayr von Lauingen nach Odessa
vom 5.9. – 25. 11. 1821 (82 Tage)

············ Rückreise des Jakob Mayr von Odessa nach Lauingen
vom 10. 12. 1821 – 14. 2. 1822. (67 Tage)

─ ─ ─ Itinerary of Friedrich Schwartz from Kupferzell to Josephst

──────── Itinerary of Jakob Mayr from Lauingen to Odessa, from 9.

············ Return Journey of Jakob Mayr from Odessa to Lauingen,

50

ear Odessa from 6. 26. to 11. 5. 1817 (133 days)

o 11. 25. 1821 (82 days)

m 12. 10. to 2. 14. 1822 (67 days)

-Courtesy of Karl Stumpp

51

of the Danube sometimes carried 300 or 400 people. Thus the emigration harmony led by miller Koch had come to Vienna in four boats and started out from there in two, but at Pest the 430 passengers were placed in a single boat. As we shall see, this overcrowding of the boats was to have disastrous consequences.

Even before the start of the long journey down the Danube there were outbreaks of discontent and dissension. The "harmonies" were split into two factions: the leaders and the misled. Some of leaders treated the people harshly, and even committed acts of dishonesty by squandering or embezzling money from the communal fund, thus shamelessly abusing the trust of their followers. In the course of the journey some emigrants, having become weary of the long and arduous trip, deserted the expedition and accepted offers of work and a livelihood among the landed gentry in Hungary. Besides the moral corruption of individual leaders, the emigrants were frequently exposed to other misdemeanors. On their way through Bavaria, Austria, and especially in the Turkish domains of Rumania, they were relieved of much of their money by swindlers and unscrupulous merchants.

But the greatest cause of discontent among the emigrants were the precarious conditions that prevailed on the boats. The roofless, single-deck "Zillen" were packed and crammed to capacity. Every available space was filled with men, women and children. There was not even enough room to sit or lie down. People had to take turns lying on the floor or on top of crates and trunks. It was an appalling scene of congested confusion: the healthy with the sick, the newborn with the dying, the living with the dead. It was a bedlam of wailing and laughter, of praying and cursing. One day the pitiful passengers were scorched by the blazing heat, the next they were drenched by a sudden downpour of rain. The nights were spent in a desolate spot near the shore where the men hastily set up some tents while the women prepared a frugal meal over the camp fire. The inevitable swarms of gnats, mosquitoes, and river flies made it difficult to eat in peace, and virtually impossible to sleep.

The slow voyage in the middle of the hot summer, the irregular meals, the lack of sanitary facilities, the consumption of too much raw fruit and spicy Turkish wine soon caused physical debility, intermittent fever, dysentery, and other illnesses. Even in the early stages of the journey while the boats were passing through Hungary, many people fell ill and died. But conditions were to become much worse before journey's end. At Galati a virulent fever broke out among the passengers. On August 24 half the people on five of the boats that had arrived there were lying around sick, and 42 of them died within five days. The dreaded plague had broken out! On a boat filled with emigrants from the Black Forest, almost all died of fever, some infected by the plague.

After arriving in Ismail the immigrants disembarked and were placed into a quarantine camp where they remained confined for a period that varied from

40 to 50 days, though there were instances when this was reduced to 24 days. The passengers from each boat were quartered in single camps which were roped off from the others, and policed by Russian soldiers.

Since no regular quarantine buildings were available, the people were put up in dingy unheated huts with re-thatched roofs and drafty walls of clay-plastered wickerwork. Hundreds of families who arrived later in the fall had to spend the entire period of quarantine in their own tents, despite the prevailing cold and rainy weather. The entire quarantine complex was located on the open steppe near the city and almost in the shadow of the old Turkish fortress. The hundreds of huts, tents, and barracks that covered the area had the appearance of an immense army camp. Some of the immigrants who had to pitch their tents close to the fortress claimed that it was the site where 20,000 soldiers, who had perished in the bloody siege of 1790, were interred in shallow graves.

The living conditions of immigrants quarantined in these primitively wretched camps almost defy description. The quarters were squalid, damp, and cold. The weather had become dreadfully inclement, for at that season of the year violent rainstorms, high winds, and even frost prevailed in the Danube delta. Rare were the days when there was a bit of sunshine.

The lack of sufficient food and warm clothing aggravated the general misery of the people from day to day. Some food could be purchased in the city, but the prices were exorbitant and not within reach of the poorer people. By order of the Czar the quarantined immigrants were to be provided with bread, flour, meat, butter, rice, barley, coffee, and sugar; also wine, brandy, and vinegar. However, the available supplies were far from being sufficient for the thousands of half-starved, fever-ridden people. Most of them had already spent almost all their money; many were forced to sell some of their belongings in order to obtain food. Unscrupulous middlemen took advantage of their plight and fleeced them for the sake of easy profits.

Soon after the arrival of the first boats at Ismail an epidemic of virulent fever broke out in the quarantine camps. One witness speaks of "nerve and other fevers, yellow and black dysentery accompanied by large boils on head and neck." The death toll mounted from day to day. One of the survivors who had arrived in the Swiss-Alsatian boat reported in a letter[2] of April 12, 1818: "In our camp a great many people died. There were bereaved widowers and widows and orphans. Oftentimes from 10 to 20, sometimes even 30 people died in a single day, and were buried in mass graves."

---

[2] Anon. *"Merkwürdige und vollständige Reisebeschreibung"*, originally published in Germanien in 1818; re-edited by Friedrich Fiechtner and republished in 1970 by the Landsmannschaft der Bessarabiendeutschen, Stuttgart. An English edition was published by Theodore C. Wenzlaff in 1973 under the title, *Fateful Danube Joruney.*

The immigration authorities and the military made honest efforts to alleviate the appalling situation. The critically ill were taken to the city hospital which had heated rooms, though the accommodations were limited. A number of larger huts in the quarantine encampment were therefore converted into emergency lazarets which provided room for 50 or 60 beds. But these wickerwork barracks were not only unheated but also drafty and leaky. According to one eyewitness: "Whenever it rained, the water ran through the (thatched) roof into the beds." Since there were not enough hospital attendants, the still healthy immigrants were generally permitted to attend to the needs of their sick relatives.

A number of doctors were sent into the quarantine camps by the government, but they were virtually helpless in stemming the tide of the ravaging epidemic. Their efforts were largely limited to dispensing medicine of dubious efficacy. They visited the field hospitals, inquired about the sickness of the patients, and gave everyone a spoonful of an unidentified liquid from a large wooden container that was carried by two attendants. They also advised the patients to drink malaga wine and a hot punch made of wine, lemon juice, and nutmeg.

But the constant thirst of the fever-wracked patients was particularly aggravated by the fact that there was not a drop of good water in the entire Ismail area. Since all the quarantine hospitals had only the loathsome river water from the Danube, the doctors advised the patients to drink it only with a liberal admixture of wine vinegar. In their delirious attempt to alleviate their tormenting thirst, many patients drank unsterilized river water, and this may have contributed substantially to their death.

Under these circumstances the epidemic raged on for several weeks, and the death toll continued to mount. At the height of the epidemic over 1,200 people died within a period of 24 days. Entire families were wiped out, and in a large number of families only one or two members survived.

The immigrants themselves had to bury their dead. Every morning a number of volunteer gravediggers went through the camps, inquiring at each hut and tent whether anyone had died. They then placed all the corpses on a pile, removed them by wagons, and hauled them in a boat across the river, where they were wrapped in reeds and interred in mass graves. There were no funeral services. Each gravedigger received from the government a burial fee of one Turkish guilder (about 36 Kreuzer) for each adult, and 24 Kreuzer for each child.

The total number of immigrants who perished in that fateful fall of 1817 in the quarantine camps of Ismail has never been definitely established. According to a letter written April 20, 1820, by the immigrant Johann Georg Höhn of Karlstal near Odessa, 1,328 immigrants were buried at Ismail. An additional 800 out of a contingent of 1,500 people who were en route from Ismail to Odessa died on the steppes of Moldavia (Bessarabia) or in the quarantine barracks of Ovidiopol. The Separatists leaders Frick and Reuer, who visited Czar Alexander at Moscow in the winter of 1818, were probably correct when they reported to him that almost 3,000 immigrants had perished.

In those traumatic weeks many of the leaders of the ill-fated Swabian expedition also succumbed. The following are known to have died at Ismail: Johannes Leibbrandt of Unterweissach (July 24), his wife (Sept 11), and his 2 daughters (Oct 3 and 10); only Immanuel-Jakob, the eleven-year-old son survived; Jakob Philipp Koch of Marbach; Johann Jakob Koch of Schluchtern; Konrad Eppinger and Jakob Lutz of Plochingen; Johann Georg Bidlingmayer of Ötlingen (Sept 15); Johann Melchior Lindenmayer of Bietigheim; Gottlieb Jäger of Gross-Heppach; and unidentified others, among them the leader of the Swiss-Alsatian contingent.

For the immigrants who survived the horrors of Ismail there was still a final excruciating ordeal. Upon their release from quarantine they were required to carry all their clothing and baggage into a closed-in boat for fumigation. After this was accomplished, the poor people — men, women, and children — had to undress completely on the chilly, wind-swept shore, and return to the boat to put on "disinfected" clothes and take their other belongings with them.

The government officials now provided the immigrants with transportation to the old fortress town of Ovidiopol on the east bank of the Dniester liman. The transportation facilities consisted of ox-drawn wagons which were driven by Russian or Moldavian peasants who had been requisitioned for compulsory service. As described by a Swiss immigrant, these vehicles were "small, poorly-constructed wagons, with wheels that had no iron rims and axles. It was difficult to imagine how anyone would venture to drive them 60 paces, much less a distance of 50 or 60 hours." Since the open wagons provided no shelter against the rain and the wind, the immigrants found it necessary to attach wooden bows and stretch a tent over them. Before departure each family received three Turkish coins from the officials as food and travel money for the next two weeks.

The Russian wagon trains were usually made up of 120 vehicles. However, because of their small size, they transported only 60 families, since half of the wagons were needed to haul the baggage. The journey from Ismail to Akkerman, which lay on the west shore of the Dniester liman, required from 50 to 60 hours of travel time. By driving at least 15 hours a day, the Russian teamsters were sometimes able to make the trip in 4 or 5 days. They often started out at 3 a. m., and made only brief stops in the early morning and about noon, in order to cook a hasty meal and allow their oxen to graze a while. The wagon train then rolled on again until the late evening hours. At about midnight the drivers stopped for a few hours of rest. Wrapped in their thick sheepskin coats, they slept on the ground or under the wagon, while the oxen grazed nearby. The poor immigrants had to remain in their wagons where they were too miserably cramped to lie down and too cold to have a restful sleep.

For the weary, run-down wayfarers the jolting journey across the freezing, trackless steppe was an exhausting, harrowing experience; for the critically ill, many of whom became delirious and demented, it was a fatal ordeal. More than 300 people died in their wagons and were buried along the lonesome road that led across the alien steppe of Bessarabia.

A day or two after the wagon train arrived at Akkerman, the immigrants and their baggage were loaded on a ferry boat that took them, in 3 or 4 hours, across the wide estuary to Ovidiopol. Here they were again placed into quarantine for shorter or longer periods of time, depending on the state of their health or the available accommodations. In contrast to the situation confronting the immigrants of 1804, Ovidiopol now had large quarantine buildings, with many well-furnished and even heated rooms. However, with the unusually large influx of immigrant colonists, the rooms were soon overcrowded. A large proportion of the survivors of the Ismail calamity were still sick and ailing. The first contingent that arrived were in such wretched condition that the officers of the Kamchatka regiment immediately took up a collection of 920 rubles to provide the hapless people with food and warm clothing. But the number of dying mounted from day to day, as people succumbed to dysentery and other infectious diseases. Soon the death toll reached 400, and the end was not in sight. Because of the lack of gravediggers and coffins, the dead were interred in mass graves at a site that became known as the "Pesthügel", the hill of the plague.

Count Langeron, who had succeeded his fellow countryman Duc de Richelieu as governor of Odessa, made every effort to relieve the deplorable situation. He gave orders that the old unused cloth factory of Grossliebental be converted into an emergency hospital to accommodate the most critically ill who were languishing in the Ovidiopol quarantine. Most of the families who were still on their feet were transported by the German colonists to their villages in the Grossliebental[3] and Kutschurgan districts, where they were placed into winter quarters. There was hardly a single home in those villages that did not take in at least one family.

It should be mentioned here that one group of 98 families had already decided in Ismail that they would not migrate to the Caucasus but intended to settle in the Odessa region. The government readily offered them a tract of land in the Kogelnik valley in Bessarabia, 125 versts from the town of Kishineff. However, soon after their arrival at the site where the new colony of Elft (later renamed

---

[3] The duration of the journey from Ulm to Odessa via the Danube route ranged from 90 to 130 days, depending on the lenght of the stop-overs (at Vienna, Galati, Akkerman, and Ovidiopol) and the length of the quarantine at Ismail (40—50 days). The actual journey-time on the Danube was as follows: From Ulm to Vienna   7 days
                                                                          From Vienna to Ismail   40 days
Thus the duration of the stop-overs and the quarantine equalled, and often exceeded, the length of the journey.

Teplitz) was to be established, almost all the settlers became ill of dysentery and fever, and 100 died within the first four months.

In the spring of 1818 a considerable number of immigrants who had decided to remain in the Odessa area were settled in the villages of Grossliebental, Alexanderhilf, and Neuburg. A number of immigrant artisans who were willing to forego the privileged status of colonists were established as craftsmen in the city of Odessa. Another group who had arrived under the leadership of Koch, Nusser, and Stockinger were settled in the newly established colonies of Stuttgart, Friedrichstal, and Waterloo in the Beresan district. Twenty-seven families from the parties of Stephan Schmidt and Johann Gugel were settled in the colony of Johannestal. Sixty-four families from the Weissach and Ötlingen harmonies, who had been quartered for many months in the Catholic villages of the Kutschurgan district, were settled in the new colony of Hoffnungstal, 50 versts west of Tiraspol on the Dniester. They were later joined by several members of the Backnang and Marbach harmonies.

As we indicated earlier, the Schwaikheimer harmony, which was the first to emigrate to Russia, arrived at Odessa on December 31, 1816. While 300 dissident families decided to settle in the Odessa area, 31 families were determined to continue their journey to the "haven of refuge" in the Caucasus. They set out in a wagon train in July of 1817 and after a hazardous journey across the Caucasus mountain range they arrived safely in Tiflis on the 20th of September, and were settled in the colony of Marienfeld, 35 versts east of the city.

Heartened by this successful expedition, 400 Chiliast families who had spent the winter of 1817/18 in the Grossliebental villages insisted on being settled in the Caucasus, despite the opposition of the immigration authorities. In midwinter two of their leaders, Reuer and Frick, journeyed to Moscow to present their petition to the Czar. Alexander was so overwhelmed by their obdurate faith that he decided to permit them and their followers to settle near Tiflis. Another 100 families who had already been settled in the Grossliebental district sold their property and joined the Chiliast expedition.

The 500 families were divided into 10 parties, and the first wagon trains departed from Odessa near the end of May. The first parties arrived in Tiflis in September and October, and were established in three villages not too far from the city. The last two parties, comprising 125 families, arrived in November and were settled at Katharinenfeld, 200 versts east of Tiflis. They endured much tribulation and hardship, and 256 people died in the course of the year. Disorder and dissension broke out among the dissatisfied and disillusioned colonists. Frick died a few years later, and one of the principal leaders, Jakob Koch of Bössingen, unable to endure their reproaches, sought refuge with the Moravian Brethren at Sarepta on the Volga, where (it was said) he bitterly lamented the part he had played.

But the tribulations of the Chiliast colonists were not yet at an end. During the war between the Persians and the Russians, their villages were ruthlessly attacked and devastated. On August 26, 1826, a horde of Turkish and Kurdish horsemen descended upon the colony of Katharinental and perpetrated a scene of horrifying violence and cruelty. A missionary named Saltete described[4] it in these words: "They tore the infants from the arms of their mothers, and spiked them with their lances; they ravished wives and maidens; they tied old men to the tails of their horses, and dragged them after them. Upwards of 30 young and old they butchered. They burned down the houses, cornfields, and gardens. Depriving 250 families of house and home, they turned the whole district into a desert. They carried away every article of value, but worst of all, they dragged 140 men, women, and children into slavery."

Another report gives the following details: "No human tongue can describe the misery which, in the course of a few hours, overwhelmed the settlement. Some of the colonists, in attempting to escape, were caught with long cords, in the same manner as wild cattle. Whoever was thus taken was immediately stripped of his clothing, and either killed on the spot, or allowed to run away naked. Little children were bound together in pairs and then slung across the horses' backs, like articles of baggage. If any of them disturbed their persecutors by their cries, they were instantly dispatched, before the face of their parents. Every sense of shame, and every feeling of humanity, was extinguished in these barbarians; the brutal hordes set no limits to their licentious passions. A young woman of acknowledged piety, in trying to escape from the robbers, was fired at and shot in the spine, so that she instantly fell and slowly expired in the most excruciating agonies. A man, while endeavoring to intercede for the lives of his wife and children, was murdered at the foot of a tree to which his wife had fled for shelter. The latter, with an infant at her breast, was spared, but with a bleeding heart she saw her two little ones carried away into slavery. Three girls, about fifteen years of age, thought themselves happy in having reached the river, at a distance of about 7 or 8 versts, when two Tartars overtook them, and cruelly wreaked their vengeance on two of them. Among the wounded who were afterwards taken up and attended to was one who had his skull laid open, and was wounded in the back with no less than twenty-two thrusts of a lance. A Kurd ordered another of the colonists to throw himself on the ground, in which situation he pierced him twice with a lance, in the same manner as fish are caught by spearing them in the water. Another Kurd hurled a large stone at him, so that he was eventually left half dead.

The most deplorable situation was that of the poor captives who were treated like beasts, and inhumanly butchered if they did not immediately obey the cruel

---

[4] cf. Pinkerton, Robert, D. D., *Russia*, London, 1833, pp. 149—51.

orders of their plunderers. A part of them have been carried away and sold in Turkey, and the remainder are in slavery in Persia. The almighty hand of the Lord, however, preserved the lives of 240 persons, but upwards of 30 were put to death, and about 140 were carried away into slavery."

Of the 1,500 emigrant families who had set out on the ill-fated expedition to the mouth of the seven-streamed Danube, only a remnant of 400 made it to the Caucasus. The Chiliast dream of the pious pilgrims who had hoped to see the coming of the glorious millenium lay shattered in the dust. Along the Danube route nearly 3,000 souls were doomed to an early tragic death in the perilous ports of Galati and Ismail or at the precarious way-stations of Teplitz, Tatar-Bunar, Akkerman, Ovidiopol, and Grossliebental. The majority of the fortunate survivors found a haven of refuge and a land of promise on the fertile steppe above the Black Sea.

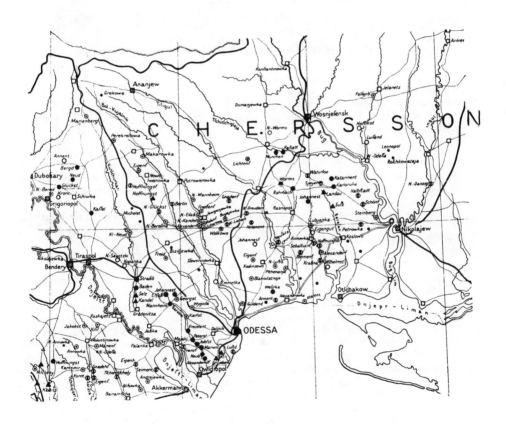

Of the hardships and tribulations endured by the emigrants during their long, long journey down the Danube, we have several eyewitness accounts in the form of diaries or letters written by certain passengers. To provide the reader with detailed first-hand information about the enormous difficulties and dangers of that epic journey, I have selected three of the most significant documents: 1. The *Schwarz* Travel Account; 2. The *Bidlingsmaier* Letter; and 3. The *Höhn* Letter. (Cf. also J. B., *"Fateful Danube Journey"*, published by Theodore C. Wenzlaff).

1. The Second Travelogue[1] to Russia by Friedrich Schwarz and his family

1817 Thursday, June 26. It was on this day that I set out, with my wife and 9 children, from *Kupferzell,* and had to taste the bitterest pain of separation.

27. We arrived at *Unterkochen.*

28. As far as *Allbek* (Alpeck, near Ulm).

29. Sunday morning at 8 o'clock we arrived safe and sound in *Ulm* and were lodged in the inn "To the Golden Goose".

July

2. I have to pay the boat fare to Vienna, namely 4.30 florins per person under 8 years, 5.30 fl. from 8—16 years, and 6.30 fl. for adults. It cost me 58.30 fl. Our baggage was loaded in the evening.

3. In the afternoon, aboard the boat, a beautiful song was sung with music, a prayer was said, and brother Bayer gave a brief but fitting address to the travellers as well as the spectators. At 2 o'clock we departed amid ardent tears and prayers for God's blessing. We safely reached *Lauingen* in the evening.

4. We got as far as two stations from *Ingolstadt* when a thunderstorm prevented us from continuing. We had to stay on an island, where it rained hard all night and the next day.

5. We reached *Regensburg,* where we had to remain aboard the boat because of the continuing rain. We spent a miserable night because of the lack of room.

6. We reached *Straubing* at noon, and *Deggendorf* in the evening.

7. In the morning, from 4—8 we were delayed because of the fog, and at noon we reached *Passau* where we stopped for two hours. In the evening we arrived in *Engelhardtszell,* where our passports were inspected. Brother Jakob and I stayed overnight with our families in the inn "To the Lamb", and had good, inexpensive accommodation. I should mention that from here to Ismail I never got out of my pants, socks and boots, as this was the last time I slept in a regular bed until I reached Russia.

8. Because of the rainy weather we could not depart until 11 o'clock in the morning. We reached *Aschbach* at 2 p. m. and had another passport inspection.

9. We left at 6 in the morning and arrived at *Linz* at 11 o'clock. Here we had to show our

---

[1] cf. Karl Stumpp's detailed map of the itinerary appearing in chapter 2. My translation of the travel account and the subsequent two letters is based on the German texts that were provided by Dr. Stumpp.

Ulmer Schachtel

passports a third time. In the evening we came to *Persenbeug* where there is an imperial castle.

10. We departed at 3.30 in the morning of a beautiful day and at 4 o'clock we arrived at *Nussdorf*, where we had to wait until we were directed to a landing pier in *Vienna* ...

11. I went into the city with my children who were so amazed with wonder that they hardly knew what to gaze at.

12. There were thunderstorms all day, and we had to stay in our room, where I had the chance to write to my dear brothers in Kupferzell ...

14. Again I had to pay boat fare, this time to Galatz, about 700 hours' journey. All the passengers in the five ships were divided in 3 classes: the first class fare was 16 florins, the second 17, and the third 18 fl. We again departed at 3 o'clock and at 10 we reached *Rustschuk*, which is a fortress that was heavily damaged by the Russians in 1811.

15. We had to move into a larger ship, but we now have less room, because 121 more people were added, making 309 souls in all.

16. We departed again, in God's name, at 6 a. m. and at 12 we reached *Diem* (Theben, Hung. Deveny, Slovak. Devin) on the Hungarian border, where the ship was again to be inspected. And so we left our dear German fatherland behind, but we did not forget it ... At 3 p. m. we arrived in *Pressburg*. Since we had to provide ourselves with food for three days, we stayed here overnight.

17. We were supposed to start early, but a wind arose which blew so violently all day that we had to remain another night.

18. Because of the wind we could not depart until 9 a. m., but an hour later we ran into such a storm that the boatmen had the greatest difficulty in getting the ship out of the current. We reached *Karlsburg* (Karlburg) at 11.15 p. m.

19. We started at 4 a. m. and passed *Gomoren* (Komorn) at 11. *Waitzen* at 1, and at 3 p. m. we arrived in *Pest*, where we again had to have our passports inspected ...

21. We had to purchase provisions for 8 days, and obtained the finest bread.

22. We departed at 2 p. m. and landed at an uninhabited place at 9.30.

23. We started at 1.30 a. m. and travelled all day in the finest weather. At 10 p. m. we landed at *Turnau* (Tolna) where many Württemberger have been living for 20 years and doing very well.
24. We set out at 4 a. m. and landed near *Mogatschau* (Mohacs) at 9 p. m.
25. We stayed there until 2 p. m., because a woman who died had to be buried. We landed near *Monassa* (Monastarsceg) at 9 p. m.
26. We departed at 3 p. m. and arrived at 3 p. m. in *Neusatz,* across from the fortress of *Peterwardein.* We again had to buy provisions for several days which were somewhat more expensive that at Pest.
28. We set out at 2 p. m., but after half an hour we had to anchor until 6, because of the wind. At 10 we landed at an uninhabited place, where we found so many fruit trees laden with plums that the branches almost broke.
29. We departed at 4 a. m., and at 11 we reached *Semlin,* where we again had to buy some food and show our passports.
30. At 6 a. m. we passed the famous fortress *(Belgrad)* and reached *Panschua* (Pancsova) at 9; the leaders alone went to the town to have our passports inspected. We thought we would be able to depart by noon, but the commandant was so strict and wanted to ascertain if the number of passengers corresponded with the passports.
31. Stormy weather set in, and we had to remain. On this day the following accident occurred: A man named Reiber was bathing his child alongside the ship when his feet slipped and a large wave carried him under the boat, and he could not be found. The lack of precaution was to blame for this unfortunate mishap.

August

1. The storm let up a bit during the night, but next morning it grew so much stronger that we had to remain in the same place. Only at the risk of one's life could we get to the town in our small boats, in order to obtain provisions.
2. The storm began to abate and about noon it was over. We had the finest weather as we departed from this desolate island at 2 p. m., thanking God for his infinite goodness. At 9 p. m. we landed at an uninhabited spot across from the Turkish fortress of *Sementria* (Semendria).
3. We departed at 4 a. m. and at 6 we stopped at *Cobin* (Kubin), where we again had to have our passports inspected. Here we also buried an old man and an old woman who had died during the night. We departed at 2 p. m. and landed near *Tobrawaz* (Dubravca) at 8 in the evening.
4. Departure was at 4 a. m., and we landed near *Neu Molda* (Neu Moldava) at 10 p. m. In this area there are silver and copper mines. In the evening we landed at an uninhabited spot.
5. We departed at 4 a. m., but had to lie at anchor from 6 to 9 because of the fog. From 2 to 5 p. m. we travelled through the *Gasan* (Kasan) Pass, which is a narrow gorge enclosed on both sides by huge rock walls, where the changing rapids and torrents are much more dangerous than those at Linz. At 6 p. m. we reached *Orsowa,* which is the last Christian locality on our route.
6. We remained here, because our leaders had to go to the pasha in *Neu-Orsowa,* three-quarters of an hour from here, in order to have our passports inspected.
7. We departed at 9 a. m. and passed Neu-Orsowa, a crescent-shaped fortress in the middle of the Danube. From 10 to 11 a. m. we passed through the most dangerous place on the Danube, namely the *Iron Gate.* The water there is in such an uproar that one naturally doubts one can get through safety. The whole Danube at this spot is so strewn with boulders that one can see them protrude wherever the water shoots upward. The ships had to be steered right and left between the boulders, but one heard them scraping over low rocks, so that one became faint-hearted and frightened. At 12 o'clock we landed across from the Turkish fortress of *Glatuwa* (Kladowa), where we again had to show our passports, and so were compelled to stay overnight.
8. We had to remain another day, because the newly-arrived boatmen were so intoxicated with brandy that we could not entrust ourselves to them.

9. We departed at noon in the most delightful weather, but at 1 p. m. we had to land again because of the wind. We started again at 5 and landed at an uninhabited spot at 9 p. m.

10. We set out at 3 a. m. and came to *Vittin* (Vidin) at 3, where our passports had to be taken at once to the pasha.

11. Our departure was at 3 p. m. and we landed at a desolate place at 8 in the evening.

12. We travelled from 3 a. m. to 8 p. m., and during the whole day we saw only two villages on the shore. But the Danube was swarming with bustards and wild ducks. We again landed at a uninhabited place.

13. We departed again at 3 a. m. and throughout the day we had an almost unbearable heat. At ten p. m. we landed in a desolate place.

14. We departed at 3 a. m. and at 10 we reached *Ruschtschuk* (Rustschuk), a fortress which the Russians laid in ruins in 1811...

15. We set out at 6 a. m., but had to stop from 8 a. m. to 3 p. m., because of the wind. We made it to *Popina* and landed at 7. For the last three days my wife has been very sick. Johann, Rosina, and Leonhard are also complaining a lot about headache, fatigue, and rheumatic pains...

16. We departed at 8 a. m., and the heat is again very intense. At 4 p. m. we passed *Silistria* and landed at an uninhabited spot at 8 in the evening.

17. We started out at 3 a. m., and it was another hot day. In the evening we landed across from the fortress of *Chursowa* (Harsowa) at an uninhabited place.

18. Some men from each ship went across to Chursowa to show the passports and buy food supplies. We departed at 10 a. m. and landed at an uninhabited place at 10 that evening.

19. We left at 5 a. m. in very hot weather and arrived safely in *Galatz*. Towards evening there was a cool wind which developed into a storm during the night.

20. The storm is continuing and there is a bit of rain. Our leaders are dining today with the Russian consul in the city.

21. The consul and his family came out to visit us and dined with our leaders in a tent. The day was pleasant.

22. We again had a bit of rain, which was a great boon for us, since we had many sick people and some were dying daily.

23. It was very hot again. We still do not know when we are going to get away from here.

24. On Sunday we had Communion service ... Half of the people in the 5 ships are lying around sick. Many elderly people are dying, also those who have some chronic ailment soon succumb.

25. Very hot. Otherwise nothing special ...

26. Another very hot day. At nine o'clock in the evening I had a protracted attack of diarrhea, violent vomiting, and cramps in all my limbs. I became so weak that night that I could scarcely walk a few steps.

29. God be praised, we departed again at 10 a. m. During the days we spent in Galatz, 42 people in our 5 ships died.

30. We started at midnight under a bright moon, but at 3 a. m. we had to land in a desolate spot because of stormy weather. The storm lasted the entire day and the following night.

31. There was continuing bad weather, and in the evening we had a thunderstorm and a heavy rain all during the night.

September

1. The storm continued throughout the day and night with incredibly loud thunder, and we had to remain where we were.

2. We departed in rainy weather and reached *Ismail* (Ismail) at 3 p. m. and had to land on an island.

3. It was a beautiful day, and we were able to get dry again ...

6. The bodies of my sons Leonhard and Albrecht are completely swollen.

7. Also Margarete's body is beginning to swell; Josef is becoming thinner day by day; Johann is also sick in bed.

8. We left the island today and were supposed to go into quarantine. But when we arrived, there was not enough room for us, and we had to remain on the shore of the Danube.

9. Again we had to remain here. We can scarcely obtain any food for our money, and there is no medicine at all. I have nothing but river water to help quench the thirst of my many sick people ...

12. This morning at 8 o'clock, my dear son Leonhard fell so peacefully asleep in the Lord that we were long in doubt that he was really dead. This evening brother Jakob's daughter Friederike died just as peacefully.

13. Today my dear Margarete is deathly sick and Katharina is unable to be on her feet.

14. Today all my children feel much better, praise and thanks to our dear Savior.

16. At 4 p. m. my dear son Josef fell peacefully asleep in the Lord.

17. We were obliged to bring all our clothes and bed linen on the ship for fumigation, and as it was quite cold, we froze terribly while we were undressed.

18. It is again quite cold, and there is fumigation again today ...

27. It rained again. Today 400 souls arrived on 3 ships which are in quarantine near us.

October

1. It now seems as if the quarantine will soon be over. I had more fever today ...

4. We moved out of quarantine into an open camp outside the city gate.

5. I had much fever again today. My dear brother-in-law Busch died today of bilious fever.

6. We had a terrible night of storm and rain; all our tents were soaked and the water ran through our bedding. The rainstorm lasted all day and the following night. Sister Sophie's tent was ripped apart and covered her and the children.

7. In the morning they crawled out and crept into my tent and under my wet blankets. Today I was so worn out with fever that I could no longer sustain myself on my feet.

November

1. We were loaded, together with our baggage, on a ship which transported us across the *Dniester River* in two hours. We were then given quarters in the barracks at *Ovidiopol*, where we had to spend 3 days in quarantine.

5. We received wagon transportation and were brought in four hours to *Josephstal*, where we were given lodging in the home of a colonist settler. This was really the end of our 133-day journey.

8. Jakob and I drove to Odessa to have a look at the far-famed city. But our expectations were greatly deceived when we saw the many desolate places, the numerous huts of earth, the poor houses, and particularly the knee-deep mud. We stayed overnight, but since we were not clothed in large sheepskin coats in the manner of the natives, we had to sleep on a cold hard table.

9. Sunday. We were greatly astonished to see how the Sunday was desecrated. The bartering and bustling in the deep mire was even much more frantic than on Saturday. This and many other things created such a revolting impression upon me that I firmly resolved to go to the Caucasus in the spring.

December

5. We were visited by the doctor and the inspector from Grossliebental, and since we were all infected by mange, we were immediately removed to the hospital in Grossliebental.

27. We came back to our former quarters in Josephstal. I now wrote a 3-page letter to my dear brothers in Kupferzell and included some excepts from this diary. And so we lived quietly, content with our lot.

March 1818

8. I and my son Johann went to Odessa to work in Hoffmann's harness shop, while my five other children remained behind in Josephstal. This separation from my children caused me the greatest grief. But with the small salary Hoffmann was giving me — it was only 32 rubles — it was virtually impossible for me to bring the children to the city and pay for their food and lodging.

2. We moved, with all our belongings, to Grossliebental. But here our misery began all over again. One after the other, we all fell sick again. Things finally became so bad that all of us were bedridden and none could do anything for the others, not even cook a bowl of soup. In our forlorn situation the good Lord found for us a helper and consoler in the butcher Sanzenbach and his kindhearted wife who were at that time living in Grossliebental. Without having even known about our sad condition, she brought us a large bowl of rice and meat, and as none of us could get up, she waited on all of us, whereby we were all moved to tears of deepest gratitude. Little by little, we began to regain our health.

Ulmer Schachtel
on the Danube

2. Letter of Joh. Chr. Bidlingsmaier, leader from Oetlingen, regarding the journey from Ulm to the Black Sea

Galatz, July 18, 1817

Here, dear friends and faithful brothers and sisters in Christ Jesus Our Lord, we must describe to you the entire journey from our home as far as Galatz, because we believe that you are eagerly looking forward to some news from us. Well, we departed from *Ulm* between 11 and 12 o'clock on June 2 (s. Ulmer barge). We arrived safely at *Blendenheim* the same evening, and all the timorous ones were abashed. On June 3 they embarked with more confidence, and we arrived safely at *Marching* the same day. On the fourth we reached *Regensburg*, but had to remain here for 4 hours because of high wind. After we were able to continue we came to *Pfaden* and reached *Passau* on the fifth, *Linz* on the sixth, and remained there the following day. On the 8th we continued our journey to *Marbach*, and on the 9th we arrived safely, through God's gracious guidance, in *Vienna*, where we met the first boats. Here we encountered a new problem, because we were supposed to continue our journey by land to *Pordia* and *Razivili*, where we had already lost half of our women and children. Even if we had sold half of our belongings, we would now have had to pay 9,000 Gulden for transportation costs, apart from the difficulties that confronted us. However, in the last hour a letter arrived from one of our deputies with the message that we should travel by boat as far as Galatz. Tears of joy filled our hearts and we recognized that God's hand was guiding us. During our four-day stop-over, the people of the city came out to see us and generously brought many gifts for our children, saying that our exodus was similar to that of the children of Israel. In the afternoon of the 14th we continued our journey and reached *Theben* in the evening. I can scarcely describe our astonishment as we passed through the woodland with its vineyards and grapes. In all our life, not even in the most bountiful harvest, did we ever see such lofty vines so full of grapes. We had to spend a sleepless night, however, because of the gnats, which were identical with the Rhine mosquitoes. They came in such swarms that we could not help think of the Egyptian plague of insects. Early on the 17th we departed and passed *Pressburg*, the first Hungarian town, and reached *Seehn;* on the 18th we came to *Gross-Marusch,* where we encountered only Germans; on the 19th we made it to *Pest* and *Ofen,* where we had to re-negotiate for the boat fare. We then got the boat ready and made it to *Erdschin* on the evening of the 20th. But on the 21st we again lay at anchor for 8 hours because of high wind, and came to *Földwar;* on the 22nd we reached *Dull* and a good deal farther, but had to spend the night on the water, where the gnats tormented us greatly. On the 26th we came to *Peterwardein,* a Hungarian fortress called *Scharengrad.* After inspection at the Chief Commissariate we had to travel another half-hour to the courts of Peterwardein. On the 27th we reached Semlin, where we had to stay for a day; on the 29th we came to *Bauschua* (= Panesova), where we again had to spend the night between earth and sky. On the 30th we came to *Semendria,* a Turkish fortress, and stayed on the water overnight. On July I, we were in *Alt-Balanka,* where we remained at anchor for six hours because of high wind; then we passed through the rapids which one could hear roaring from an hour's distance, whereas the rapids near Vienna are hardly remarkable. Praise God, we came through them safely. Some of our children hoped that the whole journey might be like that — now they were being rocked in a cradle. We came to *Moldauen* the same day. On the 3rd we came to *Alt-Urschua* (Orsowa), a border town of the Austrian Empire, where we had to stay for two days. We departed on the 5th and after an hour we passed through the *Iron Gate,* where the raging water resembled a vortex. We also passed through it safely. At 8 o'clock we arrived at the first Turkish border fortress, called *Kladua* (Kladowa) where we had to wait four hours to pass the Turkish customs inspection, so that we made it only as far as *Kladua.* We departed on the 6th when it was unbearably hot. On the 7th we had to remain in the same place all day, because of high wind. We had to go ashore to buy provisions in a nearby locality. We bought two pigs for 5 Gulden, 12 Kronen; one weighed 104 lbs and the other 96 lbs. Thus we paid only 2 Kr. per lb. Things are getting cheaper day by day. In this area we bought 1 lb. of bread for 2 Kr., 3 pints of wine acc. to Württemberg measure for 7 Kr., 6 Kr., 5 Kr., splendid good wine with fire, similiar to that of the year eleven. *In fact, as regards our physical needs we have been doing well all the way from Ulm to here, so that we often think of how poorly you may be living. If only we could supply you with the things we can buy so cheaply here. But that is impossible.* At 8 o'clock in the morning of the 8th we passed by the town of *Achriwa* (Oryechowo). We continued our journey on the 9th and came close to the fortress of *Gelobel* (Wikopol); on the 10th we reached *Rustschuk,* another fortress; on the 11th we made it to Glifhin; but in the evening of the 12th we again had to cast anchor and spend the night on the water; on the 13th we reached *Hirsova.* There Andreas Spindler's child died of convulsions. On the 14th we came to *Orschua,* a Turkish fortress, on the 15th to *Braila,* the last Turkish fortress. On the 16th we arrived *Galatz,* where our journey has been terminated for the time being. We cannot tell you anything definite. We have no report from the deputies except that we are to travel to *Ismail* and to *Odessa.*

Everything is cheaper here; we buy the finest one-pound loaf of bread for 1 Kr. or about 1 penny; a tankard of wine, like brandy, for 6 to 8 Kronen. We often think and say: If only we could supply some of your wants. The lands through which we travel are all so productive, from Vienna to here, that we have had to marvel at the sight. We have seen many districts where the vines stand in thickets or grow to the tops of trees in the woods, where people obtain their grapes without planting them. The people do poor work. We often said: *This is where our Württemberger ought to be!* One easily recognizes from afar where Germans are living, but in many things they imitate the lazy people. They generally live in wretched huts. In Hungary and in Turkish districts the huts are dug into the ground. Everything lies about in confusion: geese, pigs, chickens, sheep, cattle. The towns do not even look like a regular village back home, and there are lots of uninhabited areas. Especially after we left Belgrad we often-times said: *Some Württemberger could make such a good living here, but so many of them back home do not even have a foot of land!* I must close; we have so little time.

Attested by
Johann Christoph Bidlingsmaier of Oetlingen

3. The fate of those who emigrated to Russia in 1817 from Rosenfeld, district of Sulz, and vicinity (Abridged)

Excerpted letter from Carlsthal near Odessa on the Black Sea, written April 20, 1820, by Johann Georg *Höhn,* locksmith by trade and a son-in-law of Andre Diesterle, a tile-maker in Rosenfeld.

"We had a good journey from *Ulm* to *Vienna,* except that Höhn's children got the measles, but they recuperated during our 8-day stay in Vienna. From there we travelled on another boat as far as *Pest,* where the 430 passengers from two boats were loaded together into one. The journey now continued until we reached the beautiful fortress at *Peterwardein* and *Neusatz* where Höhn's brother and several other families who had enough of travelling decided to let themselves be recruited by a nobleman for settlement in a colony in Slavonia. As the others continued their journey, Höhn's brother-in-law Caspar became ill with brain fever and died four weeks later. He was buried at *Orsowa* near the Hungarian border. In *Widdin* (Vidin) Höhn still bought food supplies. However, because of the intense heat that prevailed, more and more sickness occurred, and both he and his wife fell ill. In *Galatz* his mother-in-law died and also the son of his brother-in-law John Hörter, together with many other people. After stopping for four days, the boat continued on to *Ismail.* In this first Russian town the immigrants had to remain in quarantine under the open sky for seven weeks, but upon the order of the Czar they received daily rations of bread, flour, meat, butter, rice, barley, coffee and sugar; also wine, brandy, vinegar, olive oil, and soap. There was no lack of doctors and medicines, but here were violent outbreaks of typhus and other fever, yellow and red dysentery, large ulcers on head and neck. Two of Höhn's children, Anne and Maria-Rosine, died; his brother-in-law Hörter lost four children: Andreas, Johann, Anne-Elisabeth, and Daniel who was born in Galatz; also the stocking-weaver Jakob Nagel and his wife. In Ismail alone 1,328 immigrants are said to lie buried. Fortunately, Höhn's two older daughters remained in good health.

From Ismail they continued the journey overland on Russian farm-wagons and arrived in *Akiermann* (Akkerman) in three days, 60 hours. While they were camping for the night on the open steppe, Höhn ran away in his feverish condition while his wife was asleep, and wandered about all night. However, through God's grace he again came close to the camp the next morning, so that the anxious searchers succeeded in finding and rescuing him. When they came to Akiermann the next day, he was put to bed and he slept for a whole day, whereby he began to recover.

After a 5-day stop the journey was continued from here to the fortress of *Wiederbohlen* (Ovidiopol) on board a boat which crossed the Dniester River and an arm of the Black Sea. At midnight they were overtaken by a rain-and-snow storm, and only the next morning they passed through the dreaded breakers to reach dry land. During another quarantine of 14 days many people again became sick; Höhn's father-in-law Dieterle and his daughter Christine died.

... From here German settlers brought them to their homes where they were given living quarters. When one of the settlers, the mayor of his colony, asked Höhn's tearful wife the cause of her sorrow, she replied that no one would provide accommodation for her husband and herself, because both were sick and were bringing along four children of their own and two of the stocking-weaver's orphans. But the mayor said: "As mayor I shouldn't take anybody, but I shall take you with me and give you an entire room for yourselves." He forthwith provided three wagons for them and took them to *Peterstal,* where they found kind people and recovered from their illness. The other people who were fever-stricken were given quarters in the German colonies, whereas those who were gravely ill were taken to the hospital at Grossliebental, in which, despite good care, Höhn's brother-in-law Joh. Martin Dieterle and his sister Catherina died. The immigrants who survived received winter quarters in the German villages in the vicinity of Odessa until St. James Day (July 20).

Höhn plied his trade, with good earnings, in the employ of a smith. The families who went to the Caucasus received 500 rubles to buy a wagon and horses, and each person received 40 kopecks (= 12 Kr.) for daily food rations. Five hundred families, divided into 10 parties, set out. Among them were Andreas Dieterle and Joh. Hörter, Elisabeth Dieterlin, Höhn's brother-in-law and sister-in-law.

Carlsthal, where Höhn lives, is a nobleman's village, two hour's distant from Peterstal, four hours from Odessa, and two from the Dniester. More Germans than Russians are living in this area. It was the pastor of Peterstal, in whose house Höhn had his workshop, who recommended him to the nobleman in Carlsthal. From the latter Höhn received a fine house, a smithy equipped with coal and tools, and he soon had much work that paid well.

The colonists (of Carlsthal) can obtain as much land as they desire; they pay no taxes, nor do any labor service, but have to deliver the tithe. The landlord of this village owns 6,000 dessiatines of land. In the first year of his residence there, Höhn harvested 9 Scheffel (= 50 bu.) of wheat from a field which a peasant had given him because he had no time to reap it himself. Höhn now (1818) also owns 10 head of cattle and 7 horses, and works his own fields. Höhn's son-in-law Joh. Hörter, whose father is living in Erzingen, was sick for a long time, as was his wife, and lost all of his children, excepting the oldest daughter who went with him to the Caucasus.

The two sons of the deceased stocking-weaver were adopted by two colonists in Peterstal. Johann Holweger of Leidringen and his wife and children were in good health on the entire journey. From a man who went to the Caucasus he received the free gift of a house, land, and cattle located about 30 hours from Odessa. The other emigrants from Leidringen all died on the journey, excepting the two daughters of Friedrich Bäcker. Also Bäckle (Böckle) of Isingen and his family died, except two grown sons. Ursula and Kath. Schneckenburger of Schura, who had emigrated to Poland, moved from there to the Molochna (Taurida) and are living in Catharinoslav.

Ex. 2/3. d. Ven. 1821

Greift hinein ins volle Menschenleben
Ein jeder lebt's, nicht Vielen ist's bekannt,
Doch wo ihr's packt, da ist es int'ressant.

Goethe

IV. Duc de Richelieu, Father of the Colonists

Armand Emmanuel Sophie Septimanie du Plessis[1] was born in Paris on Sept. 25, 1766, the son of Louis du Plessis, duc de Fronsac, and grandson of the marshal of Richelieu. The comte de Chinon, as the young Armand was called, was married at fifteen to Rosalie de Rochechouart, a deformed young girl of twelve, but his relations with her were never more than formal. Soon after the marriage he travelled for a couple of years with his tutor l'abbé Labdan through Italy, Switzerland, and Germany. On his return to Paris he was made a lieutenant of a regiment of the Queen's dragoons and received a position at the court of Louis XVI.

Duc de Richelieu 1766—1822

The life at the court of Versailles was not to his liking. He frowned on the frivolities of the courtiers and gallants, and even though the young men esteemed him, they kept their distance. For the comte de Chinon was of serious mind, retiring and reserved, with an air of pedantry and almost puritanical austerity.

---

[1] For the account of Richelieu's career in Russia, particularly his participation in the siege of Ismail, I am largely indebted to Alfred Rambaud, *Le duc de Richelieu*, Revue de deux mondes (1887), p. 618—662.

He had made excellent classical studies, and had acquired a fluent command of German, Italian, English, and later also Russian. An adherent of the physiocratic school, he was familiar with the new political economy of the time.

Physically, he was tall and gaunt, and somewhat stooped, but he had a charming face that he retained until the end of his life. He had large dark eyes that were nearsighted but full of fire. His complexion was likewise dark, and his hair jet-black but started to turn gray prematurely. Though his physique was distinctively from the South, his moral temper was undeniably from the North. His bravery was that of cool intrepidity rather than that of ardor and passion. Count Langeron once remarked that he loved the Germans and their "Gemüt-lichkeit", as well as their sententious, sombre formality.

In 1787, the 21-year-old lieutenant became intensely interested in the news that the Russians had declared war on the Turks. Bored and depressed by the idle life at the court, he requested the King to permit him to enter Russian serv-ice. The permission was refused, and he remained in France, where the Revolu-tion found him. In the fall of 1790 he fled with some Royalist émigrés to Ger-many, where he attended the coronation of Emperor Leopold II in the Römer at Frankfurt in early September.

At Vienna he met Prince Charles de Ligne and Count de Langeron. One evening, while the three young men were dining with the aged prince de Ligne, a Russian officer announced that General Suvarov was preparing to lay siege to the Turkish fortress at Ismail, and added that "it would be a very lively and hot affair". Richelieu and Prince Charles looked at each other and read each other's thoughts. "Let's go", said Richelieu, and Charles at once responded, "A coward who backs down!" And the decision was made then and there. The old prince wept, but encouraged his son, while Richelieu remarked: "I'm tired of always wearing a uniform, without having once received a shot."

The journey of 500 leagues (1,500 miles) was anything but an outing, partic-ularly since they had to travel in cold weather, without equipage and baggage, and, in the case of Richelieu, with hardly any money. The dinner had been on November 10; at two in the morning of the 12th, Richelieu and Charles set out in an open carriage; Langeron had departed the day before. They travelled night and day through Moravia, Silesia, and Galicia, without becoming demoralized by the cold and snow and hunger, and reached Jassy on November 20, where they met Langeron long enough to transmit letters of introduction to General Potemkin. The following day they continued their journey through the more barbarous and savage lands of Bukowina and Moldavia. But even when they found themselves stuck in a snowdrift in the middle of the night, the thought of regretting their departure from Vienna never entered their minds. What worried them was the possibility of arriving too late for the storming of Ismail. After a few days they reached Bender on the Dniester, where Prince Potemkin

70

had established his headquarters. Here they met other French emigrés, among them the valiant Count Roger de Damas, with whom Richelieu was closely befriended.

Richelieu met Potemkin and was astonished to see a man who looked more like on oriental grand vizier of the Christian sultana Catherine than the general of a Euopean army. He describes[2] his headquarters as "a salon furnished with a divan of gold beneath a magnificent baldachino, surrounded by six charming ladies clad in unimaginable splendor and reclining on cushions in the oriental fashion. In front of them sat Potemkin, dressed in a full-flowing pelisse similar to our robes de chambre. He liked this attire the best, in fact it is all he usually wore. Fifty officers of every rank adorned the other end of the salon which was illuminated by scores of candles.

Potemkin, the absolute ruler of the army, was an extraordinary man, a mixture of grandeur and weakness, of genius and the ridiculous. But his physical and moral stature evoked respect and obedience. Though illiterate and untravelled, he was very knowledgeable in many things. He could not read books but men. He sought information from everyone he met, and had a remarkable memory to retain it all. Human respect meant nothing to him. His power was unlimited, for he not only ruled from the Danube to the Caucasus, but also shared with the Czarina the rest of the imperial government. His wealth was immense, and he took what he wished from all the treasuries. He had many tables of guests, and was magnificently served by a retinue of valets of every kind, comedians, dancers, and musicians — all in the midst of the military campaign."

Potemkin received the French noblemen from Versailles "in a very distinguished manner", and had them at him table for three days. On the evening of the third day he sent them to Ismail. He himself, as Richelieu remarks, "remained behind for political reasons, but perhaps most of all because he did not wish to leave Princess Dolgorouki, with whom he was very much taken."

At Ismail the Russians were making extensive preparations for the impending siege. The large Turkish fortress, constructed like an amphitheater, stood on the left bank of one of the arms of the Danube, about 20 leagues from its mouth. The town itself formed a semicircle 6 miles in length, while a segment of the Danube some 800 fathoms in length formed the diameter.

It was the plan of General Potemkin to assault the fortress both by land and from the river. An Italian named Ribas commanded the naval forces which comprised 120 boats of various types, of which the largest were equipped with 16 cannons. A battery of 100 cannons was emplaced on a large island in the middle of the river. Four thousand soldiers manned the flotilla which had succeeded in breaking through the mouth of the Danube and approaching to within

---

[2] *Journal de mon voyage en Allemagne, par le duc de Richelieu*, Société impériale d'Histoire de Russie, t. LIV, p. 148

a mere 900 fathoms from the fortress. The land forces comprised 20,000 infantry and from 7 to 8 thousand Cossack regulars. One division was commanded by major-general Kutusov, the other by generals Gudewitsch and Paul Potemkin. A third corps, under the command of General Samoilow, was brought in from the army camp at Lilia. The Turkish forces were estimated to have been about 40,000.

Richelieu considered the Russian troops "the best soldiers in Europe", but he was astonished at the poor leadership and the barbarous disorder that prevailed in all operations. "Sometimes more Russians were killed by their own bullets than by those of the enemy. Life was cheap. The soldiers' blood was spilled as though it had no value. The medical corps was so poor and the ignorance of the doctors so great that every wounded soldier was as good as dead. The gaps were easily filled with drafted serfs. Time and lives were wasted in a series of ill-conceived and badly executed attacks. Indeed, after eight unsuccessful assaults upon the fortress, the army chiefs were about to raise the siege, when an order came from Bender "not to *attack*, but to *take* the fortress."

The top commander in the field was Count Suvorov, a war hero who resembled a Cossack or a Tartar chieftain rather than a European general. But he really was an extremely bold and intrepid leader. In his journal Richelieu remarked : "He lives in his tent, sits on a mat, and eats the most detestable food. He sleeps a few hours, and then spends the rest of the night singing. At dawn he emerges from his tent almost in the nude, and rolls in the wet grass, ostensibly to preserve himself from rheumatism.

He does not have a horse of his own, but whenever he goes on reconnaisance he simply mounts the first Cossack horse near him, and rides full speed right up to the moat, utterly indifferent to cannon fire or danger of capture. He acts as though he were mad, but he is really just lucky."

On the morning of December 21, the Russians began an all-out bombardment of the fortress which continued without let-up for 24 hours. According to Richelieu, it was "the most terrible cannonade ever recorded in history. The fortress of Ismail appeared to be a veritable volcano with fire shooting out on all sides." On the following day, before sunrise, the Russian troops, divided into three massive columns, launched their assault. Richelieu, who was then still known as Comte de Fronsac, was placed in charge of a corps of infantry under the command of General Lacsy. In his description of the "bloody day" he later wrote: "All over the town one heard the universal cry of 'Allah', the furious war cries of the Russians, the sustained firing of muskets by the frantic soldiers, until they had expended the last cartridges, the appalling screams of the women and children who were being massacred. One could see the brave Turkish defenders go to their death with imperturbable fatalism, one could witness the fighting ardor of Polotski's regiment whose officers were all killed, and the zealous army chaplain who led the regiment forward with a crucifix in one hand and a musket in the other, offering a martyr's crown to all who marched ahead, and the threat of hell to all who retreated. So great was the frenzy of the soldiers that not even the Empress Caterina herself could have prevented them from sparing the life of a single Turk."

The death toll had indeed been enormous. Richelieu estimated the Turkish losses at 30,800 men, plus 2,000 women and children. Langeron noted that 38,000 corpses lay in the blood-soaked streets of the town. Even Potemkin was shocked. In their successful attempt to take the fortress of Ismail, the Russians also sustained heavy losses. Several generals were killed, 33 lieutenant-colonels, 396 of the 650 officers, 4,100 soldiers who were killed in combat, 4,000 who died of their wounds, and 2,000 who suffered minor injuries.

In the mad confusion of the fighting Richelieu chanced to see a ten-year-old Turkish girl who was trying to escape from two Cossacks by hiding among the bodies of four women who had their throats cut. The soldiers were on the point of killing her when Richelieu intervened by snatching her in his arms and resisting the attempts of the Cossacks to get at her. He threatened them with punishment, and they left. The girl had a slight cut on her cheek which was probably caused by the sword that had pierced her mother. Richelieu also noticed that she wore a small gold medal around her neck bearing the image of the king of France. This circumstance caused him to become deeply attached to her. "She trusted me", says Richelieu, "and I carried her away from the frightful scene of slaughter, to spare her the horror of having to step over the bodies of her slain compatriots." Enchanted by the graceful child, he decided to adopt her. Unfortunately, while he was on his way, he met Colonel Ribas who was conferring with 700 Turkish soldiers who were confined in the stone bastions. On seeing the girl, they demanded her back with loud outcries. Her would-be protector was unable to decide to give her up, until Ribas gave him his word that she would be returned to him the following day. But Richelieu never saw her again, and for a long time he was unconsolable[4].

The French volunteers came through the ordeal at Ismail without serious harm. Charles was wounded in the knee. Richelieu had two bullet holes in his uniform; and Langeron was unscathed. They stayed at Ismail for 15 days while Charles was recuperating from his wound, and returned to Bender on January 1, 1791. Prince Potemkin received them most graciously, and after a few days accompanied them to Jassy, where the victory at Ismail was celebrated by numerous festivities. On January 25, Richelieu, Prince Charles, and Roger de Damas de-

---

[4] *Mémoires inéditis de Langeron*, Archives des Affaires étrangères. Russie. Mémoires et Documents, t. XXX.

parted for Vienna, to rejoin Prince de Ligne. In early February Richelieu received the news of his father's death and hastened back to Paris. With the renowned title of Duc de Richelieu, he also inherited an immense fortune that bore a revenue of almost half a million livres, but he also was burdened with the heavy liabilities incurred by his father. In May the duke travelled to England, but was soon recalled by the King who was now confined to the Tuileries. Richelieu obeyed the royal summons, but in a letter[5] to his wife, he averred: "I assure you that I needed more courage and devotion to decide to return than a fool needed to join the assault on Ismail."

Richelieu did not stay long in France. On July 27, 1791, he submitted a request to the National Assembly for a passport in order to fulfill his engagement in the Russian service, in the hope of being able to use his acquired military knowledge in the service of France. The passport was granted, and he returned to Russia in August. His stay at St. Petersburg fell into the winter of 1791—92. Catharine received him graciously, and for his services in the Ismail campaign she conferred on him the Order of the Cross of St. George and presented him a golden sword. He was admitted to her intimate circle at the Hermitage and promoted to the rank of an officer of the état-major russe.

In the spring of 1792 the Czarina commissioned Richelieu to deliver 60,000 ducats to Prince de Condé, the general of the Royalist forces at Coblenz, to help support the émigrés who were assembled in the Breisgau area of the Black Forest. Ostensibly as an observer for the Russian General Staff, but in actuality as a soldier of de Condé, Richelieu participated in the campaigns of 1792/3/4. He assisted at the siege of Valenciennes, and helped direct operations in the campaigns of Dunkerque, Mauberge, and du Quesnoy; there and in the Austrian-Prussian campaign of 1793, he charged the Republican columns at the head of Austrian troops. He was an émigré in fact and at heart.

In May of 1792 Duc de Richelieu received the news that his wife had been imprisoned by the Revolutionaries and all of his property confiscated. As a result she and the duke were in grave financial difficulties. In the spring of 1794, after the Austrian and Prussian forces were forced to retreat beyond the Rhine, Richelieu and his friend Langeron again departed for Russia. Potemkin was dead, but they were fortunate in finding another protector in the person of the old marshal Rumantzov, a renowned hero of the Turkish wars. The old marshal graciously appointed Richelieu second colonel of his regiment of cuirassiers, and made Langeron vice-colonel of his regiment of grenadiers. Both men were happy and indeed lucky, for Russia no longer offered the French émigrés the customary kindnesses, now that the cause of the Bourbons was lost. The Hermitage was now

---

[5] cf. Leon de Crozsaz-Crétet: *Le duc de Richelieu en Russie et en France* (1766—1822) Paris, 1897, p. 59 et seq.

closed even to Richelieu, and his letters to Catherine's favorites proved to be useless.

While Richelieu and Langeron were in their garrisons in Volhynia, they received the startling news of Catherine's death (1796) and of the succession of Paul. The new ruler made Richelieu major general and colonel of the imperial cuirassiers. In 1799 he was promoted to the rank of lieutenant general. However, while Richelieu was a military man he was not a corporal; neither he nor his men "were very advanced in the art of parading". The young Czar, who demanded frequent parades, was infuriated at Richelieu's inept performances, and criticized every blunder. The duke was constantly reprimanded, fired, rehired, exposed to all disgraces. One day he marched his regiment, without the Czar's orders, to extinguish a fire. The Czar became enraged, and the duke fell into disgrace and reduced to the condition of having to live on 30 sous a day. He wrote to his wife, saying that the height of his ambition was now to receive from his immense fortune a mere 1,000 écus of rent. She was sad that she was unable to give him even that pittance from her dowry which was still confiscated.

Without regret Richelieu quit the Russian service and returned to Vienna in 1800. The following year he retired to Poland, hoping to obtain a passport to get back to France, for he realized that his name was still on the list of émigrés. Meanwhile Napoleon had become first consul, and Richelieu decided that the time had come for him to return home to reclaim at least part of his property.

On January 2, 1802 his wife, on her way home, saw a German coach driving down the street. Her heart at once told her that it was he. "He arrived home before I did", she later remarked, "and it was he who greeted me. A crowd of simple people gathered to congratulate him on his return and celebrate the joyous event."

Bonaparte had indeed granted him a passport to return to Russia, but refused to erase his name from the list of émigrés, a formality which would have permitted Richelieu to regain his property. Before granting this favor, the first consul demanded that Richelieu accept an amnesty and make a promise of submission, but the duke refused. He also declined to enter the service of France, for he considered the Corsican a usurper.

To Richelieu the course of honor was paramount; no sacrifice was too great to pursue that course. He had no alternative but to leave his home, his friends, and his fortune, and return to Russia. Only through the personal appeal of his friend Czar Alexander I and the diplomatic negotiations of the Russian envoy with Talleyrand did Napoleon finally remove Richelieu's name from the list of émigrés. After being reinstated in his possessions, the duke asked his wife to manage his financial affairs and satisfy all the creditors, adding: "If nothing is left for me, well and good. I can walk with my head high, and that which I shall own I shall owe only to myself."

Upon Alexander's invitation to come to Russia, Richelieu arrived in Petersburg in September of 1802, and was received with great kindness and affection. He was permitted to see him often and familiarly, for the young Czar esteemed the duke highly, and once said of him, "He is a lovable and closely attached man, such as I have known only a few". He gave him a gift of 10,000 francs and a sizable estate in Courland with a large revenue. The following year (1803) Alexander appointed him civil governor of Odessa, and in 1805 he was promoted to the position of Governor-general of New Russia, a vast territory that was larger than the whole of France.

When Richelieu came to Odessa in March of 1803, it was still a small, sprawling town of some 4,000 inhabitants who lived in lowly reed-thatched adobe huts that covered a wide expanse of the steppe plateau overlooking the Black Sea. But it was an important frontier town that stood on the threshold of remarkable development. Indeed, it was about to become a booming city whose growth would exceed that of any city in Europe. Large numbers of people were beginning to flow into the young city not only from Old Russia but also from various countries on the Mediterranean and in western Europe. There was an influx of Italian and Great Russian masons and construction workers, of Greek, Turkish, and French merchants, and of Polish laborers and shopkeepers. In 1803 some 300 Jewish families from the Polish city of Czernowitz were established in the city.

View of
Odessa
in 1828

Although the large harbor was still undeveloped, Odessa was rapidly becoming an important seaport with increasing shipments of grain, hides, and tallow. In

1803, 280 vessels arrived from Constantinople and the Levant, and departed with 300,000 chetvert (1,800,000 bu.) of wheat. The following year 449 vessels arrived, and in 1805 the number rose to 643. The steady growth of the city was also accompanied by the settling of immigrant farmers on the neighboring steppelands. While there were still only 500 families (Russian, Bulgarian, Greek, and Armenian) in the environs of Odessa in 1802, this number was substantially increased by the arrival of more than 650 German families who were settled in 1803 and 1804 in the newly developed Liebental district.

Besides the German colonies, Richelieu also established many Bulgarian settlements, and directed the founding of settlements for the Greeks at Mariupol, the Armenians at Nachitchevan, the Jews in the provinces of Cherson and Yekaterinoslav, and even the semi-nomadic Nagaians at Nagaisk.

In Odessa Governor Richelieu occupied a small, unpretentious one-story house with five plain rooms. The furniture consisted of a few crude wooden tables and benches. When he wished to give himself the luxury of a dozen chairs he had to import them from the town of Cherson, for the city still had no craftsmen to manufacture them.

The duke's daily routine of work and diversion has been aptly described[6] by the French biographer Leon de Crousaz-Crétet: "Winter and summer, he rose at 6 o'clock, had a cup of coffee with milk at eight, gave an hour's audience to all who came to see him, and worked with his secretaries until twelve-thirty. He opened all the mail himself, read all the petitions, jotted his decisions on the margin, and drafted all papers of importance. He wrote everything extemporaneously and without blunder, whether it was in Russian, French, English or German, almost always while singing or humming to himself. He often worked this way for eight or ten hours a day. He carried on a very extensive correspondence, read all the journals and reviews that came to him. Reading was a real passion for him, he devoured books, and at the end of the day Virgil and Cicero were always on his night table.

At one o'clock, after he had dinner, the duke usually went out until evening. He was always on foot, on horseback, or in a *droshki,* like any other private person. He was never seen in a closed carriage, even in bad weather. He frequently scoured the environs of the city, visiting agricultural establishments and chatting with gardeners, farmers, herdsmen, and fishermen.

In the evening he never refused invitations; he was present at all public and private balls. He always had with him a score of table-companions. Ordinarily these included his three aides-de-camp, the captain in charge of the troops under his command, his kinsman Count de Rochecouart, a Livonian named Stempowski, the 3 secretaries of the gouvernements, the city secretary, the French doctor Scudéry, the venerable abbé Labdan who was his former teacher, the foreign consuls, distinguished visitors to the city, and the chief businessmen.

Richelieu Plaza (Kohl, 1838) The governor of Odessa (1803–1814) pointing to the harbor.

On Sundays there was a grand reception of all the government dignitaries and a review of the garrisoned troops. The duke then visited the lyceum, listened to the report on the conduct of the students, and took two of the outstanding ones with him to attend Mass, went on an outing, had dinner with them in the evening, and escorted them back to the school. He retired at eleven in his study where one of the couches had been prepared for a bed."

The management of the household was in the hands of his kinsman Roche-chouart, who was also in charge of the numerous domestic servants and stable-boys. Living was very cheap in Odessa in the early years. Meat cost only 3 sous (pennies) a pound; the Black Sea provided fish in great variety and abundance; fresh vegetables and fruit arrived from the Crimea in every season; the wines of France and Spain were imported duty-free. The duke's income from regular salary and emoluments from the czar ranged between 15 and 20 thousand rubles. manners, which did not compromise his dignified bearing as a grand seigneur. He manners, which did not compromise his dignified bearing as a grand seigneur. He loved to stroll along the broad streets of the town, to visit the stores and factories, and to chat with the common laborers and peasants. It was said that he knew by name the heads of almost all the families and most of the citizens. Since he spoke with ease the major languages of Europe, he conversed with each in his native tongue.

This aimiable simplicity accompanied him everywhere, and people invariably felt at ease in his presence. A certain businessman once made a complaint about Richelieu to the Czar. The duke paid the man a visit and graciously accepted the frugal repast that was offered him. After his departure he said to the companion who had come with him, "When I met that man I tried to make him understand that I bore him no grudge for making a complaint against me." To anyone who had a grievance he simply replied: "Come to me and you shall receive justice and protection." In view of the new country's booming growth which was constantly curbed by officious bureaucrats, he adopted the judicious motto: "Don't regulate too much." Sicard speaks of Richelieu's "gentle government and friendly rule".

The duke was also known for his love of trees and made every effort to provide people with all kinds of seeds and young saplings. He took care of his own garden and encouraged others to plant trees in front of their homes and along the streets. One day the duke was passing in front of the house of a citizen when he noticed that the two acacia trees planted there were suffering from the heat. Calling the owner, he said: "I beg you to give those poor trees a bit of water. You'll be doing me a great pleasure. If you don't want to do it, let me water them myself."

In the month of May, duc de Richelieu, accompanied by chief mayor Brittner, travelled through the German colonies on a tour of inspection of the homes and the yards. Beloved by all the people, he had a paternal interest in their welfare and progress, listened to their grievances, gave them friendly counsel and encouragement, settled their disputes, and distributed alms to the poor. On the other hand, he was strict in matters relating to discipline, thrift, and industry, and was known to have a keen eye for every kind of disorder and slovenliness. No wonder that even the tidiest German housewife could never be sure whether her kitchen and pantry would pass his inspection.

During Richelieu's eleven-year tenure in office the old Turkish fishing village of Hadyi-Bey (renamed Odessa by the Czarina Catherine in 1792) developed into a flourishing city, and the duke is justly regarded as the "founder of Odessa", the Queen of the Black Sea. Under his energetic and enterprising administration two large harbors separated by two moles were constructed, one for the imperial navy and the other for merchant vessels. Since Odessa had become a free port, trade and commerce increased by leaps and bounds. Impressive two-story buildings of stone adorned the wide, treelined boulevard of Odessa, and a magnificent flight of 200 limestone steps 90 feet wide led from it down to the harbor. Among his first projects was the construction of churches for each of the principal denominations, Orthodox, Lutheran, and Catholic. He also established a city hospital and a sanctuary for the poor. With the help of his friend and mentor, Father Nicolle, he founded the imperial lyceum of higher education, which was later to become the University of Odessa. He also promoted the

City plan of Odessa 1828

building of shops and bazaars, and provided the city with a theatre and opera
house, a park, and a botanical nursery. He also established a colony of German
artisans in a section of the city, to develop a variety of useful crafts and industries. Under his efficient administration the population of Odessa grew from
4,000 to 35,000, and that of New Russia from 300,000 to 2 million. In the spring
of 1811, Alexander called Richelieu to St. Petersburg, where he was awarded the
Grande Cordon of St. Alexander Nevski with a diamond-studded plaque, along
with a gift of 50,000 rubles in compensation for his frequent travelling expenses.

After 11 years and 6 months of fruitful activity Duc de Richelieu was called
back to his fatherland, which had been freed from the domination of the
"usurper" Napoleon who was now exiled to the island of Elba. The people of
Odessa and in the surrounding villages were shocked and grieved at the news of
his departure. As he was leaving the city in September 1814 an immense crowd
accompanied him until he reached the suburbs, and more than 200 people kept
following him for 20 versts on the Tiraspol Road until he reached the station of
Hederim, where they shared a farewell repast and drank a toast to him, wishing

him a safe journey and an early return. Cries of hurrah resounded through the steppe, but were soon extinguished by sobs and lamentation. The people crowded around him, trying to embrace him, to kiss his hands and the flaps of his coat. Each expressed his grief, his good wishes and farewell. Encircled and compressed by the crowd, the duke burst into tears, and said, "My friends, spare me. Take me away from this sad scene!" A couple of men carried him to the coach, and he departed. And the fateful presentiment was to be realized: they would never again see the man who was so justly esteemed, revered, loved, and adored[7].

In Paris the duke found it difficult to get used to his new life and surroundings. In a letter[8] to his friend Count Langeron, who had become his successor as governor-general, he wrote nostalgically: "At Odessa the sight of a new village, a plantation of trees, or even a growing sapling delighted my heart and consoled me for the hardships I had to endure. Here I have no compensation. I would be willing, on my honor, to have my left arm cut off, if I could get away from here. For all that, perhaps I shall return to Odessa, and sooner than you think. Perhaps I can again occupy myself with the welfare of that country where everything is new, and where people have room to expand, whereas here one is chained together with others, so that one suffocates. If you could see the life I lead you would really pity me. It is not the work that frightens me, but for all the privations and suffering one needs some compensation. Here I have none, for the kinds of pleasure which abound in Paris do not exist for me. Alas, my dear friend, I am disconsolate, I am dying alive, I don't eat and sleep anymore, and shall soon resemble a skeleton." And in a subsequent letter[9] written to Cobley, he exclaims: "Poor Odessa! Poor Crimea! The shores of the Black Sea became for me a new fatherland, dear to my heart. The good will and the gratitude which the inhabitants extended to me for the feeble attention I gave to their interests have forever bound me to that country. As great as that recognition is the pain of separation, and it would be unendurable for me, if I did not console myself with the hope of again seeing the Odessa that I love so much."

When Napoleon suddenly returned from Elba, Richelieu fled with the new Bourbon king, Louis XVIII, to the city of Lille, then set out for Vienna to join the Russian army. As a personal friend of Czar Alexander, he was able to exert considerable influence in the councils of the Allies. After Napoleon's ultimate defeat at Waterloo and his permanent exile on St. Helena, Louis XVIII appointed Richelieu premier ministre of his cabinet. In this important position the duke was able to gain favorable conditions at the Congress of Aix-la-Chapelle in

[7] Sicard, *Lettre sur Odessa,* quoted by L. Pinguad, Les Francais en Russie, p. 416.
[8] *Duc de Richelieu to the governor of Odessa,* Paris, Dec. 10, 1815, quoted by de Crousaz-Crétet, p. 175.
[9] *Letter to Cobley* quoted by L. Pingaud, ibidem, p. 437.

1818. Not only was Alsace returned to France, but most of the occupation troops of the Five Powers were removed from the country. Richelieu also succeeded in getting the national war debt reduced from a billion to only 265 million francs. Moreover, with grain imported from his "beloved Odessa" he was able to feed France, and offset the crop failure that had threatened to produce a national famine. In 1818 Czar Alexander, in grateful recognition of Richelieu's many years of devoted service in Russia, bestowed on him the distinguished Grand Ribbon of the Order of St. Andrew.

Owing to the cabinet's rejection of his proposal to modify the electoral laws, Richelieu resigned his office in December 1818, and returned to private life, after donating his annual pension of 50,000 francs to the founding of a hospital at Bordeaux. He again became president of the council (Feb. 21, 1821), but his position became untenable because of the attacks by both the "Ultras" and the Liberals, and he resigned on Dec. 12, 1822. His health was impaired, and on May 17, 1822, he died of apoplexy, at the age of 54, in the arms of his faithful friend, Father Nicolle.

Czar Alexander, hearing of his death, paid him a last loving tribute: "I mourn for the Duc de Richelieu as the only friend who made me listen to the truth. He was a model of honor and loyalty." On another occasion he remarked: "The French Revolution caused a great deal of harm, but I have to be grateful to it for giving me such men as Richelieu, Langeron, and Traverse." The French historian, Alfred Rambaud[10], honored Richelieu with the words: "This Frenchman was one of the great statesmen of Russia. He prevented the dismemberment of France and restored orderly government to the new monarchy. He was one of the founders in France of political liberty and parliamentary government."

In 1828 the city of Odessa erected a bronze statue of Richelieu in the center of the Grand Boulevard. The illustrious Frenchman is there represented, dressed in a Roman toga and wearing a citizen's wreath on his head. His right hand is extended towards the seaport, as if to show Russia the edifices he had caused to rise and the roadsteads which he had opened for commerce into the Mediterranean and the Near East.

On behalf of the German colonists who honored and cherished the noble name of Richelieu for many generations, the noted historian Fr. C. Keller[11] of Sulz paid him the fine tribute: "The memory of this noble man remained dear to all the colonists of South Russia, for through his love and dedication he deserved, like his friend State Councillor Kantenius, the outstanding president of the Colonist Welfare Committee, to be acclaimed the greatest benefactor in the history of the colonies."

---

[10] op. cit., p. 662.
[11] Conrad Keller, *Die deutschen Kolonien in Südrussland*, Bd. I, Stadelmaier, Odessa, 1905, p. 55.

V.   Early Accounts of Colonist Life

1. The Mariental Report of 1818

The earliest report on the status and life of the German colonist in the district of Grossliebental appeared in 1817, only 13 years after the first colonies were established near Odessa. The report was contained in a lengthy letter[1] which a Swiss immigrant, known only by his initials as J. B., sent to his relatives back home. The letter was first published in 1818 in "Germanien" under the title "Merkwürdige Reisebeschreibung." The section appearing here in translation will give the interested reader a fascinating and informative eyewitness account of the achievements of the first German settlers who pioneered on the virgin steppes above the Black Sea.

1. Arrival in Mariental

When the three days of quarantine in Ovidiopolis were over, many wagons arrived from the neighboring German village to take us into winterquarters. The farmer who loaded up our belongings was from the village of Mariental where we are staying at the present time. When he saw there were only three of us, he gave us to understand that he would be pleased if we were willing to stay with him, because he feared that he might have to take in more people. Mariental is a three-hour walk from Ovidiopolis. Our acquaintances now became separated. The people who had come with us were mostly Alsatians; a good many of them had to stay behind in the hospital at Ismail.

As we drove away from Ovidiopolis, a strong and very cold wind was blowing, and during the fast drive we became quite numb and almost froze to death. We reached Mariental on Sunday night, the 16th of November

---

[1]The letter written by J. B. was published in 1818 in "Germanien" under the title: *Merkwürdige und vollständige Reisebeschreibung der im Jahre 1817 ausgewanderten Württemberger, Badenser und Schweizer, nach Kaukasien.* The translated passages appearing in this book were made from the edition published in 1970 by the Landsmannschaft der Bessarabiendeutschen (Stuttgart), and edited by Friedrich Fiechtner, to whom I am indebted for the extensive use of his text.

(New Style). As soon as we came into the warm room, the farmer's wife served us a hot meal consisting of excellent meat and potatoes. We ate with ravenous appetite and since we were also very thirsty we also drank a lot of water, and all of us became sick that same night. We had much abdominal flatulence which was followed by violent diarrhea. I had the strongest attacks and in a few days I felt so weak that I couldn't get out of bed. The weakness increased so much from day to day that we thought we would have to die. However my father and my wife soon got better, but we all found it difficult to walk.

Grossliebental
Kleinliebental
Lustdorf
Alexanderhilf
Neuburg
Josephstal
Mariental
Franzfeld
Peterstal
Freudental

The German Colonies near Odessa

All our money was now spent and we were at a loss what to do. We decided to make an agreement with our farmer host regarding our board for a certain period of time, and it was agreed that we pay half a ruble a day for each of us. The meals were good, for they consisted of substantial portions of meat and noodles every day. However, this was obviously too heavy a diet for us sick people, and on some days I hardly ate anything at all. But we observed on many occasions that our hosts really liked us.

The area where we are now living lies a little above the 46th degree of North Latitude, which does not differ greatly from yours. But it gets much hotter here in the summer than it does in Switzerland, since there are no mountains here. If Switzerland did not have its high snowcapped mountains, it would also be warmer. The winter is much colder than yours and there are prevailing strong winds, for there are no obstructive barriers, neither hills, nor forests, nor valleys, but only very level plains. Only rarely do we have two or three windless days. Often it blows so hard and cold across the Black Sea that no one would think of being on the road for even an hour without a fur coat. But the last winter was quite mild, and if the winds had not blown so vehemently, the weather would have been like yours in spring. Snow fell only a few times. The local people say that when there is much snow and prevailing strong wind (and it often blows so hard that some people have been flung to the ground right in front of their own doorsteps), it gets so cold that one's face can easily become frostbitten. Strong winds generally also prevail in the summer. If this were not so, the German settlers would not be able to stand the heat. The nights are mostly quite cool, for the wind also blows at night. However, the frequent winds are really a great boon to the country, for without them no grain could be ground, since only windmills are in general use. Near Odessa there are a hundred of them, standing side by side.

The area around our village is somewhat hilly, and from a nearby hillock one has a beautiful view of Odessa. The countryside has very fertile soil. Everything grows here that one could wish for, and it grows without much labor. The soil is completely black, with a high saltpeter content; when dry, it crumbles in the wind like ashes. All kinds of grass and plants that you have back home are also found here and many others besides. However, because of the fertility of the soil they grow twice as large. One cannot find a single stone in the tilled fields, but there are many stone quarries, all of them of the same type, namely limestone. These stones are wondrous to behold, for they are composed of tiny seashells that have the appearance of small fossilized leaves of some exotic plant.

A characteristic of our environment is that not even the smallest stalk of wood grows here. From Ismail to here we didn't see a single tree or shrub, except near Akkerman. One could, of course, plant trees and establish some woodlands, and for this purpose the first colonists were provided with seeds of the acacia and of other trees, but so far nothing has been planted except some willows that grow like weeds in humid places. The colonists are wholly content with farming and think that this is all that needs to be done.

Instead of firewood, the people here use *burian*, bulrushes, straw, and cow manure for fuel. *Burian* is a collective term for the large, stalky weeds that grow on the steppe. Among them are various kinds of wormwood that grow to a large, sturdy size. Many other kinds of *burian* are also combustible. Tall bulrushes or river reeds grow profusely along the Dniester. They are frequently gathered in the fall and in the winter, and, like *burian,* many thousands of wagonloads of them are sold. Everyone is permitted to cut and gather as much reed as he can use; the rest is burned at the end of winter. The resulting conflagration produces a red glow in the sky that can be seen for two or three weeks. In spite of this massive burning, very large quantities of reed remain. After the bulrushes are cut they are tied together in bundles and sold in lots of one hundred in the city. A hundred bundles cost from five to eight rubles in the country, and from eight to thirteen in the city.

Cow manure, free of all straw, is dried in the summer for fuel and the surplus is sold in the city, but this fuel is more expensive than the river reeds, for it is as combustible as peat. Wood is very expensive here, but it is available in Odessa. Coal, which is used by blacksmiths, has to be imported from the Russian interior and from Poland.

There are very many wolves in this region. One often sees them in packs of ten or twenty, and they appear almost daily in the villages, both at night and in broad daylight. Last winter three cows and several calves were torn up by them in our village of Mariental. No one, therefore, leaves the village at night, and whoever has some business to attend to in winter, even if it's only 15 minutes away from the village, either rides there on his horse or in his wagon. The people here travel very fast and their horses have to run, even when they are hauling heavy loads. But this is not done just because of the wolves; it's simply common usage. One could easily take measures to gradually exterminate these harmful animals, but the authorities would have to help by issuing an order that this has to be done. But no one ever thinks of that, neither the authorities, nor the subjects, regardless of the fact that no one can safely walk the streets in winter and in spite of the fact that many people have been mangled by the wolves. Except for the wolves, I have so far not seen any animals here with which you are not familiar. There are, however, small turtles which, it is said, have such a hard shell that a heavily loaded wagon can run over them without causing them any injury. There are also very many dogs here, but not as many as in Turkey. They run about wild and undomesticated, and one can catch as many as one wants, but one never sees a single small dog, for the type here consists mostly of large hunting dogs.

It is very good to live in this country, once you get used to the climate. Indeed, it's a pity that there are not more German people here to cultivate the fertile land. The colonists here possess a very large acreage, but they only plant the fields they like best, while the remaining area is not cultivated. The chief grains that are sown are winter wheat, spring wheat, rye, barley, oats, and maize. Spelt wheat isn't grown here, but the winter wheat is as good as your spelt. The best fields near the houses remain untilled. The fields that are used are plowed only once a year, namely in the spring just before seeding time. Potatoes are planted in the spring, but no additional work is done on them—no hiving or hoeing. The people simply accept what nature itself provides. In such a potato field one sees more *burian* and all kinds of weeds than potatoes, and these are generally of very poor quality. If the people did only half as much work on them as you do back home, they would have excellent crops. The fields here are never fertilized with manure. Vegetable and other plants are never watered; instead, everything is allowed to dry up in the heat.

During the winter very little work is done. The farmer, his hired man, and the servant girl sit around most of the time in the warm *Stube*. They find it very burdensome that the cattle produce manure. They haul it to a pile on a field closest to the house, and there it stays. The ashes from the stoves are likewise dumped there. When the sowing, haying, and harvesting is done the colonists' work is finished, except that they have to tread out some wheat during the winter. If one speaks to them about improving their farming methods, they laugh right in your face. They are satisfied with what they have, and in fact, most of them are very well off. To be sure, they could be much more prosperous if they adopted better methods of farming.

Anyone who is willing to exert himself a bit can easily amass a sizable fortune in a few years. One seldom sees families who are very poor, still less does one find beggars among the colonists. Nor is there any lack of money, for everything that the farmers want to sell fetches a good price in the city. Everything is very expensive here, and this is the reason that so much money is in circulation. Almost every Saturday the local farmer hauls a load of wheat into the city, and when he has no more wheat to sell he hauls bulrushes, *burian,* cow manure, butter, eggs and the like, all of which brings a good price. You can make as much hay here as you like and also keep a lot of live stock, for the fertile steppe provides more fodder than can be used. The livestock is always kept out on the open steppe to graze, even in wintertime when the ground is frozen hard and covered with frost. This does not harm the animals in the least; on the contrary, they thrive on it and grow fat. The livestock is kept at home only when the ground is covered with snow. Horses and cattle are not much cheaper here than they are in your country. There are also wild horses here which are caught on the open steppe and tamed with great effort. In the winter they find their fodder on the steppe even when the snow is deep, for they scrape it away with their hooves and feed upon a certain wild shrub called *Hexenkraut*.

The wages for farm labor are very good, as can be seen from the following figures: the horse herder receives an annual wage of 1300 rubles; the cow herder gets 900; the ox and the swine herders make 400 rubles. In addition, the farmers also provide free board.

Our village of Mariental has no sheep, but there are large sheep farms in the neighboring villages. The daylaborers, of whom there are very few, earn two or three rubles a day, plus free board. In the haying season and at harvest time they earn up to five rubles a day. In those seasons many needy Polish laborers travel two or three hundred hours to earn some money in these parts, and are able to return to Poland with 200-300 rubles. All grain is seeded in the beginning of spring; what is sown later is burned by the heat. During seeding time the farmers do not return home from fields from Monday till Saturday. Wrapped in their fur coats, they sleep on the open steppe, even when the ground is frozen. They take their provisions with them and cook their meals in the field. Since there are no springs of water anywhere, they also haul barrels of water for themselves and the horses. They also take along their guns and pistols, on account of the numerous wolves. All these things are done also at haying and harvest time.

There are no granaries on the steppe. At harvest time a large part of the wheat crop is treaded out by horses on the field; it is then winnowed and cleaned. Since there are no winnowing mills, the threshed wheat is tossed into the air with large wooden scoops, and the strong wind separates the wheat from the chaff and dust. The sheaves that are not threshed in the field are hauled home and stacked in the grain yard, to be treaded out during the winter. Many farmers also leave some of the grain sheaves and the straw in large stacks on open steppe until the following spring. If the straw is no longer needed it is burned, many hundreds of tons of it. The most distant fields are often a two-hour drive from the village. Much hay is also stacked in the fields and then hauled home in the winter. What the colonists don't need is sold to the Russians at a very cheap price.

Here on the steppe a great deal of grain is lost in a variety of ways. At harvest time all the grain is mowed by Russian and Polish laborers who do not perform a proper job, for much of the wheat and other grain is left lying in the fields. Indeed, hundreds of poor people support themselves from the leavings, but nobody else thinks of gathering them up, for no one has any need to do so. In addition, much of the grain that is stacked in the open fields over winter begins to rot; much of it is devoured by wild game, cattle, and field mice; and much is lost when it is treaded out. Finally, the grain is not thoroughly ground in the windmills. An indescribable loss is also caused by the fact that the colonists fail to utilize the unground grain for the production of distilled spirits. Moreover, the miller returns to the farmer only as much of the milled grain as he pleases. In these various ways the amount of grain that is lost is greater than what you harvest back home.

From all this you can readily conclude that a state of superabundance prevails here. We have very few crafts, however, since the colonists consider this profession too insignificant. All manufactured goods are very expensive. Shoemakers and tailors will not do any kind of work for you for less than two or three rubles. Hence all the manufactured goods must be bought in the city at a very high price. You can obtain everything from the shopkeepers and tradesmen, but they expect to make at least a 50 percent profit. The immigrants in the German villages were almost all artisans before they came here, but now everyone wants to become a farmer. You can easily imagine what a disadvantage this is for the economy, and yet everyone is doing well and making a good living. My dearest wish is that a few experienced and industrious farmers from your area would be here. Even if they worked only half as much land as the farmer works here, they would become wealthy people in a few years. If a person did nothing more than establish a small tree nursery, he would become the most prosperous man around here. Such an enterprise would cost him very little, for there is a great abundance of small wild trees along the shore of the Black Sea. In Grossliebental, only two hours from here, there is a plant nursery called the *Krongarten* where anyone who wants trees can obtain them, but he has to pay a high price. Hence there would be no lack of sales for trees, especially since an order has been issued by a high-ranking authority that trees must be planted. What a great benefit it would be for our region, if this order would be carried out.

In the city everyone is involved in business and trade, and no one gives any thought to manufacturing. For this reason all the goods you buy in the city are very expensive. That is understandable, for all the goods are brought in from France, England, Italy, and Germany, and at such great distances the freight alone is already high.[2] Fifteen years ago Odessa was still a small village, but now it's a large city and one of the foremost commercial centers in Europe. It is really remarkable how a recently established town could develop so much in such a short time. Everybody in it is engaged in commerce, and it boasts of having several millionaires. A large number of Jews, Greeks, Turks, Armenians, Italians, Frenchmen, Englishmen, even Egyptians and Moors from Africa, have business establishments there. There are also many Germans, among them several distinguished Swiss, who came here quite poor a few years ago, but now own elegant houses and some of them even ocean-going vessels. In this city you can obtain everything imaginable. There are many large grain storage depots in the city, and every year several hundred vessels laden with wheat sail into the Mediterranean and to adjoining countries. Both wheat and flour are transported to Odessa from a distance of 200 or even 300 travel hours. There is also extensive commerce in wood and all kinds of wood products, such as furniture, wagons, plows and wheels. Every day is a big market day, but the biggest is held on Sundays. Every kind of opulence and luxury prevails, just as in every larger city in Germany. The houses are beautifully constructed of stone, but are generally only two stories high and attractively roofed with small boards or thick shingles. To date, the streets are not yet paved, so that the morass in the spring and fall is so deep that the horses and wagons often get stuck. But it is rumored that the streets will soon be paved with stone.

The colonists in the ten German villages in this area are mostly Alsatians, Württemberger, and so forth. When they arrived thirteen years ago they had thought of settling in the Crimea. At that time many Swiss emigrants also arrived under the leadership of a man from Zurich by the name of Escher, and were settled in the Crimea. According to reliable reports, all of these immigrants are faring very well there. This peninsula is only forty hours' travel distance from here by sea. When the aforesaid Alsatians and Württemberger arrived 13 years ago in the Odessa area that was being developed at that time, the authorities were most interested in establishing several villages in the environs of the city and getting the countryside under cultivation. For this reason the immigrants were encouraged to settle in this area. They were glad to accept the offer, for the Czar also granted them a sizable advance loan to help them get established. He also gave them enough fertile land and

---

[2] As examples for the high prices prevailing in 1818, the Swiss immigrant J. B. adduces the following items: work shoes, 5-7 rubles; boots, 7-20 rubles; a cotton handkerchief, 2-3 rubles; an embroidered muslin shawl, 10-15 rubles; a lb. of granulated sugar, 1-2 rubles; a lb. of pepper, 2 rubles. However, he also notes that fruit, including imported oranges, lemons, and figs, was very cheap. Liquor was also inexpensive; an *oka* (1.35 U.S. quarts) of beer or mead was only 20-30 kopecks; an *oka* of good wine or fruit brandy was from 70 kopecks to 1 ruble; excellent French brandy was 2-3 rubles.

money to build their homes and purchase both livestock and farm equipment. In addition, they were granted daily food money until they were able to provide for themselves.

In this way, forty German villages were established in the Odessa region, consisting of four districts. One lies near the seashore, one to the east of Odessa in the direction of Nikolaiev, one in the direction of Tiraspol and one to the north of Odessa. The locality where we are living was formerly occupied by several Russians, but they were assigned to another region. Since there is still a lot of room, new colonists are still accepted in the same way as the first colonists and we ourselves were accepted. In fact, many of the colonists who came here with us and who are still receiving daily food money are being settled in this area, since many of them do not want to move into the Caucasus. We don't want to go there either, nor do we want to be settled as farmers. In the first place, we do not have anyone to work for us in the fields; secondly, we are earning enough money with our bakery.

Since wood is so very expensive here, the pioneer colonists cannot build their houses in the German manner. However, since plenty of stone can be quarried near the villages, their houses are constructed of stone, but are only one-story high and thatched with bulrushes. The houses have a very long extension and are surrounded by stone walls, giving them the appearance of monasteries. However, despite their great length, the houses generally have only two rooms, namely the living room and the kitchen. The remainder of the building is divided into stables and barns. The walls are constructed of limestone which is plastered with clay. Lime, which is very expensive here, is only used to whitewash the walls inside and out.

All the houses are ranged in a straight line on both sides of the street. Every house has two large yards which are enclosed by stone walls. In the front yard you find the house with attached barn and a good well from which the water is drawn by means of a balance beam. In this yard you also find a large number of poultry. The Russians, on the other hand, let all their livestock run around the front yard since they have no barns, but let their cattle and horses roam freely under the open sky even when the weather turns very cold. The German settlers own a lot of livestock; almost every farmer has from 4 to 8 horses and from 20 to 40 head of cattle. In the second yard at the rear, called the grain yard, you find stacks of grain, hay, and straw which tower above the houses and give the village a peculiar appearance.

It is rumored that the Czar is going to visit Odessa in May and, on this occasion, will also inspect the German villages and their economic condition. The report alarmed the officials, for they feared the Emperor's displeasure, because in many of the villages no trees have yet been planted and no wood-lands established. The authorities, therefore, issued stringent orders that drainage ditches had to be dug on either side of the sidewalks, allowing for crosswalks at the gate entrances that led into the yards. Moreover, straight rows of shade trees had to be planted along each side of the street and all houses had to be neatly whitewashed. The officials received seeds from the government to establish acacia plantations. Without delay, the people started to plant trees, dig ditches, and pave pathways. Some of the earlier colonists had already done this twelve years ago and now have very beautiful avenues of trees, as well as cherry, plum, and mulberry trees, so that it's a real delight to travel through such a village. In our village of Mariental, however, all is still devoid of such ornaments, but now it will doubtless also become beautiful. In general, the German villages are really beginning to have the aspect of a city. All the streets are over 100 decimal feet (or 47 yards) wide; all the houses are built in a straight line; and rows of shade trees are planted along the walls parallel to the street and protected by wooden railings. On the wall facing the street, entrance gates are being erected which are framed by two pillars supporting a painted crossbeam. In this way each village gains an attractive appearance, and in the largest village you can survey everything at a glance from the first to the last house on the street.

In every village where there is no parish church, you find a chapel or house of prayer. All the parochial churches are beautifully constructed, and both the roof of the church and the steeple are covered with copper. In each belfry there is only a single bell. The graveyards are all outside the villages. With this brief description, you can easily visualize how things look around here.

2. The Colonists greet Czar Alexander

The following interesting episode was related in the memoirs[3] of the German immigrant Friedrich Doering, who was in the employ of the Duke of Württemberg on his large estate at Karlstal located 7 versts from the colony of Freudental.

"In April of 1821 the town of Tiraspol on the Dniester became the scene of great activity and excitement, for it was made known that His Imperial Majesty Czar Alexander I would be coming through the town in the course of his journey to the Crimea. For days the military from Odessa and the gouvernement of Cherson were marching through our steppe on their way to the camp near Tiraspol, where some 30,000 troops were to hold maneuvers in honor of the visiting monarch.

For a whole week the distant sound of the cannon could be heard. One day, however, as the sound grew louder, the superintendent Schellenberg called me and directed me to drive several flocks of sheep to the post station of Hederim, about 7 versts away, since the Czar would be passing through that place on his way from Tiraspol to Odessa, and would perhaps be able to see the sheep while the stagecoach horses were being changed at the post station.

After I had brought the sheep to the designated place, I rode along the post road, and when I was still two versts from the station, I saw several hundred horsemen, all dressed in blue uniforms, riding towards me. As they approached, I discovered, to my amazement, that they were colonist farmers from Freudental and Peterstal riding forth to meet the Czar. They were former emigrants from Hungary, and for this reason they wore the Hungarian national costume. They tried to ride in proper rank and formation, but their well-fed horses, frightened of this strange equine association, kept kicking and biting each other. The mayor of Freudental rode ahead, as the commander of the cavalcade.

At the post station several hundred people from the surrounding district had gathered, eagerly awaiting the Czar's arrival. Had I known this earlier, I would have come here by wagon, and brought along my wife. About four in the afternoon, when the people were already quite tired of waiting, the stagecoach came down the sloping road, preceded by the cavalcade of German farmers.

Two gentlemen descended from the coach, and I did not have to guess which one was the Czar. His tall, slender figure and his stately walk permitted me to identify him the moment I saw his face, for I had seen it portrayed in pictures a hundred times.

Many women from Freudental, Peterstal, and other colonies had assembled at one place. The Czar walked towards them, and asked how they liked it in this country, whether they had good crops, and if they were in good health. One of the women who came forward spoke for all of them. She was stout-hearted, and frankly told the Czar that many people had died on the Danube river on their

[3] The "Memoiren" were published by his son, Dr. Eduard Döring, Russian Councilor of State (Verlag E. Pierson).

way here by boat, and that many were even now still lying in the lazaret at Ovidiopol. This was true, for the boats were overcrowded, thereby causing the outbreak of epidemic disease that took the lives of a great part of the passengers. The woman also told the Czar that those immigrants did not receive all of the daily food-money that had been allotted to them by the Crown.

The Czar replied: "Dear people, you should not have come along the Danube waterway." He then asked them to be patient, and assured them that everything would get better, for every beginning is difficult. In conclusion, he asked them from what part of Germany they had come, and now you should have heard the women. One shouted, "Württemberg"; another, "Bavarian Pfalz"; a third, "Alsace"; a fourth, "Hungary", and so on.

After the brief interview Schellenberg came forward and presented to the Czar a folder in which samples of wool had been pasted, and pointing to the flocks of sheep, he indicated that they belonged to Prince Eugen of Württemberg. The Czar opened the folder, examined the samples of wool, and then looked at the flocks of sheep through his small field glasses.

He then returned to his coach. Suddenly the mayor of Freudental shouted a vivat: "Es lebe der Kaiser Alexander Pawlowitsch!" But since no one joined in the acclamation, I thought it would have been better if he had kept his mouth shut, for the people who had come here were not interested at that moment in shouting but in getting a look at him, as no one wanted to go home without having seen the *Kaiser*. He was indeed very handsome, perhaps the most handsome man of his time. As the Emperor drove away, he raised his shako in farewell, and everyone in the crowd shouted a lively *"Lebewohl!"*

On another occasion Czar Alexander, who was profoundly respected and indeed revered by his subjects, had a more humorous encounter. While driving through the countryside in a common carriage and dressed in a plain, unofficial overcoat, he came to a Russian post station. Wishing to speak to an elderly man standing near the road, he called out: "Hey, *muzhik* (peasant), come here!" But the man retorted, "No, I'm not a *muzhik*; higher up, brother." "Well then, a *dessetnik* (assembly man)" — "No, higher up!" — "Well, *Vuibornui* (elector), come here!" — "Higher, higher." — "Perchance even the *golova* (chief mayor)?" — "At your service, little father", the man replied, "I'm the mayor of this place. What can I do for you, Captain?" — "No, brother", the Czar responded, "not a captain; higher up!" — "Perchance a major or a colonel?" — "No, brother, higher up!" — "Oh, perhaps a general?" — "Higher up." — "What? surely not a field marshal? Pardon me, Your Excellency, that I ..." — "Higher up, brother, higher up!" — "God in Heaven! Do I see right? You are ...?" — "At your service, little father, your Czar." The mayor sank to his knees with such fright that the Emperor had great difficulty getting him back on his feet again.

3. By Troika to Odessa

It was a sun-resplendent dawn in mid-May, the roads were excellent and the twelve hooves of our troika were continually in the air, as we sped across the steppe above the Black Sea in the direction of Odessa. Towards morning a cool breeze rose from the south, and Kun-lei, my coachman and companion, suddenly aroused me with the cry, *"Voilà la brise de la mer noire."*[1] The arrival on the coast of a new sea is always an exciting moment for the traveller, and it was not long before we gazed upon the broad expanse of water and heard the surge of the white-crested surf. As we drove along the steep bank of the steppe plateau we recalled fond memories of youth and school days, and now we were able to greet in spirit the 10,000 Greeks of yore who finally reached this sea after their long and arduous campaign.

A Russian troika (1818).

The first post station by the sea was Troitzkoye, which is located at the mouth of the Teligul Liman. This was the first time I was able to view the remarkable geological formation that was completely unknown to me. However, since our road to Odessa would lead us past four more limans, namely the Little and the Big Buyulik and the Little and the Big Kuyalnik, we would have excellent opportunities to study the formation that is peculiar to the steppes and the northwest coastal area of the Black Sea. The Teligul Liman is over ten German *Meilen* (i.e. 45 English miles) long and from two to four *versts* wide. From here on the road runs constantly close to the seashore. At

---

[1] "Here it is! The breeze from the Black Sea."

the post station we saw several *semelyankas* of the Cossack soldiers who are posted here to guard the coast against smugglers and the dread plague. No ships or boats are allowed to land without a permit from the Odessa quarantine authority. In fact, nothing may be taken from the sea, not even driftwood, and the boatmen are restricted by law from going beyond the limit of one verst.

The post station at the second liman at the mouth of the Little Buyulik was located high up on the steppe plateau. From there I took a walk on the *peressip,*[2] the long sand bank, to get a close-up view of the curious formation. With a tumultuous surge the sea rolled into the *gheerl,* the sluice that provided an opening in the *peressip.* Two stone bridges lay in ruins near the sluice, and a third bridge made of wood was under construction. At the ferry a large number of people with wagons and herds of cattle were gathered. Naturally, there was a great deal of traffic and tumult on the *peressip,* since detours had to be made from all sides in order to go around the *liman.* Between the *gheerl* and the onset of the breakers a sand bar has been formed in fairly shallow water, and many teamsters take the chance of driving their wagons along the submerged sand bar, in order to get to the other side of the *liman.*

I was greatly astonished when, amid all the tumult and the roaring of the breakers, I heard voices which one would ordinarily only expect to hear on the banks of the Neckar or the Lech. "Seid gschäut," a teamster was shouting to his companions, "hier am *Liman* können wir die Pferde mit tränke! Wir hätten's obe am Brünneli tun solle."[3] They were Swabian colonists who had come from München,[4] Worms, Rohrbach and Stuttgart and were hauling grain to Odessa. The localities are the names of colonies they had established to the north of the Teligul Liman. They all had large wagons that were drawn by four horses. They freely praised their life on the steppe and were very satisfied with their livelihood and their relationship with their Russian neighbors. One of them remarked, "Oh, we get along well with the Russians. We have fewer quarrels with them than with our German neighbors."

They were just as astonished when they heard that the stranger in the bearskin coat was addressing them in standard German, as I was utterly surprised when I heard the Swabian dialect coming forth from their sheep-

---

[2] peressip, from the Russian ssipatj, to stride; hence, a ford or crossing.

[3] "Don't be silly, we can't water our horses here in the liman; we should have done it back at the little well."

[4] München was a Catholic colony; the others were Lutheran. All of them were established in 1809, Stuttgart, however, was later abandoned because of lack of water.

skin overcoats and Crimean karagul caps. Outwardly, we all had the appearance of Russians, but inside we were, of course, very good Germans—at least as far as my inner self was concerned. I let them transport me on one of their wagons to the other side of the *Liman* and I remained with them until Kun-lei and our troika caught up with me. We talked about the *limans* and they gave me an interesting account of the beautiful salt crop which they and the entire region had harvested in the Big Kuyalnik Liman several years ago.

It was not long before we reached the city of Odessa, the Queen of the Black Sea. Like all the cities of New Russia, Odessa is constructed on a regular plan and laid out on a truly grand scale. Except for a few gullies, the terrain on which the city is built is perfectly flat, and the streets extremely wide. However, because of their great width they remained unpaved for many years, and it was only through the efforts of governors like Richelieu, Langeron, and Voronzov that the main avenues were eventually paved with stone that had to be imported from Italy and Malta. Rows of acacia trees adorn all the streets, but they are unable to protect the city from the frequent winds and the pitiless rays of the summer sun. In earlier decades the prevailing steppe winds that swept through the broad dirt streets raised such frightful dust storms that life for the citizens became just as intolerable as the swarms of mosquitoes that afflicted Humboldt during his sojourn on the Orinoco. On the other hand, during the rainy season the dusty streets of Odessa were turned into a quagmire of mud that paralysed all pedestrian and vehicular traffic.

The main street of the city is the Odessa Boulevard that runs along the edge of the steppe plateau overlooking the harbor. It is lined with avenues

View of the Black Sea near
the Odessa harbor

of acacia trees and beautiful walks. On the inner side of the boulevard there is a long row of elegant hotels and shops, and the palatial residence of Count Voronzov, the present governor of the city. From the spacious Plaza de Richelieu there extends a grandiose limestone stairway to a width of 100 feet and descends 130 feet down the side of the steep embankment to the seashore.

The Grand Staircase at Odessa

Among the principal public buildings that deserve to be mentioned are the Imperial Lyceum founded by Duc de Richelieu and later renamed the University of Odessa; the Odessa Theater, in which operas and plays are performed in five languages; the stock market with its elegant Casino del Commercio; and the various foreign shops on Richelieu Street. There are also many churches, the chief of which are the Russian Orthodox, the Catholic, and the Lutheran.

A noteworthy establishment is the Botanical Garden with its extensive nurseries which contain over four million young and older trees. In sharp contrast with the beautiful garden is the large city cemetery which presents a scene of utter desolation and neglect, typical of other Russian cemeteries. Crumbling and decayed monuments of the detestable local limestone stand so deep in wild-growing steppe grass that one might easily assume that the place was intended to be a cattle pasture instead of a cemetery. One can, however, make the happy observation that all denominations and races lie together here in communal peace. To my great satisfaction, I also saw that the graves in the German section were definitely well-tended. They were also surrounded by beautiful trees and adorned with shrubs of acacia.

Although Odessa scarcely had 8,000 inhabitants at the beginning of the century, it has now (in 1838) almost ten times that number. Its population is very cosmopolitan. The languages that are most frequently heard on the streets are Russian and Italian. Even the street signs appear in these two languages. While Russian is the language of government, the marketplace, and the harbor, Italian is the language of trade and commerce. The architecture of the public buildings is also Italianate. French is the language of high society. The Jews of Odessa, some 12,000 in number, all speak Yiddish, but most of them came here from Poland. Besides these languages, you can hear at least another dozen on the streets of Odessa, namely German, Polish, Tartar, Turkish, Greek, Bulgarian, Moldavian (Rumanian), Hungarian, Dalmatian, Swedish, and Spanish. English is of no importance.

The commercial product with which Odessa is primarily concerned is the wheat from Podolia, Bessarabia, and New Russia. All other products, excepting tallow and wool, are of lesser interest to the lords of commerce. Almost all the wheat is exported to England and to Italy. In 1837, for example, 121 English sailing ships arrived in the Odessa harbor to take on their cargoes of Russian wheat. The time required to transport it to England was from 60 to 70 days. Italy is the next largest importer of wheat, but Odessa also has three large factories that produce every kind of macroni and *galetti* for export. Tallow, used for candles and lamps, is also exported in large quantities to England, Italy, and Greece.

The grain that is hauled into Odessa from the vast steppelands of South Russia is stored in hundreds of stone granaries that are constructed like ordinary houses and located on the streets all over the city. As the city continues to grow and expand these granaries are readily converted into regular dwellings. Some of the granaries are veritable palaces, as for example those of the wealthy grain dealer Count Potocki and the Polish nobleman Sabanski. But the grain palace of the latter was appropriated by the Imperial Crown after he was convicted of having been a leader in the Polish Rebellion of 1829. At the present, the granaries in Odessa are said to have a storage capacity of 80,000 wagonloads of grain. In regard to its total import-export trade, Odessa now stands in third place, being surpassed only by Petersburg and Riga.

4. Nationalities in New Russia

Among the numerous peoples and nationalities of New Russia, the principal and basic ethnic group was that of the so-called Malorussians or Little Russians, better known in modern times as the Ukrainians. In distinction from these, the Muscovite Russians were known as the Great Russians or by the common nickname *"Kazappi,"* a Tartar word which had the meaning of "butchers." In return, the Little Russians were given the sobriquet *"Cacholl,"*—pigtail, because when they cut their hair they let a long tuff of hair grow in the middle.

The highly interesting ethnic group of Ukrainians expanded, a couple of centuries ago, in a most remarkable way from their aborigenal habitat into neighboring regions. Their original settlements were located largely in the lands around the middle Dnieper, and in the regions of Kiev, Poltava, and Chernigov. From there they spread to the Carpathians where a group of them known as the *Rusnacks* lived under Austrian rule. However, in these lands, as in the Ukraine itself, the Ukrainians constituted the major portion of the population, not only in the open country but also in the market towns and the cities.

From these places, the Malorussians spread southward as far as the Black Sea and through all of "New Russia," and also as far as the Volga, particularly the farming region around Saratov. In the middle of the nineteenth century, the Ukrainian nationality constituted the largest agricultural population in all the southern steppes of Russia as far as Moldavia, the Crimea, and the Caucasus.

This remarkable peaceful expansion and settlement was in certain respects a fairly modern development. For even though the former members of the Cossack settlements were mostly of Ukrainian stock, it was only after the decisive victory of Russian arms over the Turks and the Tartars that the Ukrainians were able to become the inheritors of the Tartars.

In South Russia, the Ukrainians are considered more honest, industrious, and moral in every respect than the Muscovite Russian. The Great Russians frequently pursue the trade of carpenters, architects, masons, plasterers, and interior decorators, while the Ukrainians tend to be civil servants, tailors, and shoemakers.

The Russian, generally speaking, designates the refined Germans who live in the cities as *"Niemtzi,"* whereas the German colonists were called *"Schwabui,"*—Schwaben, a term which had come to denote the lower class Germans, in general. He calls them all *"Schwabui,"* no matter if they originally came from the Danube, the Elbe, or the Rhine. The Poles, incidentally, also use the same term, and from Cracow to the Volga all German colonists are called *"Schwabui"* by the common people. In Odessa, a widely used nickname for the Germans was *"Kartoski,"* from the German term *"Kartoffel,"* for the colonists were known as avid potato-eaters. In Moscow, the German foreigners were nicknamed *"Kalabassniki,"* the sausage-makers.

The chief inhabitants of Bessarabia are known as *"Moldavaneshti."* They are descendants of Daco-Rumanians of the ancient Roman province of Dacia, and their language is a derivative of Moldavan-Latin. The land known as Bessarabia, originally and long before the Turkish hegemony, comprised the territory of eastern Moldavia between the Pruth and the Dniester, when the Bessarab family occupied the Moldavian throne. However, under the growing might of the Austrian and Russian eagles, the poor Moldavia with its five million inhabitants was divided up into four principal sections: 1. The *Bukowina* under Austrian sovereignty in 1780; 2. *Bessarabia* under Russian domination since 1812; 3. *Moldavia* under the independent Prince of Jassy; 4. *Wallachia* or "La Mantia" under the independent Prince of Bucharest. The extreme southern part of Bessarabia was also known by its old Tartar name *"Budyak."*

5. Colonist Calendar of Major Events

1801-1825	Reign of Alexander I, grandson of Catherine the Great.
1803	Alexander publishes Rescript on the colonization of "New Russia." Richelieu appointed governor of Odessa. Kantenius becomes president of the Colonist Welfare Office.
1804-1807	Founding of German colonies near Odessa, in the Crimea and in the Taurida.
1805	Richelieu appointed governor of New Russia.
1806-1812	The third Russo-Turkish War.
1808-1809	Founding of the six Kutschurgen villages and the four villages in the Glückstal area.
1809-1810	Founding of 8 settlements in the Beresan district.
1811	The first census of the colonists.
1812	Napoleon invades Russia. Russia annexes Bessarabia. The outbreak of the Odessa plague.
1814	The founding of the German colonies in Bessarabia. Richelieu returns to Paris. Langeron becomes governor of Odessa.
1815	Russia conquers the Duchy of Warsaw.
1815-1820	The "golden years" of colonist prosperity.
1817	1,360 emigrant families from Württemberg arrive at Ismail. Over 1,300 people perish in the quarantine camps.
1817-1818	Founding of German colonies in the South Caucasus.
1818	Colonist Welfare Office is established in Odessa. Inspectorates introduced in the colonies.
1820	The Jesuits expelled from Russia.
1822	Langeron returns to Paris. Vorontzov becomes governor of Odessa. The death of Duc de Richelieu.
1822-1831	Founding of German colonies near Berdyansk (Sea of Azov).
1823-1824	Locust plague in the Odessa area, poor crops.
1823-1842	Founding of the "Planer" colonies in Mariupol district.
1825	Alexander I visits South Russia. Dies at Toganrog. His brother, Nicholas I, becomes Czar of Russia.
1825-1829	Good crops in the colonies. Building of new homes.
1829	Platzer's plan to establish Central (secondary) schools.
1828-1829	Fourth Russo-Turkish War. German colonists provide labor services.
1830-1831	The Polish revolt.
1833	The "Black Year." No rain, no crops; famine and food relief.
1835	Colonial affairs placed under the Ministry of Imperial Domains.
1839	Russian silver currency established.
1842	First Central School established.

1845-1848	Gen. Hahn becomes president of Colonist Welfare Office.
1845	Czar Nicholas I visits Pope Gregory XVI.
1846-1848	Years of colonist prosperity.
1848	Colonist Codex established. The writing of Community Reports.
1849	Johann Ludwig Bette and 21 families from the Odessa district arrive on the *Constantia* in New York on Oct. 22 and settle in Ohio.
1850	Helanus Kahn becomes first bishop of Tiraspol diocese.
1853-1856	The Crimean War. The German colonists of South Russia provide essential labor services.
1855	Cholera epidemic.
1855	Death of Nicholas I. Alexander II becomes Czar of Russia.
1857	Catholic seminary established in Saratov.
1861	Emmancipation of the serfs. Land distribution. Redemption payments.
1862	The first German newspaper, *Unterhaltungsblatt,* published.
1863	Prohibition of corporal punishment for schoolchildren.
1864	Zemstvo (municipal) government established. Bishop Kahn dies. Lipski becomes administrator.
1865	Corporal punishment of women abolished.
1869	Central School established at Grossliebental/Od.
1871	Colonist Codex abrogated. Privileges of colonists granted by Catherine and Alexander repealed.
1872	Joh-Ludwig Bette visits colonies of Johannestal, Worms, and Rohrbach, urging emigration to America. From 30-40 families winter in Sandusky, Ohio, and settle at Yankton, SD in spring.
1873	Fifty-five families from Worms and Rohrbach emigrate to the U.S.A. and settle near Sutton, Nebraska and in Dakota Terr.
1874	On Jan. 13, Imp. Russian government introduces compulsory military conscription of German colonists.
1877	Colonist Welfare Office abolished.
1880	Abolition of the salt tax.
1881	German colonist schools placed under Ministry of Public Enlightenment. Czar Alexander II assassinated. He is succeeded by Czar Alexander III.
1883	Antonius Zerr, native son of Franzfeld/Od. becomes bishop of Tiraspol. Increase of colonist priests.
1885	The beginning of Catholic emigration to USA and Canada.
1892	Famine in Russia.
1893	Wave of Russian nationalism. German village names Russianized.
1894-1917	Reign of Czar Nicholas II. Deposed in 1917, imprisoned, and executed with his family on July 16, 1918.

1901	Basilika church built in Seltz.
1902	Bishop Zerr resigns. Baron van Ropp, fourth bishop of Tiraspol.
1904-1905	The Russo-Japanese War.
1904	Joseph Kessler, Volga German, becomes 5th bishop of Tiraspol.
1907	Central School established in Landau.
1908	Progymnasium established in Landau by Fr. Scherr.
1914-18	First World War. German colonists serve on the southern front. Suppression of the German language and cultural activities.
1917	Bolshevik Revolution of Nikolai Lenin and the beginning of the Soviet regime.
1919	Enforced requisition of grain. The Red massacre in Selz.
1920	The closing of the seminary. Bishop Kessler leaves Russia.
1920-1923	The Great Famine. 300,000 German colonists starve to death. Hoover's American Relief Fund. Lenin's looting of the Russian churches.
1921	Lenin's "New Economic Policy."
1923	The Soviet registration of all churches.
1924	Stalin becomes supreme dictator.
1928	The first Five Year Plan. Liquidation of the kulaks and the collectivization of all farming. Millions sent to the slave labor camps.
1929-1931	The deportation of priests and intellectuals.
1929	Bishop Frison appointed administrator of the Crimea.
1932-1933	The second Soviet Famine.
1932	Bishop Zerr dies in Kandel; is buried in Selz/Od.
1933	Bishop Kessler dies in a monastery in Prussia.
1934	The sham trials of the priests in Landau.
1937	Bishop Frison executed in a Crimean prison.
1941	The Nazis invade the Ukraine. The capture of Odessa. The deportation of the Volga Germans to labor camps in Siberia.
1943	Bishop Glaser appointed administrator of Transnistria. Churches in the Odessa region reopened.
1944	The retreat of the German Wehrmacht. The flight of 350,000 colonists to the West.
1945	Soviet army captures and deports 260,000 German-Russian refugees to Siberia and Central Asia. Only 90,000 make their escape to Germany.
1950	Bishop Glaser dies in a Communist prison in Rumania.
1964	Krushchev grants amnesty, without reparations, to the deported German-Russians in the slave labor camps.
1977	About 2 million Soviet Germans still live in the USSR.

VI. The Emigration from Alsace to Russia (1803–1809)

Until recent years the history of Alsatian immigration to Russia was inadequately researched and the number of Alsatian colonists greatly underestimated. An extensive survey of the number of German families who had migrated to Russia in the years 1803-1817 from the provinces of Württemberg, Baden, the Palatinate, and Alsace was published by Dr. K. Stumpp in 1961. In this survey he reached the conclusion that the emigrants from Alsace came from 110 villages and numbered 449 families, with a total of 1,568 souls.

However, subsequent research undertaken by Prof. Jean Schweitzer of Strasbourg and myself showed that those estimates were far too low and needed to be corrected. My own calculations demonstrated that the number of Alsatian families who emigrated from the principal 88 villages in the *arrondissement* (district) of Weissenburg and settled in the 16 Catholic mother colonies of the Odessa district exceeded 550 families with an estimated 2,475 souls. This number, it must be noted, does not include the Alsatian families who settled in other parts of South Russia, v.g., in the Crimea, the Molotchna, and the Caucasus. Nor does it include the sizable number of Alsatian who came from the Lutheran villages of Lower Alsace and settled in the Odessa district, particularly in the mother colonies of Rohbach, Worms, Neudorf, Kassel, Bergdorf, and Glückstal.

There has been a tendency among some German scholars to minimize the number of Alsatian settlers in the Evangelical-Lutheran colonies of the Odessa area by calling into question the validity of an early historical source which specifically indicated that there were 60 Alsatian pioneer families in Kassel, 57 in Rohrbach, 37 in Neudorf, 36 in Worms, 21 in Bergdorf, and 10 in Glückstal.

Unfortunately, only about 15 of these Alsatian families have been identified from other sources. Virtually all the rest fall into the category of "village of emigration unknown." In considering the question of those Alsatian families we must take into account the fact that the Palatinate was under French domination during the years of emigration to Russia and was therefore administratively incorporated into Lower Alsace. However, that does not justify the assumption that all the Alsatians alleged to have settled in the Lutheran colonies were from the Palatinate, unless such an assumption is confirmed by supporting evidence. In the light of the large number of

105

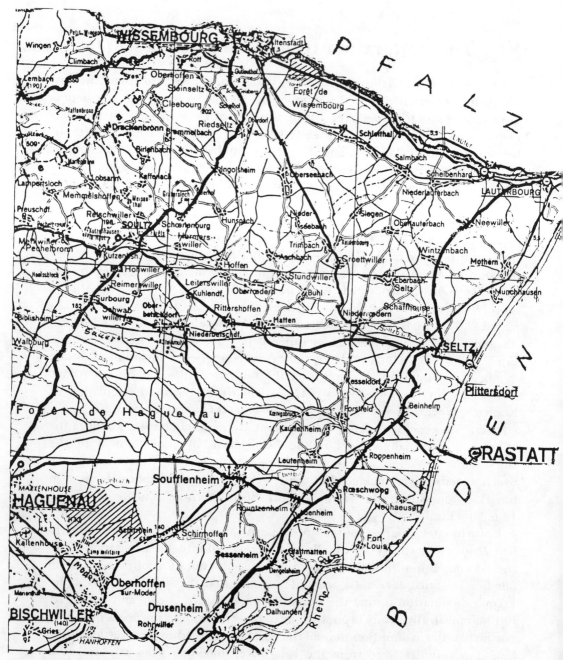

The villages of Lower Alsace in the areas of Weissenburg and Hagenau

Alsatians who emigrated from the Catholic villages in the Weissenburg department, it is a most plausible assumption that a comparatively large number of Lutheran Alsatians emigrated from the same area.

This would mean that at least another 200 Alsatian families, with an estimated total of 900 souls, must be added to the Catholic group of 550 families, which would make a total of 770 families numbering about 3,275 souls. We probably need to add another 100 Alsatians families who were settled in the Crimea, the Molotchna, and the Caucasus.

In the present investigation, I have not included Alsatian villages from which only one family emigrated. It should also be borne in mind that the number of emigrant families indicated for a particular village is not definitive. In many instances, the necessary records are not available to determine the identity of certain families, for their native villages remain unknown.

1. CANTON SELTZ

ASCHBACH

Fischer, Michael 37, son of Anton, chief mayor of the Beresan district, Margareta 28, dau. of Philipp Paul from Kapsweyer, Alsace; daughter from 1st wife: Margareta 8; children from the second wife Barbara: Johann 2, Gottlieb 1 yr. To Landau/Odessa
Fischer, Johannes 23, Rosine 21 nee Ostermaier, Mathias ½ yr. To Selz/Od.
Herzog, Johann 59, Anna 59, Johann 17, Matheus 17, Maria 20, Martin 26. To Kleinliebental/Od.
Hoffart, Joseph 31, Agnes 27, Maria-Eva 3, Johann 1½. To Mannheim/Od.
Hoffart, Ottilie 62, widow, Franz 26, Johannes 23, wife Regina 22, Ignatz 4½, Barbara ½. To Mannh.
Mayer, Jakob 44, Eva 34, Georg 12, Eva 10, Marianna 8, Jakob 4½, Joseph 2½, to Kandel/Od.
Weiss, Ferdinand 37, s. of Georg, Katharina 24, d. of Joh. Fleck of Wingen/Als.,Franz 7. To Sulz.

BEINHEIM

Duchscherer, Christoph 27, Elisabeth 24 nee Gregory, Joseph 3½, Elisabeth +1813. To Mannheim/Od.
Duchscherer, Dionysius 33, weaver, Elisabeth 23, Phil-Martin 4½, Barbara 3, Johann 1 day. Mannhm.
Elter, Augustin 57, Klara 41, Joseph 10, Ludwig 6, Magd.+1816. To Mannheim/Od.
Fahner, Ludwig 40, Maria 41, Elisabeth 16, Maria 11, Margaretha 1½. To Mannheim/Od.
Ganje, Joseph 40, volost mayor, Magdalena 38, Peter 14, Joseph +1812 at age 10, Dionys 7, Christine 4½, Rosine +1816. To Mannheim/Od.
Roth, Nikolaus 31, mason, Christine 28 nee Ostermaier; bro-in-law Balthasar & Rosa 37. To Mannhm.
Schneider, Ludwig 46, Elisabeth 41, Philipp 20, Philippina 15, Elisabeth 10. To Peterstal/Od.
Strubel, Michael 37, Elis. 32, Bernh.+1813, Maria-Eva 3¾, Kath. 2¾, Maria-Antonia ¼. To Mannh
Trautmann, Johannes 32, Elisabetha 25, Johannes 4½, Wilhelm 2½, Peter +1814. To Elsass/Od.
Vetter, Joseph +1812 at 49, Rosine +1816, Michael 34. To Mannheim/Od.
Weber, Ludwig 38, Marianna 34, Ludwig 8½, Christina 4½, Ignatius 1½. To Mannheim/Od.

BÜHL

Ball, Andreas 33, wife Katharina 33, Andreas ½ yr. To Mariental/Od.
Kocher, Georg +1811 at 56, Katharina 46, Elisabeth 14, Anton 7, to Kleinliebental/Od.
Schaub, Joseph 36, Susanna 33, Franz 9, Jakob 2, Karl ¼. To Franzfeld/Od.

EBERBACH

Lacher, Sebastian 64, teacher, Barbara 49, +1813, 2nd wife Barb 48, Franz 20,Regina 22. To Kandel.

*The ages given in these records are for the year 1816.

KAIDENBURG

Brinster, Michael 58, Eva 56, Joseph 15, Xaver 8, to Kleinliebental/Od.
Giesinger, Jakob 40, Barbara 40, Jakob 20, Barbara 14, Katharina 13, Margaretha 10,   .brosius 9,
   Georg 7, Magdalena 4½, Lorenz 2½, Konstantin ½, to Mannheim/Od.
HEIDT, Konstantin 33, Katherina 30, Jakob +1812 at 6 months, Jakob ¼, Johannes b. 1819, Konstan-
   tin b. 1823, mother-in-law Margaretha Riehl, 54, to Mannheim/Od.
Schall, Jakob +1840 at 60, eldest son Xaver 26, wife Marianna 26, Xaver 2, Johannes 21, wife El-
   isabeth 20, children Jakob +1814, Marianna +1815; Appolonia 19 mar'd Nik. Braun, to Selz/Od.

KESSELDORF

Röhl, Joseph 40, Regina 40, Martin 9, Franz +1812 at 3, Kath. +1812, Marg. 11, Jos.+1812,to Selz.
Rumbs, Ludwig 51, teacher, Margaret 53, Elis. 20, married Joh. Schall 21, Maria 14, to Selz/Od.
Rumbs, Franz 25, s. of Ludwig, Katharina 23, Franz-Joseph 4½, Marianna 3½, Elis.,1½, Marg. ¼,Selz.

KRÖTTWEILER

Zimmermann, Michael 28, Margaretha 23, Joseph 2, to Sulz/Odessa

MOTHERN

Baumgärtner, Johann 28, Elisabeth 23 nee Schranz, Kath.+1812, father Peter B., 67, to Strassburg.
Baumgärtner, Georg 30, Josepha-Eva 29, Franz 6½, Marianna 4½, Rosine·1½, to Strassburg/Od.
Baumgärtner, Friedrich 44, Ev.-Lutheran, Elisabeth 41, Friedrich 23, to Alexanderhilf/Od.
Bechtel, Mathias 41, Margareta 33, Kath. 4. Emigrated 1809, itinerary Frankfurt a.M., 8.5., Leip-
   zig 16.5, Dresden 19.5, Breslau 27.5, Babice (Pol.) 6.6, Lemberg 17.6, Radzivilov 21.6,1809.
Berstch, Anton 29 , Maria 28, Lorenz 7, Joseph + 3months, Valentin 1 yr., to Selz/Od.
Bertsch, Michael +1812 at 35, Regina 30, Barbara 7, Anna-Maria 4½, to Selz/Od.
Bertsch, Juliana 47, widow, sons Franz 25, Michael 22, to Strassburg/Od.
Fettig, Anton 29, Eva 28, Michael 6, Johannes 4, Thomas 4¼, Peter-Anton 1 yr., to Strassburg/Od.
Hochmuth, Peter 55, Elisabeth 48, Karl 25, his wife Margareta 30 nee Thomas, children: Johannes 3½,
   Barbara.2½, Michael 6 days, to Selz/Od.
Holzer, Joseph 43, Katharina 41, Katharina 14, Georg 11, Joseph 9, Johannes 6, to Strassburg/Od.
Keller, Jakob 34, Margaretha 27, Katharina 4¼, Joseph 2½, Bernard 5 months, to Selz/Od.
Keller, Joseph 36, Elisabeth 37, Johannes 16, Eva 10, Susanna 2, to Mariental/Od.
Mangold, Lorenz 70, widower, Simon 24, Franz 38, wife Walburga 27, Nikolaus 2½, Barbara ½, to Str.
Mangold, Joseph 35, s. of Lorenz, Juliana 34 nee Kohler, Kaspar 13, Johannes 8, to Selz/Od.
Mastel, Georg 64, widower, Peter 23, margaretha 23, to Selz/Od.
Mastel, Michael 35, s. of Georg, Elisabeth 30, Johannes 5½, Marianna 4, Joseph 2, to Strassburg/Od.
Maurath, Katharina, widow of Michael, +1812, Andreas 21, Maria 15, to Josephstal/Od.
Maurath, Johann 24, s. of Michael, Bernhardina 25, Philipp 2, Johannes 1, to Josephstal/Od.

Mayer, Burghard 36, Anna 35 widow of Jakob Huber, Margareta 10, Barbara 4, Maria 1½, step-
   children: Regina Huber 11, Johannes Huber +1815 at 7, Ludwig Huber 6, to Selz/Od.
Sailer, Mathias +1811 at 53, Johann 7, Philippina 19, to Selz/Od.
Schlosser, Thomas 54, Maria 47, Lorenz 22, Benedikt 18, Michael 15, Ludwig 9, Jos 7, to Strbrg.
Schweitzer, Anton 40, Christina 35,Markus 14, Mariana 12, Peter 11, Mich. 10, Anton 8, Strassburg.
Seiler, Lorenz 37, Magdalena 33, Katharina 4½, Maria-Eva 3¼, Stephan 1 yr., to Strassburg/Od.
Solway, Michael 44, Elisabeth 29, Nikolaus 6, Katharina 4, Eva 2, to Selz/Od.
Streifel, Michael 44, Franziska 22, Adelheid 13, Kath 10, Mariana 8, Mich 4, Elis ¼,-- Strassburg,.
Weissenburger, Berhard 35, Maria 40, Peter 11, Eurosinia 8, Marg 5½, Bernhard 3½, Kath 2 m.- Selz.

MÜNCHHAUSEN

Brauer, Joseph, to Kleinliebental/Od. Descendant Jos. Baruer was mayor of Franzfeld in 1909.
Gabel, Friedrich +1814 at 56, daughter Margaretha married in Kleinliebental/Od.
Neigel, Maria 47, widow, Franz 15, Juliana 14, Georg 24, wife Eva 19, dau. Elisabeth 1,-Josephstal.
Zimpelmann, Karl 48, Lutheran, Maria 27, Eva 14, Christoph 13, Margaretha 9, Karolina 8, Jakob 7,
   Philipp 4, Georg 2, Barbara ¼, to Rohrbach/Od.

NIEDERRÖDERN

Engelhardt, Leonhard 48, Barbara 46, Jakob 19, Georg 10, Elis 16, Kath 14 Magd 5½, to Kandel/Od.
Engelhardt, Jakob 23, s. of Leonhard, margaretha 22 nee Bitz, Magd 4, Sebastian +1813, Veronica
   1½, Elisabeth 1 month, to Kandel/Od.
Legler, Friedrich 51, Barbara 34, Barbara 13, Marg 9, Friedr. 6, Jak-Daniel 4½, Jakob ¼, Neudorf/Od.
Schmidtheisler, Adam 51, Salome 53, Magd 24, Maria 20, Richarda 11, Michael 10, Jakob 1l, to Elsass.

NIEDERSEEBACH

Hofer, Peter 38, Marg 35, Michael 16, Marg 14, Salome 11, Martin 8, Ewald 4, Magd 3½, to Neudorf.
Usselmann, Christian 23, Katharina 29 widow of Peter Hulm, Christian 1½ yrs., to Selz/Od.
Usselmann, Elisabeth 40, widow, sons: Jakob Usselmann 19, Martin U. 12, to Selz/Od.

OBERLAUTERBACH

Arth, Johannes 27, arrived in Russia June 20, 1808. First wife Eva-Rosina +1812 at 30, 2nd wife Maria 21 nee Schweitzer, Katherina +1810 at 1 yr., Genoveva +1814 at 1 yr., to Selz/Odessa.
Bohl (Boell?), Johann +1811 at 64, wife +1811, Johann 25, wife Elisabeth 26, Kath 1 yr. to Selz.
Dillmann, Matheus +1812 at 65, Marg 56, Augustin 25, wife Eva 30 nee Vogel, Maria 17, Josephstal.
Eisenmenger, Philipp 50, Kath 46, Martin 14, Michael 9, Peter 4½, Regina 15, Barb 11, to Kandel/Od.
Feist, Nikolaus 37, Margaretha 32, Alois 9, Anton 5, Margaretha ¼, to Strassburg/Od.
Feist, Johannes 27, Philippina 23, dau. of Mathias Seiler, Damian 1½, to Strassburg/Od.
Huber, Anton 39, Barbara 39, Regina 15, to Selz/Od.
Krämer, Anton 53, Magdalena 54, Magdalena 20, Marareta 10, to Kleinliebental/Od.
Lindemann, Michael 34, Katharina 33, Peter 4½, Annemaria 3¼, Magdalena 1 month, to Selz/Od.
Maier, Franz +1812 at 50, Magdalena 56, Georg 24 (married), Elisabeth 10, to Kleinliebental/Od.
Maier, Franz 30, s. of Franz, Katharina 30 nee Warter, Michael 6, Kath 3, Magd ¼, to Kl.Liebental
Maier, Georg 28, s. of Franz, Viktoria 37 nee Schan, Maria 2, to Kleinliebental/Od.
Mastio, Nikolaus 34, Maria 32, Maria 9, Philipp 6, to Franzfeld/Od.
Moser, Heinrich 34, Barbara 32, Martin 4, Johannes 1 yr., to Josephstal/Od.
Steiner, Jakob 43, Susanna 42, Magdlaena 20, Johannes 14, Elisabeth 13, to Kleinliebental/Od.
Weisbeck, Anton 23, Regina 23, widow of colonist Sebastian Hatzenbühler, to Selz/Od.
Werner, Bernhard 44, Regina 44, Franz 12, Bernhard 7, Johannes 2, Margaretha 14, to Selz/Od.
Werner, Theobald 49, Margaretha 38, Marianna 18, Michael 11, Johann 9, to Kleinliebental/Od.

SCHAFFHAUSEN

Kerner, Joseph 37, Barbara 41, Katharina 6, Margaretha 4½, stepson Johann 6, to Kandel/Od.

SELTZ

Amann, Simon 35, Barbara 35, Franz 11, Anton 7½, Barbara 2½, George ½, to Elsass/Od.
Becht, Philipp 40, tailor, Magdalena +1812 at 38, 2nd wife Margareta 23 nee Senger, Philipp 10, Sabina 3, Sebastian 9 months, to Selz/Od.
Bischof, Joseph 53, Elisabeth +1813 at 40, Joseph 22, Valentin 12, Christina 6, to Kandel/Od.
Bleyerle (Bleile?), Joseph 67, Elisabeth 67, Johann 25, wife Eva-Katharina 23, Joseph 3¼, Barbara , 1 month; adopted Peter Kuppy 6. To Kandel/Od.
Braun, Joseph +1812 at 91, Nikolaus 45, wife Maria 31; children by 1st wife: Johanna 10, children by 2nd wife: Franz 3, Maria 1, to Franzfeld/Od.
Braun, Joseph 48, Elisabeth 44, Franz 15, Elisabeth 13, Johann 6, Maria 3, Anton ¼, to Franzfeld.
Ebertz, Michael 35, Barbara 35, Franz 11, Anton 7½, Barbara 2½, Georg ½, to Elsass/Od.
Ekhelm, August 28, Juliana 28, ,other-in-law Marianna Friedmann 68. To Rastadt/Od.
Gauer (Hauer?), Dorothea, midwife, +1812 at 63, Bernhard 29, Elisabeth 31, to Baden/Od.
Gauer (Hauer/), Joseph 29, Elisabeth 31, Peter 7, Franz +1813, Joseph +1815, to Kandel/Od.
Gelzinger, Anton 29, Anastasia 29, Franz 5, foster son Joseph Lanz 15, to Rastadt/Od.
Gössel, Peter 43, Susanna 42, Joseph 22, Maria 16, Kaspar 12, to Strassburg/Od.
Harr, Adam, miller, +1812 at 40, Franziska +1815 at 35, Joseph 10, Mariana 16, Anna 13, to Baden.
Hermann, Christina 44, widow,Johann 24, Anton 18, Paul 11, Michael 7, to Grossliebental/Od.
Kirschner, Ignatz 37, Mariana 28, Magd +1814, Franziska 4½, Lenore 1½; bro. Martin K.,31. To Baden.
Kirschner, Michael 48, Elenore 42. To Kleinliebental/Od.
Leboldus (Leopoldus), Michael 44, Mariana 32, Joseph 8, Franz 6, Johann 4½, Michael 2¼. To Baden.
Märtz, Engelbert 44, stocking maker, Martina 59, Johann 13, Marg 6, Bernh. & Georg +1815. Elsass.
Mahler (Mohler/), Michael, justice of the peace, to Taurida (S. Russia).
Martin, Sebastian 51, Appolonia 41, Michael 6, Appolonia 21, Maria 11. Entire family fled 1812.
Mucker, Peter, 19 in 1812, married widow Sabina Pflieger, 32. They moved to Elsass/Od.
Nenninger, Adam 52, Barbara 39, Adrian 10, Veronica 12, Christina +1811 at I yr. Georg 3, To Baden.
Philipp, Georg 43, Gertrud 37, Georg 6, Mathias + ½yr. old, Elisabeth 10, Maria 1½. To Selz/Od.
Reinbold, Michael 20, Veronica 23 dau. of Joseph Schan. To Baden/Od.
Rengert, Peter 48, Veronika 29, Peter +1815 at 5, Adam 3, Joseph +1815, to Kandel/Od.
Rieger, Jakob 52, Christina 40, Barbara 11, to Kandel/Od.
Rieger, Andreas 44, weaver, Katharina +1813 at 40, Georg 16, Maria 14, Katharina 6. To Kandel/Od.
Rieger, Georg 39, Cecilia 39, Katarina 11, Christian 4½, Georg-Jakob 1½. To Kandel/Od.
Schatz, Ignatz 44, physician, Walburga 31, Karl 11, Batholome 10, Ignatz 7, Joseph 4¼, Franz-Joseph +1814, Walburga 3, Peter-Anton ½. Farmed with 4 horses and 4 oxen. To Mannheim/Od.
Schiffmacher, Anton 56, stocking maker, Mariana 56, Jos. 23, Teresa 21, Kath.16,Soph.9. Elsass.

Schwengler, Egidius 49, tiler, Kath. 48, Paul 20, Egidi 10, Simon =1814 at 6, Helen 14. Elsass.
Schwengler, Paul 24, s. of Egidius, Katharina 20, dau. of Georg Ziegler, Magd.+1815.˜ Strassburg.
Schwengler, Joseph 38, Maria 36, Joseph 9, to Josephstal/Od.
Wallior (Waljer), Jakob +1810, Walburga 38, Johannes 5, Walburga 10, to Baden/Od.
Walliser, Jakob, with wife an 2 children, settled in Landau/Od.
Zahn, Johann 45, Dorothea 33, Magd 19, Maria 16, Barb 13, Dorothea 10, Jakob 5, Joh 1. Kandel.

SIEGEN

Beil, Jakob died in 1814 at age of 24, in Sulz/Od.
Graf, Michael emigr. with wife and 3 children to Taurida in 1809. Itinerary: Franfurt a.M. 20.4,
    Leipzig 12.5, Babice (Pol) 31.5, Myslenice 2.6, Bochnia 3.6, Lemberg 12.6, Brody 16.6.1809.
Hartmann, Joseph 27, Kath. 29, Johann 6, Michael 4½, Magd. 2¼, to Kleinliebental/Od.
Hartmann, Jakob 26, Christina 24, Kath. 5, Theresa·½; bro. Johann Hartmann 17. To Kleinliebental
Moritz, Franz 40, Maria 25, Eva 2, to Rastadt/Od.
Thomas, Georg 43, s. of Peter, Marg 38, dau. of Jos. Blumenschein of Steinfeld/Pf. To Landau/Od.
Wagner, Mathias 21, mother Marianna 55, didter Marianna 23. To Speier/Od.

STUNDWEILER

Kaspar, Nikolaus 45, Maria 47, Katharina 21, Johann 13, to Landau/Od.
Kaspar, Michael 43, Elisabeth 37, Peter 16, Elis. 13, Mathias 8, Christian 6, Anton 1½. Landau.

TRIMBACH

Bockmeyer, Jakob Jr.,32, Agatha +1812 at 33, 2nd wife Maria 17, Marg +1812, .Magd ½. To Mannheim.
Bockmeyer, Jakob Sr. 41, Marianna 39, Anton 13, Maria 6, Magd.+1815, Mathias 3½. To Mannhe·m/Od.
Bockmeyer, Adam 24, Katharina 26, daughter Franziska ½ yr. To Landau/Od.
Gerhardt, Jakob, tailor, +1813 at 77, Eva 54, Paul 27, his wife Katharina 25, Katharina 2; Magd-
    alena ¼, stepson Anton Martin 5½. To Elsass/Od.
Mattern, Georg 27, Maria 27, Katharina 2. Also bro. Valentin Mattern 21. To Mariental/Od.
    Also colonists with unknown destination: Martin Adet, Jakob Birkel, Johann Heitz, Michael Kurtz.

WINZENBACH

Aschenbrenner, Joseph 45, Margaretha 41, Joseph 6, Georg 1, Johann ¼, to Josephstal/Od.
Bauer, Anton 33, Barbara 27, Balthasar ½, to Mariental/Od.
Becker, Georg +1815 at 68, son Georg 28, wife Veronika 26, Moritz 4, Franziska 2, to Selz/Od.
Billmann, Adam 37, Eva +1815, Gertrude 15, Joseph +1813 at 17. To Speier/Od.
Billmann, Johannes 35, Barbara 29. To Sulz/Od.
Deck, Johann 24, first wife Maria +1814, second wife Sibilla 24, Elisabeth 1 yr., to Josephstal/Od.
Ehrmantraut, Georg 23, teacher, Barbara 29, Margaret 5, Joseph 3, Adolf 1½. To Landau/Od.
Geringer, Simon 45, Margaretha 41, to Josephstal/Od.
Gutenberg, Johann 46, carpenter, Agnes 32, Magdalena 10, Michael 7, Elisabeth 2½, to Strassburg/Od.
Heinz, Georg48, Margaretha 54, Franz +1811 at 19, to Mariental/Od.
Held, Balthasar 36, Mariana 30, Franziska 11, Christina 7, Johannes 4½, Anton 2, to Selz/Od.
Keller, Egidius 48, miller, Katharina 43, Joseph 20, Johanna 11, Barbara 9, Valentin 18, his wife
    Maria 21 nee Germann, son Joseph 2. To Selz/Od.
Reinhard, Michael 43, Christina 45, Joseph 20, Georg 13, Elisabeth 9. To Stra-sburg/Od.
Schneider, Joseph 70, widower, Melchior 27, wife Elisabeth 23, son Wendlin 1¼. To Strassburg/Od.
Schmidtheisler, Magdalena 59, widow, Peter 21, Christian 19. To Josephstal/Od.
Schwengler, Wendel 43, Franziska 27 nee Fuhrmann, Franziska 10, Maria 9, Joseph 5½, Elisabeth 2¼,
    Katharina 1½; brother-in-law Joseph Fuhrmann 20. To Kandel/Od.
Stolz, Franz 26, Maria 28, Wendelin 5, Joseph 3, Margaretha 8, Maria-Eva 1½/ To Selz/Od.
Welk, Moritz 31, tailor, b. in Erlach (Baden), Magdalena 29, daughter of Georg Arth of Winzenbach,
    Kaspar 11, Johannes 4, Georg 1½. To Selz/Od.

2. CANTON LAUTERBURG

LAUTERBURG

Adam, Georg 49, Elisabeth 33, Kath. 8, Elis. 5, Rosine +1812, Magd. 1½, Kath. 2 mon. →Elsass/Od.
Germann, Wilhelm 53, Magdalena 44, Wilhelm 17, Sebastian 16, Johann 4½, Margareta 22, Katharina
   12, Marianna 9, Magdalena 3, Egidius 2. To Elsass/Od.
Grossmann, Johannes 53, plasterer, widower, Rosine 20, Ottilia 13, to Elsass/Od.
   The passport record of 1808 shows that Johann Grossmann travelled with his wife and 8 children,
   and two brothers and a sister via Vienna to Taurida (= South Russia). The visa stamp entries
   indicate that he travelled on the Danube from Ulm to Vienna, then via Bohemia and southern Po-
   land to Russia: Regensburg, Oct. 16, Linz, Oct. 21, Vienna, Oct. 25, Brünn (Bohemia), Oct. 30,
   Brody (Poland), Nov. 15 and Radizivilov (Russia), Nov. 19. In the census records of 1811, there
   is no mention of his wife, and only 2 of the 8 children are listed. The family name died out.
Keiber, Peter 42, Lutheran, Elisabeth 31, Peter 10, Margaretha 5. To Grossliebental/Od.
Miller, Franz 38, hatmaker, Rosine 36, Johann +1814 at 9, Franz 6, Rosine 2½, Magd. 1½. To Elsass.
Ripplinger, Peter 24, Rosine 20 nee Grossmann. Franz Ripplinger 22, wife Magdalena 18. To Elsass.
Ross (Rosso?), Johann 65, hatmaker, Sophia 52, Jakob 9, Barbara 19, Veronika 12. To Elsass/Od.
Wild, Johannes 42, cabinet maker, Salomea 44, Elisabeth 4. To Elsass/Od.
Wild, Joseph 44, Maria 33, Joseph 18, Maria 16, Walburga 14, Regina 7, Jakob ½ yr. To Mariental.
Zayky, Johann 61, Margaretha 49, Johann +1814 at 18, Maria 12, Agatha 11. To Elsass/Od.

NEEWEILER

Baumstark, Johann 36, Katharina 36, Kath 15, Magd 11, Mariana 6, Theresa 4. To Strassburg/Od.
Baumstark, Anton 31, Margaretha 31, Paul 5½, Anton 3½, Magdalena 1¼, to Selz/Od.
Brendel, Michael 27, Regina 24, Johann 4½, Anton 1 month, to Selz/Od.
Brendel, Johannes 28, Theresa 28, nee Kiefel, Anton 6, Michael 2½, to Selz/Od.
Brossart, Valentin 44, Maria 40, Franz 8, Marianna 12, Regina 10, Maria-Eva 1½, to Selz/Od.
Bullach,Andreas 30, Martha 26, Michael 4, to Kandel/Od.
Demelet, Johannes 31, Maria 25, Balthasar 10, Elisabeth =1814, Annemaria 3½, to Selz/Od.
Eckstand, Jakob +18]2 age 25, Annemaria 34, Joseph +1812 at 3 months, to Kandel/Od.
Eichenlaub, Balthasar 37, Anna 34, Helena 11, Margareta 4, Annamaria 2½, Johann 2 mths. To Selz.
Eichenlaub, Franz 49, Maria 49, Katharina 16, Georg 13, Franziska 10, to Landau/Od.
Eisenzimmer, Johann 27, Magd. 39, Valentin 16, Cecilia 14, Mariana 13, Baptist 11, Franz 4. Str.
Eisenzimmer, Georg 47, Maria 47, Lorenz 17, Jos. 13, Johann 9, Georg 7, Marg 15, Magd 11. To Selz.
Feller (Voeller), Martin 58, Kath. 55, Joseph 22, Anton 19, Mich. 11, Martin 9, Kath 14. To Selz.
Fetsch (Vetsch), Ludwig 29, Maria 29, Franz 7, Elisabeth 2, Jakobina 1 yr.To Josephstal/Od.
Fetsch, Margaret, widow, +1816, Peter 20, Georg 7, Franz 31, wife Veronika 21. To Kleinliebental.
Fetsch, Michael 30, Elisabeth 22, Joseph 6, Franz-Georg 2½, Michael 4½. To Selz/Od.
Fix, Franz 34, Katherina 34, Jakob 6, Georg ¼ yr., to Franzfeld/Od.
Fix, Johann 33, Katherina 30, Katherina 10, Joseph 8, Johann 6, Magdalena 1. To Kleinliebental.
Fix, Xaver 51, Klara 58, Bernhard 18, Margaretha 14, Magdalena 12, Jakob 8, to Kleinliebental/Od.
Fix Jakob 59, Eva 58, Georg 26, Michael 17, Kornelius 27, wife Theresa 23, Franz 1. To Franzfeld.
Helm, Maria 47, widow, Adam 17, Anton 15, Katharina 20, Maria 7, Elisabeth 6, to Selz/Od.
Heisler, Georg 53, Maria 37, Valentin 9, Johanna 7, Elisabeth 3, to Franzfeld/Od.
Heisler, Anton 28, Christina 26, Marianna 3½, Katharina 1½, to Baden/Od.
Heisler, Peter 25, Barbara 31, Barbara 4, Elisabeth 2, to Franzfeld/Od.
Heisler, Franz 35, Maria 34, Johann 9, Marianna 8, Nikolaus 7, Elisabeth 3, Georg 1. To Franzfeld.
Hermann, Sebastian 34, Magdalena 34, Marg. 8, Ursual 4½, Marianna 2½, Johann 2 mnths. To Kandel.
Hoffart, Joseph 41, Kath. +1815 at 27, Margareta 13, Johann 11, Anton 9, Stephan 3¼. To Selz/Od.
Jakob, Joseph 47, Barbara 48, Michael 19, Adam 17, Seb. 14, Georg 9, Maria 2½, Mariana ¼. To Selz.
Kaiser, Johann 45, 1st wife Maria +1811, 2nd wife Kath. 27, Joh...21, Joseph 3, Adam 1. Franzfeld.
Kiefel, Stephan 31, Maria 30, Philipp 5, Elisabeth 7, Johannes 3½, Annemaria 1 yr. To Selz/Od.
Ostermaier, Anton 38, Marg. 34, Sebastian 14, Maria 11, Kath 6, Johann 11, Anton 9. To Selz/Od.
Reiss, Michael +1814, Margareta 57, widow, Sebastian 21, Jakob 16, Katharina 12. To Selz/Od.
Thomas, Franz 42, Maria 52, Marg.20, Jos. 21, Martin 13, Wilhelm 23, wife Maria 17. To-Selz.
Wagner, Anton 56, Eva +1811 at 50, Barbara 18, Magd. 17, Joseph 26, wife Barbara 17. Kl.Liebental.
Wagner, Johann 45, Maria +1811, 2nd wife Magd 44, Kath. 18, Marg. 15, Jakob 14, Maria 11. Kl.Lieb.
Wagner, Johann 29, Anna 28, Eva 4, Georg 1 yr. To Franzfeld/Od.
Wingerter, Anton 57, widower,Franz 18, married in Speier, Georg. 20, wife Elisabet 19. To Landau.
Wingerter, Peter 32, Marianna 25 nee Brendel, Kasimir 7, Peter 1, Kath. 6, Christina 4. Elsass.
Zerr, Georg 58, Rosine +1812, with 4 following sons; also ancestor of Bishop Anton Zerr. Franzfeld
Zerr, Joseph 34, Franziska 38, Joseph 9, Johann 6, Katherina 4, Franz ¼, to Franzfeld/Od.
Zerr, Anton 28, Margaretha 26, Katherina 9, Peter 6, Maria 4, Michael 1, to Franzfeld/Od.
Zerr, Johann-Michael, 32, Franziska 28, Peter 7, Margarete 6, Katharina 1, to Franzfeld/Od.
Zerr, Johannes 24, Katherina 18, Anton 1, Margarete ¼ yr., to Franzfeld/Od.
Zerr, Andreas 27, Katharina 26, Elisabeth 3½, Margareta +1812 age 2, Michael 2, to Selz/Od.

NIEDERLAUTERBACH

Baumstark, Georg 38, Eva +1811 age 26, 2nd wife Marianna 22, nee Kerzinger, from Winzenbach, Franz +1812, Joseph +1815, to Selz/Od.
Bohl, Jakob 32, Susanna 38, nee Kunz, Adam 3, Elisabeth 1 yr., to Mariental/Od.
Feller (Voeller), Michael 29, Barbara 21, daughter of Silvester Wald, to Strassburg/Od.
Fetsch, Johannes 44, Appolonia 37, Johann 3½, Maria-Eva 1 yr., to Selz/Od.
Herrbein, Jakob 45, Magdalena 47, nee Nieder, Katharina 15, to Kleinliebental/Od.
Krämer, Jakob 28, Margaretha 27, Maria +1812, 1 yr. old, Rosine 4, Kath. +1815, to Kandel.
Leibel, Sebastian +1814 at 41, Eva +1813, Jakob 23, Sebastian 18, Eva 17, Anton 13, Anna 9, to Josephstal/Od,
Lochert, Paul 29, Magdalena 25, Barbara +1812, Joseph 2, to Selz/Od.
Rother, Joseph +1814 age 55, Elisabeth 37, Regina 7, Elis +1813, Magd.+1815, to Kandel.
Schäfer, Peter 48, Maria 47, Valentin 20, Peter 15, Eva 18, Elisabeth 16, to Josephstal/Od.
Strauss, Ludwig 44, Elisabeth 40, widow of + Johann Miller, Genoveva 3½; stepsons Jakob Usselmann 15, Martin Usselmann 8, stepsons: Thomas Miller 18, Michael M.,16, Markus M. 18, Salome M. 14, Appolonia M. 6, to Selz/Od.
Springer, Jakob 27, son of Christian, Barbara +1812 age 24, Joseph +1812 at 3 months, Jakob's brother Georg, 30, to Kandel/Od.
Wald, Silvester 48, village mayor, Margaretha 44, Adam 19, Rosine 17, Lukas 11, Balthasar 9, Katherina 4, Hanna 1½, to Strassburg/Od.
Weigel (Weichel), Philipp 49, Magdalena 49, Ludwig 18, Anton 6, Sabina 16, Margaretha 13, Maria 10, to Selz/Od.
Weigel, Michael 35, Barbara 31, nee Schmidt, Peter 8, Margaret 6, Michael 4, to Selz/Od.
Veigel, Michael 36, Katharina +1811, sec. wife Maria 52, Peter 8, to Josephstal/Od.

SALMBACH

Acker, Nikolaus 31, rope-maker, Elisabeth 36, Barbara 10, Mariana 8, to Kandel.
Andres, Hubert 33, Franziska 26 nee Meier, Philip 5, Peter 2¼, Elisabeth 8, to Speier.
Bär, Johannes 25, Eva 45, Margarete 13, Jakob 11, Barbara 7, to Speier.
Bartelmann, Franz 38, Barbara 34, to Mariental.
Bosch, Johannes 32 in 1812. Left country with wife and 2 children from Karlsruhe.
Ehretsmann 30, Barbara 32 nee Reichert, Margaret 4½, Ignatius 4½, Maria-Eva 1 wk. To Kandel.
Ehrenwein +1814 age 54, Anna +1815 age 42, Margaretha 26. To Kandel.
Ereth, Georg 45, Elisabeth 42, Katherina 15, Franziska 13, Anton 11. To Speier.
Fritz, Maria, 43, widow of +Ignatz, 33, Joseph 13, Maria 10, Michael 9, to Landau.
Fritz, Georg, wife Marianna and 4 children settled in Elsass.
Funk, Justina, 39, widow of + Xaver, Jakob 19, Peter 13, Xaver 8, Maria 15. To Selz.
Gerber, Christian 45, Maria 63, Regina 15, Marianna 12, Georg 3. To Speier.
Gerber, Johannes 32, son of Adam, Maria 28, Kath. 7, Wendel 8, Maria 4½, Rosine 2, To Speier.
Glass, Michael 36, teacher, Barbara 37, Georg 14, Josef 9, Max 6½, Mariana 10, to Elsass.
Hulm, Georg 41, Maria +1813, Kath. 17, Philip 15, Martin 9, Maria 13, Eva 11, to Franzfeld.
Hulm, Maria, 51, widow, Anton 19, Maria 11, Elis. 10, Adam, 21,wife Euphrosine, 21. To Selz.
Hulm, Adam 21, son of Maria, wife Euphrosine nee Baumann 21, son Simon 1 yr. To Kandel.
Hulm, Peter +1812 at 23, wife Katherina 29, son Simon 1. To Selz.
Joos, Georg 45, Susanna 33 nee Schweissgut, Jakob 10, Christian 8, Mariana 5. To. Kleinliebental.
Lacher, Heinrich 49, Franziska 52, Philipp 16, Elisabeth 23, Gertrude 14, Katharina 7. To Kandel.
Miller, Margaret 54 2idow, Friedrich 22, wife Katharina 18 nee Rink. To Selz.
Moser, Lorenz +1816 age 40, cabinet maker, Kath 28, Jos 9, Lorenz 7, Franz 4½, Sebast 2, To Selz.
Nold, Philipp 35, Maria 31, Maria 12, Franz 10, Jos 8, Geo 4, Nickolaus 6, Kath 1. To Franzfeld.
Pfalzgraph, Philip 43 (Luth.), Marianna 42, Philip 11, Georg 4½, Kath. 21, Elis. 19. Mannheim.
Rappold, Christoph 51, Elisabeth 47, Regina 13, Magdalena 10, Georg 23, wifeMariana 24. To Selz.
Reichert, Jos. 37, Margareta 27, Michael 8, Elisabeth 4½, Josef +1815, Franz ¼ yr. To Kandel.
Röbrich, Kaspar 4o, Elisabeth 46, son Wendel 9. To Josephstal.
Röhrich (Rerich), Anton 38, Helena 34, Georg 12, Eva 10, Franz 5½, Johann 3, Nick ¼. To Strassburg.
Richter, Johann 30, Marianna 34, Eliz. 11, Johann 9, Mariana 7, Kath 4¼, Eva-Rosina 2. Strassburg.
Scheibel, Michael 47,son of Georg-Jakob, Maria 37, Maria 5, Anton 1 yr. To Landau.
Scherer, Jakob 64, Magdalena 56, Mathias 19, Joseph 14. To Strassburg.
Schlick, Jakob 50, Eliz. +1815 at 42, Franz 14, Johann 13, Appolonia 4½. To Kandel & Mariental.
Schmalz, Christian 45, Maria 63, Regina 15, Marianna 12, Jakob 7, Georg 3. To To Speier.
Stein Peter 33, Cecilia 33, Johann 10, Cecilia 8, Marg 6, Eliz. 3 Marianna 1, Peter 1. Kl.liebental.
Vogel, Johann 30, Marianna 28 nee Acker, Johann 3½, Sebastian 8 days, to Kandel.
Wagner, Leonhard 43, Magdalena 39, Georg 7, Maria 12, Theresa 9, Eva 4. To Elsass.

112

3. CANTON WEISSENBURG

ALTENSTADT/Als & Pf)

Kunz, Franz 29, Magdalena 41, son Franz 7; Martin Kunz, brother of Franz, to Landau/Od.
Nollet (Nuollet), Michael 24, Margareta, 30, Katharina 8, Michael 4 Johann 2, to Landau/Od.
Schaf, Peter +1814 at age 45, his sons: Jakob 2 in 1812 and Joseph 1 in 1812 moved to Sulz/Od.
Weber, Leonard 42, son of Joseph, Margaret 35, son Georg 15, to Landau/Od.
Weisgerber, Jakob 37, Magdalena 27, Lorenz 12, Kath. 10, Elis. 8, Jakob 6, Joh. 3, Phil. 1. To Landau.

CLEEBURG

Hagelsberger, Jakob, locksmith, with wife Margaretha and 2 children to Odessa.
Haller, Georg 61, Margareta, 62, Georg 18, Magdalena 16, Elis.13, Eva 10, Marg 18. To Bergdorf/Od.
Haussauer, Johann-Jakob 52, Margaretha 34, to Kassel/Od.
Haussauer, Balthasar 33, Katharina 31, Balthasar 10, Jakob 9, Georg 2½, to Glückstal/Od.
Michael, Jakob 39 in 1812, Elisabeth 26, Jakob 7, Magdalena, Elisabeth, Margaretha, to Glückstal
Michael, Jakob, with wife and 4 children, to Sulz/Od.
Siffermann, Lorenz 45, Lutheran, Dorothea 45, Johannes 18, Lorenz 3½, to Bergdorf/Od.

KLIMBACH

Berger, Johann-Peter, +1813 age 43, Magd., 37 nee Urlacher, Mich 11, Seb 7, Peter 3. To Landau.
Dosch, Jakob 42, Greta 43, Philipp 13, Johannes 9, Peter 3, to Kandel/Od.
Maas, Michael 30, Lutheran, Katharina 27, Michael 5, Ludwig 2, to Johannestal/Od.
Neuhart, Valentin 30, Dorothea 33, Eva-Margaret 7, Barbara 5, Daniel 3½, Ludwig 1½, to Kassel/Od.
Scheibel, Michael 47, Maria 37, Anton 1 yr., to Landau/Od.
Schmidt, Johann 54, Katharina 45, Magdalena 21, Georg 17, Katharina 14, Franz 12, to Landau/Od.
Schmidt, Michael 31, Elisabeth 31, nee Bullach, to Landau/Od.
Stein, Jakob 54, Elisabeth 50, Georg 23, Katharina 15, Peter 21, his wife Barbara 23, to Landau.
Urlacher, Joseph 21, wife's name unknown, sons:Ignatz b. 1819, Martin b. 1823, to Landau/Od.

LEMBACH

Breitenreicher, Christian 57, son of Karl, Maria-Eva 53, dau. of Martin Warter. To Sulz/Od.
Gratz, Anton 43, son of Martin, Salomea 32, Martin 10, Magd. 8, Jakob 6, Phil. 5, Peter 2. Landau.
Hirschspiegel, Adam 32, Magdalena 40, Margareta ½; son Johann, born in 1831, to Landau/Od.
Koch, Johann +1811 at 35, Magdalena 33m Johannes 11, Georg 7, Katharina 5, to Landau/Od.
Kühlwein, Ludwig 35, his wife Christina 23, to Landau/Od.
Siegwart, Michael son of Johann, +1812 at 45, Margaretha 43, Michael 14, Magdalena 13, to Sulz.
Schirek, Karl 29, son of Thomas, Maria 29, nee Strohmeier, to Landau/Od.

OBERSEEBACH

Derschan (Dessam) , Nikolaus 39, Maria 31, Ursula , Juliana, Maria, Johann. To Josephstal/Od.
Frey, Philipp 27, Katharina 30, Magdalena 3½, to Selz/Od.
Frison, Valentin 41, miller, +1814 age 43, Maria 45, Johann 18, Ludwig 15, Stephan 12. To Selz/Od
    was the ancestor of Alexander Frison, bishop of the Crimea 1929-1937 .Killed by Communists.
Knittel, Lorenz 43, Magdalena 42, Joseph 5, Jakob +1815. Magdalena 3, to Mannheim/Od.
Knittel, Jakob 29, son of Adam, Regina 30, dau. of Georg Lauber (Luber?) from Altenstadt/Alsace,Mar-
    garetha, 2, Martin, born 1822, to Sulz/Od.
Marbach. Philipp 37, shoemaker, Antonia 37, Magdalena +1812, to Selz/Od.
Marbach , Barbara 41, widow (2nd husband Joseph Kerner), Franziska Marbach 15, Johann 10.To Kandel.
Senn, Michael 50, Kathatina 45, Elisabeth 7, Margarete 4, Maria 14, Martin 10, Mich 14. To Speier.
Senn, Martin, son of Michael, married Eva-Margarete, daughter of Johann Fäth.

OBERSTEINBACH

Fischer, Georg 43, Margaretha 43 nee Siegwart, Peter 3, to Sulz/Od.
Keller, Georg 35, Maria 30, Georg 6, Ludwig 2, to Speier/Od.

RIEDSELZ

Fichter, Maria 41, widow, Valentin 11, Joseph 4, Maria 19, Eva 15, Elisabeth 7, to Landau/Od.
Fischer, Michael 59, Marianna 44, Michael 18, Marianna 15, Joseph 12, Elis .10, Anton 8, Strbg.

Fischer, Andreas 49, Anna 52, Magdalena 20, married, and Georg 16, to Kleinliebental/Od.
Fischer, Johann 40, Elisabeth 29 nee Heilig, Anton 17, Georg 3, Franz 1. To Josephstal/Od.
Hegel (Häckel),Joseph 49, Maria 43, Margaretha 21, Jakob 19, Franz 11, to Landau.
Huffner, Jakob and his wife Maria and 2 children settled 1809 in Landau/Od.
Hummel, Franz 45, Maria 32, Magdalena 15, Franziska 13, to Karlsruhe/Od.
Hummel, Jakob 18, sister Katharina 16, and brother Michael 8, to Landau/Od.
Jülch, Daniel , b. 1810, his wife Maria b. 1811; 3 male descendants, to Neudorf/Od.
Lauinger, Ignatz +1815, age 56, Barbara 42, Anton 16, Egidius 12, Mathias 2½, to Strassburg/Od.
Senger, Paul 45, Elisabeth 33, Marianna 9, Paul 5½, to Strassburg/Od.
Senger, Georg 46, Marianna 44, Johannes 16, Joseph 13, Ludwig 6, Elisabeth 3½, to Strassburg/Od.
Senger, Damian 26, Barbara 22, daughter of Joseph Schneider, to Strassburg/Od.
Senger, Johann 62, arr. in Russia 1803, Rosina 43, Kunigunde 6, Katharina 3, to Kleinliebental·
Senger, Jakob 18, Johann S. 16, Maria S. 17, to Josephstal/Od.
Stephan, Jakob 52, Rosina 51, Philipp 19, Marie 16, Dorothea married 1813, to Alexanderhilf/Od.
Stumpf, Jakob 27, Elisabeth 30, son Franz, 1 month old, to Speier/Od.
Streicher, Anton went with wife and 3 children to South Russia . Lived in Grossliebental/Od.
Streicher, Peter, 63, Katharina 50, Johann 23, Maria 16, Magd. 13, Kath. 21. To Kleinliebental.

SCHLEITHAL

Armbrust, Anton 28, moved from Liebental area in 1813, his wife Maria 23, to Sulz/Od.
Burk (Birk), 24, Barbara 20, Stephan 1, to Kleinliebental/Od.
Bösherz, Daniel 29, Eva 28, Konrad 3, Kaspar 1, to Landau/Od.
Bösherz, Kaspar 39, Katharina 37, Katharina 18, Michael 9, Maria 3, Barbara 1, to Landau/Od.
Daniel, Katharina 50, widow, Martin 18, Katharina 9, Ursula 8. To Kleinliebental/Od
Eckert, Joseph 46, Katharina +1812; sec. wife Maria 32, son by 1st wife: Joseph 19,Josephstal.
Eckert, Michael 32, Crescentia 27, Johannes 9, to Josephstal/Od.
Fäth, Wendel 49, Barbara 39, Martin 17, Ludwig 8, Christina 3, to Rastadt/Od.
Fäth, Wendel 40, widower, Benedikt 7, Georg +1812 age i, to Zürichtal/Crimea.
Heinrich, Adam 27, Katharina 27, Katharina 6, Michael 2½, Franziska 14, to Speier/Od.
Holtzmann, Joseph 28, widower, Elisabeth 15, to Kleinliebental/Od.
Klaus, Martin 52, Maria 48, Kaspar 21, Kath 16, Marg 9, Joh.4. To Kandel. Ran away.
Melle, Adam 48, Maria 43, Johannes 11, Regina 19, Maria 9, Martin +1813, tu Kandel/Od.
Mock (Moog), Michael 34, Maria nee Röhl, +1815 at 40, 2nd wife Kath 36, Marg 9, Joh 4. To Kandel.
Mock, Stefan 57 in 1811, Rosine (no age given) Kaspar 23 in 1811, Elis and Regina.
Peter (Pierre), Bernhard 33, s. of Mathias, Barbara 27 nee Thomas; Barbara 11, Kaspar 3. Landau.
Richter, Anton 26, Theresa 33, widow of +Dietrich, Anton +1813, Joseph 1½, Philippina 4, To Kande
Spielmann, Mathias 30 in 1811, Christina 28, Jakob 6, Barbara 2. To Grossliebental/Od. Departed.
Schweitzer, Adam 33, Elisabeth 24, Georg 4, Barbara 1, to Josephstal/Od.
Schweitzer, Joseph 38, Maria 36, Joseph 9, to Josephstal/Od.
Schwengler, Joseph 38, Maria 36, Joseph 9, to Josephstal/Od.
Thomas, Kaspar 31, Katharina 28, Joseph 5½, Juliana 3¼, Johann-Adam 1¼. To Kandel/Od.
Thomas, Maria 52, widow, Joseph 21, Georg +1813 at 14, Martin 13, Margareta 26 married Karl
   Hochmuth; Wilhelm Thomas 25, wife Maria 17 nee Herle. To Selz/Od.
Weiss, Michael 42, wine grower, Anna 43, Anna 16, Maria 14, Magd 8, Mich 3. Kromental/Crimea.
Weisgerber, Martin 25, Katharina 20, Katharina 1, Maria ¼ yr., to Josephstal.
Weisgerber, Heinrich 40, Magd 39, Kath 12, Barbara 11, Joh. 10, Philip 3, Georg 1. Josephstal.
Wilhelm, Michael 56, Barbara 46, Joseph 21, Philipp 25, his wife Katharina 20. To Josephstal/Od.
   Other settlers; with destination uncertain. Franz Ekling; Johann Hemmerle, Martin and Jakob
   Kauf; Johann Korst, Michael Ranion, Theobald Rühl, Valentin Schmidt to Sulz?/Od. Franz
   Walliser and family to Landau?/Od.

STEINSELZ

Bauer, Konrad 35, Katharina 28, Barbara 9, Anton 7, Marg. 2, Stephan ¼. To Sulz/Od.
Bäuerle, Konrad 40, Lutheran, Magdalena 42, Jakob, 12, Magd 9, Philipp 7, Susanna 5. To Rohrbach.
Maire (Maier), 26, shoemaker, Margareta 27, Sebastian 2½, Joseph 1, Annemaria +1812.To Kandel/Od.

WEISSENBURG

Anton, Joseph 29, Elisabeth 22, Joseph 1 yr., to Rastadt/Od.
Bauer, Kaspar 35, Katharina 28, Barbara 9, Anton 7, Margaretha 2, Stephan ¼ yr., to Sulz/Od.
Erk, Adam 30, schoolmaster, Marianna 26, Maria 7, Valentin 4, to Kleinliebental/Od.
Erk, Franz 50, Barbara 51, Joseph 16 yrs., to Strassburg/Od.
Odenbach, Adam 26, married in Landau/Od. 1816.
Zahnbrecher, Peter 55, Elisabeth 41, Peter 7, to Rastadt/Od.

114

WINGEN

Burgard, Franz 24, Katharina 20, nee Schwan, Katharina 1 yr. To Strassburg/Od.
Burgard, Nikolaus 31, JOhanna 29, Franziska 4, Elisabeth 1½. To Strassburg/Od.
Burghard, Joseph 26, son of Theobald, Elisabeth 23, Johann 3½, Salomea 1¼. To Landau/Od.
Fleck, Johann +1801 at 34, Margaretha 40, widow, dau. of Adam Schlick, Christian. 20, Margareta
    18, Georg 15. Mathias 13 (chief mayor of Beresan volost 1841-1864). To Landau/Od.
Fath, Wendel 49, Barbara 39, Martin 17, Ludwig 8, Christiana 3. To Rastadt/Od.
Gustin, Johann 41, Magdalena 35, Katharina 20, Franz 13, Michael 10, Johann 5. To Rastadt/Od.
Guthmiller, Ludwig 26, Lutheran, Elisabeth 26, Ludiwg 3½. To Neudorf/Od.
Helbling, Johann 55, widower, Christian 23, Barbara 22, Franziska 21, Joseph 19, Elisabeth 15,
    Ludwig 12, to Speier/Od.
Helbling, Michael 29, son of Johann, Eva 29, Johannes ½ yr. To Speier/Od.
Kost, Kaspar , born c. 1800, and his sons Kaspar, b. 1825, and Georg, b. 1830.   To Landau/Od.
Maffenbeier, Magdalena 55, widow, Philipp 22, Johann 24, wife Katharina 20, to Kleinliebental/Od.
Maffenbeier, Hermann 32, Johanna 28, Magdalena 7, Anna 5, Valentin 3, to Kleinliebental/Od.
Marsal, Christian 49, Maria 41, Johann 16, Marg. 10, Christian 23, wife Marg. 21. To Landau/Od.
Miller, Lorenz 60, Marianna 50, Michael 24, wife Marg. 23 nee Baumann, Jos.+1813, to Kandel/Od.
Morschhäuser, Peter with wife and 2 children to Landau/Od. in 1809.
Rohrbach, Nikolaus 23, Lutheran, Eva-Barbara 32, Johann-Nikolaus ½ yr. To Neudorf/Od.
Samtmann, Christian 31, Katharina 28, Franziska 3, Christiana ½ yr. To Speier/Od.
Schmalz, Georg 27, from Liebental area, his wife Mariana 23. To Landau/Od.
Schreiber, Michael , 35, and son Jakob, 10.   To Landau/Od.
Schwarz, Karl,33, and son Anton 11 yrs. To Landau.
Walter, Johann 32, Helena 31, Georg 0, Maria-Eva 4½, Johannes 2½. To Kandel/Od.
Walter, Christian, with wife and 8 children, and his mother and sister, to Landau/Od.
Westermeyer, Martin 50, his wife Magdalena 45. To Landau/Od.
    Other emigrants from Wingen were single men: Bernhard Schaf, 23, to Sulz/Od. and Joseph Zent,
    23, to Speier/Od.

4. CANTON BISCHWEILER

AULNHEIM

Hettler, Sebastian 46, (3rd wife) Kathatina 23, Matheus 13, Martin 3. To Josephstal/Od.
Franz Lehnert, 18, to Rastadt. Georg Epinal, 13, to Rastadt/Od.

FORT LOUIS (also known as Fort Vauban and Fort Libre).

Adler, Sebastian 51, Ursula 44, Elisabeth 14, Andreas 8, Johann 6, Lorenz 4, Georg 2,→Kl.Liebental.
Becker, Jakob 54, saddler, Eva 46, Joseph 28, Magd.21, Maria 19, Elis 17, Franz 9, Jak 7. → Kandel.
Gisi, Anton 48, Katharina 27, Anton 20, Katharina 16, to Mariental/Od.
Gisi, Leonard 43, Marianna 56 nee Schuler, to Mariental/Od.
Hegele, Jakob 35, carpenter, Magdalena 28, Magdalena 6, Johann-Jakob 4, Franziska 2½, to Elsass.
Hegele, Christian 40, Maria 36, Christian 17, Vaxeri 16, Bernhard 14, to Elsass/Od.
Zentner, Christian 69, Marianna 44, Maria 4½, Bernhard 29, returned to Germany in 1812, to Selz.
Zentner, Mathias +1814 age 27, Evª 32, Margaretha 6, Martin 4¼, Katharina 2½, to Strassburg/Od.

LEUTENHEIM

Heinrich, Jakob 66, widower, Alexander 24, wife Veronika 26, Martin +18.5 at 3, Marg 2½, Barb 1¼.Mh.
Kaiser, Michael 64, Maria 58, Joseph 13, Anton 12, Heinrich 11, Peter 8, Elisabeth, Christina.
Klötzel, Leonard 38, tailor, Christina 30, Bernh.7, Heinr 4½, Johann 2½, Elis. 1½. To Mannheim/Od.
Schnell, Joseph 40, Magdalena 40, Margaret 11, Joseph 5, Georg 2, Maria 1, to Landau/Od.
Weber, Michael 69, Dorothea +1814 age 52, Michael 15, Helena 9, to Baden/Od.
Weber, Bernhard 40, Magdalena 30, Magdalena 5, Barbara 2½, Alexander 9 months, to Mannheim/Od.

NEUHÄUSEL

Erhard, Anton 33, son of Karl, Elisabeth 30, dau. of Peter Frenzel. To Landau/Od.
Erhard, Anton 33, Margaretha 23, Peter 3 yrs. To Rastadt/Od.
Hettler, Sebastian 51, third wife Katharina 23, Matheus 13, Martin 3, Marianna 1. To Josephstal.
Naas, Georg 44, Lutheran, Maria 42, Friedrich 15. To Bergdorf/Od.

RÖSCHWOOG

Kocher, Georg +1811 at 56, Katharina 46, Elisabeth 16, Magdalena 14, Anton 7, To Kl.Liebental.
Schmidt, Paul +1813 at 52, Katharina 41, Franz 21, Peter 18, Jakob 13, Mathias 9, Martin 5,
    Franz 3. To Karlsruhe/Od.
Sprauer, Michael 60, Maria 45, Valentin +1813 at 28 yrs. To München/Od.

ROHRWEILER

Borschneck, Michael 59, tailor, Magd. 49, Wendelin 19, Franz 16, Regina 24. To Kandel/Od.
Borschneck, Christian 35, s. of Michael, Marianna 22, Joseph 1 yr., to Josephstal/Od.
Kupfer, Jakob 53, 2nd wife Eva 29, Kath. 14, Jakob 11, Lorenz 8, Michael 3½, Joh 1½. Kandel.
Schmidt, Michael 51, Elis. 41, Martin 12, Nikolaus 9, Elis. 7, Kath. 3¾, Philip +1815. Kandel.

ROPPENHEIM

Bitz, Johannes 47, Katharina 51, Lukas 17, Adam 14, Bernhard 10, Magd 18, Marg 12. To Kandel/Od.
Schwarz, Heinrich 61, Magd. 41, Philipp 19, Christian 17, Martin 12, Ursula 4, Valentin 1. Selz.
Stoller, Gotthard, 27 in 1812, Josepha 25, daughters Karolina & Mariana. Fled 1811 from Speier.

RUNZENHEIM

Maier, Georg 45, 1st wife Kath. +1812, 2nd Barbara 26 nee Ring, Bernhard 11, Magdalena 9, Georg
    2, Barbara 6. To Elsass/Od.
Marquart, Joseph 50, Marianna 48, Joseph 19, Peter 18, wife Elisabeth 18 nee Fieger, Marianna 15,
    Michael 12, Margaretha 11, Ludwig +1815. To Kandel/Od.

SCHIRRHEIN

Halter, Anton 27, Eva 34 nee Heck +1815, Anton 5, Joseph 3, Maria-Eva 2½, to Baden/Od.
Rieder, Joseph 43, Juliane 36, Regina 7, Eva 5, Joseph +1813, Lorenz 1½. To Kandel/Od.
Scherer, Jakob 64, Magdalena 56, Johann 24, wife Katharina 22, Mathias 19, Jos. 14. To Elsass/Od.
Scherer, Valentin 30, Magdalena 30, Joseph 3½, to Baden/Od.
Scherer, Michael 54, baker, Elisabeth 34, son Joseph 18. To Kandel/Od.

SCHIRRHOFEN

Bechel, Ludwig 47, Barbara 42, Nikolaus 19, Rosine 17, Magdalena 15, Michael 11, Nikolaus 9,
    Katharina 9, Elisabeth 7, Joseph 3½, Genoveva 1 month. To Selz/Od.
Isemann, Joseph 38, Marianna 38, Katharina 12, Mariana 7, Magd 3¾, Johann +1812. To Kandel/Od.

5. CANTON SULZ

BIRLENBACH

Leitner, Georg 45, Katharina 50, Michael 19, Eva 16, Barbara 10, to München/Od.
Opp, Urban 39, Maria-Anna +1814, Daniel 9, Heinrich 6, Karl-Franz 3½, Johann 1.→Glückstal.
Schaffner, Peter +1812 at age of 31, his children: Ignatz 9, Margaretha 7, to Zürichtal/Crimea
Mayer, Simon 21, his wife Angelika 27 nee Tost, to Rastadt/Od.

HOHWEILER

 Acker, Philipp + before 1811, Elisabeth, widow, +1811, Joseph +1812 at 12, Lorenz 21, Andreas 28,
    his wife Juliana 21. To Mariental/Od.
 Schütt, Anton 44, Dorothea 33, Dorothea 8, Joseph 3, Barbara +1816. To Mariental/Od.

HÖLSCHLOCH

Bauer, Kaspar 32, Regina 28, Barbara 9, Anton 7, Margaretha 2, Stephan ½, to Sulz/Od.
Bauer, Anton 33, Barbara 27, Balthasar ½, to Mariental/Od.
Illner, Anton 44, Katharina 36, Karolina 3, Barbara 1 yr., to Rastatt/Od.
Wandler, Franz 38, Friedericka 36, Joseph +1811, ½ yr. old., to Kleinliebental/Od.

INGOLSHEIM
Hofer, Theobald 22, Katharina 18, to Neudorf/Od.
Haster, Theobald with wife and 3 children, to Taurida (S. Russia).
Marzolff, Georg, Lutheran, +1815 age 38, Maria 38, Bernhard +1812 age 13, Georg +1814 age 13, Jakob 13, Johann 9,
    Margaretha 4, Elisabeth 1½, to Neudorf/Od.
Preitz, Peter, single, day-laborer, to Taurida (S. Russia).
Solline, Catherina, widow with 3 children, to Taurida.
Weste, Jakob, with three children to Taurida

OBERRÖDERN

Schaller, Georg 44, Magdalena 42, Georg 11, Johann-Adam 1, Margaretha 17 married Jakob Bockmeyer, to Mannheim/Od.
    Itinerary to Russia: Rastatt 24.9.1808, Vaihingen 1.10.1808, Ulm 7.10.1808, Regensburg 12.10, Linz 17.10.1808,
    Vienna 20.10,1808, Lemberg 5.11.1808, Brody 9.11.1808, Radzivilov 12.11.1808. Total of 50 days to Russian border.
    Also: Johannes Sudel (5 in family) and son Georg Sudel, to Taurida (=So. Russia)

REIMERSWEILER

Bastian, Philipp 46, his 2nd wife Katharina 31, Philipp 13, Magdalena +1813. To Neuburg/Od.
Gress, Anton 32, s. of Mathias, Elis. 31 nee Schmidt, Marianna 5, Peter 3, Mich. 1½. To Landau.
Gress, Johann 23, son of Franz, Margaretha 24, Peter, 2 yrs. To Kleinliebental/Od.
Kost, Franz-Joseph 34, Barbara 33, Joseph 10, Magd 8, Eva 5; Barthel, bro. of Fr-Jos.To Mariental.
Moser, Christian + ca. 1816, his son Joseph, b. 1800, married Christina Vollmer 1820. To Landau/Od.

SCHÖNENBURG

Deiss, Philipp 46, Barbara +1811, Katharina 15, Philipp 14. To Josephstal/Od.
Deiss, Franz 44, shepherd, Margaret 39, Johann 14, Ludwig 6, Eva 11, Magd. 2. To Mannheim/Od.
Deiss, Johann +1810 at 54, Katherina 50, Theresa 18, Dominik 14, Marg. 10, Franziska 8. Sulz.
Deiss, Matheus 40, Theresa 34, Ignatius 10, Georg +1812, Joseph 2½, Xaver 2 mon. To Kandel/Od.
Freidig, Peter 26, son of Peter, Theresia 22. To Landau/Od.

SCHWABWEILER

Bachmann, Johann-Georg +1811, Magdalena 48, widow, Georg 23, Mathias 23, Thekla +1815, Magd-
    alena 18, Anton 17, Joseph 15. To Josephstal/Od.
Fassel, Jakob 38, widower, Peter 17, Joseph 14, Maria 14, Lorenz 12. To Mariental/Od.
Fassenach (Fassnacht), Johann 52, Maria 48, Barbara 22, Johannes 16, Philipp 7. To Lustdorf/Od.
Griener, Georg 34, shoemaker, wife Charlotte 24. To Prischib/Raurida.
Schäfer, Michael 38, Elisabeth 23, son from first wife: Michael 15. To Mariental/Od.
Schnellbach, Jakob 52, Eva 50, Heinrich 20, Walburga 30.Jakob's bro. Joseph 42. To Mariental/Od.

Also the following heads of families, with undetermined destination: Jakob Heuselmann, Lorenz and Georg-Heinrich Hölzel, Michael Seiler and son Joseph, and Lorenz Trauter.

SULZ

Deibele, Johannes 57, Maria 47, Joseph 14, Philipp 11, Regina 8, to Rastadt/Od.
Hell, Katharina 33, widow, Dorothea 21, Georg 19, Friedrich 8, Katharina 7, to Glückstal/Od.
Lehmann, Daniel +1812, Katharina 41, widow, Matheus 21, Anna 18, Karl 17,Andr. 11. Josephstal.
Weimer, Benedikt 54, Barbara 56, Michael 22, his wife Katharina 22, to Mariental/Od.
Weimer, Nikolaus 27, son of Benedikt, Margarete 25, Augustin 4, Katharina ½, to Mariental/Od.
 Other settlers: Jakob Nagel, Martin Neuhard, Johannes Rau. David Rosenbach, Andreas Schwerer.

SURBURG

Auquer (Oger, Ocker), Martin 36, s. of Peter, Magd. 27, Johann 2 yrs. To Leitershausen/Taurida.
Bachmann, Georg 28, Maria 24, Stanislaus 1, Maria 1. To Josephstal/Od.
Bachmann, Magdalena 58, widow, Georg 23, Matheus 23, Magd. 18, Anton 17, Joseph 15. To Josephstal.
Gustin, Johann 41, Magdalena 35, Katharina 20, Franz 13, Michael 10, Johann 5. To Rastadt/Od.
Löwenstein, Anton +1814 at 40, Joseph 18, Felix 16, Johann 13, Karl 8. To Mariental/Od.
Millius, Jakob 50, Marianna 37, Theresa 17, Anton 12, Magd. 18, Ignatz 3. To Karlsruhe/Od.
Millius Jakob, 27, Elisabeth 25, to Marinetal/Od.
Popp, Anton 37, Katharina 25, Maria 13, Anton 11, Michael 9. To Speier/Od.
Ramburg, Joseph 38, Margaret 36, Joseph 6, Kaspar 4, Michael 1. To Speier/Od.
Warter, Katharina 59, widow, Philipp +1811 at 27, Adam 25, Karolina 23. To Sulz/Od.
Warter, Georg 26, Walburga 23, Magdalena 5, Michael 3. To Sulz/Od.
 Other settlers with unknown destination in South Russia: Pater Bauer, Heinrich Huber, Michael Howil, Jakob Karlin, Matheus Rastatter.

FROM OTHER CANTONS:

HAGENAU

Baumann, Jakob 53, Maria 52, Martin 18, Barbara 7; Margaret 21 married Michael Miller, to Kandel.
Deis, Mathias 40, Theresa 34, Ignatius 10, Georg +1812, Joseph 2½, Xaver 2 months, to Kandel/Od.
Fischer, Mathias 28, smith, from Rundmühl/Hagenau, Theresa 26, Marianna 3½, Michael 1½, to Baden.
Götz, Johannes 46, Maria 32, Nathan 7, Katharina 1½, to Elsass/Od.
Götz, Joseph 42, (second) wife Katharina 19, Maria 9, Sebastian 6, Marianna 4. To Kleinliebental.
Götz, Ignatz 56, Barbara 44, Theresia 13, Maria 7, Christian 17, Klemens 11, From first wife:
   Xaver 25, Gabriel 27, wife Helena 23. To Kleinliebental/Od.

HÖRDT

Bader, Wilhelm 33, women's tailor, Marianna 32, Marg 9½, Sibilla 6, Barb 4. To Mannheim/Od.
Doll, Michael 39, s. of Jakob, Maria 30, Marie 7, Ursula 4, Elisabeth 1½. To Kandel/Od.
Fieger, Leonard +1815 at 47, Katharina 52, Georg 24, Elisabeth 16. To Kandel/Od.
Rengert, Peter 48, Veronica 29, Adam 3, Peter +1815 at 2, Joseph +1815. To Kandel/Od.
Riffel, Melchior 58, Maria 46, Johann 18, Peter 9, Michael 7, Rochus 2½. To Kandel/Od.
Stiebich, Andreas 29, Katharina 25, Heinrich 5, Maria 2, Simon ¼ yr. To München/Od.

WALBURG

Braxmeier, Joseph 28, Magdalena 31, nee Hoffmann, Genoveva 4, Joseph 1½, to Sulz/Od.
Epp, Philipp 53, sec. wife Elisabeth 38 nee Gabriel, Leonhard 19, Lorenz 3, to Mariental/Od.
Gross, Jakob 57, Anna Barbara 47, Georg 17, Heinrich 14, to Glückstal/Od.
Millius, Jakob 50, Marianna (2nd wife) 36, Theresa 17, Anton 12, Magd 5, Ignatz 3. To Karlsruhe.
Millius, Jakob 27, son? of Jakob, Sr., Elisabeth 25. To Mariental/Od.
Pukard, Jakob 42, Marianna 30, Xaver 6, Annamaria +1814, Leonore 1½, to Selz/Od.
Wirth, Michael 39, Magdalena 35, Eva 11, Joseph 8, Eva, 1 yr., to Mariental/Od.

SCHWEIGHAUSEN

Lauber, Konrad +1815 at age 55, weaver, Elisabeth 55, Franz 22, Elisabeth 15, to Mannheim/Od.
Lauber, Martin 27, son of Konrad, Theresa 25, daughter ot Anton Hanke, to Kandel/Od.
Vetter, Michael 34, Maria 21, Martin 2, Annemaria 1 month; to Kandel/Od.

1. Canton Seltz	
Aschbach	8
Beinheim	11
Bühl	3
Eberbach	2
Kaidenburg	4
Kesseldorf	3
Kröttweiler	1
Mothern	26
Münchhausen	8
Niederrödern	4
Niederseebach	4
Oberlauterbach	18
Schaffhausen	8
Seltz	52
Siegen	8
Stundweiler	3
Trimbach	6
Winzenbach	42
18 villages; 211 families	

2. Canton Lauterburg	
Lauterburg	12
Neeweiler	45
Niederlauterbach	18
Salmbach	39
Scheibenhard	6
5 villages; 120 families	

3. Canton Weissenburg	
Altenstadt	6
Cleeburg	9
Klimbach	12
Lembach	14
Niedersteinbach	5
Oberseebach	9
Obersteinbach	7
Riedselz	20
Schleithal	35
Steinselz	3
Weissenburg	12
Wingen	25
12 villages; 157 families	

4. Canton Bischweiler	
Auenheim	4
Bischweiler	2
Fort Louis	8
Leitenheim	7
Neuheisel	2
Röschwoog	7
Rohrweiler	4
Roppenheim	4
Runzenheim	2
Schirrhein	6
Schirrhofen	2
Sesenheim	4
Sufflenheim	5
13 villages; 57 families	

5. Canton Sulz	
Birlenbach	7
Bremmelbach	2
Hatten	3
Hölschloch	3
Hohweiler	3
Kühlendorf	3
Kutzenhausen	4
Lobsann	4
Ingolsheim	6
Memmelshofen	4
Ndr.Betschdorf	3
Oberrödern	2
Reimersweiler	9
Rittershofen	2
Schönenburg	6
Schwabweiler	15
Sulz unt. Wald	21
Surburg	18
18 villages; 115 fam.	

6. Canton Hagenau	
Hagenau	6
Schweighausen	4
Mariental	3
3 villages; 13 families	

7. Canton Wörth	
Biblisheim	6
Hegeney	3
Neuweiler	3
Walburg	10
Wörth	2
5 villages; 24 families	

8. Canton Schiltigheim	
Avolsheim	1
Bischheim	2
Mundolsheim	1
Strassburg	12
4 communities; 16 fam.	

9. Canton Brumath	
Gambsheim	3
Gries	1
Hördt	4
Wanzenau	5
4 villages; 13 families	

10. Canton Niederbronn	
Bitschhofen	2
Dambach	2
Niederbronn	3
Reichshofen	2
Ueberach	1
Uhrweiler	2
6 villages; 12 families	

Summary

Canton	Communities	Families	Souls
Seltz	18	211	949
Lauterburg	5	120	540
Weissenburg	12	157	706
Bischweiler	13	57	256
Sulz	18	115	517
Hagenau	3	13	58
Wörth	5	24	108
Schiltigheim	4	16	72
Brumath	4	13	58
Niederbronn	6	12	54
	88	738	2,621

*I could not help admire that so much
was achieved in the short time since the
colonies were founded 30 years ago.*

J. G. Kohl

VII.   A Vist to the Colonies in 1838

In the summer of 1838, J. G. Kohl, an inveterate traveler and remarkable ethnologist, undertook an extensive tour of South Russia, and on this occasion also visited the German colonies in the environs of Odessa. The two-volume work that he subsequently published about his travels also contained a fascinating account of the conditions prevailing in the German colonies. Because of the historical significance of his observations and impressions, the account[1] deserves to be included in a special chapter of this book. The following is a fairly literal translation of the German original:

The special interest that every German takes in the welfare and progress of his fellow countrymen in foreign lands, and also the general interest which the German colonies in Russia evoke in anyone who is concerned with the condition of peoples and states prompted me to live for a while in one of the colonies near Odessa. Such a visit, I felt, would enable me to make some interesting comments and at the same time to observe the peculiar character of the different nationalities that populate the steppes. I therefore chose Lustdorf, a friendly German village lying right on the shore of the Black Sea, twelve versts to the south of the city.

As I had already made the necessary arrangements for room and board with the mayor of the village, I mounted my horse one morning, to ride to my summer resort on the steppe. I rode leisurely through the gardens and *khutors* of Odessa and passed by the "Little Fountain", where people, like the Danaids of old, were ceaselessly occupied with the task of hauling water. After stopping briefly near the Russian hamlet of Fontal to view the garden of a wealthy Greek, I continued my ride past a small Russian monastery and the farm of a prosperous Bulgarian colonist who owned extensive vegetable gardens.

Soon I reached the borders of my German colony of Lustdorf. Just inside the border I came across a beautiful spring, where a plant for washing wool had been established. People told me that for a long time the spring was the object of contention between the monastery and the colony. Both parties had begun a lawsuit which had even been venued to Petersburg, where it was finally decided in favor the colony. Although the stream was only as thick as one's arm, the

---

[1] J. G. Kohl, *Reisen in Südrussland*, Dresden und Leipzig (1841), Vol. I, p. 127, 134—141, 143—155.

colonists were now deriving from it an annual revenue of 500 rubles, for that was the sum the Odessa merchant, who owned the wool-washing plant, had to pay for the lease of the spring.

Night began to fall as my chestnut steed and I finally reached the small *liman* (estuary) on whose elevated banks Lustdorf is located. I rode up from the seashore and reached the mayor's house where I found two small rooms in readiness for me, and the kind people anxiously awaiting my arrival. The "Gospodin Schulz", as he is called by the neighboring Russians, who have a profound regard for the mayors of the German colonies, was a highly respected, judicious man by the name of Lang. Throughout my stay at his house he was to become my sincerely devoted friend and also my teacher in regard to many interesting conditions existing in this area.

His wife, who was tirelessly busy with the management of the house and the children, proposed to prepare my meals, while the pretty seventeen-year-old daughter Bäbele, was to be my waitress and chambermaid. The mayor's aged mother was also still living, a woman already in her seventies, who had come to this country at the age of forty, and could therefore still speak the Swabian dialect as purely and fluently as if she had just arrived from the Neckar. After her husband's death she was spending the remainder of her days with her son, mending the clothes and stockings of her young grandchildren, preparing the salad for the kitchen, peeling potatoes, shelling peas and beans, and reading the Bible in the evenings.

A German travelling through Russia once remarked: "As I approached the banks of the Volga near Sarepta I was struck by the prevalence of the German dialect on this region." Indeed, the heart of a German is thrilled when, after roaming about among all sorts of strangers, he suddenly finds himself in the midst of dear fellow-countrymen and the amenities of his homeland, as though he had come upon a small piece of his native land right in the middle of a remote desert.

I felt completely at home with these good folk, who did everything to make my stay with them most pleasant. My room had a sofa, a table and chairs, and the windows were adorned with geraniums and myrtle. On one side I had a view to the small flowergarden of my friend Bäbele; on the other side I surveyed the farmyard, where the mayor and I set up a tent that very evening and where I intended to have my coffee the following morning. In my bedroom there was, of course, only a plain bed with a layer of straw, but I soon discovered that it was wonderful to sleep on it.

After I had taken an evening stroll with the mayor through his vineyard and got a view of his establishment, his wife invited me to a snack of *Holderküchle* and milk which Bäbele had already served in my room. I in turn invited the mayor to share the snack with me, and from that moment on he remained my daily companion and my constant guide on all walks and excursions. Those

121

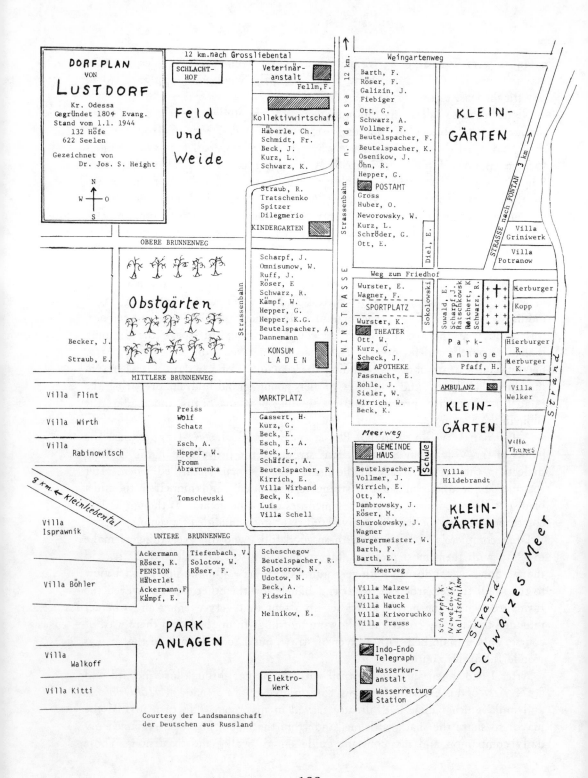

"Holderküchle" are a Swabian pastry. The people gather the blossoms of the elderberries that grow by the seashore, dip the yellow umbles into a batter of eggs and flour, bake them in butter, and eat them with sugar and appetite. This we now proceeded to do, and the mayor began to tell me the story of a shipwreck that had taken place last fall and whose sad wreckage — a ship's rump — I had seen on the beach on my way here.

In the course of such and similar stories I spent my first night in the village of Lustdorf, of which I soon grew very fond. It also happened to be a Saturday evening, which has always been my favorite evening of the week. For me, too, it came as a surprise "to hear the German dialect", and indeed in song. For the young German boys sat together half the night and sang old German songs, such as: "Freut Euch des Lebens", "Es ritten drei Reiter zum Tore hinaus", and many others which I had not heard for years, and which I certainly would not have expected to hear again on the shores of the inhospitable Pontus.

As I had anticipated, I slept very well on my straw bed (I had lain on harder beds in the Russian post stations), and when my Bäbele opened the shutters the next morning and the Sunday sun streamed through the window and the schoolmaster started to ring the bell for church, I felt so at home that I reached for my steaming coffee, enjoyed one cup after another in good German fashion, and then took a stroll through the village.

When the village was first established, the colonists had given it the name "Kaisersheim". However, when Duc de Richelieu came riding into the village one day and pondered the name, he deemed it inappropriate that this name should have been selected for no special reason and without the approval of the Czar. He therefore requested that another name be chosen, and the colonists agreed to re-baptize their village by the name it still bears.

The houses in the village are all nicely constructed of a soft conglomerate of limestone. All have only one story, spacious rooms, and green shutters on all the windows. All are kept neat and tidy. To be sure, Lustdorf has a special need for larger rooms, since suitable accommodation is required for the numerous summer guests who come here to enjoy the sea-baths. The progress of the colony is evident from the fact that in the 30 years of its existence the interior of the houses has been renovated for the third time.

In the beginning the government had provided the settlers only with reed huts, in which they practically froze to death in the wintertime. Following the example of the Russians, the colonists soon began to dig themselves into the ground and build adobe houses. Finally, when their situation improved and they had become more well-to-do, they built the present handsome houses. The same development took place in the other German colonies that I had the opportunity to visit.

The houses are situated on both sides of a broad street, and each house is surrounded by a spacious yard. In the rear part you find the unroofed threshing plot and the uncovered *skirte* (long stacks) of grain, hay, and straw. Behind these stacks are located the vineyards, orchards, and vegetable gardens. The village street is lined with two rows of beautiful acacia trees, and at the gable end of every house there is a small, well-tended flower garden, the care of which is always in the hands of the oldest daughter of the family. Decked out in their pretty Sunday clothes, these girls were now standing at the stone wall distributing larkspur and gilliflowers to their favorites among the lads of the village who were sauntering down the street and jesting with the girls.

When the schoolmaster sounded the second bell, the mayor's seventy-year-old mother, with a sparkling white bonnet on her head and a white apron over her blue cotton skirt, came out of the house to go to church. As I accompanied her on the way she told me that it took a long time and cost many a life before the colony achieved the prosperity I was now witnessing. During the first period of settlement the hardships had been great, and she was now one of the few that had survived those storms. Most of the German immigrants had, in fact, perished before they were even able to take possession of the land that had been granted them. Even the trek to Russia had been a terrifying experience. It lasted two summers and one winter. One party had come down the waterway of the Danube. They had fared worst of all, for at the delta of the Danube malignant diseases had broken out among those immigrants, and a large number of them were carried off. The other parties had come by way of Vienna, Moravia and Galicia, and after staying in the last-named province the entire winter, they continued their trek through Podolia. In the beginning all the women had been terribly frightened of the Russians, and even now she could not help tremble a bit whenever a Russian visitor comes unexpectedly into the house. There was also much fear of the Turks who, at that time, were still in possession of the west side of the Dniester. Indeed, the poor womenfolk suspected that every vessel that appeared on the river might be a part of the piratical Turkish fleet.

"The worst thing", added the mayor, who was walking along with us, "was the fact that the immigrants had found practically nothing prepared for them on their arrival. To be sure, the land was there, 25 dessiatines for each of the 40 families who were to be settled, but the available dwellings were so wretched that the colonists had to dig themselves into the earth, like the Russians. Moreover, the plows given to them were such sorry contraptions that when put to use the plowshares bent like tin. To make matters worse, the colonists really had no idea in what latitude they were now living; some even thought that the land belonged to Podolia. Nor did they know when to start work in the fields, when to sow, when to reap, whether to fertilize, or indeed what to plant and sow. The Russians, whose language they did not understand, were unable to enlighten them on these matters. Therefore, the more well-to-do among the settlers hired Russian farm hands and let them manage the farms and fields as they liked. The best food was set before them and they were almost regarded as sacred persons. People were often heard to say: "For goodness sake, let's keep the Russians contented, for on them our whole welfare depends!" The poorer settlers simply imitated the example of the well-to-do and their Russian servants, sowed and planted when they did, etc. In due time the situation changed in a twofold respect. On the one hand, the Germans not only soon learned what was needful and proper, but with hard work and their ambition to improve themselves, combined with the greater knowledge of agriculture already gained in Germany, they were soon able to improve their farm implements and farming methods to such a degree that the Russians are now often heard to exclaim: "Tak i njemtzi sdalayut!" (That's the way the Germans do it!). On the other hand, those who were formerly well-to-do now belong to the poorer class, whereas those who had practically nothing to start with are now the most prosperous in the community."

This process was repeated in all the colonies, and the cause of it was that the rich always relied on their Russian servants and squandered their money on them as well as on their unsuccessful enterprises, whereas the poor gained useful experience without incurring any losses. Indeed, in relying upon their own efforts, they had learned more and learned it better.

The schoolmaster, a native Swiss, read the sermon rather poorly, but I was nevertheless edified, for the association with a group of people for religious purposes is always uplifting. However, I believe that church affairs in the colonies are not in their best condition. The best preachers from Lithuania and Esthonia, which supply most of the preachers in the Russian interior, do not like to come this far, even though the clergymen in the colonies are not badly off. They get 120 dessiatines of land and a fairly good salary.

Since many Germans are scattered through all of Russia, the Lutherans have a certain number of superintendencies throughout the country, just as Russia (as a whole) is divided in many "gubernias" (administrative districts), or the Greek church into several eparchies. In every larger city there is a parish with its own preacher who at times is also the superintendent of a large area extending over several "gouvernements", and is therefore responsible for the supervision of religious services in the German colonies. Oftentimes the preachers come into conflict with the colonial authorities who resent their influence and place all sorts of obstacles in their path. Hence it happens that many colonies do not engage a preacher, and the church remains in an obvious state of neglect. Often the schoolmaster takes over the functions of the pastor, although on occasion a visiting missionary from Basel may stop over at a colony.

In the course of several walks among fishermen, shepherds, and colonists, I gained a much clearer understanding of this area and its people. And so the first days of my sojourn at Lustdorf were spent with many informative talks with my friend the mayor and with some innocent banter and jesting with my cheerful

Bäbele. I even came to her defense a bit against her mother who claimed that the girls born in Russia were less inclined to work as hard as those from Germany, and yet I found that the girl was quite active. However, the careworn spirit of the German women, their restles, ceaseless activity, their unflagging drudgery and worrying — this, to be sure, tends to disappear among the Russian-born girls, and for that reason all the daughters here find themselves in opposition to their mothers. I found some fault here with the mothers who, in almost German fashion, get so involved in work that they miss the joy of living. Actually, I liked the balance of German diligence and Russian ease which I detected among the young people of the colony. In fact, it was very instructive for me to compare German housewives with Russian ones, and I could not help marvelling at the striking difference in the character of each ethnic group. It seemed obvious to me that not a single exemplar of such a busy worker like the mayor's wife (and I found many others of her type in the village) could be found among the 50 million Russians, nor could such a lively product be derived from the stuff of which the Russian national character is baked.

In my opinion, there is no cause to fear that the poor management of Russian households, their customs and language will soon replace the German way of life in the colonies. The Germans are massed together here in large numbers, almost always they marry their own people, and the Russians are not permitted (by colonial law) to settle in the colonies. They still dress in the German fashion; only the winter fur coat has been adopted — because of the climate. The Swabian dialect is passed on from father to son. Russian, which of course they must learn for business reasons, is spoken only with Russians. To be sure, some young German sons, and especially some of the poorer people, have defected and established themselves outside the colony where they became Russianized, but they are comparatively few. Most of the people who find no means of livelihood in the rapidly rising population of the colonies move to the cities, were many good opportunities are open to their industry and ambition, and where they again find German communities that preserve the German spirit through churches, schools, and other associations.

In point of fact, the superiority of the Germans over the Russians is, in many respects, so great that whenever the two nationalities come into conflict it is not surprising to see the German come out on top. The German thinks, the Russian does not; the German works and forges ahead; the Russian gets stuck and easily goes backward. The German even cheats more thoroughly than the Russian, who despite his wily chicanery is invariably the dupe in the end.

Also the physical character of the Germans has certain advantages over the Russian. If the latter is more versatile and resistant to wind and weather, hunger and thirst, the German in turn is more vigorous and robust. This is apparent even in the everyday petty conflicts — I mean the fights that take place between Ger-

126

mans and Russians — in which the latter are invariably the losers. A German first is not afraid of two or three Russians, and a lone Russian will never venture to oppose a German, man to man. For the ethnologist I could adduce some interesting stories and observations, the upshot of which is that "German blows", as Schiller already noted in his Fiesco drama, are feared as much here as they are in Italy. "*Pisse Njemetzi*, devilish Germans!" the Russians shout at us, when a German comes driving along in his heavy, ironbound, chain-clanking wagon, and they make way for him because they have already discovered that in the event of a collision their own wooden cart will get the worst of it. For all these reasons the German colonist is far more feared and respected by the local Russians than he is hated, as has been falsely stated in a recent newspaper article on the German colonists in Russia. The Russian is far too conscious of the superiority of the German, to leave much room for hatred.

However, while we are discussing scrapping and fighting, we should not fail to admit that the Russians resort to this disgusting activity far less frequently than the Germans. In this regard I have heard my countrymen use expressions that are quite unknown to the Russians. On hearing them, I could not help blushing for my nationality, and the more pacific and conciliatory character of the Russians appeared to me in beautiful light.

Often enough the Germans scrap and fight until the blood flows. The Russians, in contrast, pummel each other a bit on their thick fur coats, and the matter is settled. To be sure, the poor Russian is accustomed to getting more blows than he delivers, and thus it is not merely his greater love of peace but also his lack of independence, just as it is not merely German coarseness but also the feeling of greater independence. However, even in the raising of their children I found the Germans much more apt to resort to physical punishment than was the case with the Russians. The outcries of the vigorously beaten children could be heard through the villages all day. The Russians live much more amicably with their children and they caress them more often. On the other hand, it must be observed that the Germans pay much more attention to training and discipline than is the case in Russian families that are often completely wild and unruly.

In regard to the young children I also noticed that the German children appeared less neat and clean than the Russian ones whom I always found very tidy and proper. Even the grownup German women and men did not appear to have as much personal cleanliness as the Russian mujiks. It is, however, very difficult to make general judgements about cleanliness. One nationality is more particular in this respect, the other in that. The German women work a great deal and can therefore not always appear very attractive. Hence, on workdays the women, with their wild flying hair, give one the impression of just having emerged from the sheer despair of their household drudgery. On a Sunday, the day of rest and leisure, the situation is altogether different. Then the spic-and-span German woman definitely had the advantage. In point of fact, it is characteristic of the various classes in Russia that no very great difference can be noticed between their Sunday attire and their workaday clothes. The numerous feast days make it impossible to celebrate all of them in special holiday attire, and for the Russians the weekdays are not workdays or business days to the extent that special clothes are necessary. Everything flows together in a rather chaotic way.

My Bäbele, who brought me flowers every morning from her garden for my breakfast table and found my humorous company quite congenial, had of course other admirers who took her more seriously. She was much sought after, for she was the prettiest girl in the village and the daughter of a man who held a most respected position and stood in high regard and frequent contact with Germans, Russians and Greeks in the neighborhood as well as in Odessa.

Of her admirers, one was more richly endowed with emotion, another with rank, and the third with money. The sentimental one was a young farm lad of the village; the man of rank was a Cossack officer; and the man of means, a young German who was the owner of a wine tavern in Odessa. The sentimental one called every evening and there was chatting, laughter, and teasing. The Cossack rode up to the house a couple of times, drank a glass of wine with the girl's father, ogled her from a distance, and then one fine day came right out with a proposal of marriage. He told the mayor that he had known him for some time and had also become acquainted with his daughter Bäbele (actually he had never spoken a word to her), and that he was well pleased with her diligence and good behavior. He admitted that he had only a rather poor house and a small salary, but the did possess rank and title, two medals, and a silver cross. At present he was the owner of three horses, and was planning to buy a *kaleska*, a buggy. He would, therefore, like to ask for Bäbele's hand. She would, he felt sure, do a fine job of housekeeping and on Sundays she could go out for a buggy ride. The mayor poured him another drink and suggested that the matter could be discussed some other time. The suitor, having gotten the mitten, mounted his steed and rode off.

The tavern owner from Odessa came out to the village every Sunday — to the deep vexation of the poor sentimental one — and asked permission to take Bäbele to a dance. The parents were decidedly in favor of him, and Bäbele, too, was willing. The only point that created a feeling of apprehension was the fact that this suitor had a shock of flaming red hair. I, for my part, would have liked to see the girl remain in the village and, for that matter, would have gladly granted her to the smart village lad. Since I had also made an issue of the red hair, I now began to fan the flames even higher so as to increase its repelling force, although I gradually began to doubt my success. The matter was decided shortly before I took my departure from the village. The glitter of the gold won out, the aversion to the red hair was overcome, and before I left I had to congratulate Bäbele on the happy event that declared her the fiancée of the

128

red-headed wine-seller from Odessa, and cast the poor village lad into the pit of despair.

The first longer excursion that I decided to undertake with the mayor was into the neighboring German colonies and to the mouth of the Dniester Liman. One fine morning at five the mayor's son Jakob hitched up a pair of bays and climbed on the buckboard of a Hungarian farm wagon, of the type which several Hungarian-German colonists had introduced into all the German colonies here. The mayor and I took our places in the rear on a layer of straw that was covered with a pretty multicolored Russian blanket. Our way took us first along the small, narrow *peressip* of the village liman. It was completely dried out; only here and there on its cracked and scarred surface thin layers of salt were to be seen. After crossing the broad terrain that lies between the shore and the elevated steppe, we proceeded upon the long, wide *peressip* of a much larger *liman* that always holds salt water, but breaks out into the sea about every ten years. It was the Suchoi Liman, as our map indicated. Its water is strongly salinated and contains several varieties of sea fish. On its banks we also saw countless heaps of seashells.

More interesting were the human settlements on its shores. These were so numerous and so charming in their scenic setting that I imagined I was at one of the small lakes in Holstein. The liman, which forms a connected mass towards the sea, divides into two crooked arms farther inland to the north. In the foothills of the forked area lay a large German colony, with attractive church and handsome houses, named Kleinliebental. To the right of this village lay the large village of Alexandrovka, which is inhabited by Greeks. On the left stood the Russian hamlet of Burlaktschi Balk, "Valley of the Rogues", and at the apex of one arm the Malo-Russian village of Suchoi Liman. Besides these settlements, there were several fishing huts along the shore, and the estate and country villa of Countess Potocki.

The sight of so many settlements really came to me as a surprise. I never encountered a similar scene on the steppes. On the *peressip* stood a long row of fishermen's huts and between the villages, herds of cattle and horses moved about. Enough variety of people and occupations to give us food for thought as we rode along the narrow ridge between the liman and the sea, enjoying our cigars. About midway on the long ridge, the mayor suddenly said: *"Jakob, halt's mol an, de Pferde woll'n sich amol verschnaufe!"* (Jakob, stop a while, the horses would like to catch their breath a bit). I thought to myself that life is not made that pleasant for the poor Russian horses, for a Russian never stops to worry about what his horses want or do not want.

The "Rogues' Village" got its name in the old days when marauding bandits lodged in every ravine and at the mouth of every river. Now only a few years separate us from those earlier times in this region. One must marvel at the magic power which the Russian empire has exerted on the civilization and cultivation of these vast wastelands. No matter how far we go back into history, we encounter nothing but wild, plundering hordes of nomads. But here before our eyes we now find a picture of peaceful, busy settlers. It would indeed be difficult to find any better ones in those lands that have been cultivated since the dawn of history.

Our way took us through the Greek colony of Alexandrovka. It was founded in the days of Catherine the Great, who had settled a group of unhappy Moreitoses here. The people were now all Russianized and spoke Russian much more fluently than the German colonists. They had also adopted most of the Russian customs, lived in indolence, and squandered their money in the taverns. They are inefficient farmers and even though they received much more generous grants of land from the Empress than was allotted to the Germans — depending on his rank, each Greek settler received 8 to 10 times more — they are now all in debt to the two neighboring German colonies. The latter find time, after having worked their own fields, to cultivate the fields they have leased from the Greeks. Indeed, the latter will often lease their land ten years in advance, in order to obtain ready cash. After the money is squandered, they eke out an existence in their wretched huts. The difference between the outward appearance of their village and that of the German colonists is that between night and day. Everything is in a state of unsightly decay. There are no trees and no gardens. The village church also had the same dreary aspect. Instead of a bell they simply hooked up a piece of scrap iron on which the blows of a hammer called the community together. With sad thoughts we drove on.

After a long drive across the Greek steppe we again reached German terrain — the fields and gardens of the large colony of Grossliebental which is also the administrative seat of the entire German district and the headquarters of the chief mayor. Ten other colonies belong to this district, six of them Evangelical and four Catholic. In the Odessa region of "New Russia" there are four such districts, each with its chief mayor: *Liebental,* near the mouth of the Dniester; *Kutschurgan,* farther up the Dniester; *Glückstal,* to the northwest of Odessa; and *Beresan* to the northeast. These four districts have about 25,000 inhabitants and, like other colonies in Russia, are subject to the so-called "Colonists' Welfare Committee" in Odessa, of which the president is a Russian general. All matters coming before this Committee are conducted in Russian, although all the officers also understand German. For every district there is an inspector who serves as an intermediary between the colony and the Committee. He is generally also a Russian, but the mayors are of course Germans who are elected by their own communities. The same is true of the chief mayors and also the village and district clerks. In each village two men are elected as "burgomasters" to assist the mayor in his work. An adjutant of the mayor, known as the village beadle, assembles

130

the townsmen to the regular meetings by ringing a bell through the streets. Those colonists who fail to appear are liable to pay a fine.

In addition to the colonial districts already mentioned, there are several others in South Russia. Over 30,000 colonists are settled in Bessarabia, 50,000 near the Sea of Azov, 5,000 in the Crimea, and 5,000 in the Caucasus. The most prosperous of all these German colonies are those on the banks of the Molotschna River, near the Sea of Azov. Some farmers there have herds of 20,000 sheep, and the colonists live in very attractive homes.

All the colonists in Russia are regarded as one distinct class, and when a colonist on the Volga or in the Caucasus is punished for some crime, the deed is also made known on the Dniester. They are also interested in one another in other ways, for instance when preachers from the Crimea are transferred to Bessarabia, or schoolmasters from Sarepta on the Volga come into the southern colonies. Adventurers and beggars from Germany sometimes roam from colony to colony. Occasionally, also some practices and customs spread from one colony to another. We have already mentioned the Hungarian farm-wagon which is to be found in all the colonies of South Russia. I should, indeed also mention the cattle from the Molotschna, which all the South Russian colonies are trying to introduce.

To be sure, the colonies in the different regions of this vast empire did not all obtain the same amount of land grants and government loans. As a rule, those in South Russia received 60 dessiatines (162 acres) of land per family, and a so-called "advance loan". This loan usually consisted of 2 horses, 2 cows, 2 oxen, a few farm implements, and a small sum of money. The 60 dessiatines of crown land are regarded as indivisible property for which the colonist proprietor pays taxes, which at present amount to 14 rubles. All the German colonies in Russia probably pay a total of 2 million rubles per year to the imperial treasury. The original land grant, it should be noted, may not be divided among the sons through testament; but several families may live on it, if they can secure a livelihood. Nor may any of the land be sold without the permission of the government. Every district is held responsible for the tax payments of all its settlers, and also for the long-term repayment of the advance loans.

The increase of the population in the German colonies is commensurate with the great expansion of population in the Empire as a whole; perhaps it even grows faster. Thus, the small colony of Lustdorf had 208 people at the time of the census of 1815. In the census of 1835, there were 357 people, not counting those who came into the colony from elsewhere. If one adds the 19 that moved away, we find that the population had doubled in 25 years. Similar results are indicated in the lists that I saw in other colonies. On half of the original homesteads two or more families are now living. Moreover, every year many families move away to the city. In Lustdorf one-sixth of the population has already moved to town. The younger men who can find no livelihood in the village often settle on some land that well-to-do fathers have purchased for them, somewhere among the Russians. Sometimes the landless sons became *dessiatint-schicks,* namely renters that have leased a few dessiatines from some Russian nobleman. They build an adobe house and work the land as long as they like or until they have saved enough money to buy property of their own.

To what extent the German colonists can thrive in this country is evident from the following example. A Mennonite in the Molotschna, though he came as a poor man to this country, has become so prosperous through his hard work and enterprise that his property today is valued at 2 million rubles. He owns a herd of 20,000 sheep, whose wool contributes in no small way to the flourishing commerce of Azov. I was also told of other colonists who owned 12,000 sheep and 7,000 head of cattle. To be sure, there are also many poor people, but there are no beggars or uncared-for indigents to be found in any of the German colonies. All this is, of course, not solely due to German industry but also to the favorable conditions in which they are placed. It is easy for the Germans to better themselves among the Russians.

In point of fact, every German farm establishment on the steppes is generally superior to that of the Russians. The Germans are the only inhabitants of the steppe who have developed effective means against the depredations of the grasshoppers. They have also been the chief exterminators of the snakes that formerly infested the steppes. When there is a famine in the land the Russians come to the German colonists to obtain some of the surplus grain from their granaries. The colonists cultivate the idle fields of the neighboring Greeks and other indolent peasants. They are never in arrears with their taxes and invest their capital in useful enterprises. Hence a German colonist was led to tell me with justifiable pride: "If the Czar were to come to this district, he would have to acknowledge with joy that we Germans have been largely responsible for the cultivation of the steppes." As a matter of fact, when Alexander, while passing through the Molotschna on his final trip to Toganrog, surveyed the thriving German colonies, he cried out in astonishment: "Children, we really don't need to travel to Germany anymore. We have more than Germany right here in our own empire!"

The houses in the colony of Grossliebental were on the whole very attractive and in good condition. Less so, the gardens, which were full of weeds and thistles. In truth, gardening is not making much progress in the colonies of the steppe. They were actually in better shape in the earlier years. On the one hand, farming and the raising of livestock are really more productive, while on the other hand the difficulties of gardening are too great. The gardens on the higher levels of the steppe were particularly drab and desolate. Those located in the valley were still in good condition and of such impressive size that I could not help marvel that so much has been achieved in the short period of 30 years.

Every house has its well and its fine spacious cellar. Because of the hot summers, these cellars are dug to an astonishing depth. I found it most fascinating to observe how the people store the milk to keep it cool. There is a broad staircase with numerous steps. In the early spring the milk is placed on the topmost step. As the days grow warmer it is set several steps lower down, in the beginning of the summer still lower, and finally during the greatest heat, it stands at a depth of 25 and more feet.

Since we did not find the chief mayor at home, we called on the district clerk. In the offices we found everything spacious, neat, and even elegant. We then took a look at the communal sheep ranch, the community garden and vineyards. Every district owns certain communal property: a large orchard, a vineyard, a sheep ranch, and a fishery. From the proceeds of these various enterprises a communal treasury is set up, from which the needy or those who require capital for some useful enterprise can obtain a loan against the necessary security. We have here actually a kind of loan bank of the type which some of the noblemen back home established in several areas. These community treasuries provide good services, especially in lean years. In the treasury of this colonial district (comprising ten villages) there were cash assets of 300,000 rubles. The other treasuries

The Grossliebental Colonies
Est. 1804–1807

Courtesy of
Dr. Karl Stumpp

133

of the district were in similar good condition, for the Fire Assurance Fund amounted to 197,000 rubles and the Widows' and Orphans' Fund amounted to 160,000 rubles. Thus, the total cash assets for the ten villages were 650,000 rubles. I think this is brilliant enough.

We stayed for the night with the district clerk, who had a very charming house and was indeed a man of status, married, with a nice income of 400 thalers, and as I soon discovered, the real manager of the district. During the evening we discussed a hundred topics relating to the colonies and the steppes: snakes, grasshoppers, Mongolian mounds, agriculture, etc. We finished with a discussion about egg-production and came to the surprising conclusion that the hens of the steppe lay twice as many eggs as the German ones. In Germany a hen lays no more than 60 eggs per year, while the hens here lay 120 and more.

The next day we drove through many other German colonies: Alexanderhilf, Freudental, Peterstal — all of which lay in a row along the valley of the Baraboi, a small insignificant stream that was now completely dried up, except near the villages where its water had been collected into *stavoks*, ponds. This construction of ponds is a common feature throughout the steppes of the Ukraine. Every landlord and every village builds a dam of earth across the river bed, to contain the water. A channel with sluice gate and bridge-crossing is provided to take care of the overflow in the spring. The man-made ponds are called *stavoks*, and every stream of significant size deposits its water in a large number of such *stavoks*. In this way, water for washing clothes and watering the livestock is obtained.

The colonies of Peterstal and Freudental are the most prosperous in this area. They are inhabited by German-Hungarians, that is, by Germans who had originally settled in Hungary and later emigrated to Russia. In Freudental we visited a colonist who had such a splendidly furnished home that it would scarcely be surpassed by the richest peasant houses in Switzerland. In the spacious living room we saw the finest furniture, even a large, beautiful grandfather's clock for which he had paid 200 rubles in Odessa. In the bedrooms stood the most enchanting beds, with white curtained canopies, and everything else in the house was likewise well furnished.

The preacher of Freudental, who is also the Evangelical Superintendent of all Russia, was, regrettably, not at home. He is said to be a very original character, and completely devoted to his farmers. Indeed, he is himself a big farmer and hauls his cattle, his wheat, and his *kirpitsch* (dry manure) to the markets in Odessa. He is said to have done much to improve agriculture in the colony, which, to be sure, can still stand a lot of improvement. However, as long as the grain flows abundantly into the farmers' hands, improvements will be rather slow in coming. A big farmer here usually loses as much grain on his threshing floor as a small peasant back home can manage to harvest. The threshing floors are simply open surfaces on a level patch of hard-packed earth. An unexpected rain often soaks the grain that is spread out on the floor, where it is completely ruined, because with the rapid germination that takes place it begins to sprout at once. An enormous amount of grain is also lost to the ducks and chickens that have a splendid feast, and much is also trampled and destroyed.

Threshing, which for us back home is a perspiring job for even the toughest worker, is here just mere child's play. Two or three wagons are hitched up, the young boys climb on the buckseat, their sisters and the neighbor's children pile in the back of the wagon, and they drive round and round over the grain that is spread out on the threshing floor. In Freudental I was shown the strangest threshing rig I have ever seen — a Bulgarian one. It consisted of several boards set together on the same plane, curved in front like a sleigh runner and studded on its lower surface with numerous flint stones. The Bulgarians around here drag this threshing sled over their grain, but I could not rightly understand how the kernels were thereby separated from the ears.

From Freudental we drove westward to the Dniester. As we came into the valley of its tributary, the Kutschurgan Liman, we saw before us two broad terraces on which large herds of livestock were grazing. These belonged to the Russian village of Majak which is located about 5 versts above the Liman. Its inhabitants are so-called *Raskolniki,* that is to say, "Old Orthodox" Russians who in earlier times had left their fatherland because of its opposition to their faith and settled in what was then Turkish territory.

Since it was getting late in the day, the mayor suggested that we ought to stay over night in the village with one of the families he was acquainted with. Just as the Scythian troglodytes in the time of Herodotus, so the native Malorussians of the steppes live in a *semelanka,* an earthen hut. Indeed, there is every likelihood that this primitive type of dwelling is still much the same as it was in antiquity. Certainly, the building material is the same.

Because of the cold in winter and the heat of summer, but particularly because of the lack of timber and wood, the steppe dwellers conceal themselves and their dwellings halfway in the earth. They excavate a cellar three to four feet deep and according to the dimensions of the proposed house. Three beams of equal height are then erected on the south elevation, one at each end and the third in the middle. A horizontal beam, called the *"swolok"* (Durchzug), is placed over them to serve as a ridge pole. From the ground level on the north side a sloping roof of reed and turf is laid out to extend as far as the ridge. Seen from the northern approach, such a house looks deceptively like a slight elevation of the landscape. On the sunny side, a wall of earth about 4 feet high is erected and a couple of pieces of glass inserted into it to serve as window panes. From this side the house gives the impression of being in the process of "growing" out of the earth.

The entrance to the *semelanka* is provided by the *peressinya*, a closed-in stairway leading from the ground level to the subterranean floor of the house. At each end of this passageway there is a door, to keep out the heat as well as the cold.

Our prospective host gave us a very friendly and hospitable reception. No sooner had we expressed our desire to be permitted to stay overnight, when everyone began to provide for us in the very best way. The young son put our horses out to pasture. The wife and the aged mother of our host set about to prepare a supper for us in the summer kitchen.

After having seen the primitive exterior of the *semelanka*, I was very pleasantly surprised to find myself in such a comfortable and attractive room. Outside it was very hot, but down here it was delightfully cool. The air was fresh and fragrant, for the clay floor was strewn with grass and the walls were festooned with bunches of aromatic herbs. Everything was so neat and tidy that one cannot sufficiently praise the Malorussians in this respect, compared with the Great Russians and the Poles. Pretty, quaintly colored quilts covered the benches and a number of plump comfortable pillows lay on the beds. The windows had gay curtains and the walls were adorned with brightly printed wall paper and several little mirrors. But nothing was more prettily decorated than the holy icon that hung in a niche in one corner of the room. The niche was bordered on three sides with small silver-edged curtains, and on a painted shelf below it lay a profusion of offerings, fruits, and flowers. In front of the icon hung a silver lamp that was kept burning night and day. The whole thing seemed like something that had been set up for the children as a surprise on Christmas Eve. What a childlike simplicity of faith must animate the hearts of these good people!

As we were chatting through the falling twilight the finest supper began to appear on the table: borscht soup, lentil pottage, egg omelet cake, and the best milk in the world. *Borscht* — the national dish of the Malorussians — is a treat for anybody, especially in the summertime. Every conceivable kind of delicious, savory herb and vegetable gets into this soup: sliced beets, parsnip, caraway, parsley, purslane, thyme, leek, etc. The base of all these ingredients are lentils and a chunk of mutton, while the common element in which everything swims is a sourish *kvass*, the well-known national beverage of the Russians. To each bowl of the steaming soup the diner adds a portion of cool thick cream.

The good people wanted to give us their own bed for the night, while they proposed to sleep in the yard. But we requested that they simply spread some straw for us in the adjoining store room, and there we had a good, if brief, night's rest. The next morning, just as the sun peered over the high grass of the steppe, we sat down for a light breakfast of tasty white bread and fresh milk. As our wagon rolled out of the yard our kind hosts sent along a thousand good wishes: *"Dai Bog wam starowie!"* — "God give you good health! God grant your body and soul happiness, salvation, and well-being!"

My last days in Lustdorf were spent visiting with all kinds of people, with colonists, gypsies, shepherds, and horse herdsmen. I also made a final longer excursion — this time to the towns of Ovidiopol and Akerman, near the mouth of the Dniester. But as I gradually noticed that the sources of new ideas and the fountains of new information were beginning to flow rather sparingly, I found myself thinking of some new region to visit. So I packed up my writing materials, took leave of my excellent host, wished my Bäbele a sweet life with the redhead from Odessa, and bade farewell to these good people. As I rode back to the city, I began to look forward to my projected excursion to the Crimean peninsula.

137. Russian droshky at Odessa (1838)

VIII.   The Achievements of the Colonists

1. The Bashtan, the Pride of the Steppe

Translator's foreword. If there is one thing that evoked frequent nostalgia among the parents and grandparents who came from the Pontic steppes of South Russia to the prairies of the Dakotas and Saskatchewan, it was doubtless the memory of the beautiful *bashtans* that flourished in every colony. But these *bashtans* did not merely survive as romantic memories of the *Heimat;* they represented a heritage of the love of gardening, of the expertise and skill that remained alive and fruitfully effective in the gardens of the prairies. The following description by the German traveller, Johann-Georg Kohl, who visited the colonies near Odessa in 1838, provides a fascinating insight into the origins and the nature of the steppeland garden. J.S.H.

"A most peculiar kind of garden that one frequently finds in the environs of Odessa and elsewhere is the melon garden of the Malorussians which is widely known in Russia as the *bashtan.* Like the garden itself, the word is of Tartar origin and was doubtless adopted by the Ukrainians (or Kleinrussen), since both are found not only among the Tartars of the Crimea and the Caucasus as far as Baku and Derbend, but also in the Great Tartary beyond the Caspian Sea and throughout the lands of the Cossocks, and everywhere in the Ukraine. Indeed, the products of the *bashtan* are intimately connected with the life of all the people in these regions, including the area of Odessa. Furthermore, this type of garden is so well suited to the nature of the soil that the *bashtan* can be said to be the most beautiful and perfect thing that the steppe has brought forth.

The principal products of the *bashtan* belong, almost without exception to the class of the *Curcurbitaceae,* namely melons, squash, cucumbers. Besides these, the *bashtan* also contains the following: sunflowers, onions, radishes, Turkish lentils, maize, tomatoes, and *baklayan,* eggplant. In other words, such vegetables as are favored by the soil and the climate, and which are really in greatest favor among the people.

138

Among all these products, the *arboose*—the watermelon, holds the first place. Nature seems to have created this excellent juicy fruit especially for the steppe, for it thrives best in the desolate dry steppeland where the slender stem draws its sweetest and most refreshing juice in the driest years. Throughout the southern steppes the *arboose* grow so large and so succulent that they must be regarded as a veritable boon for the entire country, and can be considered an excellent substitute for good spring water. That they are chiefly thought of as a thirst-quencher can be concluded from the way the Ukrainians talk when they wish to eat watermelon. "Oh, I'm so awfully thirsty," they say, and proceed to buy a watermelon and eat it.

At every breakfast and dinner there is watermelon into which they bite from time to time while they are eating their bread and pork. Indeed, the whole interior of a good watermelon consists of a smooth fleshy juice that melts completely on the tongue. The Ukrainians have a special way of cutting open a watermelon. First they slice off the outer shell where the stem is attached, and then they set the watermelon on the flat surface. Then they slice off the top and make many parallel cuts from top to bottom while the whole thing hangs together. It is then set in the middle of the table and each guest can take out one slice after the other.

Incredible quantities of watermelon are brought into the Odessa market. Even in small towns, like Poltava, one sees huge mounds of watermelons in the market place. Everybody loves and eats this beautiful refreshing fruit and it appears regularly on the tables of the rich and the poor. Many people drink their watermelon in the morning just as we drink our coffee, and whenever anyone drives into the country he certainly will not forget to put a few watermelons into his carriage. There are several localities on the steppe that are famous for their fine *arboose,* for example, Tichwin in the Ukraine and Akerman in Bessarabia, but the best come from the Crimea.

It is interesting to watch the connoisseurs shop for watermelons in the market place. They are able to judge the quality partly by the appearance of the shell and partly by the tone that is produced when they tap the shell with a finger. They keep poking at each watermelon until they find one that appears to be just right. The watermelons here are so sweet that you do not have to sprinkle them with sugar. Since they are very delicate and spoil easily, various methods have been devised to preserve them. The best method, supposedly, is to pack them in clay and store them in the cellar. In this way they will keep fresh right into the winter months. There are many varieties of *arboose.* Some have pure white meat, some are yellowish, and others are a pinkish-red. I like these the best, perhaps because of their attractive color.

Besides the sweet fountain of the *arboose,* we must mention the muskmelons. They, too, are produced here in unimaginable quantities. A German

139

colonist from the steppe told me that he first saw this kind of melon being eaten at the table of the King of Württemberg where he happened to be among the spectators. Here on the steppe he could eat as many as his heart desired. These melons are hauled by the wagonload to the market, and it is for us a remarkable sight when one sometimes sees tattered beggars on the street eating muskmelons with their dry bread. However, the muskmelons do not have the excellent quality of the watermelons. It seems that they require more special care and cultivation on the part of the gardeners than they receive here, in order to develop a finer texture and a more delicate flavor.

In the *bashtan* there are also numerous varities of *tickwi* (pumpkins) and gourds. Nowhere have I ever seen them of such size and in such odd shapes. Some of them have an ash-gray color like the steppe oxen and are as big as flour sacks. Others have deep-green stripes, invariably ten in number, on a dark background. Another variety is over an ell (21 inches) long, but only two inches in diameter. Some are distinguished by their small size and have the shape of a pear and the appearance of having been turned out on a lathe; or they have the exact size, form, and hardness of a billiard ball. But other varieties—as though nature wished to play some tricks on us—emulate the color, shape, and size of an orange. The most marvellous type I discovered had a circular flat shape. On the lower side it had the form of a dainty foot and on the topside there were ten identically formed knobs arranged in a circle while at the center there was a larger knob shaped like a handle. All these gourds in contrast to the pumpkins, have a dry woody interior that is not edible. They only serve as novelties and ornaments, and people put them into their china closets, like the Dutch their conch shells. The rest are sold to the children as playthings.

After the pumpkins one must mention the cucumbers which likewise play a significant role in the Russian household. Indeed, it is the favorite vegetable of the Russians. Even among the nobler classes, nothing but cucumbers are served with roast meat. On my travels I have often had to eat cold cucumbers at midnight, because there was nothing else available in the pantry of the wayside inn. The Russians sometimes chide the Greeks as *"sellenoi Grek"* (you grassgreen Greek), because they eat so many raw vegetables. But the epithet is also applicable to the Russians. One often sees women and girls of all classes picking cucumbers in the garden and eating them with pleasure. Similarly, all Russians love to eat raw onions. But there is a difference in the way in which they are eaten. While the Muscovite Russian (der Grossrusse) simply bites into the onion that he is eating with his bread, the Ukrainian slices the onion and puts the slices on his bread. In a Ukrainian cook book there is an onion sauce that is regarded as the queen of all sauces. They crush

140

onions, garlic and pork together, let the mixture melt on the fire, and pour the sauce on all foods that are naturally dry.

The *"Paradeisäpfel"* or *"pommes d'amour"* (tomatoes) thrive in the *bastans* and grow remarkably large and beautiful. Of course, one may often see this fruit in German lands, for instance in the markets of Vienna, but the Viennese "apples of Paradise" are veritable cripples and dwarfs compared with the tomatoes of Odessa and the steppes of Russia. In the fall they are hauled by the wagonboxful to the Odessa market, all of them flawlessly beautiful, bright scarlet-red in hue and bigger than a man's fist.

Everybody eats them here baked in butter, in sauces, in gravies and in soups. They have an excellent though somewhat tart in taste. Just to see this delicious fruit in the market place excites one's appetite and evokes the same kind of joy that one feels in viewing any object that is perfect. Here in Odessa the fruit is generally called *"Pommador,"* an Italian term that is apparently a corruption of the French *"pomme d'amour,"* the apple of love. In all likelihood, it has also a Tartar name. From Russians I also heard the designation *"applitschane,"* namely "apples of China." The German colonists invariably call it *"Paradeisapfel,"* the apple of Paradise.

In addition to all these products, there is also the *baklayan,* the eggplant, which is very often seen in the Odessa market and in all the Tartar markets of the Crimea. It is a dark purplish fruit, similar in shape and size to the cucumber. There is only one way in which it can be eaten, namely filled with minced meat and baked. Thus it consists of vegetable and meat at the same time and is, so to speak, similar to the *pirogi* of the Moscovite Russians.

Of the seed-bearing plants that are grown in the *bashtan,* the most distinguished are definitely the sunflowers. This plant, which is grown only as an ornament back home—to be sure, not a particularly esthetic one—plays a significant role among the inhabitants of the steppe. These people, especially the Ukrainians, have such a nervous restlessness in their teeth that they continually need to have something to munch or to chew, so that not only nuts but also carob pods known as St. John's bread have become important articles of commerce. For this reason the people of the steppe produce large quantities of kernels that they are fond of chewing. To these also belong the sunflower seeds. They are sold on all the street corners and in the villages, along with watermelon and pumpkin seeds. There are market women who deal only in edible seeds.

The people have an amazing skill in separating the sweet kernels from the small shells or husks, and they bite and crack them incessantly the livelong day. To one who believes in the transmigration of souls, it seems clear that the Ukrainians either came from a race of seed-eating birds or will eventually enter the mortal remains of such animals. Even when they are travelling

141

across country they usually take along a large head of sunflower seeds and hold it under one arm while they pick out kernel after kernel with the other.[1]

The sunflower heads grow here to an extraordinary size. In the market place where they are stacked in large piles next to the heaps of melons, I measured some heads that were five feet in circumference. In the gardens the stalks grow as thick as a man's arm and divide into branches that bear from 20 to 30 heads. A *bashtan* is easily recognizable from afar by the yellow sunflowers, for they are the tallest plants in the garden.

Since no perennial plants are produced in the *bashtans,* new gardens have to be established every year. Usually every steppe-dweller has his own *bashtan* near his house or in a nearby field. In the environs of the city, however, the planting of a *bashtan* can be a significant business enterprise, in which Bulgarian settlers are largely involved. These people lease a parcel of land near the city or in the middle of the steppe, provide themselves with the necessary seeds, construct a small garden hut, and begin with their garden work early in April. They usually choose old steppeland that has firm soil, and after having burned off the grass they plant the seeds, each kind at its proper time. The garden area is usually not divided into plots or beds, so that the *bashtan* is the wildest, most variegated garden in the world. The melons are generally planted in the middle, and everywhere between them are sunflowers. On the perimeter they plant rows of onions and sometimes also beets and turnips, and between them cucumbers and *baklayan.* The entire field is bordered with a couple of rows of maize and lentils, or a kind of pepper (perez) whose pods are the chief condiment (paprika!) of the steppe, being used in soups and sauces, and even in brandy. Finally, the perimeter of the *bashtan* is guarded by numerous traps on account of the *suslik,* the steppe-gophers, which are very fond of watermelon seeds.

When all the work is completed, the *bashtaniks* beseech Heaven for early spring rains and dry weather afterwards, and let everything sprout and grow and bloom and ripen. They have very little work to do, for when they are not asleep in their hut they stroll around the *bashtan* merely to guard it. In the late summer when the melons begin to ripen they have to protect them especially from the numerous dogs that roam over the steppe and greedily devour the muskmelons. In the beginning of October the harvest is over and the livestock is free to graze in the *bashtans.* In good years when the moisture and the dryness come at the right time, the *bashtaniks* are well rewarded for

---

[1] The German-Russian settlers on the prairies continued to grow large quantities of sunflowers year after year. The roasted seeds were frequently and profusely chewed ("gekneffert") by young and old during the long winter months, and became widely known as "Russian peanuts."

their efforts. But occasionally they fare badly when there is a crop failure, for the cost of purchasing a large amount of seeds may be quite high.

Maize is, of course, also grown in larger quantities in regular fields. This cereal is sometimes called "Turkish wheat," probably because the Turks first introduced it into the southern steppes of Russia. But the cereal has also other names. The Ukrainians call it *"kukurutz."* To the Moldavians in Bessarabia it is known as *"popescho"* and the German colonists use the term *Welschkorn,* which means as much as "foreign" (Italian) corn. It is extensively grown in South Russia, particularly in Bessarabia, where it is the principal crop and the staple food for man and beast. The stalks and leaves are fed to the livestock and the shredded corn to the barnyard fowl. The people of the steppe eat it in various forms: cooked on the cob and buttered, or roasted. A popular dish is *mamaliga,* a corn mush prepared with butter and eggs. Corn bread is also made, but cannot compare in quality with wheat or rye bread.

2. Labor Services in the Life of the Colonist

It is a well-known fact that the German colonists in Russia were exempt from all military service, a privilege that had been originally granted them by the Empress Catherine II and which was later confirmed by Czar Alexander I. However, as we shall see in the present inquiry, the colonists were not exempt from the statutory labor services that were incumbent on all Russian citizens. This obligation was already clearly stated in Catherine's Manifesto of July 22, 1763, the official text of which was printed by the Senate and distributed to the resident ministers and emigration agents in Germany. The two pertinent passages read as follows:

7. Solche in Russland sich niedergelassenen Ausländer sollen während der ganzen Zeit ihres Hierseins, ausser dem gewöhnlichen Land-Dienste, wider Willen weder in Militär noch Civil-Dienst genommen werden; ja auch zur Leistung dieses Land-Dienstes soll keines eher als nach Verfliessung obenangesetzten Freyjahre verbunden seyen.
8. Nach Verfliessung obenangestzter Freyjahre sind alle in Russland sich niedergelassene Ausländer verpflichtet, die gewöhnlichen und mit gar keiner Beschwerlichkeit verknüpft. Abgiften zu entrichten, und gleich unsern andern Unterthanen, Landes-Dienste leisten."

In my translation of Catherine's Manifesto, which was included in Dr. K. Stumpp's "The German Emigration to Russia," and which seems to have been the first English text to appear in print, I rendered the two passages as follows:

7. The foreigners who have settled in Russia shall not be drafted against their will into the military or the civil service during their entire stay here. Only after the lapse of the years of tax exemption can they be required to provide labor service for the country.

8. After the lapse of the stipulated years of exemption, all the foreigners who have settled in Russia are required to pay moderate contributions (taxes) and, like all our other subjects, to provide labor services for the country."

Since the appearance of that translation the meaning of the term, *Landes-Dienst*—which I had interpreted as "labor service for the country,"—has been variously construed by other translators as "military service" or as "duties of administrations to the country" (Landesverwaltungspflichten). However, these interpretations do not only stand in flat contradiction to the context, but also lack the confirmative evidence of historical fact. On the other hand, my own interpretation had been corroborated by the noted German-Russian historian, Dr. Josef Malinowski, who paraphrased the term *"Landesdienst"* (in the Rescript of Alexander I, published Feb. 20, 1804) as *"Tragung des Landeslasten,"* the bearing of onerous tasks for the country.

What is more important from the historical point of view is that his interpretation, like my own, is solidly confirmed by the *Colonist Codex,* which has a special section under the rubric, *Allgemeine Landschaftsnaturalverpflichtungen der Kolonisten.* (Chap. 2. Sec. 2). These "General natural obligations to the country" are precisely the labor services mentioned in the manifestoes of Catherine and Alexander. The *Colonist Codex* deals with the following statutory labor services:

1. The construction and maintenance of roads, bridges, and dams. The colonists are required to work on those sections of highways that traverse the land area of a particular community.

2. In accord with the stipulation of Catherine's Manifesto, the colonists are required to provide lodging for a night to soldiers who were passing through on the line of march.

3. The furnishing of vehicles for the transportation of public officials and also for the delivery of official letters or packages from village to village could also be demanded. The Czar, of course, had the prerogative of commanding any kind of natural service, such as the transportation of soldiers and provisions in case of emergencies—such as war, epidemics, natural disasters—for the regional or general welfare of the country.

In view of the nature of these services, it becomes evident that the *Landesdienste* must be interpreted as "regional or provincial" labor services. This interpretation receives additional confirmation from the Russian term *sluzhby zemskiya,* which was used in the original Russian text of the Manifesto. The noun *sluzhby* means service work, labor. The term *zemskiya,* with the base *zemlya* (land) is an adjective related to *zemstvo,* which denoted, in Czarist times, the district or municipal government. Hence, it would at least be co-extensive with *volost* or even *gubernie.*

In time of war, the colonists of a certain region would be obliged like all other Russian subjects, to perform certain services in support of the military forces mobilized in that region. Fortunately, we do not have to speculate on this matter, for the noted German-Russian historian, Conrad Keller, has given us a most graphic ten-page account of the *Frohnen* (servile labor) and *Leistungen* (achievements) that were provided by the German colonists of South Russia during the Russo-Turkish War of 1828 and the Crimean War of 1853-1856.

We are informed that Czar Nicholas I declared war against Turkey on April 14, 1828 and that 130,000 Russian soldiers marched to the southern border where preparations for military operations had already been completed. In the early part of February, the Czar had confirmed the proposal of the Minister of Public Domains and issued the order that all German colonists participate in a general effort to help with the transportation of troops in the event of a possible emergency. Accordingly, the Colonist Welfare Committee ordained that all the German colonists in the southern area had to equip a certain number of wagons, horses, and teamsters, according to specifications laid down by the government. The wagons, for example, had to be the sturdy, iron-axled colonist wagons, also known as the Hungarian or Molotchna wagons. The teamsters had to take along a supply of new clothes, a sheepskin sleeping blanket, and provisions for two weeks.

The district of Grossliebental had to furnish 18 wagon transports, and a comparable number were provided by the Kutschurgan and the Beresan colonists. The colonists were assured that the government would compensate them for the use of the wagons and the cost of equipping them, by deducting the total cost from their tax assessment. The average cost of furnishing a wagon transport was 250 rubles. All vehicles had to appear fully equipped in the village of Grossliebental on February 10, 1828. From the fact that the wagons had to have a load capacity of 1,200 pounds, it appears that they were used to haul military equipment and provisions.

Keller's report of the *Leistungen* of the colonists during the Crimean War is even more informative. On March 2, 1855, the president of the colonist Welfare Committee, Baron Mestmacher, issued the following significant

145

ordinance: "For the prompt evacuation of the hospitals which are over-crowded with sick soldiers, bases are to be established in various localities for a certain number of transport vehicles, so that the sick can be continuously moved from base to base until they reach a determined destination. The colonists are called upon to provide the transportation, since they alone possess the necessary horse-drawn vehicles and the most comfortable wagons. Consequently, after determining that 30 vehicles are to be provided by the colonists of Liebental, the Committee ordains the following:

1. The vehicles must be equipped without delay. On every vehicle there must be a linen cover mounted over hoops for the protection of the sick against bad weather and the heat.
2. A village elder must be selected to accompany the vehicles and be responsible for the maintaining order and the necessary maintenance of the vehicles.
3. The vehicles are to be stationed at the bases in the towns of Cherson and Berislav, according as they are needed. For the present however, they are to be sent direct to Berislav.
4. For each vehicle with teamster, a monthly payment of 75 rubles in silver has been determined, with the condition that the colonist will not fail to provide a continuous supply of 30 vehicles.
5. After arriving at the designated base, the vehicles will come under the management of the director of the hospital, and the teamsters will be subject to orders of the officers who accompany the transport of the sick soldiers. However, in the case of arising grievances, the teamsters must communicate with the Colonial Inspector Chernawsky who is permanently stationed in Cherson and has received the necessary orders in this regard.

The cost of equipping a transport team amounted to about 145 rubles, which was paid by the government. The wagon train bearing the wounded troops arrived in Odessa in the beginning of March. From there it proceeded on the main road to Nikolaiev and reached Cherson on the 21st of March. At the same time the Kutschurgan and Beresan colonists arrived with 40 wagons bearing sick soldiers. After inspecting the wagon trains, the local governor extended friendly greetings to the German teamsters and remarked. "Your vehicles are excellent and everything is in good order. I thank you."

While the men were occupied with the task of transporting the sick and the wounded, the womenfolk back home were busy for four straight weeks baking biscuits (Zwieback) for the military. In the village of Josephstal, which had only a population of 725, the women baked 582 *pud* (i.e. 23,280 lbs.) of biscuit rations and donated an additional 60 *pud* (or 2,400 lbs.) to the government. The amount of labor provided by the German colonists of South Russia in the years 1854 and 1855 can perhaps be roughly estimated from the statistics that are available for the colony of Josephstal. This village provided 67 transport trips for troops passing through the region, 404 trips for troops who were stationed in other localities, 67 transport trips for hauling heavy baggage, 46 trips to haul flour for the baking of the biscuits, 238 trips to haul lumber and fascines for the construction of bridges, and 317 trips to transport wounded soldiers. The village also provided billeted soldiers with heated quarters for a total of 1,769 days.

In summing up the *Leistungen* of the colonists of Josephstal, Fr. Keller makes the significant observation: "In those years the colonists had a hard time. Scarcely a day passed on which the bailiff did not order every householder to perform some sort of *Frondienst* (statutory labor service) or some other task for the military. In the Beresan colonies, it happened that those men who had assumed all the labor services and the expenditures were given a grant of 60 dessiatines (i.e. 160 acres) of farmland."

The Czar and his government fully appreciated the contributions and achievements of the German colonists and publicly recognized the substantial services to the country. Several mayors and a goodly number of individual colonists who had distinguished themselves by extraordinary dedication and enterprise were awarded diplomas of commendation, golden or silver medals "for zeal," or gold watches valued at 80 or 100 rubles. The German districts of Chortitza, Mariupol, and Berdyansk were each awarded a certificate of highest commendation, in which the Czar stated: "After His Majesty the Emperor read the report that the Mennonite and other German communities of Chortitza, Mariupol and Berdyansk had exhibited their devotion and allegiance, in the course of the present war, through their contribution of money and their warm-hearted hospitality to the wounded soldiers by providing them with free board and lodging at the expense of the community, His Supreme Majesty is pleased to ordain as follows: In view of the exemplary zeal shown by the above-named districts, they shall be rewarded by the presentation of a special document which will serve as an eternal testimonial of their praiseworthy deed of magnanimity."

On July 7, 1858, the Colonist Welfare Office announced that the Imperial government had invited representatives of the colonies to attend the coronation ceremony of the new Emperor, Alexander II. The three representatives were Johann Kraus, chief mayor of the Liebental district; David Friesen of the Mennonite Molotchna district; and Michael Malina of Belgrad. After their arrival in Moscow the representatives were received by Count Kisselev, Minister of Imperial Domains, who thanked the German colonists of South

Russia for their services during the recent war, and added, "His Majesty the late Czar Nicholas thought of you before his death and told me that he did not have enough words to express his gratitude to you for all the services you rendered."

The representatives were given seats of honor at the coronation services, and the following day they were introduced to the new Emperor, who addressed them with the words: "I thank you sincerely for your zeal and your devotion. You have demonstrated both of these virtues in an unusual degree during the recent war. I am convinced that you will continue to render your dedication to me in the future. Pray to God that he may support me and my work. I shall also pray for you. Bring this message to your brothers, to all the colonists."

On September 1, all the chief mayors who were present were awarded silver and gold medals. The representatives were then sent on a four-day tour of St. Petersburg, to see the enchanting sights of that magnificent city. During an imperial dinner in one of the salons of the Kreml, Czar Alexander rose to drink a toast to the health of his subjects, to which the delegates replied by shouting a three-fold "Hurrah!"

The gracious reception accorded the colonist delegates by the Czar and his government remained a proud, unforgettable event. In those days, nobody in Russia had any doubts or misgivings about the patriotism and loyalty of the German colonists.

3. Colonist Impact on the Russian Peasant

By J. G. Kohl (1838)

The German colonists were brought into New Russia for a twofold reason: first, to promote agriculture on the steppe and to serve as a model for the neighboring Russians in several ways, particularly in the adoption of better methods of farming; and secondly, to provide the vast empty steppe with inhabitants and to obtain good and useful citizens for the Empire.

The question has, naturally, been raised whether the colonists have fulfilled the expectations that were entertained. Regarding the first point, some people are of the opinion that the German settlers have not been effective as educators of the Russians. The Russian, it is said, hates the Germans and this alone prevents him from emulating them. In addition, the Russian peasant is so attached to traditional habits that he seldom or never decides to do anything that differs from the way it was done by his *pradi*, his forefathers.

148

By and large, this may well be true, for in the first place all nationalities generally tend to repel each other; consequently also the Russians and the Germans. Secondly, it is very difficult to teach a people or an ethnic group to be different than it is. The Russian simply does not possess the industrious disposition to improve and perfect himself, and this quality cannot be instilled into him by any German. One would have to infuse into him a different kind of blood, which is impossible. However, in this situation everything depends upon the degree of hatred as well as the degree of indolence, and if some influence, however slight, occurs, one is not justified in saying that there is none whatsoever. We do not presume to decide this question, but we would like to adduce some simple but significant observations that we have been able to make concerning this point.

The hatred of the Russians does not appear to me to be so ardent that they would, for that reason, despise and reject everything that comes from the Germans. In actual fact, this hate very rarely finds expression in overt action, since the Russian peasant never gets in the way of the Germans; recognizing their superiority, he almost always yields the road to them. Even the Russian saying, *"Tak i Niemetzi sdälayut"* (that's the way the Germans do it), which I have heard on several occasions, seems to refute the opinion that the Russians will not adopt anything at all from the Germans.

The attachment of the Malorussian ("Ukrainian") peasant to his traditional ways is understandably very strong, just as it is in the common man everywhere, and when one travels through the villages that lie close to the German colonies, it does not *seem* that any improvement or change has taken place in the construction of their houses, the raising of their livestock, or the maintenance of their fields and gardens, in comparison with distant Russian villages. However, to discover such changes, one must do more investigating than is possible by simply passing through the villages.

—Translated by J. S. H.

4. The Germans in the Soviet Union

By Aleksandr Solzhenitsyn

Among all the deportees, the Germans were particularly hard-working. They checked off their former way of life as something irrevocable, for what kind of homeland did they really have on the Volga or on the Manitch? Just as they had formerly grown into the land that the Empress Catherine II had allotted to them, so they now became inured to Stalin's harsh, barren tracts, and they gave themselves up to the earth of the banished exiles as to something definitive and inexorable. They established themselves, not provisionally until the next amnesty or the first czarist favor, but for always.

Deported in 1941, naked and destitute, but thrifty and indefatigable, they did not despair but began, even here, to work methodically and rationally. Where on earth is there a desert which the Germans could not transform into a flourishing landscape? It was not just an empty phrase when people in Czarist times used to say: "The German is like a willow; no matter in what direction he is bent, he always takes root." Whether they worked in the mines, or at the machine and tractor stations, or in the state-owned collective farms, the managing foreman could never praise the Germans enough, for there were no better workers. In the fifties the Germans—living among the other deportees or among the native population—had the most durable, the most spacious and cleanest houses, the largest hogs, and the most productive milch cows. And the daughters grew up as most desirable brides, not because their parents happened to be well-to-do, but because of their personal purity and strict morality in the midst of a frivolous, easy-going camp environment.

—Translated from ARCHIPEL GULAG III, p. 419.

IX.   Reports and Reminiscences

1. The Trek of the Hoffnungsfelder

by Johannes Lutz

On Sunday, March 12, 1944 all was calm and quiet as usual; no one had any premonition of things to come.

Early Monday morning someone knocked at the window, and I got up and walked over. It was my brother Gottlieb. He said anxiously: "Get up quickly and get your wagon ready; we have to leave! Everything will be explained at the town hall meeting at 10 o'clock."

We got up without delay and set to work. First we emptied all the drawers on the floor, so that we could get a better idea what things to select. Clothes, bedding, and shoes were all sorted out and packed into bags. The less useful things we gave away to the Russians who had already arrived on the scene. It was now a matter of preparing the provisions for the long and distant journey. Some 20 loaves of bread were baked, 15 chickens slaughtered, roasted, and packed with lard in big cans. Jars were filled with cooking oils and grease; the smoked hams were wrapped up. Whoever still had pigs slaughtered them at once. One or two sacks of flour were loaded on the wagon. Our farm wagons were fitted out with huts made of plywood, tin, canvas, or untanned hides. Some people traded their cows for Russian horses. Toward noon the Russians were already dragging away the furniture and other household items.

At ten all the men assembled in the town hall, where the route was discussed. Every wagon was assigned a number, and the whole village was divided into 18 groups. In case of emergency on the road, the respective group had to help their people. Our group (trek) had number 403, and every group had a leader. People who had no vehicle were divided among the other wagons. Old people and families with small children had to travel by train, and were taken to the railway station at Weseli-Kut.

The weather was wet and clammy as our wagon trains started out on March 19. Ten men had to remain behind to guard the village, until the retreating German Wehrmacht arrived. Large quantities of wine, grain, livestock, bees, household and farm equipment were left behind. Many people tied a cow to their wagon, and took her along.

The following day we reached *Klein-Neudorf,* where the people were already gone. On the third day, while we were on the way to Tiraspol, we had a hard time making it up a steep hill near the village of Grebenich, and had to hitch double teams of horses. When we arrived in the city of Tiraspol on the Dniester it was raining, and we slept on our wagons during the

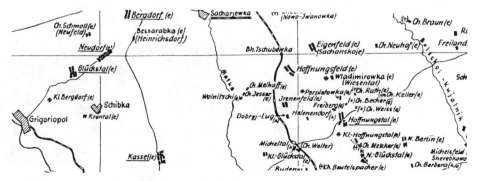

Area map of Glückstal and Hoffnungstal colonies.   Courtesy of Dr. K. Stumpp

Fateful journey

night. In the morning we crossed the Dniester bridge and stopped at *Bendery,* where we had to obtain Rumanian money to purchase the provisions and the fodder we needed. From Bendery to Kauschani (Bessarabia) we were caught in a violent rainstorm and got soaking wet. In *Kauschani* all accommodations were overcrowded, and we had difficult time finding a room or a barn for the night. Many people caught a cold that night and fell ill. The next day we had fine weather, and we stayed an extra day to dry out our clothes.

On March 25 we came to *Kubei,* where we stayed for 2 days because of high wind and intense cold. At *Gaghusen,* whose inhabitants were Christian Turks, we obtained lodging. We slept 3 families in a small room that was nice and warm. At the neighbor's place I obtained shelter for the horses, and the man asked merely for a piece of soap for looking after them. Our wagon stood out in the yard, and was not guarded. But a certain Schaffert from Weseli-Kut was robbed of all his clothes, even while he was sleeping in the wagon. We were well treated by the Moldavian people; the only bad thing was that we also got a lot of lice into the bargain.

On March 27 we came to *Borodino,* a former German colony. The village was empty, for the Bessarabian Germans had of course already moved away in 1940. The village presented a dreary

Women preparing supper

152

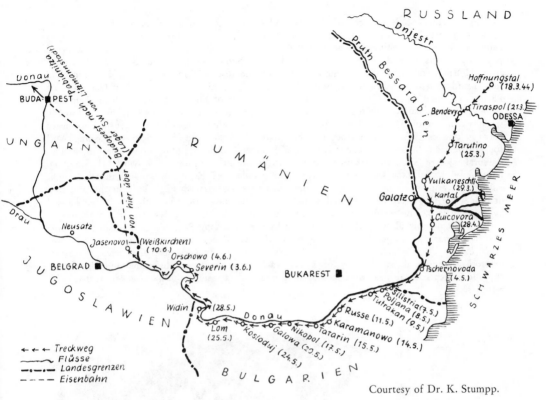

sight. Now and then we met a Karpatho-Ukrainian who had moved here in 1940. He was quite content to live the kitchen, for he didn't need the big house.

The next day we drove through *Beresina,* formerly a sizable German village, and came to *Tarutino,* a market town that used to have a large German Gymnasium (high school), and a girl's lyceum. In this town we bought some hay and corn from the fleeing Rumanians. The following day we came to *Posttal,* where we stayed overnight in an empty house whose windows were boarded shut. In the barns the mangers had been removed, so that we had to drive stakes into the ground to tie up our horses. We seldom met any people. We made beds of straw on the floor, and slept well. The women cooked in the yard. A hole was dug in the ground, stones piled around it, and a kettle placed on top. As we were driving through the village of *Württemberg,* a Moldavian passed out wine by the roadside; probably, he was also about to flee. On the stretch to Vulkaneschti many cars of the Wehrmacht roared past us. It was a lamentable situation, for many horses shied, ran off the road, and dumped the wagons in the ditch. I often witnessed such incidents.

For three and a half weeks (from April 1—25) we remained in *Vulkaneschti,* a large Moldavian village. We stayed here for such a long time because the Rumanians refused to let us travel through their country. The leader of our trek, Mr. Weingärtner, made many trips to Galatz and Bucharest to negotiate with the Rumanian authorities. On one occasion he was told that we had to give up 8 cows, in order to obtain a transit permit. In Vulkaneschti a very large number of German refugees had come together, namely the people from Hoffnungstal, Berlin, Sachansk, Neu-Glückstal, Neu-Sawitz, Klein-Neudorf, Kassel, and others. Since the people had money and the wine was cheap, there was a lot of drinking. The women had the time and opportunity to bake bread. Livestock was slaughtered and the meat sold. Weingärtner collected the money, so that there might be less drinking. People who had brought along cows

153

sold milk. Others sold yard goods, clothing, hides, etc. I sold material for a shirt for 5 liters of wine. A regular German market developed in Vulkaneschti. One yard where we stopped belonged to a rich Moldavian who had fled. He left behind many wagonloads of grain and potatoes, so that we and our horses suffered no want. Soon cases of typhus occurred. A woman from Hoffnungstal, Elisabeth Erlenbusch, died of the disease. Lina Harsch of Hoffnungsfeld fell ill and had to be taken to the hospital; she recovered, and found us later in Germany. At Easter we buried August Fichtner and Dorothea Krenzler of Hoffnungsfeld; both of them died from colds they had contracted in Kauschani. The people were hardly back from the funeral, when we heard of a third death. Woldemar Wall, of Hoffnungsfeld, was crushed to death between two cars. A German truck had halted on the road, and the driver was asking Wall for information. Suddenly a car driven by a Rumanian came speeding down the hill, and as the brakes were gone, the car smashed into the truck in front of which Wall was standing. Every day the military was in retreat, and our people were becoming worried that we might not get away in time. One day some Germans from Odessa came through Vulkaneschti and told us that while they were being ferried across the Dniester near Akkerman they were bombarded by the Russians. The people of Selz fared even worse, for after a few wagons were ferried across the remaining 60 wagons were captured by the advancing Russians. In Landau the people also had a narrow escape. A part of the population could not get any wagons, and had to be taken out by German aircraft, since the Russians were already very near. One evening we saw fireworks hanging above the city of Galatz, and soon there was lightning and thunderous explosions. Russian airmen were bombarding the railway station which was crowded with refugees.

Westward trek

The ten men who had remained behind to guard our village now arrived and told us what had happened back home. Military trains had stopped above the village, and German soldiers hauled out barrels of wine and loaded them. The remaining barrels they shot full of holes and flooded the cellars with wine. Fleeing Cossacks had come into the village, where they rounded up cows and steers and chickens, emptied the bee hives, and loaded up flour, grain, bicycles, etc. We were also told about those of our people who left by train. They had departed from Wesely-Kut about a week after we left, and travelled via Rasdelnaya to Bendery, where they were left waiting for a long time. It came to the point that they had to give bribes to the Rumanian railway officials before they could continue their journey. In Beresina the rain again stopped for a time, and Russian flyers dropped bombs during the night. Fortunately, they didn't hit anything.

At long last we were informed that we should get our wagons trains ready to continue our journey. We thought that the route would lead through Galatz and Rumania, but this plan failed. We were detoured to the south and were to drive through the Dobrudscha. After a day's journey we came to *Karagatsch* on Lake Kahul, where we remained for two days. I took my wagon to the local smith to have a broken wagon tongue repaired. On April 1 we reached *Kartal* on the Danube. We stayed here for a whole week, waiting for the arrival of the German Pioneers (soldiers) with the ferry that would take us across the river. With the Moldavian people of Karagatsch we celebrated *Provody,* the Feast of the Dead, and went to the cemetery, where the people were served wine and food. Soon after that some of our men played a stupid prank. In the yard of the village *pope* (priest) stood a wagon loaded with a barrel of wine, which he had prepared for his flight. The wine tempted several men, and during the night they hauled away several pailfuls. On a return trip the limp-footed Leonhardt Harsch was caught, and the next day there was a big scandal. For the stolen wine the *pope* had to be paid 10 kilograms of honey and a leg of ham. And each of the five culprits received several whacks on the seat of his pants.

In the beginning of May the German Pioneers finally arrived and laid a pontoon across an arm of the river right up to the Danube. We began to cross over on the 4th of May. The ferry consisted of two large boats that were lashed together side by side and covered with a big platform which offered room for 80 wagons with their teams of horses. At the front a tugboat was hooked up, which hauled the ferry across the river. In Kartal the Rumanian posted themselves on the road, searched every wagon as it drove up to the ferry, and confiscated all weapons. After the people in each wagon were counted, we drove on the platform, and were

Woman leading team

transported to the other shore, to the *Dobrudscha,* a part of Rumania. Outside the little town of *Isaktschewo* I met my brother Gottlieb, who had sustained a broken axle on his wagon. He remained behind with Wilhelm Fichtner, who had a broken wheel, and the two of them had repairs made by the local blacksmith. They again caught up with us a week later by driving mostly at night, for in the daytime one could not pass the long wagon trains of other refugees. At each village we passed through we were accosted by Rumanian soldiers who kept hurrying us onward. We were not permitted to make a stop before nightfall. They certainly took much care to get rid of us as quickly as possible. In the next few days we came through *Tschukurowo, Toporul,* and other villages. I was struck by the fact that many Russians were living in these localities, and discovered that they were descendants of Russian soldiers who had remained behind after the campaigns against the Turks. Also Saporoshian Cossacks had settled here, after Catherine II expelled them from the Saporoshian Setch.

Stalled in the mire

On May 11 we came to *Chernowody*, where we stayed for two days. Under the pretext of "air attacks" we were not permitted to stop in the little town, but had to remain in an open field, 4 km. away. The women and children huddled in the wagon-huts; the men remained on their feet. In the morning several men rode into town to get short feed and grain which had been purchased by the trek leader. Our horses were beginning to limp, and we had to decide to shoe them. I drove to the local smith, but could get only one horse shod, because he had no more nails. After a day's journey we reached the Bulgarian border, and stayed overnight in the open. The next morning, May 13, we entered the Bulgarian town of *Silistria*. The police stood off to the side and watched with curiosity. They did not even bother to ask about our passports. As we drove through the town we were greeted in a very friendly manner. Many people hurried into the shops, bought bread, and handed it to us in the wagons. They also gave us marmelade, tomatoes, and braided clusters of onions. Here we also came across many Turkish settlements, and everywhere we saw teams of buffalo. The Bulgarian horse-drawn wagons of light construction were beautifully painted, and adorned with pictures. If there was a lot of wine in Rumania, there was a great deal more here. Wherever you turned, you saw a wine tavern. The wine was of good quality, inexpensive, and generally spiced with red paprika. There was also plenty of tobacco, and it was of excellent quality. Our men bought many cartons of cigarettes. We asked some German soldiers what we should buy here, to take with us to Germany. They replied, "Buy cooking fat, eggs, and cigarettes; there's a shortage of these items in Germany." I had bad luck with eggs I had purchased. I had exchanged clothing for the eggs, and put them under the wagon for the night. There they were ruined by a dog, and partly eaten. I was able to obtain butter and lard in exchange for a record player.

On May 14 we came to *Tutrakan*. The road kept running along the Danube. Here we were supposed to obtain short feed, but we waited for it in vain, while a whole week went by. Lively bartering developed between us and the Bulgarians. Buyers kept coming around, asking for bicycles, radios, phonographs, cameras, and the like. I sold my camera for 2,000 lei. Especially hides for shoes and sandals were in great demand. I removed the hides from our wagon-hut and replaced them with mats. For two untanned hides I received 4,000 lei. For a radio I could have gotten 10,000 lei. One could buy bread in the bakeshops. A rich Bulgarian gave us potatoes, cabbages, and sour vegetables.

Every day we went down to the Danube to bathe, for the weather was already quite hot. On Sunday the young Bulgarians danced in the public square, and we watched them with intense curiosity.

On May 21 we came to *Russe*, a beautiful large town. The trees were in full bloom and enhanced the gardens around the pretty houses. We drove through the town and stopped outside, for here we had to obtain bread and fodder. During the next few days we passed through six localities: *Schischtschow, Nikolop, Orechowo, Koslodui, Lom*, and *Vidin*, where we again crossed the Danube and found ourselves back in Rumania. The weather grew warmer every day, and the heat and the dust became a torment. It was sheer drudgery to stand in line to get water from the well or to obtain fodder for our horses. A severe test of endurance was sustained by our boys and girls who drove the cows. Some of them had led their cow on a rope all the way from home as far as Serbia. All the cows were eventually driven, because we were able to graze them, but this caused some damage, and also revealed the direction our trek had taken. The wagon trains usually stopped for the night in places where the ground contained many holes, or where stones and ashes could be found. While we were stopping on the bank of the Isker, two girls, Elvira Zweygardt and Alisse Harsch almost drowned while bathing. Walter Fichtner pulled them both out by their hair.

In *Kosloduj*, where we stopped for two days, I obtained lodging in the home of a Rumanian. He wanted to trade some whiskey for my woolen jacket, whereas I wanted some butter or lard, but nothing came of the deal. While the exterior of the houses in this town did not make a bad impression, there was nothing to the interior; it didn't even contain a stove. The people simply hung a kettle on a hook in one corner of the room, and built a fire on the floor, while the smoke escaped through a hole in the roof. Bread was baked in a most curious fashion. A large stone that was hollowed out like a bowl was placed over the fire. When the stone was hot enough it was removed and placed upside down over the lump of dough until it was baked. Our next stop was at *Lom*, where the army distributed provisions and fodder to our group. We received 35 varieties of food, including such staples as flour, bread, tea, coffee, sugar, and butter; also canned meats and vegetables, dried fruit, pastries, and cigarettes. Everthing was distributed fairly, but the individual portions were rather small.

On May 30 we crossed the Danube from *Vidin* to *Kalafat* (Rumania). As we came near the little town, there was an air-raid alarm and we hid in the greenery. While we were stopping in the woods we built a fire to cook dinner. Suddenly we had a downpour that extinguished the fire. "Now the 'Strudel' are ruined," my wife said sadly. However, I set about to chop some dry wood for a new fire, and finished cooking the "strudel," which we ate with a hearty appetite. We grazed our horses in the woods. We also leased a meadow from a man, mowed it, and distributed the hay.

On June 8 we drove through *Turnu-Severin*, a city which had been damaged by air strikes. Soon afterwards we reached *Orsowa*, where we camped in a forest and distributed provisions and fodder. Nearby was the *"Iron Gate,"* where the Danube plunges through the narrow gorge of the Carpathian mountain range. British planes coming from Italy bombarded our trek, but did little damage. In the Neusatzer trek the horses became frightened and bolted, but no one was injured. The stretch Orsowa to *Basias* ran along overhanging cliffs. To avoid the risk of running into Tito's partisans, we travelled at night, with our wagons 20 yards apart, in case we should be fired upon. We now reached the border of *Yugoslavia*. Here we were again counted. After by-passing the German village of *Weisskirchen*, we came into the transit camp at *Yassenovo* in Serbia, not far from Belgrade. It was the 12th of June — 14 weeks and 2 days after our departure from Hoffnungsfeld. After going through the delousing station, we were put up in the camp, where we stayed for a week. We received good meals, took care of our horses, and packed our belongings into crates, for from here we were to continue our journey by train. We had to give up our horses, wagons, and cows, and were given an official receipt. The best horses were later loaded into trains and transported into the Warthegau (Poland). One of our men who took care of the horses en route had an unfortunate mishap. While he was asleep on the floor, a horse stepped on his chest and fractured some of his ribs. My sister Maria also suffered a serious accident. She was collecting wood to start a fire. While she was trying to break up some barrel staves that were lying about, a stave snapped back and struck her eye. She was immediately taken to the hospital and operated on, but she lost the eye. She was then brought to Würzburg in Germany until the healing was complete. Meanwhile we travelled to the Warthegau, and it took a long time until she found us again.

On June 18 the people from our village were put on two trains, and we departed. We travelled via *Budapest*, and stopped for some time at the station. I bought half a liter of whiskey for 20 Reichsmark, and a liter of wine for 10 RM. These were indeed different prices from those in Bulgaria! The following evening we stopped in *Ratibor* (upper Silesia) and the next stop was *Litzmannstadt* (Polish Lodz), where we again had to go to a delousing station.

157

On June 22 we came to *Tulischau*, in the district of Turek, and were quartered in a camp established in a school building for three weeks. We received good meals, slept on straw beds, and were able to rest up. The camp leader was a schoolteacher named Schlämer. He and commissioner Sorger resettled us in the surrounding villages. Through the mediation of our Landsmann Dr. Georg Leibbrandt, the other group of Hoffnungsfelder from the second train were also settled among us. But the men were soon being drafted into the Wehrmacht, while the women and children remained behind. Their road of tribulation was soon to begin in grim earnest.

In January of 1945 the critical moment approached. The Soviet front kept coming closer, and on January 19 we had to flee once more from the Russians. But this time we had no horses, and many of our people could not get away. Only one-third succeeded in making their way to the West; two-thirds were captured by the advancing Soviet army, and in the fall of 1945 all of them were sent in cattle cars to Siberia and the primeval forest of Northern Russia.

2. Christmas in a Soviet Slave Labor Camp
by Leo Ochs

In the German colonies on the steppe, *Weihnachten* with its *Christbaum* and *Christkindlein* had always been a season of great joy, blessed peace, and spiritual exaltation. But this high festival, like all the others of Christian tradition, was to be radically expunged from the Soviet calendar, and replaced by a day of work. However, even though Stalin and his atheist henchmen succeeded in closing the churches, silencing the bells, and extinguishing the candle-lit Christmas tree, they could not destroy the spirit of Christmas in the hearts of the faithful. That spirit survived even in the prisons, dungeons, and slave labor camps of the Soviet paradise, as can be seen from the moving account of the German-Russian refugee Leo Oks of Kleinliebental, a former inmate of such a camp. In this account, originally written under the title *"Weihnachten fern von der Heimat"*, the author states:

"Like all the other days in the Soviet labor camps, the 24th of December began with the sound of reveille.

The barracks of the camp headquarters stood right next to the gate of the compound, behind the twelve-foot-high wooden wall crowned by strands of barbed wire. Here the commandant and his staff of officers lived and worked. In front of the barracks hung a piece of iron rail, and at 5 o'clock the HQ orderly came out into the pitch darkness and the prevailing December cold, and roused the camp inmates from their sleep by pounding the primitive gong with a heavy hammer. The dull sounds, eerily reminiscent of an alarm or cries of distress, penetrated slowly and hoarsely the raw hoarfrost of the arctic air and seeped into the 16 snow-covered barracks which stood, eight in a row, on both sides of the compound. The inmates of the camp — prisoners, exiles, deportees, and civilian internees from every ethnic group in Europe — lay on crude wooden bunks that rose in three tiers and extended some 150 feet along the length of both walls. On the bare, lice-infested bunks the inmates used their clothes to provide themselves with mattresses, pillows, bed sheets, and blankets.

As soon as the sound of the gong reached the ear of the camp warder — a strong, healthy Russian worker from the east — he roused the dead-tired and debilitated sleepers with the repulsive, soul-wrenching cry: *"Podyom,"* — Get up! In 15 minutes every inmate who was

Soviet slave labor camp in the area of Archangelsk

alive and able to walk (almost every night some had died in their bunks) had to be sitting on the edge of his bunk, ready for roll call the moment the camp officer appeared. If the number of inmates checked out, and no one was missing, all who could walk were marched off, in separate groups, to the mess hall for breakfast. As quickly as possible, they all received and consumed their bread ration for the day, namely a pound of soggy rye, and their bowl of *balanda*, a gruel of cabbage leaves and fish bones. Then the men were marched, in groups of six, to the exit gate, where they were checked and frisked before a dozen and more escort guards equipped with tommy guns and big sheepdogs, conducted the column to their ten or twelve hours of work. After reaching the work area, everyone was assigned to his brigade — a work force of 15—20 men supervised by armed escort guards.

Like all the preceding 360 days, the morning of this day went by without any notable incidents. However, as we gazed towards the east we could see the distinguishing traits of the long-awaited coming day. The brightly glittering stars gradually began to pale and very soon they were blotted out by the golden rays of the rising sun.

As we had all wished, the sun rose bright and clear, and all the clouds disappeared from the sky. The air became strangely transparent. That was a good sign, and we all heaved a deep sigh of relief.

Not a breath of wind stirred, and the blue sky radiated a wondrous ethereal purity that filled our wounded hearts. And in our great misery, aggravated by hunger and cold, we rejoiced in the depths of our souls to have lived to see the day on which Christ was born for us. While we worked in deep silence, we summoned our last reserves of strength, so that we would not have to do overtime. But the day was very long and never seemed to end, and when the end came we were utterly exhausted.

The afternoon gradually merged into evening. The sun disappeared in the West, where our thoughts continued to linger. The darkness from the East was already covering the whole sky. It grew dark again, and the stars gazed so delightfully but coldly upon the earth.

Closely watched by the escort guards, we trudged with weary footsteps through the crunching snow to the general assembling place. Strengthened by some invisible power, as though on winged footsteps, we proceeded faster than usual on our way home — to the camp. But several weaker men fell behind, and we had to slow down our pace.

After the roll call and the supper — a single bowl of sour cabbage broth — five of us who had our bunks in one corner of the barracks sat down together in a circle, and celebrated Christmas Eve. We celebrated the long-awaited first Holy Night, but only in our hearts, in memory of the beautiful Christmases we had enjoyed while we were still living in freedom. It was a Christmas Eve without a Christmas tree, without sweetmeats and gifts, a Christmas far from home in an alien, desolate place. In whispering tones we sang "Silent night, holy night," and told one another the stories of Christmas in our childhood, and our souls were flooded with the warm glow of joyfulness, love, and happiness that relieved all our sorrows and doubts, our lack of faith and poverty of heart. Peace of soul and a childlike faith was enkindled within us. We wondered about the animals who, it was believed, were able to speak to each other in their stable on Christmas Eve, about the lambs who kept softly bleating: "Bethlehem, Bethlehem," about the place where St. Nickolas lived, and how he always managed to fulfill all the children's dearest wishes.

Shortly before the *Otboi*, the ten-o'clock signal for "lights out," was to be given, we walked outside the barracks and gazed out to the West, towards home where the sun would now be still shining and where relatives and friends would perhaps at the very moment be also gazing to the East and thinking of those who were deported or missing or who had already perished; and we hoped that our gaze and theirs would meet on some distant star or planet. But no one heard our weeping and pleading which was like that of a small child who had lost its mother. No one knew of the conversations of our bruised hearts and grief-stricken souls.

We returned to the barracks, happy and content to have lived to see the day of the Savior's birth. We also kept hoping for a salvation. It came later, but it came. We spent the following day, December 25 — Christmas Day — just as we had spent all the other days of our banishment. Only one peculiarity was noticeable: the number of camp guards was doubled, and the work quota for the day was increased."

160

3. A Mother Returns from Siberia

A report by Wolfgang Meyer. Translated by Jos. S. Height

After spending 30 years in a Siberian labor camp, a mother was again able to embrace her only son. The 69-year-old Maria Burghart, who is now living with her son Alexander in Gieboldehausen, near Göttingen, weeps alternately for joy over her reunion with her son, and with grief over her past experiences. The husband of the late returnee did not live to enjoy the reunion for which he had been yearning for three long decades. A few months before the Soviet authorities granted the emigration permit, Jakob Burghart died at the age of sixty-seven in Krasnoyarsk in Central Siberia.

The ancestors of Maria Burghart had emigrated from Germany in the beginning of the 19. century and settled in the Ukraine. Maria, Jakob, and Alexander lived in Strassburg in the area of Odessa during the Second World War. When the German troops withdrew from the Ukraine in 1944 the Burgharts were at first lucky. They reached the Warthegau in Poland and in 1945 they came to Alsleben, which was occupied by American troops. However, when these forces withdrew from the area in compliance with the Yalta Agreement, Maria and Jakob were forcibly deported to Siberia, but their son Alexander, who was then only sixteen years old, made his escape to the West. Recalling those fateful days, Maria remarked, "The Russians declared that we were Soviet citizens. Our journey, which we were compelled to make in cattle cars, lasted three months. While the 40 German passengers were asleep the Poles robbed them of all their belongings. The first years in Siberia were terrible for us, but later on we got along well with the Russians. My father was employed as a tile-maker and I worked as a milkmaid. Together we earned 120 rubles a month, which sufficed for a simple livelihood. In the course of time we were able to buy a large table, a sewing machine, a samovar, a washing machine, and even a refrigerator for 200 rubles."

In 1956 the Burgharts, together with 500 Germans in Krasnoyarsk, filed the first applications for emigration permits, but all of them were turned down by the Soviets. "Most of our German people," says Mrs. Burghart, "are still living there. It's quite impossible to figure out who will be permitted to emigrate. It's just a matter of sheer luck." Maria became one of the lucky ones almost 19 years after she had filed her first application. A corresponding effort by her son Alexander last April was finally successful.

Several months later, Maria Burghart had to pay 400 rubles for her emigration papers and another 86 rubles for her ticket to the border transit camp at Friedland, Germany, where she again saw her son. The 69-year-old mother had to leave behind all her possessions in Krasnoyarsk, and a Russian

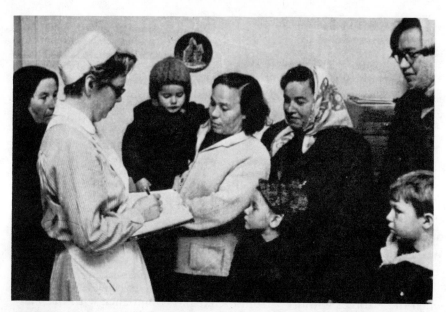

Emigrants from the USSR in Friedland

family immediately moved into her vacated apartment. The Soviet authorities let her take along 70 rubles for pocket money. When Maria Burghart arrived in the West all she owned was a small suitcase containing two skirts, two blouses, a bit of medicine, and some articles of food.

"My heart was thrilled with excitement and apprehension," said Maria Burghart in somewhat awkward German, "but I was well taken care of in Friedland and all the people there were very kind to me." But Maria was worried about her pension, for the Soviet government did not allow her to take along her Work Record Book or any other papers. Nor did the government pay her a single ruble of pension money for all the years that she worked for the Soviet state. The district councilor of Göttingen, Willi Doering, cheered her up, saying, "Take heart, for this matter will also be taken care of." By way of initial aid, the Federal Ministry for Lower Saxony granted her 500 marks and a similar sum was collected for her by the people of the village of Gieboldehausen. The returnee Maria Burghart told me joyfully, "I have already bought a quilt for my bed and some clothes to wear."

162

4. Exodus from the Soviet Paradise

A report in the *Spiegel* in 1972.

With their grandparents and a bevy of children, with wooden suitcases and bulging sacks they arrived at the old Merchants' Palace in Moscow's Grusinia Street, No. 17, the seat of the Bonn Embassy. The Federal border guard at the porter's desk has already observed them on the monitor of a TV camera that is focused on the gate of the Soviet police station. The Soviet citizens of German nationality, dressed in fur caps, head shawls, and padded jackets, are allowed to pass. These possess the little blue card with the emigration visa and also a passport that has cost each returnee 400 rubles ($640.00). They have sold their woodframe house, the cow and the pigs, after the Soviet government granted the request they had made many years ago, to be re-united with their relatives in West Germany. At the State bank they were permitted to exchange 90 rubles for 360 West German marks.

At the Embassy they receive the passport of the Federal government. At the present time practically only those German Russians are permitted to emigrate who have at one time or another been German citizens. This happened most often through enforced repatriation during the time of the German occupation or after their resettlement from the Ukraine into the Warthegau (western Poland), where the Red Army again recaptured them.

They get something to eat and are provided with sleeping quarters in the movie room of the Embassy or, for six rubles a person, a room in the suburban hotel "Sarya." Four Red Cross nurses take care of them, and an official transmits their retirement papers to West Germany and provides them with railway fares. Three times a week, a special coach at the Moscow Belorussian railway station is attached to the train bound for Berlin. There they board a train that takes them to Friedland. The sick and the aged are transported by *Lufthansa*.

In the reception camp at Friedland they hear a brief address of welcome and receive 50 marks for interim pocket money and 150 marks as "a welcoming gift from the Federal Republic." After four or five days the immigrants are processed and placed into a transit camp until they can be permanently established in their new homes.

Relatives in Westphalia are waiting for Jakob Janzen, 57, and his family who originally lived in the Ukraine. He has now come from Dnepropetrovsk which was taken by the *Wehrmacht* in 1947 when he was drafted into the German army. At the end of the war he was in active duty at Aachen, but was captured by the Americans, who delivered him up to the Russians in

163

1945. He was deported to Novosibirsk where he married a woman who had been deported there from the Warthegau. He was able later to earn the equivalent of $360 a month in a margarine factory, while his wife earned $280 in a textile concern. The son was a student, but the daughter also had a job. Ten years ago the Janzens bought a small woodframe house for about $6,400.

The family lived securely, but Jakob Janzen really never felt at home in the USSR. Like thousands of his fellow countrymen, he submitted applications for an exit visa, but at the government offices he was invariably told, "You will be allowed to go, but not all at one time." Janzen's sixth application was accepted on October 30, 1972. Two weeks later the family started out on the seven-day journey by train. Each ticket from Novosibirsk to the Braunschweig station in Berlin cost 90 rubles (about $160), but the money was refunded to them by the Federal government. The Janzens invested the remainder of their Russian money in a gold necklace costing $320, but the jewelry was confiscated by the Soviet customs officials.

It is uncertain whether Janzen, who is close to the retirement age, will be able to obtain a job; his young wife stands a better chance. The chances of a job for the daughter are difficult because of her emigration, for she was compelled, after the final application to emigrate, to discontinue her training as a surveyor. The son, age 17, cannot continue his studies in mathematics until he has passed the German *"Abitur"* examinations. He is the only one in the family who is hardly able to speak German.

The relatives in Westphalia had advised the Janzens to bring along only their very best clothes and leave behind the local type of clothing, "so that," says Janzen, "we won't stand out so conspicuously in this elegant country."

Since 1957 about 26,000 persons have come to Germany. In 1970 there were only 340, the following year 1150, and in 1972 there were about 3500. A police major in Esthonia handed a German-Russian construction worker six passports for the entire family and remarked: "Now you are allowed to go over to join your relatives, because the Russian government and the Federal Republic are on good terms. The better the relationship, the more people will be permitted to emigrate." More than 40,000 are still waiting for the little blue card and are said to come in the next five years. That is approximately 2% of the two million Germans living in the Soviet Union. To be sure, most of them never had German citizenship, have no relatives in Germany, and have no wish to emigrate. Their life is fairly good in the Soviet state. They are in demand as workers, mostly in agriculture, in construction, and in factories. Because of overtime, they often earn more money than their Soviet colleagues, according to a German foreman in Irkutsk, a tractorist in central Bukara, and a lady teacher in Omsk.

The Soviet Germans often live in small settlements in Siberia or Central Asia, speak German with each other, marry among themselves, cultivate traditional customs, and pay the Moscow government the necessary respect. Only a few have a higher education, so that only ten German resettlers were recently expected to pay the Soviet state the costs of their education.

In the new frontier region of Kasakhstan, in the district of Zelinograd, there are German areas. There is a German village on the shore of the Baikal Sea, which is exhibited to the West German tourists as a typical Russian datcha-colony. There the reporters of Spiegel met a group of children in the midst of the taiga: one third of them had German names, but understood only Russian. Today, two-thirds of the Soviet Germans live in the region of Novosibirsk, in houses which they had built in 1954. Three-fourths of the people own their own little house and 12% have their own quarters. Almost every family has three or four children.

Although most of the Germans are engaged in manual labor, some have made it into higher professions. Alexander Frank is the top doctor in a hospital. Alexander Eisenach is the director of a large firm. Rosalinde Lauth is an opera singer in Usbekistan, and Axel Berg, an Admiral Engineer, was Vice Defense Minister of the USSR from 1963 to 1957. Locomotive engineer Siegfried Dorn was granted the Order of Merit, and farmer Karl Schmidt and chicken-raiser Alexandra Stensel have become "Heroes of Socialist Labor." Heinrich Barzel, president of a club in Pawlovka, received the "Order of the Red Labor Banner." Woldemar Lein is the Soviet Minister of Food Industry. Twelve German-Russian authors who write in German belong to the Soviet Authors Association. Swiatoslav Richter, who was not allowed to perform abroad until the early fifties, has become a world-renowned pianist. His father was a victim of the Soviet Secret Police, his mother succeeded in escaping to Germany after the war.

Today several radio stations bring special programs in the German language. The Moscow *Pravda* publishes a German weekly *"Neues Leben."* There are also two other papers *"Rote Fahne"* published in Slavgorod, and *"Freundschaft"* which appears in Zelinograd. A German folklore group has recently gone on tours to perform German songs and dances. But they have not been permitted to have their own cultural organization.

According to the census of 1970, there are 840,000 Germans in the Soviet Republic of Kazakhstan, which has a total population of 12.8 million. Thus they represent the largest ethnic group after the Russians, Kazakhs, and Ukrainians. In Kazakhstan, six Germans are in the Supreme Soviet, and the

In the pioneer region of Zelinograd every eighth inhabitant is a German; in Karaganda every tenth. But only two-thirds of the people gave German as their mother tongue. There are no German schools for the children of German parents in the entire Soviet Union. Only when ten or more students desire German are they able to study German as a foreign language in a special course. In Kazakhstan 40,884 children take such a course in 343 schools. But there are hardly any text books and very few teachers. The students who take German must be content to use whatever materials are at hand, for the officials are not interested in making much material available.

The older generation generally refuses to use official Soviet educational material; they have their Bible. A German pastor is a rarity, and when there is an officially licensed prayer hall, it is usually crowded with adults, especially women. The old clergy were collectively arrested in 1941 and deported en masse to places unknown. The militant godless destroyed most of the churches in the German villages on the Volga and the Black Sea, or converted them to secular uses.

—From SPIEGEL, Nr. 50, 1972

Border Transit Camp at Friedland

5. The Sorrows of a Refugee Mother

Reminiscences of my life
in the Soviet Union, Germany, and Western Canada*

By Magdalene Volk nee Zeiler

My ancestors were among the first German pioneer settlers who established the colony of Mariental, which was located on the Baraboi River 25 versts (16 miles) west of Odessa. The earliest references to the Zeiler immigrant are found in the census records of 1815, but these are scanty. There is mention of a certain Jakob Zeiler, a builder by trade, who emigrated from Linz on the Danube in 1809, and settled in Mariental, which had been established in 1804. He appears to have been unmarried, for he is not listed among the land-owning colonists (1816). However, a later reference indicates that he inherited a farmstead and a portion of crown land that originally belonged to the colonist widow Maria Kost, presumably by marriage. A relative, Johann Zeiler, probably the son of Jakob, subsequently inherited the estate of Joseph Kost. Unfortunately, there is no later information about the second and third generations of the Zeiler kinship.

My father, Emmeran Zeiler, a son of Felix, was born in Mariental in 1888 and was married to Katherina Weimer, who was born the same year. The marriage was blest with seven children, four boys and three girls. I was the oldest of the children, having been born on September 25, 1909. The next two children, Alois and Elisabeth, died in infancy in 1917 and 1918. Maria, my only surviving sister, was born in 1918. She is married to a man named Keller and is living in Karaganda, Russia. The oldest boy in the family was named Stefan; he was born in 1913, and is also living in Karaganda. My brother Felix, born in 1923, died in Mariental in 1927; and my youngest brother, Nikolaus, who was also born in 1923, died in Mariental in 1941.

In 1923, when I was 14 years old, I contracted malaria and was confined to bed with a high fever. My father got up early in the morning and got ready to drive to Odessa. Before leaving the house, he came once more to my bed and looked at me sadly for awhile, and wondered, since I looked so poorly, if he would find his sick child still alive upon his return.

Evening came, the weather was calm, and the sky was serene and clear as the sun went down. The church bell had just sounded the Angelus when we were startled by a far-off cry. No one knew from where the sound came and

*This report was translated into English from the original German manuscript and edited by JSH.

167

who was crying out as if in mortal terror. Our hearts were stricken with pity for the poor soul. Some time later a man came to our house, inquired about

Father Emmeran Zeiler, born 1888 in Mariental (Photo 1908)

Mother Catharina Zeiler, with children Magdalena, Daniel, Stefan, and Aloysius (1914)

our name, and said to my mother "Do not be frightened, dear woman, at the message that I am bringing you. Your husband Emmeran is seriously hurt. On his way back from the city he was attacked by a bandit who robbed him of everything." Just then some men carried our poor father into the room. He was covered with blood and appeared dead. The bandit had shot at him and hit him twice. One bullet went through his mouth and the other through his stomach. Mother and her five children stood there and wept. Fourteen days after father was borne to the graveyard she gave birth to her sixth child.

Now that father was taken from us, what could my mother do, since the oldest girl was only fourteen years old and the baby only 14 days? Without a provider, how could we feed all the hungry mouths? Since we had to sell all our grain in order to pay the hospital and the doctor bills, where could we get the bread we needed to feed the family? It was terribly hard for me to see my mother so full of anxiety and constant worry, and I wanted so much to share the burden and to help her.

I slowly got well again, and when spring came I was determined to help provide our daily bread. But where would I be able to get work that would pay sufficient wages? After all, there were simply no jobs available for 14-year-old girls. There seemed to be no opportunity of earning any money, except perhaps in the stone quarry, but the work there was often too hard even for many men. Nevertheless I said to my mother: "Now I must go and break stones, so that we might have bread to eat. There's no other way." But my mother protested and said: "My dear child, may God forbid! You cannot do that. You're much too young and too weak." But I had no peace of mind, and hunger hurts. I saw no other alternative.

The next morning I got up very early, slipped quietly out of the house, walked to the stone quarry, and began to work. I had to remove the top layer of earth to a depth of three feet before I came to the rock that I intended to break. But that took considerable time and much sweat and effort. But even more difficult was the job of selling the stone I had quarried. However, I finally succeeded in selling it to Wilhelm Herz, a miller in the Lutheran village of Neuburg, and I received some flour in exchange. Well, that was a great help, and I thanked God that He had not forsaken us. I really felt happy, even though my meals often consisted merely of bread and water.

I kept working at this job for four years, and my mother Katherina was able to set the breakfast table for all of her children: Magdalena, Daniel, Stefan, Maria, Felix, and Nikolaus. One morning when I was working in the stone quarry, my limbs suddenly began to feel so heavy and my head go so dizzy that I had to stop working. I decided to drag myself over to my grandmother's house which was in the neighborhood, but I made it only to the nearby house of my aunt Malvina. I told her that I couldn't work today, because I felt so poorly. My aunt made me lie down to take a rest and urged me to give up the hard work I was doing. "You work too much," she warned me, "you are just digging your own grave."

While we were talking we were startled by frightful outcries on the street. Someone, apparently, was involved in an accident. We hurried out of the house and—God have mercy—the boy that lay dead in the middle of the street was my brother Felix! He had been driving a wagon, when the horses shied and bolted. The wagon overturned and fell on Felix, crushing his bones and causing internal injuries. He regained consciousness for a few minutes and cried pitifully for his mother. Father Wolf who happened to be nearby

Mariental. Main street

came and administered the last sacraments. Mother arrived at the scene as quickly as she could and was with her seven-year-old son for three minutes before he died. This was the second terrible accident I was to witness in my young years.

We now had enough to live on for the next few years, for my older brothers and sisters were now able to help with the work, and we had good harvests. We were able to buy two horses and a wagon, and also some farm equipment, so that we could work our own land. We planted a vineyard of the best grapes, but were unable to harvest much of them, since we were compelled to deliver up everything to the collective. We were permitted to keep only a cow, a pig, and a few chickens, but even on these animals we had to pay taxes. We also had to give up a portion of the milk that we obtained from the cow, and also the hides of the pigs that we slaughtered. All that we had left of our land was a small patch of garden. We now had to work in the collective every day, from early morning until late at night. That's how the Soviets calculated a "day's work." We did not receive any wages until after the harvest, and even then only a part of our wages were paid in money; the rest was paid in wheat and some grapes; we also received some straw for our cow. But all this was frequently quite insufficient when the crops were poor. For fuel we used the

Mariental church without tower (1914)

170

View of Kleinliebental

cow manure we were able to gather in the open fields where the livestock was permitted to graze in the fall. It was a hard, sad life.

In 1929 came the deportation of the *kulaks,* that is, the well-to-do farmers, who were arrested in the middle of the night and sent in cattle cars to Siberia. What grief and misery this caused in all our villages!

In 1933, when I was 23, I was married to Valentin Kocher of Kleinliebental, a neighboring village. It was the year we had a famine. Since my husband had lost his parents when he was still a young boy, he lived with strangers from the time he was eleven years old. He first worked as a farm hand, but later learned the trade of a cabinetmaker. He owned a house in Kleinliebental and here we had a happy home in the peace of God. He had to go all the way to Odessa to work at his trade, while I worked on the collective farm. After three months I had to quit for reasons of ill health and a five-month pregnancy. However, the Soviet taskmasters penalized me for quitting my job by not paying me any wages for my three months of work. Such cruel injustice was hard to take.

The first offspring that God granted us were triplets: Eva, Maria, and Joseph. Eva lived only two days, and Joseph only two years. Maria is still living. In 1937 I gave birth to our fourth child, a boy whom we also called Joseph and who is still living.

In the thirties we suffered much grief and tribulation. Our churches were taken from us. All the bells and crosses were removed. Only in the cemetery

Kleinliebental church

the large crucifix, minus one arm, was left standing, and there we could go to pray. But we were not allowed to pray in our homes. On one occasion when we met for a prayer meeting in the home of my uncle George, it was reported to the Soviet authorities, and he was deported to Siberia. Also several sisters were taken away. Since no nunneries were allowed, the sisters who had taken their vows lived with their parents in Kleinliebental.

Valentin Kocher, wife Magdalena, with Maria and Josef (Odessa 1944)

The outbreak of the war between Germany and Russia brought new hardships and trials upon our people. After the German Wehrmacht succeeded in crossing the Russian border our men were rounded up by the Soviet functionaries and removed from our villages. The women were forced to dig trenches six kilometers long all the way from our village to Grossliebental. This was extremely hard work, since the trenches had to be two fathoms (14 feet) wide and two fathoms deep. We had to leave our children at home all day, and when we returned late in the evening they had all cried themselves to sleep, because they had no supper. One day I decided to quit digging trenches and take up easier work in a collective vegetable garden. At eleven o'clock a big truck stopped beside me on the road. Suddenly an armed guard jumped out and drew his gun on me. I was so frightened that I couldn't utter a word. I was ordered to get into the truck and taken to the trenches.

We often endured much fear and anxiety, for none of us could be sure where we would be the following day. Every morning there were outcries and lamentations on the streets. Women suddenly found themselves left alone with their children, for the husbands had been hauled away in the dead of night, without cause, to some unknown destination. Sometimes the relatives again heard from them, but generally they did not.

In 1941 the German and Rumanian armies appeared. Again we lived in great terror when their aircraft came over and dropped bombs that killed many of our people. And later on came the persecution of the Jews. With my own eyes I saw how men, women, and children were imprisoned in granaries, which were then covered with benzine and set on fire. Many more people were hanged on improvised gallows and their bodies were laid out along the road that we travelled whenever we went to Odessa. The stench of the corpses reached as far as Kleinliebental. Oh, what dreadful cruelty was inflicted on all those poor people!

We were unable to harvest our crops because the front passed through Kleinliebental. We had to flee from the village and go to Mariental. But here we had to scour the wheat fields looking for the nests of the field mice, in order to find the grain that the poor things had stored up for the winter, and this grain provided us with our daily bread. After a month we were able to return to our home in Kleinliebental, where we began to dig out our potatoes.

In the fall of 1941 my brother Nikolaus fell gravely ill of diphtheria. He was 18 years old but had never received Holy Communion, for we no longer had any priests. When I visited him I brought him some food which I had earned as a seamstress, instead of money which was very scarce. I had to go

15 kilometers on foot and when I saw him the last time his fever had subsided somewhat, and I was alone with him in the room. Since he knew very little about praying—for this was strictly forbidden in recent years—I asked him if he would be willing to say the rosary with me. He at once agreed and said sadly: "I'll gladly pray with you, sister Magdalena, because our good Lord has been living in my heart and soul since my baptism."

We prayed slowly and fervently but after we were finished he began to weep bitterly. I was filled with sorrow and asked him why he was crying so pitifully. He turned to me and said, "Dear sister, I'm going to die in three days. There are only three days left of my life." With a heavy heart, I tried to console him, and said, "Why don't you want to die?" He replied, "I'm still so young and have not had anything good in my life!" I felt a surge of pain in my heart as I said: "Be comforted, dear brother, who knows what we shall all still have to suffer in this life. You are in God's protective hands."

I returned the same day to my family and on the third day at 11 o'clock at night my dear brother began to call for his mother. As the wife of my brother Stefan was looking after him while my mother was resting, he said, "Dear Katharina, call Mother and give me a bit of holy water to drink, so that there might be something sacred with me, for I must soon die; it must be almost 12:30." After he had swallowed the holy water he said farewell to Mother and asked if I were present. At 12:30 he expired.

Since we had no doctor and no priest to attend him, we gave him a befitting funeral, without any solemnity. When Father Pieger arrived some time later, he said a Mass for the repose of his soul. On three occasions my brother appeared to me in a dream and each time he said to me, "Dear sister, I am completely pure and white."

During the German occupation we enjoyed three happy and peaceful years. We opened our church again, cleaned and adorned it, and were once more able to worship God with a calm heart. In 1942 I gave birth to our fifth child whom we named Peter. All our children were now baptized by the visiting missionary, Father Nikolaus Pieger, and all made their First Communion. All were subsequently confirmed in Odessa by Bishop Markus Glaser, a native son of Landau. Many couples also had their marriage blessed, and there were general confessions for all the faithful.

But the few good years already came to an end in 1944, and a new terrifying ordeal confronted us. In the spring the German military command gave the order that all the inhabitants of German descent living in the area between the Dnieper and the Dniester had to depart for Germany. Who can possibly imagine how deeply that grieved us, or how difficult it was for us to leave our dear homeland where we were born and raised! We were now told that we had to go to a foreign country, without knowing to what place. We were ordered to provide ourselves with food for two weeks and to take along only the most essential belongings.

We put a makeshift hut of boards over our wagon and loaded it with our clothes and bedding, along with 2 sacks of flour, 12 loaves of bread, some cured pork and fried sausages preserved in lard; also a few utensils and tools, and my sewing machine. There was also a sack full of chopped feed for the horses, and behind the wagon we hitched a young steer. When the caravan of loaded wagons drove out through the gates, people began to cry because they had to forsake their beloved homes and leave behind all their furniture and other household belongings.

Soon the first day of the journey was over. It was the 28th of March, 1944. We had driven 30 kilometers to Ovidiopol, a town on the Dniester Liman, a large estuary formed by the Dniester river before it flows out into the Black Sea. But here the good Lord sent us another tribulation. For an entire week we had such a violent siege of storm and rain that the ferry was unable to transport us across the Liman. Many tears were shed and even the heavens wept with us. The children cried and wanted to sleep in their familiar beds, but these were now far behind us. Mother earth was now our bed and the open sky was the canopy. Sometimes we slept under the wagon, sometimes in it.

At long last we were able to undertake the crossing. My husband led the team of horses while I sat with the children in the wagon, praying that God would not forsake us. Suddenly our trek leader appeared and took the horses by the reins and led them onto the ferry. As if by a miracle we all made it safely across the *Liman* and found ourselves safely on the opposite shore, in Bessarabia. We were just about to prepare a meal when a terrifying shooting began. My God, what is happening now? It was a bombing attack by the Russians. Some grabbed whatever they could carry and left their wagons and horses behind. What a bedlam there was!

Then the trek continued through Bessarabia and along the course of the Danube, through Rumania and Bulgaria and Hungary. Some days we had to cover 60 and more kilometers. So it went for three months, and most of our people had to make the long trek on foot. Whenever we stopped in the evening, tired and beaten, there was no house where we could find shelter; we had to spend the night in the open fields. Both we and the children longed for a warm meal, but how were we to prepare it? There was no water for cooking far and wide, and no wood with which to build a fire. Sometimes after a long search, you might find a bit of kindling, but first a fireplace had to be built on which you could set the cooking pot. We simply dug a hole in the ground and that served both as a stove and an oven in which we could bake some bread. By digging a slanting hole in the ground you could bake as many as eight loaves. The kneading trough that we had brought along also served as a washtub as well as a feedbox for the horses. We thank God that He always sustained us, and our bread always turned out well, as is befitting for a German-Russian housewife. But on many days we could neither cook nor bake, because it was already dark when the wagon train came to a halt. We were hungry and dead tired; we had had nothing to eat for many hours, not even any bread. The children were crying because they were hungry, but they were too tired and wanted to sleep. It was enough to drive one to despair. We simply fell down on the naked earth, but we hardly were lying down and trying to sleep when it suddenly began to rain, sometimes without letup. Our clothes became soaking wet, but where and how could we get them dry again?

Despite all these hardships and troubles, we did not lose our trust in God. Often when the day's trek was over and we reached our camping place while it was still light and the weather was fair, we quickly built an altar and decorated it with evergreen and wild flowers, and there we held our devotions. Pius Hemmerling who was formerly our sacristan, conducted the prayer service. The first Mass that we attended on our journey was held in a cemetery in Bulgaria, when a Bavarian priest visited our camp. On that occasion he also baptized all the children who were born on the trek. But another grievous ordeal afflicted us when our youngest child Peter became gravely ill.

He suffered from an infection of the inner ear, but we had neither a doctor nor any medicine. We were given shelter in a barn where I made a bed for him on the straw. As I sat there crying bitterly, the sick child came once more into my arms, gasped for a few moments, and died. How heavy was my heart as I held the poor lifeless form on my breast. We had the good fortune to be able to bury him in a small coffin in the local cemetery and to place a beautiful cross with his epitaph over the grave. When the funeral was over we thanked God that the boy had a decent burial and was not, as it often happened, simply wrapped in a blanket and interred by the side of the road. But alas, it was not to be. Shortly after the funeral, a local Bulgarian priest showed up and ordered us to exhume the body of our boy and bury it somewhere else. But we were determined not to do his bidding. We had done our Christian duty and were confident that God would preserve his resting place. We had to leave this place and resume our journey. What happened afterwards, God alone knows and, probably, the uncharitable priest. How bitter and hard this experience had been for us.

In a forest in Rumania we attended the second Mass during our long journey. The Mass was celebrated by two priests whom we knew back in our village, and we had been expecting their arrival. They were Father Pieger and Bishop Glaser. The occasion was the Feast of Corpus Christi. A beautiful altar was erected beneath the green trees to enhance the celebration.

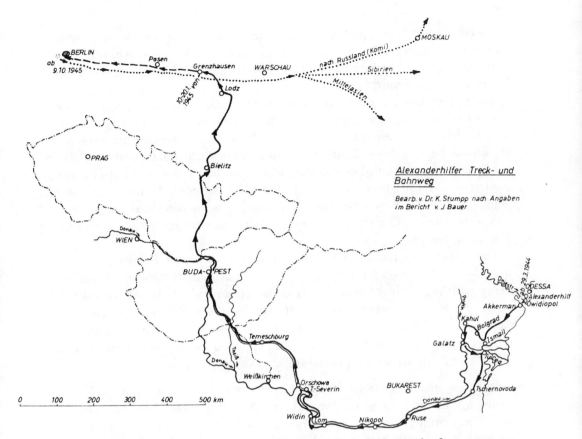

Alexanderhilfer Treck- und Bahnweg

Bearb. v. Dr. K. Stumpp nach Angaben im Bericht v. J Bauer

We continued on our trek and reached Serbia and the end of our wagon train journey. Here we had to surrender our horses, cows, and wagons. From now on we travelled by train to Poland, taking with us the few belongings that we still had. We were on the way for eight days, since our journey was delayed for some time in Budapest when we were bombarded by the Russians. But we were well taken care of by kind people who awaited us and served us and the children coffee and cake. One night as we were travelling through Poland we were unloaded from the train and transported by rail to the town of Mühlental and from there to Josephsberg in the district of Warthegau.

This was journey's end. However, we did not receive a house or even a shed where we could stay for the night, but were assigned to a mortuary chapel in the Catholic cemetery. We shuddered at the very thought of entering and sleeping there, but our protests were of no avail. For two months we lived among the graves, until we finally obtained a more suitable dwelling. It was only a small room, about 14 by 14 feet, but it had a cook stove. In this room two families, comprising nine people, lived and slept. We all slept on the bare floor of clean wet sand. We had no firewood for the stove, but had to burn straw. But we often said, "Thank God that we don't have to live any longer in the graveyard."

We had endured everything with patience and resignation, but our long road of tribulation had not yet come to an end. On October 15, 1944, my dear husband was called to Berlin to work as a cabinetmaker but soon after his arrival he was drafted into the *Wehrmacht*. With much persistent effort we finally received another dwelling where we had somewhat better accommodation. At Christmas we set up a nicely ornamented thorn tree, which delighted our children very much. But our joy was again short-lived, for this was to be the last Christmas I would be spending with my two dear children, Maria and Joseph.

One morning in January I travelled to Berlin to visit my husband. The very next day while I was still with him, the village of Mühlental where I had been living with my children was evacuated by command of the *Wehrmacht,* because the Russians were approaching. During the evacuation my children—eleven-year-old Maria and seven-year-old Joseph—were taken along by some relatives, but I could not discover what happened to them or where they had been taken. All my search proved to be in vain.

But fate dealt me another cruel blow when my husband perished at the young age of only 33 years. He had always been a God-fearing man, honest, and hard-working. He died on April 27, 1945, the death of a martyr. I was on my way to visit him in the Finkenstein Barracks where he was staying, and was only a fifteen-minute walk away from the place when the Russians suddenly unleashed a terrible bombardment upon the establishment. I didn't know what to do or where to turn. Not a soul could be seen in the street. Suddenly a boy about five years old was standing in front of me and said to me, "Dear lady, where are you going in this heavy bombardment?" I replied, "I would like to see my husband once more." But the boy continued: "Dear lady, please stay away from the place. If you go in there to visit your husband, you will lose an arm or a leg." With that, he disappeared. I was utterly bewildered and stunned. I hardly realized what had happened, but I retraced my steps and thanked God for the warning I had received.

How difficult all this was for me, for now I was utterly alone, and on June 20, 1945, I gave birth to a baby boy, whom I named Valentine, after his father. He was baptized by Father Puf in the Church of the Madonna on the Gardenschützenweg. His sponsors were Luzia Puf and Anneliese Bauer of Berlin. The little child now needs me in his helplessness and brings me hope and consolation. But will I ever find my lost children again? I ask myself this question, day and night. I keep on hoping that God, who cannot be cruel, will send them back to me, if they are still living on earth. I shall no longer lament the loss of my last wordly belongings in Mühlental in the Warthegau, although I now possess nothing but the clothes on my back. That was all I owned. No matter, all I want is to have my children back.

That's how life was for the ethnic Germans who were up-rooted from their homeland and forced to flee into the Reich. God will make his reckoning with those who did these things to us, for we have become impoverished and disheartened, and keep yearning for the things we once loved and cherished.

I have now been living here in Berlin in a state of tormenting uncertainty for four years, but I am deeply grateful to God and to the kindhearted people for all their generous aid and support. I am especially grateful to Mr. and Mrs. Richter and to Anneliese Bauer, who took me in and did so many good things for me.

I kept on searching for my children without any let-up. I went to the Search Bureau every week and also to the Caritas Society of the Catholic Priests. Everybody wanted to help me find my children, but all efforts proved fruitless. Through the Red Cross I was able to obtain the address of my uncle, Rochus Zeiler who was living in Canada. In response to my very first letter, he asked me if I was willing to come to Canada with my child. I accepted the offer and hoped that I might find my lost children over there. After a long and impatient period of waiting in the refugee camp at Milenberg, near Hanover, I received an immigration visa and a prepaid ticket. In the beginning of January, 1949, I and my little boy left Germany and embarked at Bremerhaven on the good ship Arosa. On January 14 we reached Halifax and set foot on our new homeland. After going through the immigration office where our passport was checked, we were placed on a train that took us to Winnipeg. Here we boarded another train that brought us to the village of Allan, Sask., where my uncle Rochus was living. We arrived at 5 a.m., and my uncle and Mr. John Weninger were at the station waiting for us with great anticipation, for we had not seen each other for 21 years. Our joy was great. First we were taken to the farm of Joseph Weninger, where we had a big breakfast, thanks to our gracious hosts, Johanna and Joseph. Later in the forenoon, we drove seven miles further to the farm of my uncle Rochus and my aunt Helen, to whom we are so appreciative and grateful for having gotten us out of our wretched situation. After we had eaten dinner, I marvelled at the beautiful life people have here, and it took some time for me to realize that this is the normal way of things in this land.

In the following weeks we visited all our friends in Allan. During that time I also became acquainted with Johannes Volk, who was on a visit here from Revenue where he had been a pioneer settler back in 1906, after having emigrated from the village of Baden in the Kutschurgan district near Odessa. I became engaged to this fine *Landsmann* and we were married in the beautiful church at Allan on March 20; and Father Shahun performed the nuptial ceremony. My husband John had been a widower with eight children, of whom the eldest was 21 and the youngest only one year old. I now have a home again on a farm and I like it very much. Our marriage is a very happy one, and I get along nicely with the children. In 1950 a baby girl was born to us and we named her Emma Audrey.

Life on the Saskatchewan prairie was wonderful and there was no lack of anything whatsoever. But I still kept worrying about my two lost children, where they might be, whether they had enough to eat and to wear, or if they had a decent place to live in. I kept thinking of them day and night, and could not give up hope of finding them some day. I prayed every day that the good Lord would send them back to me, or at least let me hear from them.

One day in the fall of 1955, I was reading the weekly edition of a German-language newspaper and came across a letter to the editor which was written by Nikolaus Weisgerber of Schuler, Alberta. I immediately became very interested, for the letter was written by a man whose parents must have come from the village of Josephstal/Odessa, which was close to my own native village of Mariental. The letter proved to be all the more exciting when I discovered that Mr. Weisgerber was in correspondence with a relative who was living in Kasakhstan in Central Asia. I immediately wrote to this *Landsmann* in Schuler and told him of my long and fruitless search for the two children I had lost at the time of the Soviet advance through Poland. I begged him to ask his kinsman whether he might by chance have heard of a man named Joseph Kocher and his sister Maria, and if so, whether he could obtain their present address.

About three weeks later, I received the most gratifying news that I could have hoped for. Yes, these two people were living in Kasakhstan, the young man near the city of Frunse and his sister near Karaganda. I lost no time in writing to my son Joseph and revealing to him and to my daughter the good news that I was alive and well in Saskatchewan. A couple of weeks later I received a letter with a photo of the long lost children. They told me of the many tribulations and hardships they had endured over the years, how they almost starved to death, and how much they needed help even in their present circumstances. I read the previous letter with many tears and a heavy heart in the realization that we were living so far apart from each other. Over the years we have sent them many parcels of food and clothing which were either not available in their stores or which they could not afford to buy.

My daughter Maria is married to a man named Albert Uslag, and they have two children: Joseph who is eighteen and Johannes who is nine years old.

My son Joseph is married to Josephina née Bachmann, and they have two children, Magdalena and George. My dear mother was taken out of Poland to Russia and deported to Siberia where she starved to death. We have no news of the fate of my brother Daniel since the end of the war, but his wife is living in Russia. My brother Stefan is living in Karaganda with his wife and three children. My sister Maria Koehler, who lost her husband and her four children, is also living there.

In 1966 my husband gave up his farm to two of his sons and built a house in the town of Wilkie where we live in retirement. But my trials were not yet over. I fell ill and had one operation after another, until there were thirteen. In January, 1973, I suffered a serious heart attack and was quite sick for a time. My son Valentine graduated from the University and is now teaching at a High School. Audrey also completed her University studies and is a registered nurse at the Misericordia Hospital in Edmonton. She married Wayne Wilson in June, 1973.

Though I continued to correspond frequently with my two forlorn children in Russia, our desire to see each other face to face grew constantly stronger with each passing year. I was now 68 years old and it was 32 years since I last saw my children in Poland in January of 1945. I therefore decided to send an application to the Russian consul in Canada with the request that I am anxious to see my son and my daughter after a fateful separation of thirty-two years. I was granted a permit to live in the home of my son for two weeks, but was not allowed to travel to the place where my daughter resided; she would have to visit me at my son's home.

My son Valentine and I received our visas and tickets on June 25, 1977, and on July 11 we left Wilkie for Saskatoon where we boarded an *Air Canada* plane that took us to Montreal. The next morning we got on a Russian plane and arrived in Moscow at 1 p.m. After we picked up our suitcases and passed through the gate, a man rushed up to me, hugged and kissed me, saying: "Dear Mama!" I really didn't recognize him right away as my son Joseph, for I hadn't seen him for 32 years. He had hired a taxi and we drove through the city to see many of the interesting sights before we drove out to another airport. We left Moscow at 1 a.m. and after a flight of five hours in an easterly direction we landed in Frunse in the Republic of Kasakhstan. Here we had to surrender our passports for twenty-four hours. The next day Joseph and Valentine returned to the airport to pick them up again. At the same time they sent a telegram to my husband John back in Wilkie and to my uncle Rochus Zeiler in Allan. We now had to travel another 70 kilometers to reach the village where my son had his home and where a crowd of relatives was awaiting us.

181

My daughter Maria, now 44 years old, met me with a bouquet of lovely flowers, and as she hugged and kissed me she exclaimed, "Dear sweet mother, is it really true? Are you my mother or is all this just a dream?"— "No, dear child," I replied, "it's not a dream. It's your mother." She then asked, "Can my brother speak German?" I said, "Indeed he can," and they embraced and kissed each other. Next we met Maria's husband Albert and their two children, Joseph and Wanya. Then we greeted Joseph's wife Josephine and their three children: Magdalena, George, and little Irna Kocher, and her mother Regina Bachmann who was a native of Josephstal. I next greeted my brother Stefan (born 1913), his wife Katharina née Zeiler, my sister Maria Koehler, and Mrs. Hauck, a cousin. They had all come a distance of 900 kilometers from Karaganda by plane. Like my daughter Maria, Mechtilda Bohl who was a sister of my deceased husband Valentine had also travelled with her family a distance of almost 2,000 km. from Aktyubinsk by train on a journey that took two days and two nights. No effort, no expense was too great to be re-united with the loved ones after a long separation of 32 years.

We sat down for a festive meal and joyfully celebrated our family re-union with many toasts of wine, vodka, brandy, and beer. All the relatives who had come from distant places had brought with them quantities of food of various kinds, especially chickens, eggs, butter, cream, and cheese, since they could not expect Joseph to provide food for so many people during their long visit. Moreover, they also knew that only fruit and vegetables were usually available in local food stores.

And so we spent day after day together exchanging reminiscences of our experiences and tribulations in the last three or four decades. We often sang the time-honored songs of our homeland, laughed over all the humorous incidents we could remember, and cried freely over all the tribulations and suffering we had endured in our former homeland and on the long trek to the West. All too soon the day of departure (July 26) arrived, and we were confronted with the sad moment of bidding the first farewell to Joseph's family while the other relatives were able to accompany us as far as Frunse where a second farewell became even harder for us all. Only Joseph stayed with us until we reached Moscow. This was the last farewell, and I wondered whether I would ever see my dear children again. But I consoled myself with the thought, if God grants me life and my health permits, I shall fulfill my children's dearest wish and visit them once more. Be that as God wills, I am filled with undying gratitude that He has granted me the inexpressible happiness of finding and seeing my long lost children again.

X.   Customs and Traditions
1. Nursery Rhymes

An interesting and instructive facet of German-Russian folklore are the traditional *Kinderreime*, the cradle songs and nursery rhymes which our mothers and grandmothers used to recite to the pre-schoolchildren gathered around them on the long winter evenings. Today most of these time-honored childrens' rhymes are probably nothing more than dim memories of a long-gone childhood, and for the youngest generation the old *Kinderreime* have inevitably been replaced by the well-known Mother Goose Rhymes.

The simplest and earliest form of the nursery rhyme is the lullaby or cradle song that the mother used to sing to her petulant infant. Indeed, it is probably the most primitive form of poetry in the history of mankind, just as the mother is the first language teacher in every civilization. An old Alsatian proverb says: "The crying of the child teaches its mother so sing." Lullabies and cradle songs are doubtless as old as motherhood, and as needful for the young child as food and drink. In the simple melodies of the mother, the infant imbibes the first sweet accents of the mother tongue. Among the favorite cradle songs of the colonists we find the following two:

Eia, bubaia,
was wusselt im Stroh?
's Kätzel isch g'schtorwe,
's Maisl isch froh.

Eia, bubaia,
what stirs in the straw?
The kitten is dead,
the little mouse is glad.

Schlof, Kindele, schlof!
Dr Vadder hüt die Schof,
Die Mudder hüt die Lämmele,
Schlof, du goldig' Engele!

Sleep, babykin, sleep!
Father tends the sheep,
Mother tends the lambkins,
Sleep, you darling angel!

When the child had the misfortune of bruising its finger or stubbing its toe, the solicitous mother would allay its fear and soothe the hurt by reciting one or the other of the following humorous jingles like an incantation:

A B C
d'Katz liggt im Schnee.
D'r Schnee geht eweg,
d'Katz liggt im Dreck,
morje frieh isch alles weg.

A B C
the cat lies in the snow.
The snow melts away,
the cat's in the dirt,
by morning it won't hurt.

Heila, heila, sega,
drei Tag Rega,
drei Tag Hammelesdreck,
morga früh isch alles weg!

Heal, heal, blessing,
three days' rain,
three days' calf dung,
tomorrow morning it's all gone!

183

The nursery rhymes varied somewhat from village to village, and even from family to family, depending on the original homeland of the colonists. Many of the old traditional rhymes were preserved by mothers and grandmothers from one generation to the next. From this childrens' treasury of verse we can reproduce only some of the various types.

A rather quaint nursery was recited by the mother as she dandled the child on her knee:

Hoppa, hoppa Rössle,	Hobby, hobby horsie,
droba steht a Schlössle,	yonder stands a castle,
droba steht a Guckahaus,	yonder stands a watch tower,
gucken drei Madame raus.	three damsels are looking out.
Eine spinnt Seida,	One is spinning silk,
die andre wickelt Weida,	the second is winding willows,
die dritte näht en rota Rock	the third is sewing a red coat
für den alta Zottelbock.	for the old tatter-goat.

To the rhythmic patting of hands, the mother recited the baker's practical "pat-a-cake" rhyme:

Backe, backe Kuchen,	Bake-a, bake-a cake,
der Bäcker hat gerufen:	the baker has declared:
Wer will guten Kuchen backen,	If you want to bake good cake,
der muss haben sieben Sachen —	seven items you must take —
Eier und Salz, Butter und Schmalz,	eggs and salt, lard and butter,
Milch und Mehl,	milk and flour,
Safrich macht den Kuchen gehl.	saffron gives the yellow color.

While some of the *Kinderlieder* had a meaningful content, others often consisted of nonsense verse or fanciful ditties that were either humorous or grotesquely absurd. The following selections are fairly representative:

Maikäfer, flieg!	Lady bug, fly!
Der Vater ist im Krieg,	Father's gone to war,
die Mutter ist im Pommerland,	Mother's in Pommerania,
Pommerland ist abgebrannt.	Pommerania has burned down.
Maikäfer, flieg!	Lady bug, fly!

Rega, Rega-Tropfe,	Rain, rain, raindrops,
die Buba muss mer klopfa,	the boys they must be spanked,
die Mädle muss mer schona,	the girls we have to spare,
wie die Zitrona.	like lemons rare.

Ena, dena, Tintenfass,	Eeny, deeny, inkwell,
gehst en d'Schul	Go off to school
und lernscht m'r was,	and learn some things;
kommst m'r hoim	If you come home
und kannscht m'r nix,	and know nothing,
nehm ich die Rut	I'll take the birch
und fitzle dich.	and switch you.

Ene, dene, dumme Kätt,
Wem'mr metzle, hem'mr Speck,
Wem'mer backe, hem'mr Brot,
Wem'mr starwe, sim'mr dot.

Bauer, bind dein Pudel an,
dass er mich net beisse kann;
Beisst er mich, so straf ich dich
um ein Rubel dreissig.
Ein Rubel dreissig ist kein Geld,
Wenn der Pudel noch so bellt.

Storch, Storch, Schniebel, Schnabel,
mit der langen Heugabel,
mit dem kurzen Rechenstiel.
Alte Weiber essen viel,
die jungen müssen fasten,
das Brot liegt im Kasten,
der Wein liegt im Keller,
Der Käs uff'm Teller,
d' Vadder isch im Wertshaus,
Sauft alle Glesser aus.

Steht a Poppale an der Wand,
hat a Gackele en d'r Hand,
möchts gern essen,
hat koi Messer.
Fällt das Messer oba h'rab,
schlagt dem Kindl 's Ärmle ab.
Die Magd springt zum Doktor,
der Doktor isch net em Haus.
Die Katz kehrt die Stuba aus,
die Maus tragt den Dreck naus.
Hockt a Vögele auf dem Dach,
hat sich halba duplich g'lacht.

Hansel am Bach
hat lauter scheen Sach,
hat's Heisel verbrennt,
hat Lumpe drum g'hängt,
hat d'Schiegle versoffe,
isch barfiesig g'loffe,
isch 's Bergl 'nuff gange,
hat Bliemle gesucht,
hat kaani nit g'funne,
hat 's Bergl verflucht.
A roti Grumbeer
un a Löchl dabei,
d'Bademer Buwe
sinn lauter Lakai.

Any, danny, silly Kate,
when we butcher, we'll have meat;
when we bake, we'll have some bread;
when we die, we shall be dead.

Farmer, tie your poodle up,
So that it cannot bite me.
If he bites, I'll make you pay
a fine of one ruble thirty.
A ruble thirty is no money,
However much the poodle barks.

Stork, stork, snipper, snapper,
with the long hay fork,
with the short rake handle.
Old women eat a lot,
the young have to fast,
the bread's in the box,
the wine is in the cellar,
the cheese on the platter,
father's in the tavern,
emptying all the glasses.

A little boy stands by the wall,
has a spring chick in his hand.
He'd like to eat it,
but has no knife.
The knife falls from above
cuts the child's arm off.
The maid runs for the doctor,
the doctor's not at home.
The cat sweeps out the room,
the mouse takes the dirt out.
A bird sitting on the roof
laughed itself half sick.

Hans by the brook
has all the nice things,
he burned down his house,
hung rags round about,
drank up his nice shoes,
walked on his bare feet,
went up on the hill,
searched for some flowers,
couldn't find any,
cursed at the hill.
A red potato
and a little hole in it,
the fellows in Baden
are all just lackeys.

Der Montag isch der Hebe-an,	Monday is the start of work,
Dienstag schaff i was i kann,	On Tuesday I do what I can,
Mittwoch isch der Wochenmarkt,	Wednesday is the weekly market,
Donnerstag schaff i au net arg,	On Thursday too I don't do much.
Freitag lass ich Freitag sein,	I let Friday be a free day,
Samstag bringt den Sonntag 'rein.	Saturday brings in Sunday.

Among other traditional types of children's rhymes were the easily memorized "relay jingle" and the alliterated "tongue-twister".

Aans, zwaa, drei,	One, two, three,
Geh ins Gässl 'nei.	Go into the alley.
Im Gässl isch a Haus,	In the alley there's a house,
beim Haus isch a Hof,	by the house is a yard,
im Hof isch a Garde,	in the yard is a garden,
im Garde isch a Baam,	in the garden is a tree,
im Baam isch a Nascht,	in the tree is a hollow,
im Nascht isch a Nescht,	in the hollow is a nest,
im Nescht isch a Ei,	in the nest is an egg,
im Ei isch a Dotter,	in the egg is a yolk,
im Dotter isch a Haas,	in the yolk is a bunny,
der springt d'r uff die Nas!	he'll jump upon your nose.

Wenn Wasser Wein wär,	If water were wine,
Wu wotte welsche Weiver Windle wäsche?	where would French women wash diapers?

Hinner Hanses Hasehaus	Behind Hans's rabbit house,
hänje hunnert Hase h'aus,	hundred hares are hanging out;
hunnert Hase hänje h'aus	hundred hares are hanging out
hinner Hanses Hasehaus.	behind Hans's rabbit house.

Children asking silly questions were likely to get a silly answer. Typical silly question-and-answer gags were invariably in the form of nonsense rhymes:

Was isch? Mehn Wasser als Fisch.	What is it? More water than fish.
Was machen'r? Ebb's Ung'machtes;	What are you doing? Something unmade,
wenn's zwaa gebbt, kriegsch aa aans.	if there are two, you'll get one.
Wu gehner 'na? Immer dr Nas nooch.	Where are you going? Always following my nose.
Wer? Hans Bär.	Who? Hans Bär.
Wie haasch? Hans Gaas.	What's your name? Hans Gaas.
Wie noch? Hans Bloch.	What else? Hans Bloch.
Hasch Hunger? Schlupf in e Gagumer.	Are you hungry? Crawl in a cucumber.
Hasch Dorscht? Schlupf in e Worscht.	Are you thirsty? Crawl in a sausage.

2. Handstreich und Verlobung

Der Kunrad un d'Lisbeth sinn schun lang aanich worre, as se gleich nooch dr Erne Hochzich mache. Dr heiradsluschtige Kunrad muss jetzert dr *Handstreich* mache, des maant er muss seine zukinftige Schwiegereldere um die Hand ihrer Dochter bitte. So verlangt's a alder deitsche Brauch. Weil des awwer far dr Bua a kitzliche Sach isch, muss sein Vedder Michel, der a gut's Mundwarik hat, mit'em gehe als Freiersmann.

Um Owed, als schun duschter isch un die Gasse leer sinn, mache sich die zween uff dr Weg zum Haus dr Brauteldere. Sie gehn gl ich in d'Vörderstubb, die hell beleicht isch—a Zäche, as d'Alde drhaam sinn. Nooch'em Owedgruss sagt d'Hausmudder, um a G'spräch anzuknipfe: "Grad hem'mer weg geh welle un jetz griege m'r noch Maastubb!"—"Mir sinn nit grad wejer dr Maastubb kumme, maant dr Vedder Michael, awwer wejer e wichtigere Sach Dr Kunrad will sein Anlieje vorbringe."

Dr Kunrad isch uff emol ganz bleed, sein G'sicht ward rot bis iwer die Ohre un er waas nit, wu er sein Händ na due sell. Er sagt halblaut: "Ich dät eier Lisbeth heirade, wenn'r m'r se gewwe däte." D'Hausmudder lugt niwwer zu ihrem Mann, dr vorne am Disch huckt, und sie sagt: "Ich waas nit, was dr Vadder maant, ob er se schun heirade lasse will oder nit."

D'r Alt, dr sich jetz so richtig als dr Harr im Haus fiehlt, hebbt der Kopf a bissel un maant: "Ja, ich hätt halt nix dergeje, awer d'Erne isch des Johr so schlecht ausg'falle und d'Mudder fiehlt sich alleweil aa nit so gut. Sie kennt d'Lisbeth so needich im Haus un Hof brauche. Un wemmer's richtig bedenkt, isch s'Madel so wie so noch a bissel zu jung zum heirade. Was sie selwer maant, waas ich nit."

"Na ja, die kam'mer jo froje," sagt dr Vedder Michel gleich und holt die Dochter aus dr Kich, wu se die ganz Zeit mit gespitzte Ohre hinner dr Deer g'lauert hat. S'Madel stellt sich bei dr Mutter newe dr Offe, ihre Aaje unnerschich g'senkt. "Lisbeth," sagt der Freiersmann, "eier Leit hätte nix drgeje. wenn du dr Kunrad nemmsch. Was maansch du drzue?" Weil's ihr arich schwer fallt, die richtig Antwort zu finne, um ihr Zugeständnis zu mache, sagt se aanfach: 'Warum nit?'

Nodert lasse sich die zwaa junge Leit zuredde, einanner die Hand zu gewwe (des isch dr "Handstreich") un dr Breitigam drickt dr Braut a Goldruwwel in d'recht Hand un sie sinn verlobt. Jetz steht dr Vadder uff un holt a Flasch Schnaps aus'em Glasschrank un d'Mudder stellt a Deller mit frischgebackenem Zuckerkuche uff dr Disch. Kaum hat jeder a Gläsel Schnaps zum Wohl des verlobten Paars getrunke, do falle draus vor 'em

Fenschter etliche Schuss, die vum Breitigam seine Kumerade abg'feiert worre sinn. M'r lasst die Buwe in d'Stubb 'rein, sie beglickwinsche das junge Brautpaar. Nodert drinkt m'r Schnaps un Wein, esst Kuche un Kiechle, un macht scheeni Maastubb bis Middernacht. So hat m'r in d'r gute alte Zeit in Russland die Verlobung g'feiert.

–J.S.H.

3. A Three-day Krasna Wedding

In the Catholic colony of Krasna, the girls usually married between the ages of 17 and 22, the young men at the ages between 21 and 24. A girl who was still single in her mid-twenties was practically regarded as an old maid. The young men of the village quite often married their school-day sweethearts or one of the girls from the appropriate comradeship, of which there were three classes, namely the rich, the middle class, and the poor. Marriages to partners from one of the neighboring villages were likewise fairly common. What was extremely rare were marriages to persons of another faith or to Russian nationals.

Opportunities for young men to become acquainted with marriageable girls were, of course, rather limited by social custom and circumstance, and the practice of dating or going steady was utterly unknown. Indeed, young couples never even ventured to walk arm in arm down the street. On the other hand, they were able to associate on the occasion of folk festivals and at the spinning bees. To be sure, the lads would often see the damsels in church on Sundays, but it was not the custom to converse with them or to escort them home. Haying and harvest time, when the older girls helped with the work in the fields, meadows, and vineyards, also provided the young people with frequent opportunities of meeting and associating.

1. The Engagement

Although the young man and the girl of his choice had agreed long ago to get married, their engagement remained a closely guarded secret that was known only to their parents. Then, on a Friday evening in the fall when the harvest was completed, the prospective groom, accompanied by two Freiersmänner who played the role of matchmakers, appeared at the home of the girl's parents, who had of course already been apprised of the visit.

While his comrades remained outside, the suitor and his two spokesmen entered the house. After first trying to conceal the real purpose of their visit, they came to the point and asked the master of the house and his wife, if they were in favor of the marriage. Upon receiving an affirmative reply, they called in the girl, who had been eavesdropping behind the door. She was then asked if she wished to marry the young man. The couple then stood in the middle of the room and the spokesman asked them: "Do you love each other and do you want to get married?" The couple replied, "Yes," and the spokesman said, "Then clasp your right hands and give each other a kiss." This was the traditional ceremony known as the *Handstreich* which confirmed the engagement. The groom then placed a silver coin (or a necklace or pair of earrings) into her right hand. This was the traditional *Handgeld* which was the seal and token of the betrothal. No engagement rings were exchanged.

While the engagement ceremony was taking place, some of the groom's comrades who were lurking outside fired several volleys from their shotguns into the air. The bridegroom then went out to treat his friends to wine and pastries, and also gave them some money. The young couple then repaired to the home of the groom's parents to invite them, along with the children and the neighbors, to the home of the bride for a special celebration, during which wine and brandy, pastries and snacks were served.

On the following day, a Saturday, the young couple went to the parish priest to give notice of their intention to get married, and the fathers went to the mayor's office to have them registered. The following Sunday the first banns were published in the church.

2. *The Brautschau*

It was not always an easy matter for a young man to find a marriage partner in his own village. In such a situation he had to look for one in a neighboring village. This search for a bride, known as the *Brautschau*, was not a simple undertaking, particularly in earlier times, for the prospective groom had to employ the services of a middleman who played the role of matchmaker. Generally the role was assumed by a kinsman or a close friend who began to make discreet inquiries in a neighboring village about a suitable mate for the young suitor. When they heard of a likely prospect they made a preliminary visit to the parents of the girl and inquired whether it would be agreeable to them if the suitor came for a visit. If they were interested, a date was set for the event.

Accordingly, the young man got his carriage and horses into tip-top condition, and on the specified evening, well after sundown, he set out with his middleman for the home of the girl's parents and was introduced to them and to the daughter. After the qualities and assets of the young couple were reviewed and discussed, they were left alone for awhile to get better acquainted. If it turned out that they had no liking for each other and if the persuasion of the parents and the middleman proved fruitless, the young suitor had no option but to drive home and try again later with some other girl.

In the event that the two were attracted to each other, the parents and the girl paid a visit, known as the *B'schau,* to the parents of the young man, in order to get better acquainted and, above all, to have a look at the farm and the property of the prospective bridegroom. If this visit proved satisfactory, the formal engagement soon took place.

But even then things did not always proceed without a hitch, for where there are nubile girls there are also young men who have an eye on them. Despite the late visit of the suitor, the young men of the village soon found out that there was a *Brautschau* at the home of a certain young woman. Either because of envy or wounded local pride, some of the fellows resented the intrusion of an outside suitor into their village. They therefore ganged together to punish the impudent poacher who had ventured into their privileged preserve. The punishment consisted in the perpetration of one or more traditional pranks or dirty tricks. Either the young men waylaid the foreign suitor and beat him up, or they cropped the tails of his horses. It also happened that his carriage was pushed into the pond or loaded with manure and hauled to the outskirts of the village. Sometimes the carriage was taken apart and reassembled on the rooftops of a barn; or the nuts on the axles would be loosened, so that the poor suitor 'accidentally' landed in a ditch. Quite often, however, the village comradeship informed the suitor that his visit would be welcomed with joy, if he was willing to pay an appropriate indemnity in the form of 10 gallons of wine and 4 bottles of brandy.

Girls who gave the mitten to local suitors or haughtily ignored them were also liable to become the victim of some humiliating prank or dirty trick. Either the jilted fellows smeared her window with tar at Eastertime or strewed a line of straw and chaff from her house to the hut of the swineherder or the cowherd. In this drastic way they gave vent to their resentment at the girl's haughty behavior.

Of course, not all marriages came about by the persuasion or the wilfulness of the parents. There were also marriages of love where a rich girl married a poor lad, or a rich lad married a poor girl. However, in many instances, the young couple got married because both parties were of a similar social or financial status, or because the parents insisted on that kind of marriage.

3. Preparations for the Wedding

In the following week, the *Hochzeitsväter,* the "fathers of the wedding," got together to make plans for the festive event. On the Sunday evening on which the second banns were proclaimed, the bride and the groom selected

Bridesmaids and Bestmen

the bridal attendants, namely four *Brautmädel* (the bridesmaids) and four *Brautdiener* (the bestmen), of whom the first *Brautdiener* and the first *Brautmädel* were usually the nearest of kin. Besides the bridal attendants, there were the two *Ehrenväter* and the two *Ehrenmütter,* namely the god-parents of the bride and the groom. The godmother of the bride was also called the *Brautfrau,* for she played a prominent role during the wedding festivities.

During the week, the bestmen brought their caps, bridles, and riding whips to the bridesmaids who adorned them with colored ribbons and flowers. The bride herself trimmed the groom's headgear with a wide band of white satin and small wax bouquets. The bestmen also provided gifts for the bridesmaids, such as cologne, perfumed soap, brooches, or handkerchiefs.

Throughout the week the parents of the bridal couple were kept busy with the preparations for the wedding feast. A fattened steer, one or two pigs, and two sheep were slaughtered. Each of the *Hochzeitsväter* provided a sixty-gallon barrel of wine and numerous bottles of brandy and vodka. Two reliable men were chosen as chief stewards in charge of all refreshments. They

191

were assisted by several waiters and waitresses whose task it was to serve the drinks and pastries to the guests. In the days preceding the wedding, the womenfolk in the kinship were engaged in baking immense quantities of wedding cakes and pastries.

It was customary to extend wedding invitations to all relatives, friends, and neighbors, and also to the village officials, namely the priest, the mayor, the schoolmaster, the church organist, and the village secretary. Accordingly, there was rarely a wedding to which less than 60 families would be invited. The invitation to the guests was a formal affair that took place on the Monday following the third proclamation of the banns. The chief bestman was given a list of the prospective wedding guests by the parents of the bridal couple. The four bestmen on their gaily beribboned horses then rode through the village, stopping at all the households where invitations were to be delivered. After appearing at the front door, they doffed their caps as the master of the house and his wife came out to greet them. The chief bestman, holding an ornamental mace in his right hand, recited the official invitation in a solemn voice and generally in the form of rhymed verse:

> Bride and groom make kind request
> that you become their wedding guest
> and to the festive table come
> that will be decked at the . . . . . home.
> Don't leave your fork and spoon behind,
> or with your fingers you must dine.
> And if you bring a fair young daughter,
> our joy will be so much the greater.
> So, if you have a ribbon to spare
> attach it to the mace I bear.
> And now we must be on our way,
> we'll see you on the wedding day.

The master of the house poured a glass of wine for each of the bestmen and they rode out of the yard to invite the next guests. In the evening each of the invited families sent a boy with a live chicken to the wedding house where a group of women were engaged in preparing them for the wedding feast. Each of the errand boys were treated to a piece of cake and a glass of wine.

4. The Brautabend

Later in the evening, the so-called *Brautabend,* also known as the *Polterabend,* was celebrated. It was the occasion when all the young men and women of the village gathered for a farewell party in honor of the bride and the groom who were now about to enter the married state. On this evening, the first wedding wine and cakes were served. There was dancing, singing, and exuberant merrymaking until far into the night. An outsider coming upon this scene might easily assume that the actual wedding festivities were taking place.

5. The Wedding

The wedding was traditionally held on a Tuesday and generally took place at the home of the bride's parents. At seven o'clock in the morning, the *Brautfrau,* the four bridesmaids, and a few other women came to the house to clothe the bride in her festive attire. In the olden days, she was dressed in the traditional blue or black gown and she wore an embroidered shawl and a bonnet or coif. In later times, she was clad in a gown of white silk and a long veil that was fastened to her head with a crescent-shaped wreath of rosemary and myrtle—the time-honored symbols of virginity and fidelity. Around her waist she wore a silken sash which was tied in a large bow with long streamers. In her hand she carried her prayer book, a rosary, and a bouquet of myrtle.

The groom donned his wedding suit at the home of his parents and arrived at the bride's home in the bridal carriage, attended by the four bestmen. He wore a suit of black serge, and on the left side of his coat he wore a bouquet of small myrtle flowers to which were fastened two long streamers of white ribbon. His brimmed cap was adorned with a band of white satin and small sprigs of myrtle.

After the immediate relatives and friends had gathered together, the bridal couple appeared in the living room, where a table with a crucifix, two candles, and a glass of holy water had been placed. As they stood before the table all present joined in the prayer, "Hail Mary, full of grace," and sang one or two stanzas of the well-known hymn, *"Maria zu lieben."* The first bestman then stepped forward and delivered a farewell address in rhymed verse:

> *"Den schönsten Tag, die schönste Stunde*
> *Habt ihr erleb, ihr Brautleut, heut.*
> *Ihr werdet durch den Kranz verbunden*
> *Fur eure ganze Lebenszeit. . . ."*

Dear bride and groom, for you has come
The fairest day, the finest hour.
By the wedding wreath you're bound
Together as long as you shall live.

And weep tears of silent sorrow,
Call to mind these blessed hours
Which today the wreath entwines.
But now proceed in Jesus' name,

But you must leave your parents now,
Who loved you with such tender care.
O thank them for all that they have done.
The wreath that now unites your heads
Press to your hearts with blessed joy.
It will bring you peace and happiness,
Perchance also much pain and sorrow.
But if some day you feel distressed

And let him bless your married state,
While the congregation sings Amen.
Pray to Jesus for his blessing,
Invite him to your marriage feast.
So much of the happiness you seek
Depends upon his heavenly grace.
Rejoice, O bridal pair, and love each other,
Until the end of your earthly days.

After the bridal couple took leave of the parents they were accompanied into the yard where several light carriages were waiting to take them and the assembled guests to the church. On the first vehicle, known as the *"Leiterwagen"* (ladder wagon), rode the musicians and the leading bestman. In the second carriage were seated the bride and the bridesmaids, while the groom and the bestmen rode in the third carriage. Then came the parents, brothers, and sisters, and finally the remaining guests. Before the bridal procession got under way, the leading bestman delivered the *Spruch:*

Dear people, honored wedding guests,
May I have your kind attention.
In Jesus' name we go from this house
To the house of God, and back again.
Let us step with joy before the altar
And humbly pray for the bridal pair,
That God may keep them from all harm
And lead them into his Kingdom.

Dear people, I should also like to ask
That you do not tarry too long in church,
Lest the bride become tired and weary,
And the cooks and waiters in the kitchen
Begin to grow impatient with waiting.
And now, young fellows and companions,
Get your guns and pistols loaded,
And I shall fire the first salvo!
Play, musicians, play'

The bridal coach

The musicians strike up a wedding march as the procession gets under way, accompanied by intermittent salvos of shotgun fire, until it reaches the festively decorated church. After the nuptial service the choir intones the hymn: "Singt mit fröhlichem Gemüt, Bräutigam mit deiner Braut." As the bridal party and the guests leave the church two mass servers, who have stretched a cord or ribbon across the exit door, extend their plates to take up the traditional collection.

The musicians again led the procession and played lively march music. The bride was now escorted by the bestmen, and the groom by the brides-maids. In the yard at the front of the wedding house, the stewards and stewardesses, the former with a bottle of brandy in the hand, the latter with a plate of pastries, were already waiting for the reception of the bridal party. After congratulating the bride and the groom and wishing them *"Viel Glück im Ehestand,"* each guest received a jigger of brandy and some pastry. After the reception the bridal pair was led to a small table on which lay a loaf of bread and a dish of salt. The two attending stewardesses then offered each of them a bite from the loaf, a pinch of salt, and a glass of wine.

6. The Dances of Honor

When all the guests were assembled in the wedding house and the groom was seated with the bride in the place of honor, the senior bestman led the bridal attendants and the musicians into the room. From the middle of the room, he then proceeded with the so-called *"Rausbitte,"* that is "the calling forth." He solemnly announces: "I stand in a golden wreath of roses and beg the bride to appear for the first dance of honor. Play, musicians, play!" The band strikes up some dance music while the bridal attendants walk in pairs in a circle. Only after the third invitation does the bride finally come for-ward and is escorted by the bestman in a circle while the music plays. The groom is similarly "called forth" three times and when he comes forward he joins the bride. In the same way the invitation goes out to the *Brautfrau* (the godmother of the bride), the fathers of honor, and all four bridesmaids, and all appear at the first bidding.

The bride and groom now dance the dance of honor in the midst of the guests. Then the bride's godmother, the fathers of honor, and the bestmen take turns dancing a brief waltz measure with the bride. The bridal couple are then seated in their place of honor while the bestmen and the brides-maids dance with each other amid shouts of joy and jubilation.

As soon as the dances of honor were completed the bridal party and the guests were seated at the tables for the festive dinner which consisted of chicken soup and roast fowl. For dessert there was the traditional rice pudding with raisins, sugar, and spices. After the meal the tables were cleared and the stewards served wine and pastries. General dancing now began and continued almost without interruption until suppertime. At this meal the main course consisted of pork and beef roast. Near the end of the meal the time-honored custom of stealing the bride's shoe was enacted. A couple of young fellows usually managed to snatch one of the bride's shoes which was then publicly displayed for all to see. It was now up to the *Brautfrau* to redeem the shoe by paying the fellows a ransom of two or three bottles of brandy.

After the tables were cleared, the chief bestman accompanied by his associates again entered the room for the ceremony known as the *"Tellerbitte,"* the invitation of the plate. Standing in the middle of the room and facing the bridal couple, he made the following proclamation:

I enter here, boldly striding,
Had I a horse, I'd come ariding.
Had I a coach, I'd come driving.
But since I lack both, forsooth,
I have to come to you on foot.
I've been to Hesse now and then,
They've got big bowls but little in them.
In Posen, too, I been by chance,
Where many a man has no pants.
I've even been to Saxony
Where pretty girls grow on trees.
If only I had thought of that,
I would have brought a dozen back.
But of the groom I often thought,
For him the fairest girl I brought.
I hope that he will cherish that
And present me with a nice straw hat.

In my hands this plate I hold,
Neatly rimmed with a band of gold,
And on it are three golden letters.
The first one is a capital A:
May the groom love his bride always.

The second letter is a B:
How sad the groom would be
Were he to lose his bride.
C is letter number three:
He clings to her as fast
As a branch to a tree,
As a bird to its nest,
None but God can separate the twain.

Dear friends and well-known guests,
Raise your glasses filled with wine
And drink with me to the happiness
Of the fair bride and her groom,
As the bridesmaids sing a joyful song.

Now let me step before the groom,
He'll remember my kindness to him
And give his bride a piece of gold,
For to him she is so very dear.
And you, dear friends, one and all,
Lest your coin rusts in your purse,
Let it ring out upon this plate,
As we sing out merrily:
Play, musicians, play!

The musicians play a march while the four bestmen pick up their plates to take up the collection among the male wedding guests. The dancing and merriment continue until eleven-thirty when the time arrives for the so-called *"Abtanzen der Braut,"* that is, the final dance with the bride. A group

196

of young men request the favor of the last dance and succeed, despite the alertness of the bestmen, to steal the unsuspecting bride and abduct her through an open window. The bestmen are now confronted with the penalty of having to ransom her from her captors for the price of several bottles of brandy.

7. *The Unwreathing of the Bride*

With the approach of the midnight hour comes the time for the traditional ceremonial of the *"Abbinden"* or *"Abschmücken"* of the bride, namely the removal of the bridal wreath. A chair is placed in the middle of the room and there the groom is seated with the bride upon his lap. The bride's godmother removes the wreath from the girl's head and hands it to her mother. Meanwhile the band strikes up the melody and all the wedding guests sing the traditional song:

"Den Ehestand hat kein Mensch erdicht,   No man ordained the married state,
Gott selber hat ihn eingericht.   God Himself did institute it.
Er nahm ein Ripp aus Adams Leib   He took a rib from Adam's side
Und machte ihm daraus ein Weib.   And formed a woman from it,
Setzt' ein die Eh', setzt' ein die Eh' "   And instituted marriage.

A wedding party

197

During the singing the bridal attendants moved in a circle around the bridal pair, teasing them again and again by playfully tugging their hair.

At the end of the ceremony the groom took his bride by the hand and they departed from the wedding party amid joyous acclamations and best wishes. All the young unmarried people, excepting the stewards of the wedding, also took their leave. The remaining guests continued the wedding celebration until daybreak when everyone went home.

8. The Second Wedding Day

On the second wedding day, usually a Wednesday, all the invited guests returned to the wedding house about eleven o'clock in the forenoon. The stewards again stood near the front door entrance to offer the guests a drink of brandy and some pastries. The same ceremonies were observed as on the previous day.

The guests were then seated for breakfast which consisted of steamed chicken parts and giblets. After the meal wine and cakes were served, the celebration continued. At three o'clock dinner was served which consisted of beef soup and roast. The groom and the bride, who were now dressed in their ordinary Sunday clothes, donned white aprons and waited on the guests.

After the dinner the tables were cleared and all the single people had to disappear. The bride's godmother now appeared on the scene with a large plate on which lay the bridal wreath which had been sprinkled with eau de cologne. She was accompanied by two young ladies, one of whom carried a bottle of whiskey, while the other held a plate of pastries. The *Brautfrau* now went up to each male wedding guest and as she held the perfumed wreath under his nose she emitted a whoop of ecstatic delight. The cajoled guest graciously placed a coin in the extended plate, or simply made a pledge to donate a sheep, a small pig, a few chickens, or a measure of wheat or corn—whatever he wished. He was now treated to a jigger or two of vodka, and the pledge was duly recorded by one of the attendants.

After the ceremony of the perfumed bridal wreath was over, the chief cook emerged from the kitchen, her face full of soot, her right hand in a bandage, and in her left a large wooden ladle with which she collected tips from the assembled guests for herself and her culinary staff. Then the dancing and general merriment continued until suppertime when pork and beef roast were served, followed by wine and sweetmeats. Dancing and singing was then underway until far into the night.

9. The Third Wedding Day

On the third wedding day most of the guests again showed up in the late forenoon. The waiters now served mostly leftovers which were washed down with wine. In the afternoon, two wagons fancifully festooned with ropes of straw and garlands of colored rags were hitched up. Several wedding guests, disguised in freakish attire, were seated with the bride in one wagon, and a number of stewards and waitresses in the other, drove up and down the village streets to collect the gifts that had been pledged to the bride and groom the day before during the ceremonial of the perfumed bridal wreath. The gifts were then brought back to the wedding house. The newlyweds often obtained so many gifts that they could pay the entire cost of the three-day wedding. But the collectors also managed to bring back a quantity of edible gifts, such as sausages and pastries, so that the wedding celebration could be prolonged for several more hours. Some of the younger guests who had donned masks and outlandish disguises were in the mood to amuse the guests with all kinds of pranks and tomfoolery. Some crawled on the roof of the neighbor's house and one delivered a witty speech that evoked outbursts of raucous laughter. In the meantime some other pranksters had unhitched the wagon of an itinerant Russian or Jewish peddlar. While the horses were placed in the neighbor's barn, the wagon was rolled into a ditch. The peddler was generously treated to wine and vodka, and when he was fairly plastered his face was blackened with soot or his beard trimmed. And so the celebration continued for another night until the weary guests dispersed to their homes in the wee hours of the morning.

4. Christbaum and Christkindel

The historical origin and meaning of two German traditions

1. Theory, Myth, and Legend

As inevitable as the annual appearance of the Christmas tree is the pro-
liferation of theories about its origin. While the German origin is generally
accepted, amateur folklorists and freelance writers, ostensibly richer in
imagination than in erudition, come up with all sorts of fanciful theories that
have not a shred of historical or factual evidence to support them. Their
chief interest seems to be to find the origin of the Christmas tree tradition in
pagan antiquity or in some prehistorical culture. Thus one theorist finds the
origin of the Christmas tree in the sacred tree of the Druids or the ancient
Teutons; another, in the sacred tree of the Assyrians or the Babylonians,
while a third finds an analogue in the Yuletide celebrations of the ancient
Aryans. What all of these theorists obtusely overlook is the fact that the
Christmas tree is an evergreen, a fir tree, not an elm, an oak, or a palm tree.
While it is true that people in the animistic stage of culture regarded trees as
being endowed with a soul, it must be stated that this belief has no bearing
whatever on the historical significance of the Christmas tree.

Besides such fanciful and far-fetched theories on the origin of the
Christmas tree, there have also been a number of legends. One of these
maintains that Martin Luther first started the custom of setting up a Christmas tree in his home. While Luther did compose a number of Christmas
hymns that are still sung today, there is no mention in his voluminous
writings of the Christmas tree, and it is unlikely that he knew of the custom.[1]
Others have suggested that a priest strolling one night through the starlit
evergreen forest suddenly got the idea of cutting down a small fir tree and
taking it to his home on Christmas Eve. A nice thought, but without any
historical basis.

2. The Historical Evidence

All the earliest literary sources of the first appearance of the Christmas
tree point to the land of Alsace, specifically to the towns of Türkheim and
Schlettstadt, and somewhat later, to the city of Strassburg. According to
extant documents, the *Christbaum* that was set up in a certain manor hall in
the Catholic town of Türkheim was "a Tannenbaum that was decorated with
apples, hosts (wafers), and paper roses." That was on Christmas Eve of

---

[1] The Christmas tree custom did not spread into Lutheran Northern Germany until the middle of
the 19th century. It was in 1845—almost 400 years after Luther's time—that an artist named C. A.
Schweidgeburth painted Luther and his family seated around a candle-lit Christmas tree.

1596. In 1600 there is a reference to a similar tree that was set up in the *Herrenstube* (guild hall) in the town of Schlettstadt, and in 1605 the setting up of such trees was already a fairly common custom in the city of Strassburg. A traveller who saw such a tree in that city for the first time in his life wrote the following description: "At Christmas the citizens of Strassburg bring *Tannenbäume* (fir trees) into their homes, and on them they hang roses of multicolored paper, apples, hosts, tinsel, and candies, etc. The tree is usually set in a square frame." In 1650 the Lutheran minister at the Strassburg cathedral, a certain Conrad Dannhauer (lit., a fir tree cutter!), likewise stated that the "*Tannenbaum* is set up in the houses and decorated with dolls and candies," and he adds that the children enjoyed the chance to "plunder" the tree at the close of the Christmas season. In all of these early records, there is still no mention of the custom of placing lighted candles on the *Tannenbaum*.

3. The Medieval Antecedents

Although the custom of setting up a Christmas tree is not very old in this historical form, the origin of its forerunners and earlier stages go back to the pre-Christian period in Germany. In actuality, the custom is rooted in an ancient Germanic superstition of having some greenery in the house during the season of *Weihnachten,* namely the twelve sacred nights that intervened between the old year and the new. This custom, which was already widespread in the Middle Ages, was based upon the belief that the presence of green shoots from fruit trees or from grain seed was a good omen of fertility and prosperity in the coming year.

As early as 1494 the Alsatian poet Sebastian Brant, the author of the widely-read "Narrenschiff," reproached the people of his time for their superstitious belief that they would not live out the year unless they had some greenery in the house at Christmas time. It was the belief that also gave rise to the popular practice that took place on St. Barbara's Day (December 4), when people brought twigs of fruit trees called *"Barbarazweige"* and seeds of grain into the house where they were placed into water or planted into boxes, so that they might produce green shoots and leaves by the time Christmas arrived.

However, since these superstitious attempts oftentimes proved to be fruitless, people simply brought in branches of evergreen (Tannenzweige) and used them as festive decoration in the living room. This was already a common practice as early as 1500, and this custom was the historical forerunner of the introduction of the full-fledged *Tannenbaum.* Originally these fir trees were fairly small, for they were suspended in a frame that was attached to a corner of the room. As the custom became widespread in various communities and almost every family cut down a Christmas tree from the communal forest, the local mayors found it necessary to post wardens and rangers in the woods to prevent the spoliation of evergreen trees. In some communities it was forbidden to cut down any fir trees that were taller than six feet.

There are no records to indicate when the Christmas tree was first illuminated with candles. The earliest reference to a candle-lit tree occurs in a letter of the archduchess Elizabeth of Orleans, popularly known as "Liselotte von der Pfalz," who was born in Heidelberg in 1652. In this letter she states that she was familiar with the custom of having candle-lit trees at Christmas in the home of her parents when she was still a young girl.[2] According to the Baroness of Oberkirch, the candle-adorned *Christbaum* was a common sight in every home in Strassburg as early as 1785. The custom was probably known much earlier, for the Christmas cribs in Alsace had been enhanced with greenery and candlelight since the Middle Ages. The popular song *"O Tannebaum"* was not written until about 1824.

In this connection it is interesting to note that the ornamentation of the earliest known Alsatian Christmas trees had its prototype in the Biblical tree of Paradise, which appeared in the traditional pre-Christmas mystery play that dramatized the "Fall of Adam and Eve." The apples represented the fateful fruit in the garden of Eden, the hosts symbolized the grace of Christ's redemptive death on Calvary, and the colored roses alluded to the flowering branch from the root of Jesse. Thus the Christmas tree had a distinctively religious significance. The *Christbaum* was the "Christ-tree" that symbolized eternal hope and the source of all goodness. The addition of the tinsel, gold foil, candies, cookies, and toys was intended to bring Christmas joy into the hearts of the children. For them the *Christbaum* was the *Christkindelbaum,* the tree of the Christchild.

Already in the 18th century the Christmas trees were decorated with various kinds of confections, cookies, candies, fruit, and gilded nuts. In the Palatinate and in Hesse such trees were called *"Zuckerbaam"*—sugartrees. In 1769 Goethe set up such a tree for the children of a friend in Leipzig, and in his novel "The Sorrows of Werther," written in 1773, the heroine Lotte mentions "a Zuckerbaam" with fruits and sweetmeats and lighted candles.

In the Black Forest area in Baden, it was called the *"Wienechtschindl-Baum"* the Christchild tree. In his *"Allemannische Gedichte,"* (published in 1808), the dialect poet J. P. Hebel wrote two delightful Christmas poems which describe a mother who prepares a Christmas tree for her only child. On Christmas Eve, after the child is sound asleep, she brings the little tree she had hidden in a closet into the living room, and adorns it with gingerbread cookies shaped like farm animals and brightly colored flowers. She

---

[2]The letter, written in 1708, states: "Tables are fixed up like altars and outfitted for each child with all sorts of things, such as new clothes, silver, dolls, sugar candy, and so forth. Boxwood trees are set up on the tables, and a candle is fastened to each branch."

adds a beautiful apple, a dainty handkerchief, a prayer book with pretty holy pictures, a pin-cushion, and a gilded switch. On Christmas morning the child is told that the *Christchindl* had come at midnight and brought the splendid *Wiehnechtskindelbaum* with all its wondrous gifts for the child, including a gilded switch for the mother. There is no indication that the tree was a *Tannenbaum* or that it was adorned with candles. In all probability, it was a verdant *Buchsbaum,* for the box-tree was commonly used in some areas as a Christmas tree.

4. The Spreading of the Christmas Tree Custom

From Alsace, particularly from Strassburg, the *Christbaum* gradually spread to central Germany, and later to northern Germany. The custom was more readily adopted in the Lutheran communities, inasmuch as they repudiated the Catholic St. Nicolas tradition. On the other hand, the Catholic south, where the custom of the *Weihnachtskrippe*—the Christmas crib, begun by St. Francis of Assisi, was widely and well-established, was slow in accepting the Christmas tree. It did not come into vogue in Bavaria and in Austria until around 1850. Alsatians who immigrated to the interior of France introduced the custom there after 1870. The oldest French representation of the Christmas tree appeared in 1865 on the book cover of Julie Gouraud's *"La Nuit de Noël."*

It has sometimes been asserted, apparently even by scholars, that the custom of the Christmas tree was introduced to America by German and Dutch settlers in Colonial times, or by Hessian mercenaries during the Revolutionary War (1775-83). However, there is not a single piece of documentary evidence to support these assumptions. A seemingly plausible conjecture is that the custom came to America by way of England where the Christmas tree was known to the royal family in the beginning of the 19th century. Thus Victoria's grandmother, Queen Charlotte, who was the wife of King Georg III, had a Christmas tree set up in the Queen's Lodge at Windsor in 1800. Almost half a century later, Prince Albert, the consort of Queen Victoria, was responsible for popularizing the German tradition in England, but there is no truth in the widely held notion that he also introduced the custom in America. On the contrary, all the evidence conclusively proves that it was the German immigrants who brought the Christmas tree custom from their homeland into the New World.

The earliest evidence points to the fact that the Christmas tree custom was first introduced into Pennsylvania by German emigrants from the Palatinate and Alsace where the custom was well and widely established. As early as 1819, a Philadelphia artist named John Lewis Krimmel depicted a Christmas

An early illustration of a Christmas tree
in America appeared in 1836

in his sketchbook. The following year, Matthew Zahm in Lancaster County mentions in his diary that "Sally and his son Thomas and William Henzel cut down Christmas trees near Kendrich's saw mill." In 1825 the Philadelphia "Saturday Evening Post" describes "trees that were visible through the windows, whose green boughs were laden with fruit." In 1833, Dr. Constantin Hering exhibited a German Christmas tree for his friends in Philadelphia.

Soon we find Christmas trees appearing in other states. In 1833, Gustave Koerner, a German settler in St. Clair County, Illinois, decorated a sassafras (!) tree with bright paper, ribbons, candles, sweetmeats, apples, and nuts." Charles Follen, a German citizen of Bostaon, is credited with setting up the first Christmas tree in that city in 1832. A German teacher set up the first Christmas tree in Williamsburg, in the College of William and Mary. A fully decorated tree appeared in Texas as early as 1846. The first Christmas tree to appear in a church was set up by a 32-year-old immigrant, Rev. Henry Schwan, in his church in Cleveland in 1851. By 1862 Christmas trees were a common sight in San Francisco.

Strangely enough, the Christmas tree custom spread very slowly until the end of the 19th century. According to Phillip V. Snyder, "in 1900 only one American family in five had a Christmas tree in their home, although most children probably enjoyed one at their school. In the first years of the twentieth century the custom spread like wildfire, and by 1910 in many parts of America, nearly all children had a tree at home. However, there are a surprising number of Americans alive today who never saw a Christmas tree as children and never had one of their own until they became adults."[3]

President Franklin Pierce first introduced a Christmas tree into the White House, and Benjamin Harrison set up the first publicly displayed Christmas tree in front of the White House in 1891. On the other hand, the conservationist Theodore Roosevelt refused to have a Christmas tree in the White House.

The American contribution to the Christmas tree tradition has been threefold. First of all, the size of the tree was increased by placing it on the floor instead of on the table, as was the common practice in the earlier tradition. Secondly, the Americans were the first to replace the traditional Christmas candles by electric lights.[4] Thirdly, to an increasing extent, the traditional evergreen was replaced by artificial replicas of plastic.

5. The Christmas Tree in Russia

There is no historical evidence that the German pioneer settlers in Russia set up a Christmas tree in their homes. Some of them may well have known about the custom in their homeland, but were perhaps not familiar with it in their own village. Indeed, there is a strong presumption that the Christmas tree did not make its appearance in the colonies until about 1870 when it was introduced by priests, pastors, and teachers who had learned of the custom in the seminaries and theological institutes. Their presumption is confirmed by the evidence of the older Christmas custom that prevailed among the Volga Germans in the village of Anton, in the district of Balzer. Here the custom prevailed of cutting cherry or lilac branches three weeks before Christmas and placing the cuttings in water. Similarly, seeds of wheat or barley were planted in a box, so as to have lots of greenery in the house at Christmas time. The boxes with the green branches were decorated and set in the center of the dining table. This, as we have already noted, represents the earliest forerunner of the Christmas tree tradition.

Perhaps the most obvious reason why the colonists did not have a Christmas tree for several decades is the simple fact that no evergreen trees were to be found on the open steppes of the Volga and the Black Sea regions.

---

[3] Snyder, Phillip V., "The Christmas Tree Book," Viking Press, N.Y. 1976, p. 40, 41.

[4] The first Christmas tree with electric lights appeared in 1882 in New York, in the home of Edward Johnson, the vice-president of the Edison Electric Company.

When the custom finally came into vogue in the 1870's, Christmas trees were brought in by rail to the larger cities from the coniferous regions. The earliest historical evidence of the Christmas tree custom in Russia goes back to the year 1828. On Christmas Eve of that year, Count Michael Voronzov, the governor general of Odessa, had a Christmas tree set up on his palatial residence on Richelieu Boulevard. The tree is described by an English visitor as "a six-foot sapling (no doubt an acacia!) that was planted in a box and adorned with a variety of artificial flowers and gift packages. The salon in which it stood was illuminated by a large number of lighted wax candles that were placed on tables." In all likelihood, the Count had learned of this custom from his long-time friend and predecessor in office, Duc de Richelieu, who presumably observed it in Alsace or in the Palatinate. A passionate tree lover, Richelieu no doubt had a Christmas tree in his modest home during the years when he was governor of Odessa (1803-1816).

6. The St. Nicholas Tradition

The tradition of St. Nicholas as the bringer of gifts for children probably goes back to the Middle Ages. As an historical personality St. Nicholas was the bishop of Myra in Asia Minor in the fourth century. He is said to have been a generous, kind-hearted man, and on one occasion helped out three young sisters who were poor, by giving each of them a dowry that enabled them to get married. In the Middle Ages good Saint Nicholas was honored and loved as the patron saint of boys, and his feast was celebrated on December 6. In subsequent centuries he became the most popular of all saints in the church calendar. In fact, there were over 2,000 churches in Europe that were dedicated to his patronage.

St. Nicholas Day became a very special day for all the children, and it was celebrated by having the good *Sankt Nikolaus* make his appearance in the guise of a venerable bishop with a flowing white beard and in full episcopal regalia, including mitre and crozier. He was accompanied by a hulking swarthy servant known as *Knecht Ruprecht,* who was garbed in a shaggy fur coat and matching headgear, with a heavy iron chain around his waist and a big sack over his shoulder. After St. Nicholas had read the record of the boy's delinquencies from a large open book, Ruprecht would seize the young sinner and give him a taste of the switch or have him chew on the chain, after which he would be rewarded with an onion. When all the bad but now penitent boys had been suitably punished and all the children had recited their prayers, he reached into his sack and began distributing fruits and nuts and candy. In those days, many a city, like Strassburg and Nürnberg, set up special open-air markets known as *Nikolausmarkt* where all kinds of toys, gifts, and delicacies were sold. In some places it was also customary to distribute gifts to the children at Christmas time. The earliest known *Christbescherung* in Germany goes back to the year 1584.

With the coming of the Reformation, the time-honored St. Nicholas tradition lost much of its appeal. In many areas, particularly in South Germany, the episcopal figure was replaced by the secularized figure of the uncouth demonic bugbear, the *Schreckfigur* that had formerly played the role of the servant of the kind-hearted bishop. He appeared under a variety of names, some of which retained a garbled remnant of the Nikolaus name, particularly the widely used names *Nickel* or *Klaus*. Indeed, in the Bavarian and the Alemannic areas the term *Klaus* became the common designation for the masked bogeyman who appeared in many of the popular folk festivals. Some names alluded to his shaggy appearance, for he was usually clad in bearskin, sheepskin, or goatskin. Other names referred to his boisterous behavior which was characterized by the stomping of feet and the din of rattling chains. Thus we encounter various forms of the dread figure in different parts of Germany and German-speaking lands. In the Palatinate and in Baden, he is generally known as the *Belzenickel, Belzebock,* or *Belzebub.* In Alsace we encounter the figure of *Hans Trapp*; in Württemberg, the *Pelzmärtel*; in the Rhineland, *Hans Muff*; in Switzerland, the *Zantichloise*; in northern Germany, the *Bullerklas*; and in the Netherlands, the *Sinter Klos* or *Sente Kloas*—the historical forerunner of the American *Santa Claus.*

All these secularized figures had much in common, but there is a significant distinction in their character and bearing. While the shaggy types of the High German area (in the Palatinate, Baden, Alsace, and Bavaria) were fearsome, even demonic "bugbears," the *Kloas* in the Low German area of the Netherlands and the *Weihnachtsmann* of northern Germany generally exhibited a genial, good-natured character. The Dutch *Sente Kloas,* whose name was a garbled form of the older *Sankt Niklaus,* was a jovial kindhearted figure who still had the long white beard of his remote prototype, but was clad in an attractive red suit. Unlike the fur-cloaked *Pelzenickel* of the Oberrhein, he appeared without the clanking chain and the punitive switch. He did not stomp into the living room on Christmas Eve to frighten the children out of their wits, but came silently and invisibly through the chimney in the dead of night and put his gifts into the wooden shoes that were set near the fireplace.

This Dutch *Sente Kloas* was the model of the American Santa Claus whom the poet Clement C. Moore described in 1823 in his immortal poem "The Night before Christmas," as a paunchy, jolly little elf who rode through the sky in a sleigh drawn by eight tiny reindeer, and came through the chimney with his pack to fill the stockings that were hung by the fireplace. Santa's home at the North Pole and his reindeer-drawn sleigh were the only significantly new American features. Moore's pipe-smoking St. Nick has really never met with popular acceptance. Attempts have, of course, been made to enhance the image of Santa Claus by giving him a consort by punning on the name *Mary* Christmas and by adding a "red-nosed" reindeer to guide the sleigh on Santa's merry expedition. But these are just whimsical fatuities. If Santa could make his way down through the typical American chimney, he was obviously also capable of finding his way to the roof-tops without a special guide.

The Nicholas figures of European tradition were, of course, depicted in a variety of ways, depending on the particular character represented by each type. In America the traditional fur-clad Nicholas was modified to some extent by substituting more attractive and appealing features for the scary appearance of the bogeyman. The earliest attempts to depict the American Santa Claus were made by the well-known illustrator and cartoonist Thomas Nast.

Illustration of American Santa Claus
by Thomas Nast

Born in Landau in the Rhine Palatinate in 1840 and immigrated to America in 1848, Nast became a talented creator of cartoons and sketches. Besides creating the political symbols of the Democratic donkey and the Republican elephant, he also produced several illustrations of Santa Claus. In his earlier attempts he pictured Santa in costumes that were either black or green trimmed with white fur. In a later sketch which was published in Harper's Weekly in the mid-eighties, he depicted him in a bright-red suit, which was obviously more in harmony with Moore's jolly characterization of Saint Nick as a paunchy, pipe-smoking little elf.

7. The Christkindel Tradition

In the context of the Lutheran Reformation and the developing custom of the *Christbaum,* the Protestants expressed a deeply religious sentiment that the *Christchild,* not St. Nickolas, should be regarded as the donor of gifts bestowed upon children at Christmas time. Soon the custom developed of having the *Christkindel* appear in the homes on Christmas Eve. The role, however, was always played by an adult girl who was dressed in a long white gown that was embellished by streamers of colored ribbon. On her head she wore a thin veil that almost concealed her face. Generally, she also wore a wreath of rosemary or a gold-foil crown on her head, which gave her the appearance of a bride or a fairy godmother. Indeed, in some places in Alsace, she wore a circlet of lighted candles on her head, similar to the *Lucia* figure of Swedish tradition. The feast of Saint Lucia (from Latin *lux,* light) fell on December 13, both in the Catholic and the Lutheran calendars.

To heighten the children's joy of anticipation during the days of Advent, the *Christkindel* (usually the eldest daughter of the house or of the neighbor's family) appeared after dark for just a fleeting moment at the window, threw a handful of candies against the pane, quickly vanished before the children had a chance to "see what was the matter." And, sometimes, when the western sky was flooded with the fiery glow of the setting sun, the mother would exclaim to the wide-eyed children, "Ja, 's *Christkindel* backt schun Kiechle!" (Yes, the Kriss Kringle is already baking cookies). As Christmas drew near the children made pretty little cardboard baskets which were set out on the doorstep, so the *Christkindel* might find them and return them filled with good things on Christmas Eve.

In some villages the *Christkindel* was expected to arrive on a donkey. The role was usually played by one or two boys who did the impersonation under an improvised donkey costume. Accordingly, on the eve of Christmas the children observed the custom of placing a glass on the window sill and a bundle of hay near the door, while they recited the traditional jingle:

Christkindele, Christkindele, Kriss Kringle, Kriss Kringle,
Kumm du zu uns herein!   Come to visit us!
M'r henn a frisch Heibindele We've got a bundle of fresh hay
Un aah a Gläsele Wein.   And also a little glass of wine.
A Bindele far's Essele,   The bundle's for the donkey,
Far's Kindele a Gläsele,   The glass is for Kriss Kringle,
Un bedde kenne m'r aah!   And we also know our prayers!

After dusk on Christmas Eve, the *Christkindel,* accompanied by a small troupe of girl friends and boys, started on its errands from house to house. It announced its arrival by appearing at the window and ringing a small bell. The greatly excited children quickly gathered in the living room where the Christmas tree stood resplendent in the magic glow of its lighted candles. Here the children waited with mixed emotions of joy and apprehension, for they knew from past experience or from hearsay that the *Christkindel* not only brought gifts and goodies, but also carried a switch for the youngsters who had been disobedient and naughty.

Christkindel and Hans Trapp in Alsace (Theophile Schuler)

As the white celestial visitor stood in awesome silence in the middle of the room the younger tots clung tightly to their mother's apron, while the older ones huddled together in a far corner of the room. Upon inquiry by one of the *Christkindel's* escorts, the mother or father would reveal the identity of the boy or boys who had been guilty of misconduct and mischief. Two strong-armed escorts forthwith hauled the culprit before the *Christkindel,* which promptly delivered a few strokes of the switch upon his back. While the educational effect may have been minimal, the switching was always a source of much fun and amusement—for the onlookers. After this exciting interlude the younger children stepped forward at the bidding of their mother, and recited the simple rhymed prayer:

Ich bin klein,	I am little,
Mein Herzel ist rein.	My heart is pure.
Darf niemand drin wohne	May no one dwell in it
Als Jesus allein.	But Jesus alone.
Christkindlein, komm,	Kriss Kringle, come,
Mach mich fromm,	Make me be good,
Dass ich in den Himmel komm.	So that I'll get to Heaven.

Christkindl and Belzenickl (C. Spindler)

In Alsace it was not the *Christkindel* who punished the bad boys, but the masked bogeyman Hans Trapp who jumped in through the window and brandished his bundle of switches.

The moment had now arrived for the distribution of the Christmas baskets full of cookies, apples, nuts, figs, dates, and candies. As the *Christkindel* placed the baskets, one by one, at its feet, each child had to venture forth to get its own basket. Each child also received a single gift package containing a doll, a ball, a top, or a little wagon. It was not the custom for adults to exchange gifts, for Christmas was pre-eminently a children's festival. Throughout the Christmas season they would receive a *Christkindel,* a gift basket or bag of assorted cookies, nuts, and candies from the grandparents, godmothers, aunts and uncles.

Just before or immediately after the departure of the *Christkindel,* the *Belzenickel* or *Pelzmärtel,* a Nicholas in fur, stomped into the room, creating an uproar of excitement. The fearsome, almost demonic figure usually wore a grotesque mask with horns and a long scraggly beard, a heavy coat of shaggy fur (usually bearskin or goatskin), and a clanking chain around his waist. In his right hand he held a bundle of stout switches and carried a big sack over his left shoulder. His forbidding appearance and his wild, noisy antics were calculated to inspire fear and awe even among the toughest of the bad boys. Indeed, many a one found himself stuffed into the sack and dumped into a pile of snow. In the end, however, the bugbearish *Belzenickel* rewarded the youngster with a special gift as a reward for his stout-hearted resistance against insuperable odds. With a final admonition to be good and a dire promise to return next year, the shaggy Nicholas rattled his big chain and disappeared into the night.

Just as the original Saint Nicolas of Catholic tradition was ultimately replaced by the secularized figure of the fur-clad *Nickel* or *Klaus,* so was the angelic figure of the *Christkindel* of Protestant origin fated to become obsolete. In English, its German name survived in the garbled form of *"Kriss Kringle,"* which, ironically enough is mistakenly applied to Santa Claus, the character it was originally intended to replace. In an age of supermaterialism, the figure of Santa has been largely reduced to the function of a commercial advertiser for Christmas shopping.

SOURCES

Lefftz, J., Elsässische Dorfbilder, Edition Sutter (Woerth) 1958.
Lauffer, O., Der Weihnachtsbaum in Glauben und Brauch (1934).
Pfleger, Alfred, Elsässische Weihnacht, Strasbourg, 1931.
Spamer, A., Weihnachten in alter und neuer Zeit (1934).

Am Grischtowed isch's gwesst

Clement C. Moore's "Twas the Night before Christmas"
in the Franconian-Alsatian dialect of Selz/So. Russia.

Am Grischtowed isch's gwesst un durichs ganz Haus
Nix hat sich g'muckst, ka Katz un ka Maus.
D'Strimpf sinn schun g'hange am grosse Kamin,
In dr Hoffning dr Sente Klaas dut jedem ebb's bringe.

Die Kinner die lejje schun lengscht in dr Kisse
Un draame vun Spielsach un Kendy un Nisse.
Un d'Mudder im Kopfduch un ich in dr Kapp
Lejje uns schlofe uff d'lang Windernacht.

Uff amol do glebbert's un rasselt's im Hof,
Un ich aus 'em Bett noch halwer im Schlof
Laaf gleich ans Fenschter, schnell wie dr Blitz,
Hab dr Lade uffgrisse un lug was do isch.

Dr Mōn scheint so hell uff'em frisch g'fallene Schnee
Un macht alles wie Dag, so weit kam'mer seh'.
Im a Aajeblick kummt jetz, so rund wie a Karsch,
A Fuhrmann im Schlidde un acht glaane Harsch.

A Männel im e Belz so ardlich un fein,
Gleich hawwich gwisst, 's muss der Sente Klaas sein.
Wie Adler, so flieje die Harrschle scheen z'samme,
Un er pfeift un er ruft un nennt se mit Namme:

"Jetz Renner, jetz Denzler, jetzt Hexel un Fixel!
Jetz Starnel un Schetzel un Dunner un Blitzel!
Grad nuff uff die Botsch un hoch iwwer's Dach,
Voranne! Giddup mit all uns'rem Sach!"

Wie Bledder vum Baam gedriwwe vum Wind,
Wann ebbes im Weg sie himmelwarts zwingt,
So fliege die Harrschle zum Hausgewwel 'nuff
Mit em Schlidde voll Sach un dr Nick owwedruff.

Bletzlich do heer ich uff'm Dach so a G'rappel.
Die Harrschle die danze mit grossem Gedrappel.
Ich zieg mich vum Fenschter zurick ins gross Zimmer,
Un durich's Kamin do ritscht er schun 'runner.

A Belz hat er um sich vum Kopf bis zum Fuss,
Un alles versuddelt mit Esch un mit Russ.
Uff'm Buckel a Bundel mit allerhand Sache,
Un grad wie a Trevler dut er auspacke.

Sein Maul wie a Karsch, wie Rose sein Backe,
Sein Aaje die blinzle, sein Griewle die lache.
Ganz rund isch sein Mailel un rot wie dr Klee,
Un sein Bart der glitzert so weiss wie dr Schnee.

A niedliches Pfeifel hat 'r zwische dr Zähn
Un dr Raach zwarwelt 'rum un fliegt in die Heh.
A voll's G'sicht un a Baichel so rund wie a Nissel,
Des schiddelt, wenn er lacht, wie Chelly in dr Schissel.

So dick un so fett, a luschtiger G'sell,
Ich hab misse lache, kann du was ich will.
Sein Kepfel so wusslich, er blinzelt a Aag,
Ich hab mich nit g'faricht, so wohr as ich's sag.

Er redd ka laut Wartel, geht grad zu dr Strimpf
Un fillt se voll Sach und dregt sich rum g'schwind.
Nood leggt er sein Finger grad wedder die Nas
Un springt zum Kamin 'nuff so flink wie a Has.

Er hoppst in sein Schlidde un pfeift noch a Pfiffel,
Do flieje se fort wie dr Flaum vun dr Dischel.
Un wie 'r isch g'fahre, sein Gruss hat er g'macht:
"Freliche Weihnacht, ihr Leit, un a scheeni gut Nacht!"

—Translated by J. S. Height

XI.   Stories in the Kutschurgan Dialect

1. Dr Storich vun Staanfeld

M'r hat's Johr 1940 gschriwwe un s'isch anfangs Oktober gwesst im Doref Staanfeld, a Beresaner Dochderkolonie weit im Norde vun Nikolaiev. Die Bauere im Kolchos sinn schun mit dr Erne fardich gwesst un die Storiche henn schun vor etliche Woche ihre Haamet verlasse.

Do kummen amol oweds vier junge Studende zum Schulmaschter, dem Sänger Jarig, un henn em a Storich gebrocht un froge, ob m'r dene stopfe kennt. "Ja, des kammer," hat dr Lehrer gsagt, "awwer der isch jo so arich dreckich. M'r muss 'n z'erscht a zeitlang fiedere, as er sich erholt un widder saufere Feddere griegt. Awwer wu henn'r dene Storich gfunne?" Do sagt dr ältscht Student: "Uff'em Jäger Anduni sei Schornstaan. Dr Voggel wär schun lengscht mit seine Kumerade fortgezoge, awwer wie'r sehne, isch er lahm."

Dr Lehrer sehnt wie dr Voggel a roder Spiralring am linke Fuss hat un wie'r die Inschrift betracht, sagt er: "Do uff em Ring steht dr Namme "Rossitten." Des isch a Voggelwart in Deitschland."

Die Nochricht, as in Staanfeld a Storich aus Deitschland uf'gfange worre isch, hat sich wie a Laaffeier in dr ganze Geged verbraat. Am nächste Dag isch dr Lehrer zufällig beim Kollektivstall vorbei gange un heert, wie die Rosshalter iwwer dene Storich dischpudiere. "S'isch halt wunnerlich," sagt dr Lehrer, "as dr Voggel grad unser deitsches Doref ausgsucht hat."

Nochmiddags kummt dr russisch Lehrer vum Nochberdoref, um ebbs Neies vum Storich zu heere un am Owed isch dr Dorefschulz kumme un hat dr Spiralring fortgnumme. Nit lang d'rnooch hat sich die NKWD, die kommunistische Geheimpolizei ei'gschallt und hat den Jäger Anduni mit'em Storich zu sich kummediert. Der hat dem Kommisar verzähle misse, wie 'r zu dem Voggel kumme isch. Nodert henn se i'n widder geh lasse, awwer dr Storich henn se gephalde.

Jetz isch die Reih an dr Lehrer kumme. Wie'r uff die Amtsstubb kummt, frogt ihn dr Kommisar: "Wie willst Du wissen, dass dieser Storch aus Deutschland gekommen ist?" Do hat dr Lehrer sei Buch iwwer die Voggelwart hervorgezoge un dem Kommisar die Stell gezaigt, wu alles iwwer die Voggelwart Rossitte gschriwwe gwesst isch. D'r Kommisar sagt nodert ganz uffgregt: "Und wo ist der Brief, den der Storch am anderen Bein hatte?" Dr Lehrer sieht ihn verdutzt an un sagt: "Ich weiss nichts von einem Brief. In Deutschland sind die Störche als Glücksbringer, nicht als Briefträger bekannt." D'r rote Kommisar macht a schiefes Maul un bellt i'n an: "Du kannst jetzt gehen, aber ich rate Dir von dieser Sache nichts weiter zu erzählen." Un so isch d'r Schullehrer mit heiler Haut dervun kumme, awwer dr arme Storich vun Rossitte hat seine Freiheit nimmi widder erlangt.

—Noochverzählt vun J.S.H.

2. Der verflixte Fischfang

Um Mändag noch'em Dreifaldichkaatssunndag bin ich amol niwwer zum Pfeiffer Faldin un zu mei'm Schwoger, dem Mitzel Endres, um a bissel Maastubb zu mache. Weil's Wetter awwer so arich scheen gwesst isch, isch dr Faldin uff dr Gedanke kumme, mr sotte heit doch prowiere a paar Fisch im *Liman*[1] zu fange. Do hemmer halt gleich unser Angel g'holt und sinn mit dr glaane *Lotka*[2] uffs Wasser 'naus gfahre. D'Sunn hat arich gebrennt un ka Liftele Wind isch gange. M'r sinn iwwer zwaa Stund uff'em Liman rumgfahre, henn awwer nix gfange.

"Dr Deifel muss nei fahre un a Kreizmillionestarndunnerwetter a noch drzue," hat dr Pfeifer Faldin uff amol angfange zu fluche, "Ich waas nit was zum Deihenker heit los isch! Ich bin doch geschter in dr Karich gwesst un hab allegebott uff's Fische gedenkt. Du hasch sicher ah dra gedenkt, gell, Endres?"

"Ich?" hat dr Endres gsagt, "naa, ich hab nit dra gedenkt, weil ich nit wejer 'em Fische, awwer wejer 'em Bëdde in d'Karich gange bin."—"Na ja," brummt dr Faldin, "Du kannsch ruhich dei Spott bleiwe lasse. Do lug amol do na! Ganz schwarz kummt's do unne ruff vun Majaki.[3] Ich maan m'r griege a arich beeses Wetter." Awwer dr Mitzel Endres isch nit uffs Maul gfalle: "Hajo, wem'mer immer so viel Dunnerwetter im Maul hat wie due, wär's ka Wunner nit, wenn's amol kummt un dich holt."—"Lass es nar kumme," hat dr Faldin gsagt, "s'ward uns nit fresse. Un wenn Himmel un Erde zittere, ich faricht mich nit."

Uff amol hat's geblitzt un gedunnert as m'r sei eije Wort nit verstanne hat. Un a starker Wind hat die schwarze Wolke wie wiedich iwwer dr Liman gedriwwe. Awwer dr harzhafte Faldin hat gleich widder angfange zu wettere: "A fixe darike noch a mol! Die kegle awwer heit dortdrowwe! Lasse nar bollere!" Awwer dr arme Endres hat d'Händ z'sammeglegt un hat angfange: "Liewer Harrgott, wenn ich geschter ebbes unrecht gedue hab (Faldin, a Knopf haw ich m'r in d'Hosse gflickt!), so will ich's nimmi widder due."— "Waas hasch Du gmacht?" hat dr Pfeiffer Faldin ihn angergrische, "a Hosseknopf angflickt uff'em heilige Dreifaldichkaatssunndag? "Sisch ka Wunner, as m'r nix fange un in so a Wetter nei kumme sinn! Du Himmelssapperment, ich rot dr uff dr Stell, schmeiss die verdammte Hosse gleich in dr Liman 'nei, sunscht simmer meiner Seel verlore!" Un richtig, dr verschrockene Endres hat se ausgezoge un hat se 'neigschmisse un gleich hinnenoch isch a Dunnerkeil 'neigfahre un's Wetter isch bald widder ganz hell worre. Ja, un wenn er's nit glaawe welle, bis Owed hemmer noch viel Fisch gfange.

—Noochverzählt vun J.S.H.

---

[1] Liman: a lagoon or estuary.
[2] Lotka: Russian for a small boat.
[3] Majki: a Russian village south of the Kutschurgan Liman.

3. Die Heimkehrerin

Humoreske von Frau Rissling

Ach Gott! Jetz bin ich schun varzeh Dag in Deitschland! Mit basst's ganz arich do, wenn nar die Leit annerscht waren. Dr ganze Dag huk ich allaans in dr Stubbe rum; ka Mensch kummt zu aam. Drhaam do isch immer die Stubb voll gwesst mit Leit. Un 's Wiedersehne mit mei'm Jarig, des haw ich mr aah ganz annerscht vorgstellt. Ich darf gar nimmi dran denke. Wie ich vum Zug rausgstieche bin, haw ich en schun sehne steh mit'm a blooe Glaad un a gelwer Hut un die Händ voll mit Blume. Un uff jedes jungs Weibsbild, des aus'm Zug rausgstieche isch, uff des isch'r zugsprunge un ich bin newedran gstanne mit mei'm verbuckelte *Tschumedan*[1] un an mir hat er newenaus g'lugt. No haw ichs nimmi ausghalte un habb gsagt: "Ja, Jarig, kennsch mich denn nimmi?" No isch er ganz aarich verschrocke un hat gsagt: "Ja, Schwiejermutter, due?" No hawwich angfange zu brille un habb gsagt: "Du Liddricher,[2] dei eijeni Fraa dusch verlaichle?" No isch 'r noch viel aricher verschrocke un hat gsagt: "Pelachia, des bisch du? Mei Gott, wie bisch du alt un wiescht worre!" No bin ich awwer wiedich worre. "Na," haw ich gsagt: "Was bin ich? Alt bin ich worre? Geh du amol dreiunddreissig Johr uff Sibeeri, du kummsch aah nod widder riwwer wie dei eijene Grossel. Du hasch do hiwwe e lure Lewe gfiehrt un jetz hasch du noch e Graddel[3] druff? Du brauchsch dei Krage gar nit so zu strecke wie so e junger Bitschok!"

"Kum," hat 'r gsagt, "kumm, heer uff zu brille! Die Leit luge doch schun all her. Kumm, m'r fahre haam. No hemmer uns neighuckt in die Maschin un sinn gfahre un do haw ich erscht gsehne wie scheen des Deitschland isch. Die Strosse, die Heiser, die Darfer—alles so schen saufer. Un wie ich dr annere Dag in die Magazin[4] nei kumme bin un habb die viele Sache gsehne, ich hab gmaant mir bleibt dr Ochdem[5] stehe. In Hiele un Fiele hat's gewwe! Un driwwe sage die zu uns: "Warum wellt ihr uff Deitschland? Die henn jo selwer nix zu esse!"

Awwer mei Jarig, der isch nimmi der, wu er frieher gwesst isch. Ich bin aah selwer schuld, as er micht nit gekennt hat. Ich habb ihm lauter Bilder vun mir gschickt vun frieher, wu ich noch jung un scheen gwesst bin. Der hat's doch nit wisse selle, dass ich schun so alt bin, sunscht hätt er mich gschmisse un hätt sich do in Deitschland a Liebschti gnumme. Awwer jetz griddelt[6] er dr ganze Dag an m'r rum: "Zieg dei Halsduch 'rab! Zieg denne *Kazappe-Kittel*[7] aus! Greisch nit so laut, wenn redsch!" Un jetz will 'r noch, as ich mei Groll[8] abschneid un sell m'r Grussle[9] mache. Awwer er, er hat sich a Schnauzel wachse lasse. Un do maant 'r noch, ich gebb em do a Schmitzel[10] druff.

---

[1] Tschumadon: Tartar-Russian word meaning suitcase.
[2] Liddricher: good-for-nothing fellow.
[3] Graddel: conceit, vanity.
[4] Magazin: store.
[5] Ochdem: H. G. Atem, breath.
[6] Griddelt: criticizes.
[7] Kazappa-Kittel: Russian jacket.
[8] Groll: hair in roll or bun.
[9] Grussle: curls.
[10] Schmitzel: kiss, smack.

Un am Esse do griddelt 'r aah immer rum: *"Placenta,"* Offe-Grumbeere Karbseschlecksel,[12] *Bambuschka!*[13] Isch des a Esse?," greischt'r, "Ich bin a Schwob, bei uns geit's Spatze." Liewi Zeit, isch in Deitschland un will Spatze[14] esse! In dreiundreissig im Hungerjohr drhaam, do hemmer als Spatze gfange, wemmer die griegt henn. Awwer doch nit in Deitschland, wu iwwer dr Kopf naus zu esse gebbt, will der Spatze. Ich bin aah nod zum Metzler neigange un habb gsagt: "Bitte scheen, haben Sie Spatzen?" Ich kann do in dem Deitschland iwwerhaapt nit richtig einkaafe. Heit morije do bin nunner gange zum Magazin un habb gesagt—un do kumme die doch gleich so freindlich uff aanem zue un saje: "Bitte scheen, meine Dame." *"Dame"* hat 'r zu mir gsagt. Nod haw ich gsagt: "Ja, ich hätt gern ein Kilo Schmutz.[15] " Un do hat der Mannskarl mich stehn lasse un isch zu eme annere nagange un hat gsagt: "Cheef, ich glaab do isch e Vrickti, die will ein Kilo Schmutz." Do isch der Cheef zu mir her kumme un sagt: "Was winscht die Dame?"—"Ha, ich mecht a Kilo Schmutz." No hat er gsagt: "Darf ich bitte fragen, was Sie mit dem Schmutz machen wollen?" Do haw ich gsagt: "Na, was macht mer mit 'em Schmutz? Koche un backe!" Ei, do hat er sich

so uffgregt. un hat gsagt: "Meine Dame, wir sind hier ein renvoniertes Geschäft. Wir haben keinen Schmutz." Ha, jetz wisse die nit emol in Deitschland, dass Hochdeitsch Schmalz "Schmutz" haast. Des sinn Deitschlänner un kenne nit richtig deitsch. Die saje des aane un maane des annere.

Vorgeschter bin ich do bei dene Harre gwesst, die wu mer do die Andräg stelle muss, un do hat der mich ganz freindlich bewillkommenet un hat mich als erschtes gfrogt: "Frau Rissling," hat er gsagt, "haben Sie auch schon den Heimweh-Kater[16] bekommen?" No haw ich gsagt, "Bitt scheen, gell, wenn ich schun a Katz hawwe muss, hätt ich liewer a Mädiche als a Mallert."[17] Awwer wie ich nod haam kumme bin un habb des meim Jarig verzählt, nod hat 'r gsagt: "Du Rinnochs, der hat dir doch gar ka Katz gewwe welle. Der hat gmaant, ob du aah so aarich Haamweh hasch, ass krank bisch." Jetz brill ich schun widder. Dr ganze Daag brill ich. Un geschter isch meine beschte Kumerädin do gwesst un die hat g'sagt: "Un wenn nit uffheersch zu brille . . . Brille macht alt un hässlich. Un scheen mussch dich aah mache, schunscht nemt dr Jarig doch noch e Liebschti."

Un jetz haw ich mich scheen gmacht! Jetz will ich awwer sehne, ob des dr Jarig iwwerhaapt bemerkt, dass ich mich weje ihm scheen gmacht hab. Wie sell ich denn mei Maul namache? Ich glaab er kummt schun.

Jarig: "P e l a g i a ! Ei, bisch du s c h e e n !"

Frau R.: "Oh, Jarig!"

---

[11]Placenta: from Russian palatschinte: turn-overs.
[12]Karbseschlecksel: pumpkin jam.
[13]Bambuschke: Russian garlic-flavored fritters.
[14]Spatze: HG. sparrows; dim. Spätzle: Swabian dumplings.
[15]Schmutz: HG smut, dirt; in Franconian dialect: la
[16]Kater: 1. tom-cat 2. hangover.
[17]Mallert: in Franconian: tom-cat.

4. D'erscht elsässich Bredicht

(im Selzer Dialekt)

S'Evangelije vum dreizehnte Sunndag nooch Pfingschte.

"Zu sellere Zeit hat Jesus angfange zum Volk in Gleichnisse zu redde: Heert zu, wer Ohre hat zu heere! A Landmann isch uffs Feld nausgange far Frucht zu säje. Beim Säje fallt vun dr Soot newe dr Acker un wart verdrette un vun dr Veggel uffgfresse. A Daal drvun isch uff staanicher Bodde gfalle, wu nit viel Erd gwesst isch. Die Frucht isch schnell uffgange, awwer isch ball vun dr Sunn versengt warre, un weil se ka diefe Warzel g'hatt hat, isch se verdarrt. A Daal isch in dornicher Bodde neigfalle un wie die Dischdel ruffkumme sinn, henn se d'Frucht verstickt. Awwer a Daal isch uff guder Bodde gfalle, isch scheen uffgange un gut g'rode un hat a guid Erne gewwe, daals dreissich uff dr Kaerne, daals sechszich un daals hunnert." So weit die Worte vum heitiche Evangelije.

Vielgeliebte grischtliche Zuheerer!

Ich seh schun, ass aanige unner eich schmunzle odder sogar kichere misse, weil ich heit 's heiliche Evangelije uff unsere geliebte elsässiche Muddersproch, anstatt uff Hochdeitsch, vorglese hab. Awwer indem ich in unsrer Muddersproch zu eich red, folg ich ja nar dem Beispiel vun unserem liewe Heiland, als er noch in seiner Haamet Galiläa glebt hat. Er hat ka aanziches Mol uff Hochhebräisch gebredicht, awwer immer nar uff armäisch, was sei Muddersproch gwesst isch. Sunscht hätte jo sei eijene Leit ihn arich schlecht odder gar nit verstanne.

Ich waas nit, ebb ihr elsässische Brediche gern heere däte, awwer aans kann ich eich sage: die Zeit kummt—un etliche vun eich warre 's noch erlewe—wu mr ka deitsche Brediche meh heere wart in unsere Kariche. Nood wart nar noch uff englisch gebredicht un uff englisch gebett, un all die scheene deitsche Karchelieder warre ausstarwe. Ja, die alt Muddersproch, die unser Leit vun Selz un Kannel, vun Strossbarig un Bade, un vun Mann'em un Elsass iwwer hunnert siewezich Johr uff dr Stepp un dr Breerie gredt henn, ward verfliege wie a russisch Dischdel vor 'em Wind, un die Kinnerskinner warre ka Wort meh verstehe vun ihre Grossvädder un Grossle.

Im Evangelije von heit kenne mr sehne, ass unser Harr Jesus viel verstanne hat vun dr Bauerei. Ja, 's isch leicht meglich, ass er selwer manichemol uff 'em Land gschafft hat, mit 'em a Joch Ochse gepfligt hat, die Soot hat helfe ausstreie, odder die Scheef hat hiete misse. Er hat jo efters in sei scheene Gleichnisse iwwer die schwere Arwet in dr Landwartschaft gredt. Ja, die Bauere am See Genesareth henn's halt aah nit leicht g'hat. Wie eire Grossvädder uff dr Stepp henn se d'Sootfrucht ime Sack iwwers Feld drage misse un dr Same mit dr Hand ausstreie. Ka Wunner, ass so viel Frucht verlore gange isch. Vun dr Aussoot bis zur Erne geht eich jo aah efters viel Frucht verlore. Awwer wie viel Schade kenne die paar arme Veggel anrichte? Do uff dr Breerie gebbt's noch viel schrecklicheres Ungeziffer. Wer denkt do nit an die Erdhase—die *Goffer,* die manche Johre ganze Acker verdarwe; odder an die Heischrecke—die Grashopser, die mit dausete Sense d'schenscht Erne abmäje kenne.

Freilich gebbt's bei uns aah manichemol staaniches Land, wu d'Frucht nit gut g'rode kann. Un bei dr schlechte Farmer gebbt's aah genung Unkraut un Hexe un Burian, ass die gut Frucht verstjcke musss. Awwer was isch des alles gege die viel annere Misslichkaate: Schade vun dr Schloose, vum Mildau, vun Roscht un Froscht. Un dabei haw ich nit amol ebbs gsagt vun dr grossi Druckening, die allegebott d'schenscht Erne verdarwe kann.

Mir henn aah guder Bodde do uff dr Breerie, awwer wer vun eich hat schun amol 's Glick g'hat sechszich odder hunnert *bushel* vum Acker zu griege? Heitzudags muss dr Farmer schun zufridde sei, wenn er zwanzich griegt: 's hat aah schun Johre gewwe wu dr bescht Farmer nar finef odder zeh *bushel* gedrescht hat. Ja, bei uns isch dr Bodde aah gut, awwer mr henn in viele Johre so a schlechter Himmel g'hat, wu finef odder sechs Woche ka Breesel Rejje gfalle isch.

Mr henn schun viele schlechte Erne g'hat, seidem die erschte Ansiedler mit ihre Ochsewäjje im Friehjohr do uff dr nakede Breerie ankumme sinn un sich ihre Waaseheisle uff dr Haamstett gebaut henn. Awwer ka Johr isch so schlecht gwesst wie vor 'em Johr, im Johr 1933, wu die Druckening so gross gwesst isch, ass dr Himmel iwwer dr ganze Summer mit so dickem Staab verdeckt gwesst isch, ass mr gmaant hat, die Welt geht unner. Uff dr Felder isch fascht gar nix gwachse, un 's arme Viech hat ka Fuder g'hat, nit amol Stroh hat 's uff dr Felder gewwe. Awwer die russische Dischdel die sinn arich gut gwachse in sellem Johr, un mit dene hat mr nodert 's Viech fiedere misse. Ja, mr kann sage, des sinn arich dreckige Zeite gwesst in denne dreissiger Johre. Dagelang hat mr vor Staab ka Sunn un ka Mon sehne kenne. Sogar im Haus hat's so viel Staab gewwe, as mr beinoh verstickt isch.

Awwer mr selle nicht maane, ass so ebbs noch niemol in dr Welt vorkumme isch. Unsere Voreldere in Russland henn aah amol so schlechte Zeite erlebt. 'S isch grad vor hunnert Johr gwesst, im Johr 1833, in sellem unvergesslliche "Schwarze Johr," wu vum Winter bis zum spote Summer ka bissel Schnee odder Rejje gfalle isch. Uff 'em Ackerland un im Garde isch nix gwachse, ka Stengel Frucht, ka Grumbeer un ka Kraut, un 's Gras uff dr Stepp isch ganz verdarrt. Dr Bodde isch ganz schwarz gebliwwe un drucket wie Äsch. A ständicher Wind hat d'Luft mit eme feine Staab gschwängert, as mr dagelang ka Sunn hat sehne kenne. Wind hat's gewwe alle Dag, awwer d'Windmiehle henn nix zu mahle g'hat. Viel Viech isch verhungert un die Not unner dr Leit isch so gross warre, as viel Kolonischte bis nei uff Bohle gfahre sinn um Wäjjevoll Mehl un Frucht zu hole.

Awwer die arme Leit henn die Hoffning nit uffgewwe. Sie henn weiter in Gott vertraut un in Gottes Namme weiter gschafft un gscharrt. Nochher sinn widder bessere Zeite kumme un 's Land isch widder scheen uffgeblieht, Die darre Stepp isch widder zum neie Lewe erwacht un hat widder gude Erne gschenkt. So welle mr aah nit verzage in elende Zeite, awwer weiter uff Gott vertraue, denn wu die Not am greeschte isch, isch Gott am nechste.

Iwwer die Johre, wu mr uff dr Breerie wohne, hemmer genunk schlechte Erne g'hat. Awwer wer unner uns hett Grund zu klage un zu lamediere? Bei uns isch noch kaaner verhungert. Jeder hat immer sei däglich Brot g'hat. Un wemmer mol driwwe nooch denkt, isch 's uns do uff dr Breerie viel besser gange wie unsere Landsleit uff dr Stepp im alde Russland, wu 1920 unzählige Mensche verhungert sinn. Un wie isch 's unsere Leit in Selz un Kannel, in Baden un Strossbarig, un in Elsass un Mann'em gange, wu in dr dreissiger Johre dausede vun Familievädder, nochdem mr ihne ihr Land weggnumme hat, uff Sibirie in die Stroflager verbannt worre sinn un dort vor Hunger un Elend umkumme sinn.

Im Vergleich, sinn unser Leit do uff dr Breerie noch immer ime scheene Baradies gwohne. Un mr kenne all froh sei un unserm Harrgott danke, as unser Grossvädder aus dem alde Russland ausgwannert sinn un ine gelobtes Land gezoge sinn, wu mr als freie Mensche a glickliches un friedvolles Lewe fiehre kenne. Gott gebe, ass eire Kinner un Kinnerskinner uff dere Erde immer desselwe Glick erlewe, im Namme des Vadders, des Sohnes, un des heilichen Geischtes. Amen.

Poems in German and English

Die Sechs

von Popper

Eine Legende aus den deutschen Kolonien Südrusslands

Sechs Männer sassen einst beim Wein,
Ein fröhliches Gelage.
Von denen wollte jeder sein
Der Klügste heutzutage.

Der Wein war stark, der Wein war gut
Die Wirkung war zu sehen;
Bei manchem kochte schon das Blut
Und mancher konnt nicht stehen.

"Nun lasst uns singen jetzt ein Lied!
So hiess es in der Runde;
Im Chore sangen alle mit,
In vorgerückter Stunde!

Selz isch die schenschte Stadt,
Baden isch der Dudelsack,
Strossbarg isch der Leierkiwwel,
Elsass isch der Deckel driwwer,
Mannhem isch die Morjepfeift,
In Kannel sinn die dimmschte Leit."

Ein dröhnend Lachen folgte nun
In diesem feuchten Kreise.
Ein jeder glaubte Recht zu tun
Nach seiner Art und Weise.

Die Gläser waren frisch gefüllt
Und wieder ward getrunken,
Bis sie der Nebel hat umhüllt,
Bis sie zur Erd' gesunken.

Da trat ein Kobold in die Tür,
Der schüttelt sich vor Lachen:
"Was sind denn das für Ungetier,
Was sind denn das für Sachen?"

Zum ersten sprach der Kobold dann:
"Ist das ein Lebenswandel?
Du siehst ja wie ein Igel aus!"
"O naa. Ich bin aus Kannel!"

Den zweiten stiess der Kobold an:
"Ein Sandhas, ach, vergelt's!"
Da stöhnte dieser Saufkumpan:
"Na-naa, ich bin aus Selz!"

"He dritter, du, was ist denn los?
Du hast ja gelbe Füss!"
Der Gelfuss drauf der murmelt bloss:
"Aus Baade bin ich g'wiss!"

"Du vierter, was ist denn mit dir,
Du Windhund, steh doch auf!"
"Ich bin aus Strossbarg, sag ich dir;
Ich sing und danz und sauf!"

Der fünfte liegend unterm Tisch
Sah wie ein Steinpicker aus.
"Wer bist du," fragt der Kobold frisch:
"In Elsass bin ich zu Haus!"

Der sechste sprang herzwütig auf,
"Ein Wuthammel bist du!"
"Aus Mann'em bin ich!" schrie er drauf,
Dann flog die Türe zu.

Sechs Männer sassen einst beim Wein —
Ein fröhliches Gelage;
Von den wollte jeder sein
Der Klügste heutzutage.

Elsässer Maistub

v. Popper (1927)

Die beste Zeit zum Maistub halten
Ist die Zeit, wo d'Arbeit ruht.
Wenn es draussen stürmt und wettert,
Sitzt sich's in der Stub recht gut.

Hinterm Ofen sitzen d'Männer,
D'Frauen hocken umeinand;
Drüben, hüben tun sie schwätzen
Von der Politik im Land.

Von der Saat und von der Ernte —
Von der Ross und von der Säu, —
Von der Schaf und von der Hühner
Und von sonst noch allerlei.

Manches hört man da erzählen
Was man gar nicht sagen darf.
Da wird oftmals kritisieret
Ziemlich leise, — aber scharf!

Von der Küh wird auch gesprochen —
Ich trau' meinen Ohren nicht!
Und mit grossem Interesse
Hör ich folgende Geschicht':

"Einem Mann bei uns im Elsass
Ist ein Unglücksfall passiert,
Seine Kuh ist ihm verunglückt,
Sie hat sich die Hüft' lädiert.

"Was ist da zu machen?" sagt er,
"Keinen Wert hat jetzt die Kuh."
Der Verlust ist ein sehr grosser,
Er hat Tag und Nacht kei' Ruh.

Weil der Mann jedoch sehr klug ist
Kommt es ihm in seinen Sinn —
Ich werd schnell die Kuh verkaufen,
Sonst geht sie am End noch "hin."

Gesagt, getan! Er geht zum Juden,
Er geht hin zum Salomon:
"Kauf die Kuh, ich geb dir's billig,
Kauf die Kuh, Freund Salomon!"

Doch der Salomon, sehr klug und weise,
(Gott sei Lob und Dank!)
Sieht die Kuh mit einer Hüfte
Und sagt, O je, die Kuh ist krank!"

Er betracht's von vorn und hinten!
"Sie gebt Haut und sie gebt Fleisch!"
Dann beginnen sie zu handeln
Mit viel Lärm und mit Gekreisch.

"Wie viel gebst," so fragt der Eine.
"Wie viel willst," der Andere fragt;
Und so geht das Handeln weiter,
Beiden fest das Herze schlagt.

"Dreissig Rubel kannste haben,
Kein Kopek geb ich dir mehr."
"Dreissig Rubel?" denkt der Mann sich,
Die sind mir willkommen sehr!"

"Her damit, der Kauf ist fertig!"
"Gib mir's Geld gleich auf der Stell!"
Und der Salomon der Weise
Zahlt ihm die Tscherwonze[1] schnell.

So war dieser Kauf geschehen
Und der Mann der geht nach Hause —
"Dreissig Rubel ist zu wenig,
Wie krieg ich nach mehr heraus?"

Dreissig Rubel, dreissig Rubel —
Rechnet er jetzt hin und her,
Dreissig Rubel ist zu wenig,
Für die Kuh nehm ich noch mehr.

Wozu hab'n wir die "Versicherung,"
Die hier "Strachowanie" heisst?
Doch nur, dass man sie im Falle,
Wenn es möglich ist — bescheisst.

Also schnell ein Sajawlenie:[2]
"Mir ist meine Kuh verreckt,
Diese bitt ich mir zu zahlen!"
Schreibt der Mann ganz unerschreckt.

Die "Versich'rung" untersuchet
Diesen Fall und kommt zum Schluss,
Dass der Mann für die "Verreckte"
Zwanzig Rubel kriegen muss!

Zwanzig Rubel werden pünktlich
Diesem Manne ausgezahlt.
Und man sollte wirklich meinen
Dass der Mann sich damit prahlt.

Dreissig, zwanzig — geben fünfzig,
Rechnet wiederum der Mann.
"S'ist zu wenig — Himmel Herrgott!
Sicher mehr ich kriegen kann!"

Ein Gesuch als "Komnesamosch,[3]"
Viel zu hoch die Steuern sind;
Prodnalog[4] muss ich bezahlen,
Wenn ich keinen Ausweg find."

Er schreibt schnell ein Sajawlenie:
"Mir ist meine Kuh krepiert!"
Die Regierung hat's gelesen —
War auch gleich dran interessiert.

"Diesem Manne muss man helfen,
Dieser Mann ist ehrlich, rein.
Rubel sechs vom Prodnaloge
Sollen ihm erlassen sein."

Dreissig, zwanzig und noch sechse,
Sechsundfünzig — so ist's recht.
Und er freute sich ganz diebisch,
Diese Freude, die war echt.

Und der Mann in unsrem Dorfe
Macht ein freundliches Gesicht.
Wie er heisst, wollt Ihr wohl wissen?
Seinen Namen sag ich nicht.

Interessant ist die Geschichte,
Sechsundfünfzig Rubel? Schön!
Für den Schwindel wird der "Gute"
Sicher in den "Dopr[5] gehn.

---

1. ten-ruble coin
2. petition for compensation
3. a small-holder peasant
4. taxes
5. house of correction

Kutschurgan, du stilles Tal

Fern im Süd am schönen Kutschurgan,
Dort wo die Täler grün und Blumen reichlich blüh'n,
Dort wo der Vogelsang erschallet durch die Wälder,
Dort ist mein Heim, nach dem die Sehnsucht ruft.
   O Kutschurgan, du stilles Tal!
   Sei mir gegrusst viel tausendmal!

In der Heimat meiner Jugend Glück
Hab ich mein Leben wie im Traum verbracht.
Von Schöpferhand ward mir es zugeschickt
Und ich verliess sie unter Schicksalsmacht.

—Ferdinand Kraft

Kutschurgan, o peaceful vale

Far to the South on the lovely Kutschurgan,
Where the vales are green and flowers throng,
Where the song of birds in the woods resounds,
There is my home, the land for which I long.

In the homeland of my happy youth
I spent my life as in a dreamy state;
From the Creator's hand was it bestowed,
I left it only by the power of fate.

Selz

Mein schönes Kutschurganertal,
Mein schöner Heimatort!
Heut seh ich dich zum letztenmal,
Heut muss ich von dir fort.
Ich weiss, ich seh dich nimmermehr,
Drum fällt der Abschied mir so schwer.
Sei mir, mein Kutschurganertal,
gegrüsst zum letztenmal.
Viel Jahre hab ich dich geliebt,
Mein schönes Dörflein — Seltz!
Jetzt stehst du traurig und bedrückt,
Gerade so wie ich . . .
Du willst nicht bleiben hier allein,
Willst mit mir in die Welt hinein —
Komm! Zieh mit mir, geh mit mir fort,
Mein schöner, lieber Heimatort.

—E. Scherr

Selz

My lovely valley Kutschurgan,
My native town so dear!
I gaze at you this final dawn,
Today I must depart from here.
I'll never see you again, I know.
That's why I find it hard to go.
I bid you my last farewell,
My lovely Kutschurganer vale.
I have loved you many a year,
My fair Selz where I was born;
Now you stand so sad and drear,
Just as I stand all forlorn.
You do not want to stay alone
But yearn with me to go along.
Come, go with me where'er I roam,
My beautiful, beloved home.

Verlorene Heimat

Wo der klagende Wind über Weiten sang,
Wo der deutsche Bauer die Steppe bezwang,
Wo aus Nacht eine deutsche Welt entstand,
Am Schwarzen Meer und am Wolgastrand —
Oh russische Heimat!

Wir pflügten die Erde — nun pflügt uns die Not,
Wir fuhren die Garben — nun fährt uns der Tod.
Was wir tapfer errungen — ward höllischer Staub —
Und Kirche und Tenne deckt russischer Staub —
Oh russische Heimat!

Nun geht um die Erde die flüchtige Schar,
Zu künden, was deutsch in der Fremde war,
Und als uns Glück und Friede zerrann,
Der Heimat beraubte sein Volk gewann —
Oh Volk du der Deutschen!

—Verfasser unbekannt

Lost Homeland

Where the wailing wind through the wasteland swept
Where the German settlers subdued the wild steppe,
Where a German world from the night was born
On the Black Sea strand and the Volga shore —
O Russian homeland!

We plowed the earth — now distress plows us,
We gathered the sheaves — now Death garners us,
What we bravely achieved was turned to Russian dust
Church and threshing floor crushed in Russian dust
O Russian homeland!

Around the earth now roams the refugee band
To proclaim what was German in the alien land,
And when peace and happiness for us was gone,
The homeless and bereaved came home to their own
O you German people!

Verbannt

Wann bricht die dunkle Mauer,
Wann öffnet sich das Tor,
Wann fallen diese Ketten,
O Gott, hol' mich empor!

O rette mich von diesen Schrecken,
Die Du, o Herr, mir zugedacht.
Führ mich noch einmal in die Heimat
Und mach mich glücklich über Nacht.

Denn in der Heimat wartet
Meine Frau, mein Kind.
O, lass mich sie noch einmal sehen,
Eh' mein zerquältes Herz zerspringt!

—Anon.

Banished

When will the dark walls break?
When will the gate swing free?
When will these fetters fall?
O God, vouchsafe me liberty!

O save me from the terrors
That engulf me in my plight.
Lead me to my home again,
Make me happy overnight.

At home my wife and child await me,
O let me see them once again,
Before my anguished lonely heart
Begins to break and burst with pain.

226

Aufruf

Brüder, die ihr in Sibiriens Weiten
einsam erlitten den bitteren Tod,
der euch Erlösung doch war
aus klirrenden Ketten:

Erhebt euere Stimme, lasst mahnend
sie dringen ans Herz der Welt,
aufrüttelnd die Trägen
und Selbstsuchtgefangenen
zu heiligem Kampfe für Freiheit
für Freiheit und Recht.

—Johannes Schleuning

Appeal

Brothers, in Siberia's dread taigas
You suffered in silence
Bitterest death
Which was your redemption
From clattering chains.

Lift up your voices,
Cry havoc to the heart of the world,
Rousing the indolent,
Steeped in self-seeking,
To sacred struggle for freedom and justice.

Verlust der Heimat

Wir mussten die Heimat verlassen,
Denn hinter uns hetzte der Tod.
Wir wandelten eiskalte Strassen
Und assen ein kummervolles Brot.

Nun schleichen die freudlosen Tage
Im Lager so eintönig hin,
Und jeden bedrückt oft die Frage
Nach solch eines Daseins Sinn.

—H. F.

Lost homeland

Forced to forsake our homeland,
Harried by importunate Death,
We trudged on ice-cold roads
And ate our grief-stained bread.

Now in the camp drab and drear
Our days drag on joyless indeed.
All are oppressed by the sheer
Meaningless life we now lead.

Deutsche Dörfer in der Ukraine

(Eindrücke eines deutschen Soldaten).

Die Menschen reden wieder uns're Sprache
Und laden uns an ihren Tisch.
Ein wenig Heimat fasst uns unter ihrem Dache
Und macht uns nach dem heissen Marsch gleich frisch.

Die Schwalben segeln pfeilschnell durch die Strassen
Und nisten unterm trocknen Scheunendach.
Wenn wir zum Gruss die schwielen Hände fassen,
Ist uns als käme der deutsche Bauer nach.

Die Dörfer tragen deutsche Heimatnamen,
Die Höfe zeigen deutsche Bauernart.
Die kühnen Züge mancher Dörfler mahnen
An ihrer Ahnen kühne Ostlandfahrt.

227

Vergangene Ewigkeit und
Kommende Ewigkeit
Verbindet dein Leben:
Die Ahnen gaben dir
Sein und Können,
Die Enkel tragen
Dein Wollen und Sehnen,
Und zwischen beiden
Sollst wahren und mehren
Was du empfangen,
Der ewigen Kette
Ein wertvolles Glied.

      —(O. Kröpklin)

Eternity past and Eternity to come
Impinge on your life.
The ancestors gave you
Your existence and striving,
The descendants carry on
Your aspirations and yearning,
And between the two you ought
To preserve and enhance
What you have inherited,
A valuable link
In the unending chain.

Traum im Haupte, Trotz im Herzen
zogen sie in weite Welten.
Flog die Falkenbrut der Freien
zu der Wildnis armen Zelten.
Von den Schlachten, die sie schlugen,
von der Not, die sie bezwungen,
ist zum alten Vaterlande
kaum ein leiser Hauch gedrungen.

      —Horsch

A dream in their eyes, their hearts undaunted
To far-flung lands they made their way,
Like falcon brood on freedom's wings
To lowly huts of steppeland clay.
Of the hardships they sustained,
Of their staunch, victorious stand,
Scarce the faintest breath was borne
To their former fatherland.

Aus des Rheins geliebten Auen
Zogen einst mit Gottvertrauen
Unsere Ahnen in die Ferne.
Wolken, Sonne, Wind und Sterne,
Sturm und Regen
Auf den mühevollen Wegen
Waren einzige Begleiter.
Immer weiter
Zogen mühsam sie nach Osten.

      —Solo

From the lovely Rhineland plain,
With trust in God and hearts undaunted,
Our forebears journeyed long ago.
On the long and lonesome road,
With sun and stars, wind and rain,
Storm and clouds their sole companions,
They struggled onward, striving
Steadfast to the East.

Unserem neuen Vaterland*

J. ULRICH RODUNER

Russland,
Süsses Vaterland,
In dem wir Kolonisten sicher wohnen!
Theures Pfand,
Sei von uns erkannt.
Lass uns dir mit treuem Fleiss
und Eifer willig lohnen.
Herr Gott,
Erhalter Gott!
Beschütze unsres Kaisers Krone,
Jederzeit,
Wenn ihm dräut
Zerstörung seiner Krone.
Gib Herr!
Wir bitten sehr,
Unsrem Kaiser weise, treue Räthe.
Gib Herr,
Dass wie bisher
Ihr Auge wohlgefällig ruh
Auf unsrer Kolonistenstätte.
Und heut',
So wie allezeit,
Sei Gut und Leben Gott
Und unsrem neuen Vaterlande geweiht!

Apostrophe an eine Chronik*

J. ULRICH RODUNER

Ewig theuer wirst du unsrer Nachwelt bleiben,
Kurzgefasste Übersicht von Petersthal;
Wenn die Glieder unsrer jetzgen Bürgerzahl
Einstens auf dem Gottesacker längst zerstäuben,
Werden diese Rückerinnerungen, die wir der Nachwelt schreiben,
Ihr manchen düstern Winterabend nützlich wissen zu vertreiben.
Ernster, reiner wird dann ihr Bestreben
Für ihre Kinder auch das Möglichste zu thun,
Und auf dem, der diese Übersicht zu schreiben aufgegeben,
Soll Gottes Segen ewig ruhn!

---

*The two poems by J. Ulrich Roduner, village clerk of Peterstal/Od (1848) are the earliest known poems of the colonists in the Black Sea area.

To our new Fatherland

Russian land,
Sweet fatherland,
Where we colonists live in security!
O pledge that we prize
And recognize,
Let us serve with faithful zeal and industry.
Lord God,
Sustaining all,
Protect the crown of our Czar,
Whenever danger threatens,
Near or far.
Give him, O Lord,
We implore,
Faithful councilors and wise.
Grant, O Lord,
That as of yore
They look upon our colonies with gracious eyes.
And today,
As always,
May our life be devoted to God and our new Fatherland.

—Tr. by JSH

Apostrophe to a Chronicle

Forever precious you will be to our posterity,
Brief documentary of our dear Peterstal!
Long after everyone in this community
Will have turned to dust, as must we all,
Our remembered past will bring a shared delight
To our descendants on a dreary winter night.
With purer, nobler striving will they emulate
To do their best for their own children's sake.
And on him who bade me write this resumé
May God's blessing rest eternally!

—Tr. by JSH

Die Vertriebenen

Wir vertriebnen Sowjet-Deutschen
Sind zerstreut vom Heimatland,
Wo einst lebten unsre Väter,
Wo auch unsre Wiege stand.

Und am fremden Ort, vertrieben,
Weit entfernt vom Heimatland,
Nur noch unsre Lieder blieben,
Die als Kinder wir gekannt.

Die Familien sind zerrissen,
Der eine hier, der andre dort.
Viele Mütter nicht mehr wissen,
Wo jetzt ihrer Kinder Ort.

Hunger, Elend, Angst und Kummer,
Das war unser schweres Los,
Und gar viele unsrer Brüder
Ruhen längst im Erdenschoss.

All das haben wir ertragen
Ohne Murren, mit Geduld.
Wem auch sollten wir es klagen,
Wir Vertrieb'nen ohne Schuld.

Rechtlos waren wir und Knechte,
Nur zur Arbeit, wie das Vieh.
Und zum Spott nannt' man uns Schlechte,
"Frietsch," "Faschist," auch da und hie.

Doch wir werden nicht mehr schweigen!
Brüder, auf! Nun ist es Zeit!
Unsre Stimme soll erschallen,
Bis da siegt Gerechtigkeit.

—Mathias Bossert

Mein letztes Lied

Lang, lang ist's her als Glück und Sonne
Geschienen mir im Vaterhaus.
Längst sind vergangen Freud' und Wonne,
Der Heimat Lied klang längst schon aus.
Der Heimat Glanz ist längst entschwunden
Und ihre Sterne sind nicht mehr.
Der Jugend heiter frohe Stunden
Sie sind versunken tief im Meer.
Ging es zurück, nicht wollt ich säumen
Und nähm sogleich den Wanderstab.
So aber darf ich ja nur träumen
Von dem, was ich verloren hab.
Du Heimat mein am Schwarzmeerstrande,
Die Sehnsucht mit mir weiterzieht
Durch viele fremde, schöne Lande,
Doch dir gehört mein letztes Lied.

—Baumgärtner

Der Tod der Selzer'

GEORGE RATH

Gemäht ist der Weizen im sonnigen Land,
In Reihen geschockt sind die Garben,
Gesammelt die Ernte durch fleißige Hand —
Der Bauer wird heuer nicht darben.
Bald sieht er in Scheunen die goldene Flut;
Schon summen Maschinen seit frühe.
Was lange gereift in der südlichen Glut,
Wird endlich der Lohn seiner Mühe.

Doch anders beschlossen ist vom Bolschewist
Das Schicksal der goldenen Ähre:
„Den Weizen, den lieferst du mir, Kolonist,
Und fütterst damit meine Heere.
Sie stehn mit den Weißen im blutigen Krieg,
Zerlumpt und mit hungrigem Magen.
Du gibst ihnen Brot, bis errungen der Sieg.
Sonst faß ich dich unsanft am Kragen!"

Da bricht auch dem Bauer die große Geduld
Und kocht ihm der Zorn aus der Seele.
Was hat nicht der Rote doch alles verschuld't?
Wem würgt nicht der Frechling die Kehle?
Soll ewig denn herrschen die gottlose Macht?
Zu lang schon regiert das Gesindel!
Es pack' seine Lumpen, die mit es gebracht
Und geh mit dem Trotzky im Bündel!

Landauf und landab schon mit feurigem Wort
Flink Boten die Dörfer durchziehen:
„Zur Waffe, ihr Männer, Ort schar sich zu Ort!
Erhebt euch, vereint Kolonien!
Es hat euch an Gütern der rot' Kommissar
Genug schon geraubt und gestohlen;
Und braucht er den Weizen, der wuchs
                              dieses Jahr,
So mag er ihn selber sich holen!

Zu Ende ist bald nun der blutige Wahn,
Das Haus steht den Roten in Flammen!
Zu Hauf, nicht gezaudert! Vereint euch und ran,
Dann stürzt es ihm vollends zusammen.
Auf, auf, Kolonisten zum Streit, Mann für
Ein Dorf sei dem andern zur Mauer;   [Mann!
Zur Flinte greif jeder, der führen sie kann,
Und wehr dich, du Deutscher, du Bauer!"

Und sieh, gleich dem Wetter jagt dumpf
                              es einher,
Schon grollt es und flammt's in der Weite.
Vom Dnjestr zum Bug und hinunter ans Meer,
Aufstehen die Dörfer zum Streite.
„Wir kämpfen für Ehre, für Gut und für Recht
Und wollen es niemanden geben!
Wir bleiben ein frei Kolonistengeschlecht
Und wagen dafür unser Leben."

Mit andern im Bund hat die Waffen zum
Strauß, Selz Baden und Straßburg erhoben,
Und kühn ihre Streiter nun dringen hinaus
An die Bahn, wo Kanonen schon toben.
Doch zäh sind die Roten und schwer
                              mit Geschütz
Wird Straßburg von ihnen beschossen.
Schon brennt es am Norden, doch Blitz
                              folgt auf Blitz
Und dann wird das Dorf selbst umschlossen.

Und weiter nach Süden nun von Kutschurgam
zieht eilends die gierige Horde.
Besetzt alle Wege, umgeht den Liman
Und drängt in die Dörfer zum Morde.
Da sinkt auch dem Tapfersten endlich der Mut
Und Furcht schlägt die Dörfer in Ketten.
Auf Wagen die Frauen, die Kinder und Gut,
Flieht alles und sucht sich zu retten.

Besetzt sind die Dörfer. Von Posten bewacht
Sind schwer alle Brücken und Wege.
Nach Selz wird zurück, wer gefangen, gebracht
Daß Rechenschaft er von sich gäbe.
Im Schutze des Rohres zwar mancher entrinnt,
Doch achtzig und drei müssen büßen.
Der Häuptling d. Roten hat grausam bestimmt
Sie morgen beim Dorf zu erschießen.

Und blutrot empor steigt nach bangschwerer
Das Taglicht, die goldene Sonne.   [Nacht
Wenn heut doch der junge Augusttag erwacht,
Zum Schrecken ist's nur, nicht zur Wonne.
Denn sieh, von dem Dorfe schon kommt es
Zur Hutweid' mit hastigen Schritten: [heran
Viel Rote mit Waffen. — Der Häuptling voran,
Die Opfer geschart in der Mitten.

Doch nun aus den Reihen entschlossen hervor
kommt stille ein Priester getreten,
Hebt Augen u. Hand zu dem Häuptling empor
Und bittet um Ruhe zum Reden.
Er hat zum Besuche der Mutter geweilt,
An der er voll Liebe gehangen,
Da ward er vom traurigen Lose ereilt
Und schuldlos mit andern gefangen.

Und als in der Reihe mit ihnen er stand,
Da faßte ihn tiefes Erbarmen.
Da fühlt er, wie stark ihn die Liebe verband
Mit ihnen, den Brüdern, den Armen.
Sie hatten gekämpft u. gewirkt u. geschafft
Und sollten so schimpflich nun sterben,
Und sollten die Erde, der galt ihre Kraft,
Nun heut mit dem Herzblute färben.

' From "Klänge der Seele," 1960, Omaha, Nebr., p. 99-103.

„Ganz schuldlos", so spricht er, „sind
                              alle sie hier;
Ich hab' sie zum Aufstand bewogen.
Nicht straft meine Brüder! Die Strafe gilt mir,
Denn ich nur, ich hab' sie betrogen.
Und hab ich dafür eine Kugel verschuld't,
Wohlan denn, ihr mögt sie mir geben!
Mit mir nicht, mit diesen habt Gnad'
und laßt die Betrogenen leben." [und Geduld

Da stutzten die Roten und blickten sich an,
Vom Mute des Priesters betroffen.
Fast hätt' durch sein Wort dieser tapfere Mann
Ihr Herz, ihr kaltes getroffen.
Doch kurz ist d. Wallung! Nicht lange es währt
Dann sind sie auf's neu Bolschewisten.
Man hat sie stets morden und hassen gelehrt,
Das Mitleid geziemt nur den Christen.

„Und hast du's getan und geschadet dem Land
So bist du der Schuldige eben.
Dann trifft dich die rote, die rächende Hand,
Dann zahlst du es uns mit dem Leben.
Doch sie, die im Aufstande, den du entfacht,
Mit Waffen sich an dich geschlossen
Und sich widersetzt bolschewistischer Macht,
Sie werden heut mit dir erschossen!"

Da quillt aus dem Aug' ihm die Träne hervor
und furcht' sich die Stirne vor Sorgen:
Die Hände zum Segen jetzt hebt er empor,
Empor in den schimmernden Morgen.
„Euch segne ich, Brüder, in sterbender Stund',
Beim Gang zu des Ewigen Throne;
Entlassung der Sünden euch kündet mein Mund
Im Blute des Mittlers, im Sohne."

Und mutig er stellt sich zum Tode bereit,
Hinein in die Reihe zu allen.
Dann liegt's bei d. Roten. Bald sind sie soweit
Kommandos jetzt kurze erschallen.
Maschinengewehre! Schon sind sie herbei,
Schon speien sie Tod und Verderben!
Und wehrlose Deutsche im Regen von Blei
Jetzt fallen und bluten und sterben.

Zwei Kreuze nur künden auf einsamer Heid',
Wo schwer in den Tod sie gesunken.
Und stumm Mutter Erde in meertiefem Leid
Das Blut ihrer Söhne getrunken.
Wie uns ihr Gedenken die Seele durchzieht,
So sei es dir, Nachwelt, geboten.
Besing sie drum, Herz, o besing sie, mein Lied,
Die Toten, die Toten, die Toten.[2]

---

[2] According to the most reliable reports 87 men were shot. Of these 74 were from Selz, 8 from Baden, 4 from Kandel, and one from Strassburg. The following victims have been identified:

1. *From Selz*
Bartelschwarz, Ant.
Bartle, Michael
Brendel, Anton
Brendel, Franz
Deibert, Joseph
Fahn, Hans
Feller, Joseph
Fetsch, Eugenius
Fetsch, Ferdinand
Fetsch, Rochus
Funk, Martha
Herle, Rochus
Jakob, Alexander
Jakob, Bernhard
Jakob, Pius

Jundt, Joel
Jundt, Alexander
Jundt, Michael
Jundt, Timotheus
Jundt, Stanislaus
Kaiser, Frau
Kelz, Anton
Kerzenlicht, Geo.
Kiefel, Johann
Kiefelrot, Adam
Kiefelrot, Martin
Klein, Lorenz
Köhler, Andreas
Köhler, Joseph
Leibham, Casimir
Leibham, Pius

Leibham, Wendelin
Michel, Peter
Michel, Wendelin
Peter, Wendelin
Pritasegel, Joseph
Schlagen, Pius
Usselmann, Wendelin

Weigel, Georg
Weisbeck, Dominik
Weisbeck, Pius
Weissenburger, Clemens
Welk, Anton
Wetsch, Ferdinand
Wetsch, Rochus
Volk, Andreas
Ziegler, Casimir

2. *From Baden*
Braunagel, Michael
Götz, Peter
Hepfner, Joseph
Hilzendeger, Peter
Schlosser, Johann
Schlosser, Peter
Stauss, Wendelin
Volz, Michael
3. *From Kandel*
Becker, Joseph
Bosch, Michael
Heintz, Leo
Schmalz, Michael
4. *From Strassburg*
Schreiber, Hans

The two women included in the list were killed during the raid.
The four men who survived the massacre were: Wendelin *Barthle*, Ferdinand *Thomas* and his son Valtin, and Ludwig *Wald*.
The identified victims in Fischer-Franzen were: Joseph *Brossart*, Mathias *Fischer*, Valentin *Klein*, Georg *Marquardt*, Engelbert and Longinus *Meier*, Franz *Moser*, Jr., Joseph *Reiss* and his father, Nikolaus *Schergewitsch*, and Vincenz *Wilhelm*.
The identified victims in Neu-Schlössel were: Andreas *Volk*, Johannes *Fischer* and his sons, Franz and Joseph *Schiffmacher*, and Jakob *Schiffmacher* and his sons.

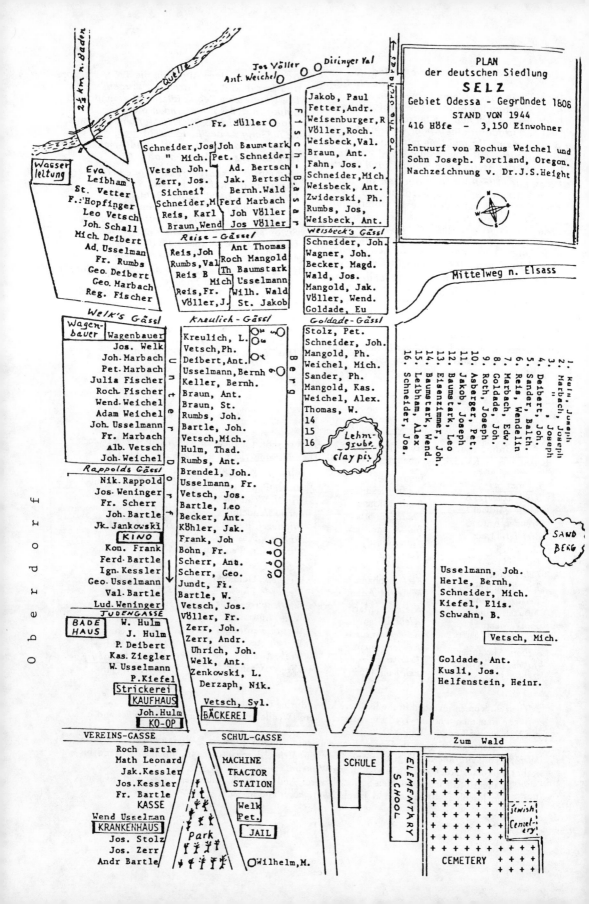

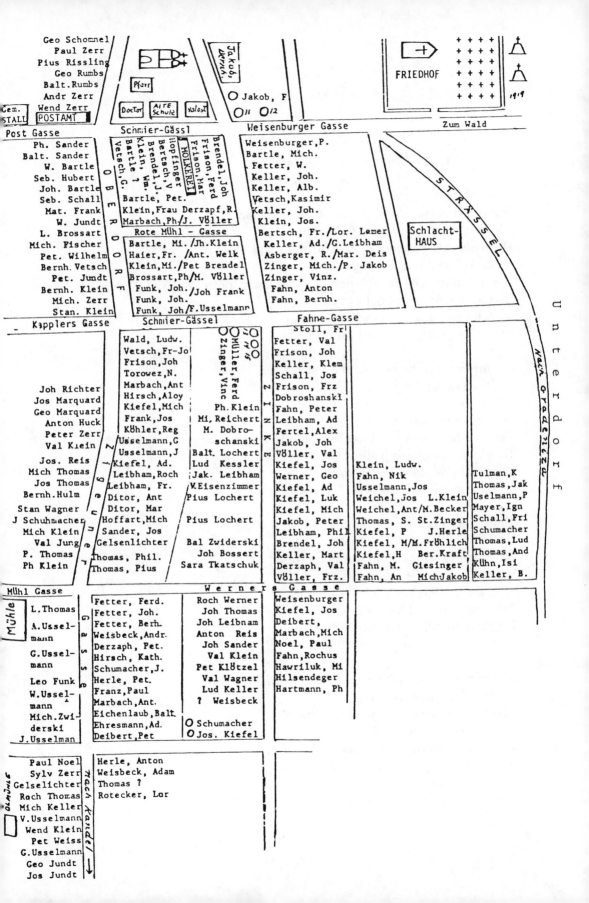

Geo Schommel
Paul Zerr
Pius Rissling
Geo Rumbs
Balt.Rumbs
Andr Zerr
Wend Zerr

Gem.
STALL   POSTAMT

Pfarr

Doctor   ALTE Schule   Valest

Jakob, Henri

Jakob, F
O 11   O 12

FRIEDHOF + + + +
+ + + +
+ + + +
+ + + +
+ + + +
1919

Weisenburger Gasse   Zum Wald

Post Gasse

Ph. Sander
Balt. Sander
W. Bartle
Seb. Hubert
Joh. Bartle
Seb. Schall
Mat. Frank
W. Jundt
L. Brossart
Mich. Fischer
Pet. Wilhelm
Bernh. Vetsch
Pet. Jundt
Bernh. Klein
Mich. Zerr
Stan. Klein

Schmier-Gässl

Vetsch, G.
Bartle, Wm.
Klein, A.
Bertsch, V.
Brendel, J.
Iliopfinger
Brendel, Joh
Frison, Ferd
Frison, Mar

MOLKEREI

Bartle, Pet.
Klein, Frau Derzapf,R.
Marbach, Ph./J. Völler

Rote Mühl - Gasse

Bartle, Mi. /Jh.Klein
Haier, Fr. /Ant. Welk
Klein,Mi./Pet Brendel
Brossart,Ph/M. Völler
Funk, Joh. /Joh Frank
Funk, Joh.
Funk, Joh/F. Usselmann

Weisenburger Gasse

Weisenburger,P.
Bartle, Mich.
Fetter, W.
Keller, Joh.
Keller, Alb.
Vetsch,Kasimir
Keller, Joh.
Klein, Jos.
Bertsch, Fr./Lor. Lemer
Keller, Ad./G.Leibham
Asberger, R./Mar. Deis
Zinger, Mich./P. Jakob
Zinger, Vinz.
Fahn, Anton
Fahn, Bernh.

STRÄSSEL

Schlacht-
HAUS

Unterdorf

Kapplers Gasse   **Schmier-Gässel**   **Fahne-Gasse**

Joh Richter
Jos Marquard
Geo Marquard
Anton Huck
Peter Zerr
Val Klein
Jos. Reis
Mich Thomas
Jos Thomas
Bernh.Hulm
Stan Wagner
J Schuhmacher
Mich Klein
Val Jung
P. Thomas
Ph Klein

Wald, Ludw.
Vetsch, Fr-Jo
Frison,Joh
Torowez,N.
Marbach,Ant
Hirsch,Aloy
Kiefel,Mich
Frank,Jos
Köhler,Reg
Usselmann,G
Usselmann,J
Kiefel, Ad.
Leibham,Roch
Leibham, Fr.
Ditor, Ant
Ditor, Mar
Hoffart,Mich
Sander, Jos
Gelsenlichter
Thomas, Phil.
Thomas, Pius

Müller, Ferd
Zinger,Vinc

Ph.Klein
Mi. Reichert
M. Dobro-
schanski
Balt.Lochert
Lud Kessler
Jak. Leibham
V.Eisenzimmer
Pius Lochert

Pius Lochert

Bal Zwiderski
Joh Bossert
Sara Tkatschuk

Stoll, Fri
Fetter, Val
Frison, Joh
Keller, Klem
Schall, Jos
Frison, Frz
Dobroshanski
Fahn, Peter
Leibham, Ad
Fertel,Alex
Jakob, Joh
Völler, Val
Kiefel, Jos
Werner, Geo
Kiefel, Ad
Kiefel, Luk
Kiefel, Mich
Jakob, Peter
Leibham, Phil
Brendel, Joh
Keller, Mart
Derzaph, Val
Völler, Frz.

Klein, Ludw.
Fahn, Nik
Usselmann,Jos
Weichel,Jos L.Klein
Weichel,Ant/M.Becker
Thomas, S. St.Zinger
Kiefel, P   J.Herle
Kiefel, M/M.Fröhlich
Kiefel,H   Ber.Kraft
Fahn, M. Giesinger
Fahn, An   MichJakob

Tulman,K
Thomas,Jak
Uselmann,P
Mayer,Ign
Schall,Fri
Schumacher
Thomas,Lud
Thomas,And
Kühn,Isi
Keller, B.

Mühl Gasse

Mühle

L.Thomas
A.Ussel-
mann
G.Ussel-
mann
Leo Funk
W.Ussel-
mann
Mich.Zwi-
derski
J.Usselman

Werners Gasse

Fetter, Ferd.
Fetter, Joh.
Fetter, Berh.
Weisbeck,Andr.
Derzaph, Pet.
Hirsch, Kath.
Schumacher,J.
Herle, Pet.
Franz,Paul
Marbach,Ant.
Eichenlaub,Balt
Ehresmann,Ad.
Deibert,Pet

Roch Werner
Joh Thomas
Joh Leibnam
Anton Reis
Joh Sander
Val Klein
Pet Klötzel
Val Wagner
Lud Keller
? Weisbeck

O Schumacher
O Jos. Kiefel

Weisenburger
Kiefel, Jos
Deibert,
Marbach,Mich
Noel, Paul
Fahn,Rochus
Hawriluk, Mi
Hilsendeger
Hartmann, Ph

Paul Noel
Sylv Zerr
Gelselichter
Roch Thomas
Mich Keller
V.Usselmann
Wend Klein
Pet Weiss
G.Usselmann
Geo Jundt
Jos Jundt

Herle, Anton
Weisbeck, Adam
Thomas ?
Rotecker, Lor

Nach Kandel

The Death of the Men of Selz

*A translation of George Rath's
"Der Tod der Selzer," by J.H.S.*

The wheat is mowed in the sun-drenched land
The sheaves stand in rows far and near.
The harvest is gathered by industrious hand,
No farmer will starve this year.
The machines have been humming since early morn
On the ripening sun-bright plains;
Soon he will haul the grain to his barn
As the long-sought reward for his pains.

But different is the plan of the Bolshevik
For the fate of the golden yield:
"You colonists all shall deliver it quick
To feed my troops in the field.
They are battling the Whites in a bloody war,
They're in rags, with bellies that bloat;
You shall give them bread till the victory is ours,
Or I'll seize you by the scruff of your throat!"

The farmer's great patience has dwindled of late,
His soul is aflame with despair.
What crimes do the Reds not perpetrate?
Whose neck do the villains spare?
Shall the godless pack forever prevail?
Too long is the rabble's reign;
Let them bundle their rags and prepare
To follow in Trotsky's train."

Across the steppe, with words flashing bright,
The couriers issue the call:
"To arms, all men, let our towns unite!
Rise up, you colonies all!
The Red commissar has plundered us bare
And looted our food, unabated.
If he wants the wheat we garnered this year,
Let him come himself and get it!

The blood illusion is fading away,
The house of the Reds is on fire.
Don't dally and waver, unite for the fray,
And topple it into the mire!
Colonists, arise and fight, everyone,
Let each village be a bulwark for others.
You men who are able, shoulder your gun
And repulse them, you German brothers!"

The turmoil now surges and seethes like the sea
In field and alley and street.
How the crowds are gathering menacingly
When the work in the fields is complete.
In the rays of the bright August sun
The fighters in groups are uniting;
Their hands tightly grip the glittering gun,
Their eyes are keen for the fighting.

Like a storm, the foe is scurrying free,
It rumbles and flares in the distance.
From Dniester to Boug and down to the sea
The villages rise in resistance.
"We're fighting for justice and honor and hearth,
And shall not surrender these rights.
We shall stay a free colonist race apart,
And on it we'll stake our lives."

With the others allied, Strassburg, Kandel and Selz
Have taken up arms for the fighting;
Boldly their fighters are moving out fast
To the railway where cannons are waiting.
But the Reds are tough, their mortars soon flash
And Strassburg is heavily pounded.
The north end's aflame, as crash follows crash,
And the town is quickly surrounded.

Farther to the south of the Kutschurgan
The horde is avidly milling.
They capture the roads, swing round the liman
And storm the towns for the killing.

237

The courage of the bravest defenders abates
And panic constricts every village.
The women with children and bundles and crates
Are fleeing to escape from the pillage.

The towns are encircled, the bridges and roads
Are guarded by Reds enterprising.
The men they have captured are brought into Selz,
To be questioned about the uprising.
Though many escaped in the sheltering reeds,
They catch eighty-three, to their sorrow,
And the chief of the Reds cruelly decrees
They'll be shot near the town on the morrow.

The dreadful night passes, the daylight breaks,
And the golden sun rises blood-red.
When this day of August dawns and awakes,
It's only for terror, not pleasure.
Behold they come marching out of the town
With hurried advance to the meadow.
The chief at the head of the well-armed band,
And the victims caught in the middle.

And when they arrived on the gruesome stage
As the dawn was turning gray,
The chief once more inquires in a rage:
"What men were involved in the fray?"
Alas, one man in trembling despair
Accuses his fellows, his eyes meekly lowered.
With scorn the chieftain grants to him there,
And to some others, their lives as reward.

But from the ranks there steps a young priest
With silent and resolute bearing.
He raises his hand and looking at the chief,
He asks for silence and a hearing.
He had just returned to his home of late
To visit his dearly loved mother,
But was overtaken by ill-starred fate
And, though innocent, seized with the others.

But now he is moved with compassion profound
As he stands in front of the others.
He feels how strongly in love he is bound
Together with all of his brothers.
They had fought and struggled, labored and loved,
And are now doomed to die disgraced
And would this day imbue with their blood
The very earth their strength had embraced.

What immeasurable grief, what unspeakable pain
Their death will cause the bereaved.
That he must now save them, is all too plain,
What matter's is that it's achieved.
With his own young life he needs to appease them
For with the Reds there's no legal appealing,
And so he assumes all the blame, just for show,
And brands himself the sole villain.

"These men," he declares, "are innocent quite,
It was I who provoked the affray.
Don't punish my brothers, mine is the guilt,
It was I who led them astray.
And if I deserve to be shot for the deed,
To me let the bullet be given.
But have patience, have pity on them, not me,
And let the misled remain living.

The Reds gaze at each other perplexed,
Amazed at the young priest's daring,
For the words of the dauntless young man
Almost touched their cold-hearted bearing.
But the emotion was brief; in a trice they will
Become real Bolsheviks again
Thoroughly trained to hate and to kill,
For compassion behooves only Christians.

"And if you have done so and stirred up the land,
You are guilty of causing the strife.
The Reds will strike you with avenging hand,
You shall pay for the deed with your life.

And all who have taken up arms for the fight,
To which you led them astray
And who dared to oppose the Bolshevist might
Shall be shot with you this day."

From the priest's eyes many tears were drawn,
With grief his brow distressing.
He raised his hands in the glimmering dawn
To bestow on the men his last blessing:
"I bless you, my brothers, in this hour of death,
As we depart to the eternal throne.
My lips proclaim God's forgiveness of sin,
In the blood of the Savior, the Son.

Adieu, you will fall on this sacred earth
As victims of dreadful proscription.
You fought for honor, for home and hearth,
For every man's right and conviction.
We shall not fear to encounter death;
Lord God, let Heaven be our inheritance.
And when amid bullets our hearts start to break,
Let us all die bravely as Germans.

Ready for death, he bravely steps back
And stands in the ranks with his brothers.
It's now up to the Reds to mount the attack,
As the chief quickly bellows the orders.
The machine guns are hastily loaded and set
To send death and destruction flying.
The defenseless Germans in a shower of lead
Now fall and lie bleeding and dying.

Two crosses stand out on the lonesome steppe
Where they sank to their death in the sod,
Where mother earth in sea-deep grief
Drank her sons' spilled blood.
And as in my soul their memory lives on,
So may it still move generations.
Sing out, my heart, sing out the song
Of the dead, the widows, the orphans.

240

Elegie an unsere Toten

George Rath

Naht ihr euch mir auf zarten, lichten Schwingen,
Die ihr zu früh, ach, dieser Welt entrückt,
Um noch einmal durch Raum und Zeit zu dringen,
Von euch beim schwersten Gange überbrückt,
Ihr Seligen? Ich hör euch Hymnen singen,
Ins helle Licht der Ewigkeit entzückt.
An eurem Leib erblick ich Nägelmal und Wunden,
Und um das Haupt die Dornenkron gewunden.

Ich seh euch in Sibiriens eis'gen Wäldern,
Im fernen Turkestan im Wüstensand,
In Knechtschaft aud ukrain'schen Weizenfeldern,
In der Verbannung an des Weissmeers Strand;
Seh Wein euch für die Unterdrücker keltern
Und sinken kalt erschossen an der Wand,
Sehzahllos euch des Hungertodes sterben,
Und fremdes Volk mit Lachen euch beerben.

Fürwahr, ihr habt zur Neige ausgetrunken
Den bittern Kelch, gleich dem, der selbst ihn trank,
Bevor im Märtyrglanz zur Gruft gesunken
Euch ist der Leib, der müde, wund und krank.
Erloschen ist des Lebens Himmelsfunken,
Mit ihm der letzte Seufzer, Schmerz und Dank,
Versiegt die letzten Tränen, letzten Klagen,
Und abgelegt die Last, die ihr getragen.

Für immer seid ihr nun dahingegangen
Aus einer Welt voll Unrict, Hass und Leid.
Wer wischte euch den Schweiss von Stirn und Wangen,
Im Angesicht der hehren Ewigkeit?
Wer stillt' der Seele heisses Trostverlangen?
O, sprecht, gab jemand euch das letzt Geleit?
Ihr schweigt und nichts und niemand in der Runde,
Gibt mir von euch und euren Gräbern Kunde.

Und doch! Ist euch genommen auch das Leben,
So blieb, was keine ird'sche Macht zerbricht:
Die Liebe, die nicht anders kann, als geben
Und in Erinn'rung noch euch Kränze flicht,
Die Hoffnung, die im stillen süssen Weben
Des Grabes Nacht verklärt im Osterlicht. --
Sie stehen über Werden und Vergehen
Und künden euch ein selig Auferstehen.

'From "Klänge der Seele," 1960, Omaha, Nebr. p. 25.

Elegy to our Dead

A translation of George Rath's
"Elegie an unsere Toten"
by Joseph S. Height

Do you come near on gentle wings sublime,
Carried off too early from this earthly sphere,
To pass once more through space and time
That you had crossed in your grievous going,
You blessed spirits? I hear you singing hymns,
Transported into light eternal-glowing.
On your body I see the marks of nails and wounds
And your head with crown of thorns is bound.

I see you in Siberia's frozen forests,
In Turkestan's dread desert sand;
Enslaved on the wheatfields of the Ukraine
And banished to the White Sea's arctic strand.
I see you press the wine for the oppressor,
Your crumpled bodies shot by ruthless hands,
I see countless thousands starve and perish
While alien nomads rape their towns and lands.

In truth, you have all drunk to the lees
The bitter cup that He Himself did consume,
Ere your bodies, weary, sick and sore,
Succumbed in martyr's splendor to the tomb.
The heavenly spark of your life is quenched
And with it the last sigh, the grief, the pain;
The final tears and plaints have ebbed and died,
And the burden that you bore is laid aside.

You have passed beyond forevermore
From a world of rank injustice, hate and pain.
Who wiped away the sweat from cheek and brow
As you faced the august eternity?
Who soothed the soul's fierce thirst for solace,
Who accompanied you on your last journey?
You are silent, and nothing, no one anywhere
Tells me of you and your last resting places.

Yet even though you were bereft of life and living,
There still remained what no earthly power shatters:
Your *love*, which knew of nothing else but giving,
And in memory still entwines wreaths for you,
Your *hope*, which in silent sweet weaving
Transfigures the dark grave in Easter light. —
These rise beyond all becoming and decay,
To proclaim for you a blessed resurrection day.

XIII   Vignettes of Catholic Colonies

1. Rosental in the Crimea

In the spring of 1803, a group of 35 families, mostly from Baden, embarked at river port of Ulm and sailed down the Danube as far as Galatz, where they remained two weeks in quarantine before they were brought by wagons to Odessa. Here they were placed in winterquarters in the city. In the following spring, 40 families were conducted by Inspector Hasper into the Crimea and 18 of the families were apportioned 2,000 dessiatines (= 5,200 acres) of land 25 versts from Simferopol and settled in the rose-abounding valley of Barantcha.

The settlers began building their houses of stone and sun-dried clay bricks in May, 1805. Another seven families from Lorraine arrived in the fall, but it was not until 1807 that all of the 25 houses were completed. Each family received a government loan of 300 rubles to enable it to purchase the necessary livestock and equipment to get settled. The first mayor, Anton Fauth, named the village Rosental, the valley of roses. With the influx of several more families the number of families rose to 56 in the year 1818.

In 1848 there were 56 households in the village, comprising 65 families that numbered 244 males and 192 females. With the exception of one adobe house, all the houses were constructed of stone. The average number of children per family was five. The plow land that had been apportioned to the colonists amounted to 615 dessiatines (= 1,660 acres). This means each land-holding family received about 11 dessiatines (= 30 acres). In addition, there were 375 dess. of communal pastureland, 185 dess. of hayland, and 1,254 woodland and forest. Thirty dessiatines were used for the farmyards. The community also had a church, an elementary school, a grain-storage depot, a water-powered grist mill, and a communal orchard.

The parish was established in 1823. Up to that time the Rosental community was affiliated with the Catholic parish in Simferopol. The first church in the village was built in 1828/30. The second church, a structure of stone in the neo-Romanesque style, was built during the tenure of Father Petraschewsky and consecrated on September 8, 1869.

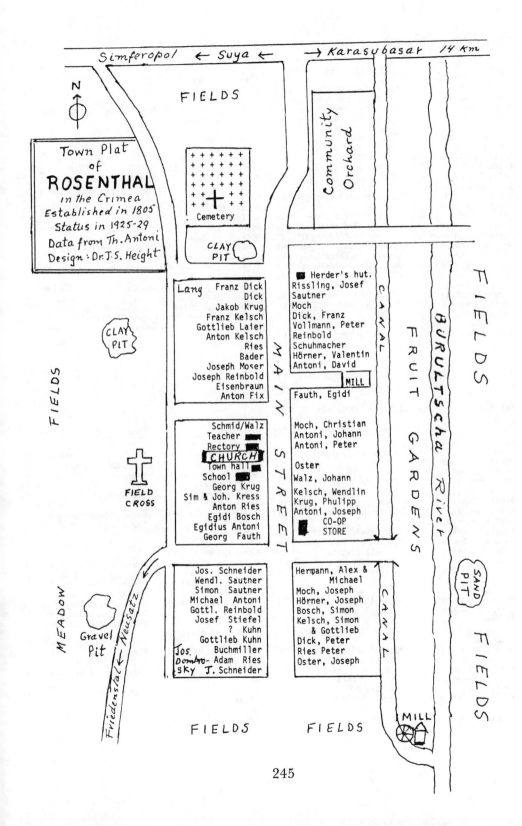

Simferopol ← Suya ← → Karasubasar 14 km

N

FIELDS

Town Plat
of
ROSENTHAL
in the Crimea
Established in 1805
Status in 1925-29
Data from Th. Antoni
Design: Dr. J.S. Height

Cemetery

CLAY
PIT

Community Orchard

CANAL

FRUIT GARDENS

BÜRÜLTSCHA River

FIELDS

CLAY
PIT

FIELDS

Lang   Franz Dick
           Dick
       Jakob Krug
       Franz Kelsch
       Gottlieb Laier
       Anton Kelsch
           Ries
           Bader
       Joseph Moser
   Joseph Reinbold
       Eisenbraun
       Anton Fix

■ Herder's hut.
Rissling, Josef
Sautner
Moch
Dick, Franz
Vollmann, Peter
Reinbold
Schuhmacher
Hörner, Valentin
Antoni, David

MILL

Fauth, Egidi

MAIN STREET

FIELD
CROSS

Schmid/Walz
Teacher ■
Rectory ■
CHURCH
Town hall
School ■
       Georg Krug
Sim & Joh. Kress
       Anton Ries
       Egidi Bosch
   Egidius Antoni
       Georg Fauth

Moch, Christian
Antoni, Johann
Antoni, Peter

Oster

Walz, Johann
Kelsch, Wendlin
Krug, Phulipp
Antoni, Joseph
       CO-OP
       STORE

MEADOW

Gravel
Pit

← Friedensfal ← Neusatz

Jos. Schneider
Wendl. Sautner
Simon Sautner
Michael Antoni
Gottl. Reinbold
Josef Stiefel
    ? Kuhn
Gottlieb Kuhn
Jos.   Buchmiller
Dombro- Adam Ries
sky J. Schneider

Hermann, Alex &
       Michael
Moch, Joseph
Hörner, Joseph
Bosch, Simon
Kelsch, Simon
    & Gottlieb
Dick, Peter
Ries Peter
Oster, Joseph

CANAL

SAND
PIT

FIELDS

FIELDS   FIELDS

MILL

245

The Founding families of Rosental/Crimea

Colonist	Home town/District	Country	Colonist	Home town/District	Country
Antoni, Melchior & Fr.		Ba	Klink, Johann		
Bader, Philipp	cj. Durmersheim/Rastatt	Ba	Klose, August		
Bast, Joseph	cj. Kuhardt/Grmshm.	Pf	König, Adam		
Bauer, Johann	cj. Uhrweiler/Ndrbronn	Als	Körner, Jakob	Walldorf/Heidelebrg	Ba
Becker, Heinrich	Reichenbach/Karlsruhe	Ba	Kranzner, Franz		
Benz, Peter	Elsenz/Sinsheim	Ba	Krug, Georg	Käfertal/Mannheim	Ba
Blatter, Joseph	Bitsch/Lothringen	Als	Kuhn, Balth. & Dan.		
Bloch, Jakob	Eichelberg/Bruchsal	Ba	Lang, Adam		
Bosch, Ignatius	Sulzbach/Mannheim	Ba	Leonhard, Johann		
Buchmiller, Andreas	Ubstadt/Bruchsal	Ba	Lehmann, Matheus		
Delhai, Alexander			Maier, Matheus	Bietigheim/Rastatt	Ba
Engesser, Johann			Moch, Peter	Kronau/Bruchsal	Ba
Erhard, Joseph	cj. Blankenborn/Bergzb	Pf	Moser, Joseph		
Fauth, Marianna			Mönch, Kasimir		
Fritz, Fideli	cj. Malsch/Karlsruhe	Ba	Neufert, Jakob		
Gerweck, Johann	Neibsheim/Bruchsal	Ba	Oster, Paul	Elsenz/Sinsheim	Ba
Hartmann, Michael	cj. Odenheim/Bruchsal	Ba	Ruckhaber, Johann		
Haselsteiner, Georg	Obermarschtal/Ehingen	Wü	Sauter, Joseph	Mühlhausen/Heidelberg	Ba
Heck, Melchior	Bietigheim/Rastatt	Ba	Schäfer, Anton		
Hörmann(Hermann) Jos.	Mühlhausen/Heidelberg	Ba	Schild, Georg	Reichenberg/Backnang?	Wü
Hörmann (")Ludwig	Mühlhausen/Heidelberg	Ba	Schlindwein, Karl		
Horle, Andreas			Schmid, Magnus	Zitzen/Graubünden	Sw
Hörner, Raphael	cj. Grombach/Sinsheim	Ba	Schmid, Johann		
Jehle, Nikolaus	Unter-Ackern (?)	Ba	Schumacher, Peter		
Kelsch, Franz			Speidel, Johann	Mössingen/Tübingen	Wü
Kettinger, , Franz			Tischler, Joseph	Freiburg	Ba
Klee, Franz	Ketsch/Mannheim	Ba	Vollmann, Matheus		
			Winter, Andreas	Forchheim/Emmendingen	Ba
			Ziegler, Franz		

The Founding families of Kronental/Crimea

Colonist	Home town/District	Country	Colonist	Home town/District	Country
Bekel, Balthasar			Minkel, Johann		
Birn, Michael	Heddesheim/Weinheim	Ba	Morast, Johann	Schriesheim/Mannheim	Ba
Bletzer, Johannes			Müller, Kaspar	Sandhausen/Heidelberg	Ba
Blöd, Joseph			Neuchum, Matheus	Neureut/Karlsruhe	Ba
Böss, Michael	Oberweier?/Rastatt	Ba	Obertshauser, Jakob	Jöhlingen/Karlsruhe	Ba
Braun, Christoph	Rohrbach?/Sinsheim	Ba	Ott, Heinrich	Grombach/Sinsheim	Ba
Breitenbücher, Michael	Erpfingen?/Reutlingen	Wü	Perle, Nikolaus		
Ehrreiser, Ignatius	Gallenbach/Bühl	Ba	Reinhard, Sebastian	Hassmersheim/Mosbach	Ba
Esslinger, Andreas			Renkert, Ludwig	Sandhausen/Heidelberg	Ba
Feist, Leonhard	Kuppenheim/Rastatt	Ba	Roth, Martin		
Gassmann, Georg	?Laudenbach/Mannheim	Ba	Schamber, Andreas	Heidelsheim/Bruchsal	Ba
Grünwald, Georg	Nehweiler/Wssbg	Als	Schmid, Georg		
Hauk, Georg	Untergrombach/Bruchsal	Ba	Schneider, Nikolaus	Obergrombach/Bruchsal	Ba
Heinert, Michael	Arzheim?/Landau	Pf	Schön, Philipp	Obergimpern?/Sinsheim	Ba
Held, Heinrich			Schweikert, Johann	Spechbach/Heidelberg	Ba
Herbst, Peter			Seiferling, Franz	Mühlhausen?/Heidelberg	Ba
Hermes, Wilhelm	Eschelbach/Sinsheim	Ba	Steinbrunner, Jak-Fr.	Graben/Karlsruhe	Ba
Hoffmann, Johann			Stern, Michael	Dossenheim/Heidelberg	Ba
Illhard, Ludwig			Thomas, Johann	Mühlhausen/Heidelberg	Ba
Jesst, Peter	?Lützelsachsen/Weinheim	Ba	Träger, Friedrich		
Klubein, Jakob			Walz, Ignatz	Jöhlingen/Karlsruhe	Ba
Knoll, Anton	?Büchelberg/Grmshm	Pf	Weidner, Wilhelm	Öhringen-Wü	
Köhler, Michael	Sandhausen/Heidelberg	Ba	Weigum, Konrad	Illingen/Rastatt	Ba
Koffler, Franz	Durmersheim/Rastatt	Ba	Weiss, Michael	Nehweiler /Weissenburg	Als
Kühn, Joseph	Obergimpern/Sinsheim	Ba	Weisser, Leonhard		
Küst, Georg	Karlsruhe	Ba	Wetzel, Matheus	Kuppenheim/Rastatt	Ba
Kuhlmann, Philipp	Rohrbach/Sinsheim	Ba	Wiederich, Peter		
Maichel, Georg			Wössnert, Salomon	Menzingen/Bruchsal	Ba
Maissel, Gottfried			Zeissler, Friedrich		

246

2. Heidelberg in the Molotchna

The colony of Heidelberg was established in 1810 by 82 families, most of whom came from the districts of Mannheim and Heidelberg, with a few from the district of Rastatt. Because of Napoleon's military campaign in the area of Vienna, the emigrants were compelled to take a roundabout route to Russia via Saxony, Silesia and Polish Galicia. They arrived in Russia in the fall of 1809 and were placed into winterquarters in the recently established German colonies near Odessa. In the spring they were conducted by their leader Franz Becht of Büchig/Karlsruhe 130 versts south-east of Yekaterinoslav and settled 18 versts northwest of the Molotchna River in the province of Taurida.

Because of the ravine that ran through the village, the layout of the streets was quite irregular, and several bridges were needed to span the ravine and make communication possible between the two sections of the village.

The land area apportioned to the new settlement was 5,132 dessiatines, or 13,856 acres. The population of the 82 founding families appears to have been 410. However, in the census revision of 1816, it is indicated that only 77 families were living in Heidelberg that year, and the total population was 348 souls (174 male and 184 female). In 1822 an additional 22 families were settled here, making a total of 99 families. For many years Joseph Ade from Büchig/Karlsruhe was the village mayor.

The years between 1825 and 1833 were difficult because of drought, locust plagues, and livestock epidemics. In 1842 the government granted the community the sum of 41,000 rubles for the construction of a large stone church. Since the colonists did most of the work in providing the building material, the cost of the church remained only moderately high. Instead of using the surplus money to furnish the interior of the church, the rather naive old-timers gave the money back to the government. For a long time Father Schamne was pastor at Heidelberg, and he became very popular not only among the Catholics but also the Lutheran people in the area.

In 1857 the land area of Heidelberg was increased to 5,520 dessiatines, probably from land purchases that were made by the community. In 1859 the population of the village had risen to 1,094. Owing to massive emigration to America in the nineties until the eve of the first World War, the population figure began to decrease. It was only 980 in 1907 and 922 in 1915. But in 1918 it reached a high point of 1,207. Animal husbandry was more highly developed in Heidelberg than in other colonies in the area. In 1912 the community owned 746 horses, 733 head of cattle, and 432 pigs. The village operated six windmills for the grinding and milling of grain; there were several general stores, a cooperage, a brick factory, and several smaller shops.

The pastors who were active in Heidelberg over the years were: Fathers Raschevsky and Ohnschinsky in the Polish period prior to the establishment of the German diocese of Tiraspol. Among the pastors who came out of the Tiraspol seminary were: Johannes Schamme, 1866-1897; Johannes Hoffman 1897-1919; Franz Kuhn 1901-1903; Markus Zimmermann 1903; Anton Fröhlich 1917; Joseph Jungkind 1920; Georg Oberowsky 1922-1923; Jakob Jaufmann 1923-24; Nikodemus Ihly 1932-1933?

The Founding families of Heidelberg/Molotchna

Colonist	Home town/District	Country	Colonist	Home town/District	Country
Ade, Joseph	Büchig/Karlsruhe	Ba	Meyhofer, Georg		
Bayer, Peter	Grombach/Sinsheim	Ba	Müller, Jos. & Peter	Hockenheim/Mannheim	Ba
Bernhardt, Simon	Obersteinbach/Wssbg	Als	Neumayer, Sebastian	Schöllbrunn/Karlsruhe	Ba
Binkmann, Jakob	Käfertal/Mannheim	Ba	Nold, Joseph	Steinmauern/Rastatt	Ba
Bopp, Jakob	Käfertal/Mannheim	Ba	Peter, Xaver	Rastatt	Ba
Brecht, Franz	Baden/Rastatt	Ba	Pfeifer, Franz-Peter	Odenheim/Bruchsal	Ba
Eisele, Valentin	Spechbach/Heidelberg	Ba	Pfund, Jakob	Jöhlingen/Karlsruhe	Ba
Eisenkrein, Martin	Dossenheim/Heidelberg	Ba	Posnak, Mathias		
Fähner, Joseph	Spechbach/Heidelberg	Ba	Reinich, Michael	Sinsheim	Ba
Fitterer, Joseph	Bischweiler/Rastatt	Ba	Resch, Georg	Schriesheim/Mannheim	Ba
Fröhlich, Johannes	Durmersheim/Rastatt	Ba	Riedel, Joseph		Ba
Geberth, Adam	?	Ba	Ritter, Lorenz	?Richen/Sinsheim	Ba
Glassner, Mathias	Aglasterhausen/Mosbach	Ba	Roos, Adam	?	Wü
Grätz, Franz		Ba	Saaneck, Joh.-Daniel	Fischbach/Biberach	Wü
Haag, Konrad	Ketsch/Mannheim	Ba	Sauer, Peter		?Ba
Härty, Nikolaus	?Herxheim/Landau	Pf	Scheid, Johann	Sandhausen/Heidelberg	Ba
Hartlieb, Thomas		Ba	Schenkel, Johannes	Mosbach	Ba
Hecht, Franz	Staffert/Karlsruhe	Ba	Schindler, Johann	Kuppenheim/Rastatt	Ba
Heid, Johannes	Eschelbronn/Sinsheim	Ba	Schleichert, Adam	Spechbach/Heidelberg	Ba
Hering, Michael	Spechbach/Heidelberg	Ba	Schrepp, Michael	?Landshausen/Sinsheim	Ba
Jasmann, Martin		Ba	Schweigert, Leonhard	Eppelheim/Heidelberg	Ba
Kailbach, Zächäus	Ketsch/Mannheim	Ba	Schröder, Jakob	?Bietigheim/Rastatt	Ba
Klab, Mathäus		Ba	Sellner, Johann	Dossenheim/Heidelberg	Ba
Klaus, Johann	Hockenheim/Mannheim	Ba	Staudenheimer, Jakob		Ba
Klumpp, Gabriel		Ba	Steinbeck, Geo. & Mich.		Ba
Köhler, Martin	Sandhausen/Heidelberg	Ba	Stelz,Christoph	Spechbach/Heidelberg	Ba
Kopp, Johann-Jakob	?Queichheim/Landau	Pf	Striebel, Johannes	Sasbach/Emmendingen	Ba
Koschny, Franz			Trenkenschuh, Friedr.		?Wü
Krämer, Georg	Menzingen/Bruchsal	Ba	Tropmann, Nikolaus	Wallstadt/Mannheim	Ba
Kress, Friedrich	Waldwimmersbach/Heidlbg	Ba	Waltz, Mathias	Kuppenheim/Rastatt	Ba
Küst, Anton	?Grünwettersbach/Krlsrh	Ba	Warth, Valentin	Kuppenheim/Rastatt	Ba
Längle, Joseph	Neibsheim/Karlsruhe	Ba	Weiler, Wendlin	Steinmauern/Rastatt	Ba
Leopold, Johann	Kuppenheim/Rastatt	Ba	Wetzel, Johann	Kuppenheim/Rastatt	Ba
Martin, Johannes	Eppelheim/Heidelberg	Ba	Wipf, Johann	Östringen/Bruchsal	Ba
Meixner, Johann	Sandhausen/Heidelberg	Ba	Wissmann, Joseph		Ba
Merkel, Georg	Rauenal/Rastatt	Ba	Wolf, Valentin	Dossenheim/Heidelberg	Ba
Metz, Valentin,	Schriesheim/Mannheim	Ba	Zeller, Andreas	Durmersheim/Rastatt	Ba
			Zerr, Stephan	?Nehweiler/Wssbg	Als

PASTORS OF HEIDELBERG

P. Easchwsky
P. Ohnschinsky
P. Johannes Schamne 1866-1897
P. Johannes Hoffmann 1897-1919
P. Franz Kuhn 1901-1903
P. Markus Zimmermann 1903

P. Anton Fröhlich 1917
P. Joseph Jungkind c. 1920
P. Georg Oborowsky 1922-1923
P. Jakob Jaufmann 1922-1923
P. Nikolaus Ohly 1932-1933?

3. Krasna in Bessarabia

According to the earliest available information provided by Malinowski, the first settlers in Krasna originally emigrated from Rhine Palatinate, particularly from the district of Münk/Mayen in the area of Coblentz. The dialect of Krasna is the East Franconian of the Moselle region. The emigrants were settled in the Polish villages of Orschokowin and Shitonitz in the Duchy of Warsaw in the years 1800-1803. However, in 1814, in response to Czar Alexander's appeal for settlers, 133 families departed from the Polish villages and migrated to Bessarabia. Ninety of the families were settled in the new colony of Krasna in 1815, and the remainder were settled in 1816.

The colony of Krasna was actually established in 1814 by a group of Lutheran immigrants from Germany on the right bank of a creek called the Kogelnik-Kunduk. It was 95 versts from the regional capital Akkerman, 100 versts from the provincial capital Kishinev, and 140 versts from Odessa. The exhausted immigrants, weary of the hardships of the long journey, had to settle in the middle of the Kogelnik Valley, which was four versts wide and overgrown with reeds, bulrushes and briars, where wolves and other wild animals had established their lairs in the bushes and the tall grass.

Most of the people arrived without any means and were completely dependent on the support extended to them by the government. The land

A stately farmstead in Krasna

250

allotted to them for agriculture was very hilly and overgrown with briar-thickets which made cultivation difficult for the pioneers. On the other hand, the well-watered valley provided excellent pasturage for the livestock, so that the settlers devoted themselves more to the raising of livestock than to grain farming.

In the early decades, the development of the colony was retarded by unfavorable conditions, mishaps, and setbacks. Diseases carried off many of the new settlers. Livestock epidemics often deprived the farmer of his last horse or cow. Because the colonists were too far away from the markets, they were unable to sell their few products at even a small profit and had to barter for the goods they needed. To sell grain, the farmer had to haul it to

Catholic Church in Krasna

Odessa, about 140 versts away. The round trip would take a week and sometimes involved the danger of being robbed on the return journey by vagrant gypsies.

As the settlers were originally partly Catholic and partly Lutheran, it was not long before the peace of the community was disturbed. Soon there were outbreaks of discord, contention, and factionalism, so that it became necessary to resettle the Lutheran group, which was in the minority, in the new village of Katzbach, which was established about eight versts from Krasna. Thus Krasna became exclusively Catholic and peace was restored to the community.

In 1865 a new parish church was built, and in 1885 a rectory was added on a spacious lot to the right of the church. To the left was the community school, with the teacher's living quarters. In 1912 the school was much too small for the number of attending pupils, for even though the building was 60 feet long and 21 feet wide, it was hardly able to accommodate the 200 school children.

The Krasna community land comprised 6910.2 dessiatines or 18,632 acres. There were 114 landholding families and 54 landless families. Before 1912 Krasna had acquired very little land by private purchase. Many families emigrated, most of them to North Dakota and to Canada. A sizable number emigrated to Rumania and settled in the town of Caramurat. The population of Krasna in 1912 was 1,864. The village had 14 blacksmiths, 8 wheelwrights, 3 cabinetmakers, 2 tailors, 8 shoemakers, two painters; 3 general stores, 3 wine taverns, two flour mills.

The Family Names in Krasna

There are no available records of the names of the pioneer settlers in Krasna, but the family names have, of course, been preserved by the descendants:

Alwinger	Hinz	Keller	Riehl	Söhn
Arnold	Janz	Koch	Ritz Rotecek	Speicher
Becker, Peter	Engel	Kraftschenko	Rückert	Spitznagel
Blotzky	Enslen	Krams	Ruscheinsky	Ternes
Bogolowska	Erker	Krenzel	Meer	Tischner
Bonjakowsky	Fenrich	Kunz	Menges	Volk
Both	Fleckenstein	Kuss	Moldenhauer	Wagner
Braun	Furch	Lauterbach	Pantschenko	Weber
Bruschinsky	Gansky	Leinz	Paul	Wetscherok
Deichert	Gedack	Löb	Plotzky	Wingenbach
Dirk	Gross	Maas	Ruth	Winter
Drefs	Gulewitsch	Mandernacht	Schäfer	Wolf
Dressler	Haag	Marte	Schreiber	Wiutschick
Hein	Habrich	Müller, Joh.	Schulkowsky	Ziebart
Heinz	Harsche	Nagel	Steinert	
Herrmann	Hartmann	Neumann	Schwalich	
Herrschaft	Kahl	Noel	Seifert	

The following families came to Krasna from some of the Catholic colonies in the Odessa area in subsequent decades:
Bachmeier and Eckert from Josephstal/Od; Braun, Materi, and Steier from Franzfeld; Hilsendeger and Ihli from Baden; Welter from Elsass; and Kopp from Rastadt.

252

4. Balmas, a Kutschurgan Village in Bessarabia

In the nineties, farmland was becoming very scarce in the Odessa area. Whatever land was still available was becoming so high in price that there were instances when a dessiatine sold for more than 100 rubles.

In the village of Kandel in the Kutschurgan district, there were numerous families who owned only a few dessiatines of land, or no land at all, and who could hardly make a living as craftsmen. They were, however, able to lease a few dessiatines to the Russian neighbors at a rather high annual rent of 10 rubles a dessiatine.

Since the land rent in Bessarabia was by comparison much cheaper—one could lease a dessiatine of land for two or three rubes a year—many colonists in Kandel and several from other Kutschurgan colonies decided to lease out their land at a high rate and obtain three or four times as much land on lease from landowners in Bessarabia.

One of these landowners was Lermantov who owned a large tract of land known as Lermannsthal, which was located about 20 versts from the city of Bender, just across the Kutschurgan Liman. About the year 1892 the name of this settlement was changed to Balmas. In the beginning, the village comprised about 50 families of which about 33 belonged to the first lease-group and 12 to the second lease-group. The land area belonging to the village measured about 3,000 dessiatines or 8,100 acres, which means that the average farmer had the use of about 120 acres.

After the initial difficulties in the pioneer years, the new settlement became quite prosperous. The community built a prayer hall and a German

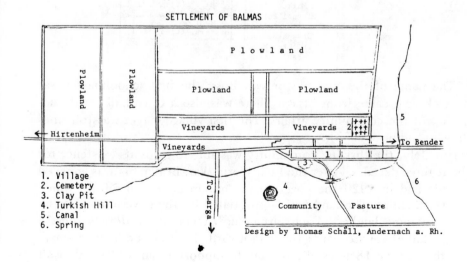

SETTLEMENT OF BALMAS

1. Village
2. Cemetery
3. Clay Pit
4. Turkish Hill
5. Canal
6. Spring

Design by Thomas Schäll, Andernach a. Rh.

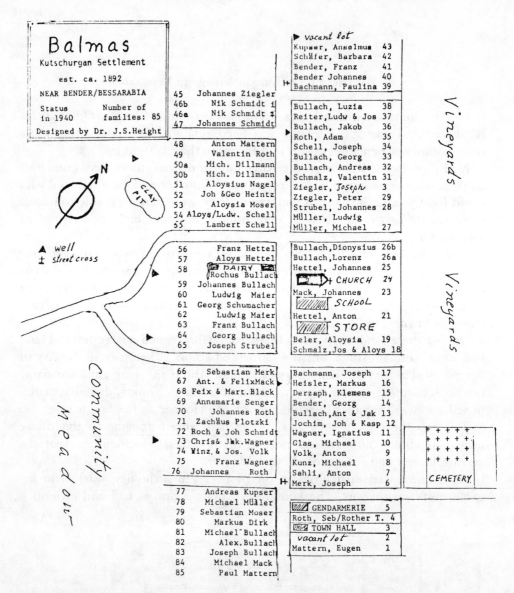

Balmas

Kutschurgan Settlement

est. ca. 1892

NEAR BENDER/BESSARABIA

Status in 1940	Number of families: 85

Designed by Dr. J.S.Height

N

CLAY PIT

▲ well
‡ street cross

Community Meadow

Vineyards

Vineyards

45	Johannes Ziegler
46b	Nik Schmidt 1
46a	Nik Schmidt 2
47	Johannes Schmidt
48	Anton Mattern
49	Valentin Roth
50a	Mich. Dillmann
50b	Mich. Dillmann
51	Aloysius Nagel
52	Joh &Geo Heintz
53	Aloysia Moser
54	Aloys/Ludw. Schell
55	Lambert Schell
56	Franz Hettel
57	Aloys Hettel
58	DAIRY (Rochus Bullach)
59	Johannes Bullach
60	Ludwig Maier
61	Georg Schumacher
62	Ludwig Maier
63	Franz Bullach
64	Georg Bullach
65	Joseph Strubel
66	Sebastian Merk
67	Ant. & FelixMack
68	Feix & Mart.Black
69	Annemarie Senger
70	Johannes Roth
71	Zachäus Plotzki
72	Roch & Joh Schmidt
73	Chris& Jak.Wagner
74	Vinz. & Jos. Volk
75	Franz Wagner
76	Johannes Roth
77	Andreas Kupser
78	Michael Müller
79	Sebastian Moser
80	Markus Dirk
81	Michael Bullach
82	Alex.Bullach
83	Joseph Bullach
84	Michael Mack
85	Paul Mattern

▶ vacant lot

Kupser, Anselmus	43
Schäfer, Barbara	42
Bender, Franz	41
Bender Johannes	40
Bachmann, Paulina	39
Bullach, Luzia	38
Reiter,Ludw & Jos	37
Bullach, Jakob	36
Roth, Adam	35
Schell, Joseph	34
Bullach, Georg	33
Bullach, Andreas	32
Schmalz, Valentin	31
Ziegler, Joseph	3
Ziegler, Peter	29
Strubel, Johannes	28
Müller, Ludwig	
Müller, Michael	27
Bullach,Dionysius	26b
Bullach,Lorenz	26a
Hettel, Johannes	
CHURCH	24
Mack, Johannes	23
SCHOOL	
Hettel, Anton	21
STORE	
Beler, Aloysia	19
Schmalz,Jos & Aloys	18
Bachmann, Joseph	17
Heisler, Markus	16
Derzaph, Klemens	15
Bender, Georg	14
Bullach,Ant & Jak	13
Jochim, Joh & Kasp	12
Wagner, Ignatius	11
Glas, Michael	10
Volk, Anton	9
Kunz, Michael	8
Sahli, Anton	7
Merk, Joseph	6
GENDARMERIE	5
Roth, Seb/Rother T.	4
TOWN HALL	3
vacant lot	2
Mattern, Eugen	1

CEMETERY

school. The name of the first pastor was Boss; the first schoolmaster was Joseph Black who came from Elsass. There was also a town hall for the administration of the community affairs. The first village mayor was Johannes Bullach, who had been an army corporal.

Unfortunately, the thriving community was able to enjoy its existence for only about three decades. After the First World War, Bessarabia was annexed by Rumania and in 1920 the government announced a land reform which also involved Balmas. The land was appropriated by the government and all the renters became landless. Each farmer now received 24 *Morgen* (i.e. 18 acres), plus 2,000 square yards for a farmyard. He was suddenly a smallholder with less than 18 acres of plowland to support a family. To add insult to injury, the Rumanian government not only made the settlers pay for the land apportioned to them, but they also had to pay the erstwhile landowner for the buildings which they themselves had constructed on their homestead. No wonder that many of the settlers became thoroughly disillusioned and emigrated from Balmas to America, especially to western Canada.

Through the Russian Revolution, the Balmaser also lost the land which they had owned in the Kutschurgan homeland. Things became even worse for the Balmaser when the Soviets again occupied Rumania and when Hitler and Stalin made an agreement to resettle all the German colonists of Bessarabia in Germany.

The Founding Families of Balmas. Est. c. 1892

Name of Settler	From...	Ancestral home	Country
Albin, Nikolaus	Kandel I*	?	
Behler, Joseph	Kandel I	Hördt/Germersheim	Pf
Bender, Franz	Mannheim I	Eschelbronn/Sinsheim	Ba
Black, Joseph	Elsass I	Seltz/Weissenburg	Als
Bullach, Johannes	Kandel I	Neeweiler/Wssnbg.	Als
Bullach, Ludwig	Kandel I	" "	Als
Bullach, Anton	Kandel II	" "	Als
Bullach, Joseph	Kandel II	" "	Als
Bullach, Michael	Kandel II	" "	Als
Dillmann, Joseph	Kandel I	Oberlauterbach/Wssnbg	Als
Dosch, Christian	Kandel II	Climbach/Wssnbg.	Als
Duni, Michael	Elsass I	?	
Engelhardt, x	Kandel I	Niederrödern/Wssnbg.	Als
Glas, Michael	Elsass I	Salmbach/Wssnbg	Als
Heintz, Leonhard	Kandel II	Salmbach/Wssnbg.	Als
Hettel, Joseph	Mannheim I	Bietigheim/Rastatt	Ba
Huck, x	Mannheim I	Herxheim/Landau	Pf
Hungele, x	Kandel I	?	
Jochim, Johannes	Kandel II	Bellheim/Germersheim	Pf
Jochim, Georg	Kandel I	" "	Pf
Keller, Anton	Elsass I	Winzenbach/Wssnbg.	Als
Laturnus, x	Mannheim I	Oberseebach/Wssnbg.	Als
Lemer, Pius	Kandel 1	Riedselz/Weissenburg	Als
Lemer, x	Kandel I	" "	Als
Mack, Sebastian	Elsass I	Obergrombach/Bruchsal	Ba
Maier, Joseph	Elsass I	Runzenheim/Bischweiler	Als
Mastel, Peter	Selz I	Mothern/Wssnbg.	Als
Merk, Johannes	Elsass II	Münchhausen/Wssnbg.	Als
Moser, Lorenz	Kandel I	Salmbach/Wssnbg.	Als
Pflieger, Anton	Elsass I	Au am Rhein/Rastatt	Ba
Roth, Anton	Kandel I	Edesheim/Landau	Pf
Roth, Valentin	Kandel I	" "	Pf
Roth, Johannes	Kandel II	" "	Pf
Reiter, Bernhard	Kandel II	Sulzbach/Rastatt	Ba
Ripplinger, Franz	Elsass I	Schwemling/Büstrich - Trier	
Sali, Aloisius	Kandel II	Waldprechtsweiler/Rastatt	Ba
Schäfer, Franz	Josephstal I	Niederlauterbach/Wssnbg.	Als
Schell, Sebastian	Elsass I	Kandel/Germersheim	Pf
Schmalz, Ludwig	Kandel II	Kapsweyer/Bergzabern	Pf
Schwarz, Adam	Selz II	Roppenheim/Bischweiler	Als
Schwengler, Anton	Kandel I	Winzenbach/Wssnbg.	Als
Strubel, Dionisius	Mannheim I	Beinheim/Wssnbg.	Als
Stückerle, Joh,	Kandel II	?	
Volk, Joseph	Bäden I	Steinmauern/Rastatt	Ba
Wagner, Joseph	Mannheim I	Salmbach/Wssnbg.	Als
Ziegler, Mathias	Elsass I	Jöhlingen/Karlsruhe	Ba

*Roman I indicates the first (earlier) lease; Roman II the second (later) lease group.

XIV. Pioneering on the Dakota Prairie

1. Reminiscences of the First Homesteaders

The first three accounts originally appeared, in German, in the *Ashley Tribune,* about the year 1912. Though written in simple, homely language, these letters to the editor contain much detailed information that deserves a place in the annals of German-Russian history of the Dakotas. The fourth account, originally written in German by Father Max Speckmaier, pastor of Strassburg, N.D., on the occasion of the 25th anniversary of that community in 1914, was largely based on the reminiscences of the first settlers. I have, however, found it expedient to abbreviate the original text in some respects. J.S.H.

Letter 1. Zeeland, N.D., McIntosh County

"It was on April 3, 1886. We drove to the railway station at Alt-Danzig, ready to depart to Schiffskohs. Pastor Pretzkau gave a stirring farewell address for the emigrating travellers, and I cannot forget how the people wept and cried. Then the time came for us to get on the train that was to take us to the port of Bremen in Germany. The very next day we embarked on the ship Dortina.

Everything went well on our ocean voyage until the third day when we were caught in a storm. We were all on the main deck, and the sailors started shouting at us, "Come, you Russians, and give us a hand!" We began to pull on the ropes and everything went better than we had expected, although our baggage went sailing from one corner of the ship to the other.

We were on the ocean for 13 days when the captain appeared and told us that land was in sight. On the 18th day we left the ship and everyone was glad to get the solid earth under his feet again. We continued on our journey to the West by train until we reached our destination, Tyndall, South Dakota, where relatives and friends awaited us. We were overjoyed to see one another again, and were deeply moved when we saw that each of us had a friend who wanted to take us along with him.

After a few days' rest from our long journey, we went to buy oxen, wagons, and other things we needed. Then we decided we would all travel together to North Dakota. I built a little hut over my wagon and we set out for the north country. You can imagine, my friends, how I felt about the prospect of a 300-mile journey with oxen into a completely unknown country. But we made it from Tyndall to Delmont, and kept going in a northerly direction. In the evenings we unhitched the oxen and let them graze on the prairie, while the men built a fire and the women prepared the meal. Sleeping was a more difficult matter, for the mosquitos were very bad. I remember that my brother covered himself with his big fur coat in the hope of escaping from his tormenters, but it was all in vain.

One day I met a man on the road and asked him if he could tell me whether I was going in the right direction and how many miles I would still have to travel. He was very friendly and after taking his whip and laying it down in the road, he said: "Stay right on this road until you reach the next town." We moved slowly forward and finally came to Ipswich. The journey had taken us ten days. We also located our land and immediately set about to build a stove of stones and clay. You will ask, dear friend, why did you put up a stove before you built a house? The answer is simply that one must first have something to eat before one can work.

We next built a large house of sod and plastered it over with clay. For the stove we used hay and *burian* (weeds) as fuel. However, in building the house we made one big mistake by putting in the door so that it opened to the outside. After every snowstorm we had considerable difficulty getting the door open.

Typical sod house on Dakota-Nebraska prairie

After the house was completed, we began picking stones and breaking the land. We succeeded in plowing about three acres and seeded them, but we harvested only five bushels. So we all went out into the prairie and collected buffalo bones near the place where Wishek now stands, and we hauled them with our oxen to Ellendale. There we sold the bones and bought provisions: flour, lard, coffee, and the like.[1] How well I remember the day when my uncle, Wilhelm Kott, and I were driving home from Ellendale where he had sold a wagonload of bones. As we were passing a farmyard my uncle noticed the beautiful chickens and he said to me: "Heinrich, this man has nice chickens, and I need a rooster." But the man was not able to understand us, nor we him. So I stood in front of him and started to flap my arms up and down, clapped my hands, and crowed like a rooster."

In 1887 we moved into the area of Zeeland, where I am still living. Here I had to begin all over again. First we built a sod barn to provide shelter for the two oxen and the cow. I also lived in the barn until our house was completed. It was also built of sod, including the roof. The walls were plastered with clay inside and out. Then I began to clear the field of stones and turned over the sod with my breaking plow. One day we saw a prairie fire approaching. I told my wife that we would have to plow a fire-break around our stack of hay. Suddenly I saw five ox-drawn wagons coming in our direction and I shouted

Homesteaders gathering buffalo bones (Public archives of Canada)

---

[1]In 1886 buffalo bones sold for 10-12 dollars a ton. A 100-lb. sack of flour cost $1.50; 25 lbs. of sugar was $1.00, and 25 lbs. of coffee was $1.00.

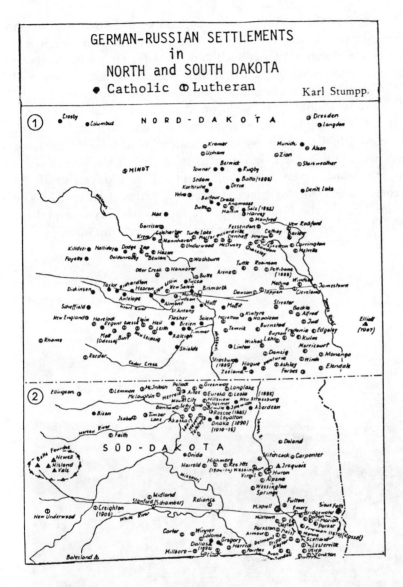

GERMAN–RUSSIAN SETTLEMENTS
in
NORTH and SOUTH DAKOTA
● Catholic ⦶ Lutheran

Karl Stumpp.

to the drivers: *"Och sto Bogi wirith!"*—that is to say, "If you believe in God, come and help!" Together we succeeded in putting out the prairie fire, but we suffered burns on our faces and hands. Another fire was approaching from the side, but fortunately it passed by without causing any damage to the hay and farm property. However, all around us the prairie was burnt black. We started again collecting bones and hauling them to the market.

Besides prairie fires, we also experienced snow storms. One day while I was on my way home from Eureka, a big snow storm came up, and I made

259

haste to get home. But the storm grew worse, and soon I could no longer make out where I was. Unexpectedly, I came across another sleigh and discovered that it was Johannes Odenbach and his wife. They had also been to Eureka and were now making a short stop. I was afraid that we might all perish and die in this storm, but he said reassuringly, "Just stay with me and we shall find our way home. I will walk on ahead." And sure enough, we finally made it to his house but we were all half-frozen. At least I was, for with my full beard I had the appearance of a snow man. In the Odenbach house, the boys were still up and they had to take care of the horses while we went into the house where it was nice and warm. I stayed until the morning and then started out for home. It was still bitter cold, and we saw other sleighs standing on the open prairie. The horses had been unhitched, and the travellers had gone forward on foot to find shelter somewhere.

Arrival of seven coaches of Russian immigrants (Nov. 13, 1892). Eureka, S.D.

Letter 2. Adolph Boschee, Zeeland, N. Dakota.

I was eight years old when we came to America. It was late in the fall of 1884 when my father Valentin Boschee with his family and several other families from the colony of Kassel, South Russia, arrived in Menno, South Dakota. We stayed with relatives and friends over the winter. In the spring of 1885 my father and my uncle Friedrich Klotz each bought a yoke of oxen, a cow, a wagon, and whatever else was needed.[2] In early May we loaded our goods and chattels into a freight car and boarded a passenger car that was to take us into the north country. Our first stop was Ipswich, S. Dakota, which at that time was the end of the railway line. Here we encountered a real Dakota blizzard and were unable to proceed until the weather improved and the snow had disappeared. We now loaded our belongings on our wagons and proceeded at a slow ox-trot pace towards North Dakota. We made a stop about 40 miles from Ipswich, where several families had arrived earlier. My father, my uncle, and several other men hired a guide who was familiar with the lay of the land and its designated sections and townships. After we had located and examined our quarter section, we returned and reloaded our wagons for the final lap of the journey to our new *Heimat*. I do not remember how long it took us to cover the stretch from Ipswich to McIntosh County, but I recall that we arrived at our destination on Pentecost Sunday, which, as I learned later, was May 17, 1885.

1888 — Eureka Roller Mill — Pfeffer and Bramaier

[2]The cost of 2 oxen, a cow, a wagon and a breaking plow was from $175 to $200.

After we had unloaded our belongings, we started getting settled. The reader may well imagine how my father and my mother felt about the prospect of living 80 miles from the nearest town, all alone under the open sky, with nothing to see but sky and prairie. We set about breaking the sod, so that we could plant some potatoes, vegetables, and a bit of flax. We did not place the seed potatoes into the newly turned furrows, as we do today, but simply spaded them into the sod. All the buildings were made of sod and then plastered with clay. The houses generally consisted of three parts: the living room, the kitchen, and the barn—all under one roof. In the kitchen we made a cook stove and oven of stone and clay, and fired it in the morning and evening with hay or *burian,* to provide us with warmth by day and night.

After the buildings were completed, we began with the haying. My father and my uncle each bought a scythe and wanted to mow the hay the way they used to do it in Russia. Alas, it didn't work out. Both of them were all worn out after half a day's work. They claimed that the grass here was too hard and too tough to be cut with a scythe. So they had to borrow a grass mower.

Then came threshing time. Since there were no threshing machines and we still had no horses, we had to do our threshing with our oxen. We cleared a large round plot of ground about 50 feet in diameter. After removing all the grass and turf we poured water on the area and packed and rolled the ground. After it got hard and dry we laid down a bed of swathed grain about two feet thick and then had the oxen 'tread' it out. When it was thoroughly treaded we removed the straw with pitch forks and winnowed the grain in the wind. This was the threshing machine of the first settlers.

Early adobe type church in the Eureka district, S.D.
(Harper's Weekly, July 11, 1896)

In the late fall my father and several other settlers drove to Ipswich to buy provisions for the coming winter. The trip ordinarily took a whole week, but by driving day and night they made it in four days. A good thing they did, for on their return journey they got into such a terrible snow storm that they were often unable to tell in what direction they were going. Luckily for them, the good old oxen knew the way home. They got home safely that night in a raging blizzard that continued for a whole week. I often heard my father say that if they had not made it home that same night, they would all have frozen to death, for the weather suddenly turned very cold and the snow was too high to get through with an ox-team.[3]

On another occasion, I believe it was in the fall of 1886 or 1887, my father had driven to Ellendale to get some provisions. On the way, one of the oxen fell sick, so that father was compelled to stay away longer than usual. At home we had no more bread or flour. The children wanted to eat, but we had nothing to give them. So my mother took some of the wheat we had in our granary and roasted it like popcorn. And that was our food for the next three days. We really enjoyed it, for it was something of a novelty. But you can easily imagine how my mother must have felt when there was neither bread nor flour in the house.

In our poverty and distress there was one thing that came to our rescue, and that was the buffalo bones. If it had not been for those bones, we would all have suffered from hunger. The crops at that time were still small and meager, and there was no way of earning a livelihood. But we were able to sell those bones. One week was spent in collecting the bones from the prairie, the following week we hauled them to town. Collecting bones was the harvest that kept us busy until the coming of winter. It was very easy to find the bones when the prairie had been burned off.

In the first years of settlement there were no churches and no schools. Religious meetings were held in the sod houses, and the attendance in those days was better, even though people had to drive with oxen, than it is today when people have cars.

These are, in brief, some of the experiences of the first settlers. One could, of course, write a great deal more about the pioneer days, but I fear that the present generation would hardly be able to get a real conception of the hardships which the old-timers had to endure in those early years.

---

[3]The "big blizzard" of 1888 began Jan. 12 and lasted for a week. In S. Dakota 112 people perished, and the neighboring states also suffered great distress.

3. *Report.* By Rev. Max Speckmaier, Strasburg, N. Dak.

"It was in the fall of the year 1888 when delegates from Strassburg, South Russia, came into Emmons County, where the town of Strasburg now stands, to look for suitable land for the arriving homesteaders. What they found was unlimited space, uninhabited and empty, but there was lots of room to settle. Far and wide nothing could be seen but a lone dwelling that belonged to a certain Mr. Petrie, who later became a prominent businessman in Linton, N.D.

After this first tour of exploration, several so-called German-Russians arrived in the spring of 1889 to take up homesteads. The first of these stalwart, stout-hearted settlers were the three Baumgartner brothers, Jakob, Johannes, and Franz; Albinus Schneider, Kaspar Feist, and two unmarried young men, Joseph Burgard and Jakob Feist. Shortly afterwards a second group arrived, namely Egidius Keller, Peter Kraft, Jakob Geffreh, Franz Giesinger, and Martin and Lorenz Schwab—all of them from the Kutschurgan district northwest of the city of Odessa.

What the first settlers found was little more than the vast naked prairie. It was, in fact, literally naked, for just prior to the arrival of the intrepid settlers a prairie fire had swept away everything except the bare earth and

Anton Masset sod house. McIntosh County, ND. c. 1900
Vestibule and low annex added later.

stones. The first settlers arrived at noon on the 7th of May, 1889, and on the same day they started plowing up the sod and building the simple lowly huts of earth and clay. That was enough of a hardship, but the very first night a heavy rain set in and the weather turned so cold that the home-steaders had to remove the boxes from the wagons to provide some shelter for themselves and their families.

When the days grew warmer a plot of prairie was plowed and prepared for the sowing of grain, but the results were meager and the crop was rather poor. The ripe flax which the men had cut with a grass mower was mostly blown away by the wind. In an attempt to save the rest of the crop, the people picked the flax by hand. Much labor was now required to convert the small crop into money wherewith to buy food. The nearest railway station was at Eureka, S. Dakota, where you could sell grain and buy provisions, but the town was at least 50 miles away.[4] The hardships that the poor settlers had to endure on this long trip, particularly when there was a rain or a snow storm, can scarcely be conceived by the younger generation today. And we

Adobe house of pioneer settler Anton Masseth.
(Northern part of McIntosh County, N. Dak.)

---

[4] The Milwaukee railroad reached Eureka in 1887 and soon trainloads of immigrants rolled into this frontier town. In the following years settlers hauled their grain to this terminus from distances of 50 and 75 miles. By 1902 Eureka became the largest inland grain market in the world, handling between one and two million bushels a year.

should not forget that the draft animals of the first settlers were not horses, but oxen.

The year 1890 arrived and with it another crop failure. The poor people were beginning to suffer want and were filled with distress and despair. The pioneers still relate even today how they used to cry all day, partly because of their poverty and misery, partly because of homesickness and longing for their native villages in Russia. Many of them would have gone back, if the way had not been so terribly far and if there had been no ocean between America and Russia.

In those times of utter distress, everybody, young and old, wandered over the desolate prairie day after day, looking for buffalo bones. These had then to be hauled to Napoleon or Steele where one could sell them and buy the needed groceries with the bit of money. One did not make much, of course, on the sale of bones. For a wagon load you could get a sack of flour, which was the most important staple at that time. One was unable to obtain any meat, except what you might occasionally get with a gun.

So it happened one day that three men went a-hunting, in the hope of shooting something that had meat and bones. The three hunters were Jakob Feist, Egidi Keller, and Lorenz Schwab. They set out in the direction of Beaver Creek where they expected to find some wild game. They walked around for a long time, without seeing or finding anything. Finally they spotted a bird, not very big and not too small; it was probably a snipe. Now it was a question of quick action, for birds fly fast. Lorenz quickly took aim, the shot rang out, and the bird fell to the ground—dead. The three men hurried to the spot. They lifted the feathered victim from the earth, but alas the poor thing was completely shot to pieces. Lorenz was about to fling it away when Egidi cried out excitedly, "Give it here. I'll take it. Meat is meat." That's how precious meat was in those times.

What was even worse than the lack of meat was the scarcity of fuel and the non-existence of roads. The following incident will provide a graphic illustration. One day Jakob Feist with his wife and his brother-in-law Egidi Keller hitched their oxen to their two wagons and drove to Beaver Creek to get some firewood. They found enough wood to load up both wagons. When they were ready to start back the sun was already setting. The return trip was slow, for the wagons were heavy and the oxen were plodding slowly and laboriously across the roadless prairie. Night fell all too quickly and it soon grew pitch dark. Since the drivers could neither see nor hear anything, they soon lost all sense of direction, but the oxen moved forward through the night. Suddenly a glimmer of light appeared in the darkness. "That's my house," exclaimed Jakob. He had the foresight to tell his people at home to set out a burning lantern in front of the house. But suddenly the light disappeared again as the nocturnal wayfarers came near an intervening hill. The drivers now separated and Jakob drove in the direction of his house which he soon reached. Egidi also drove in the direction of his house but missed it completely. For a long time he drove around aimlessly in the darkness and finally fell asleep, but the oxen kept on going. The people back home were beginning to worry, but eventually they crawled under the wagon-box and went to sleep. When they came out the next morning they saw the oxen standing in the yard with a fine load of wood, on top of which they found Egidi, still fast asleep.

In the first years there was no church in the new settlement. The nearest priests were 26 miles away. They were the Benedictine missionaries, Fathers Bernard and Franz, who were stationed at Fort Yates. The first priest to visit the settlers was Fr. Bernard who also celebrated the first Mass for the community in 1889 in the sod house of Franz Baumgartner. The joy of the settlers could not have been greater if an angel from Heaven had suddenly appeared among them. In the same year, the first resident priest, Father Schmitz, arrived at St. John's Parish in McIntosh County. However, the Benedictine Fathers from Fort Yates continued to visit the settlers from time to time."

Similar accounts of pioneer experiences could, no doubt, be multiplied a thousand times and corroborated by the oral reminiscences of many old-timers. But even the brief reports presented here enable us to draw the well-founded conclusion that the obstacles and hardships confronting the Dakota pioneers were, by all odds, even greater and more formidable than those endured by the immigrant forefathers who settled on the steppes of Russia some 90 years earlier.

To be sure, the journey from Russia to America was not as arduous and dangerous as the trek of the German emigrants to the Black Sea, and the sod house on the prairie was doubtless more comfortable than the crude *semelyanka* and the wattled clay hut of the steppe-dweller. Moreover, the homesteader in the Dakotas also had the distinct advantage of having a better wagon, plow and other farm equipment. On the other hand, he was seriously disadvantaged in several respects. While the pioneer of the steppe received an interest-free government loan of 250-300 rubles to help him get established on his homestead, the settlers in the Dakotas (and elsewhere) received no government loans, but were often at the mercy of unscrupulous loan sharks who, at times, exacted a 200% interest on short-term loans. Furthermore, while the Czarist government granted the homesteaders food-ration money until the first harvest, the settlers on the prairie were, in several instances, forced to pick buffalo bones in order to provide bread for their families. In Russia, the colonists lived together in villages which provided the facilities of mutual aid and social contacts, whereas the settlers on the prairie had to live in isolation and loneliness. Finally, whereas the Czarist government even provided a stone church for each of the colonist enclaves, the first settlers of the plains had to be content with makeshift sod churches for several years. What both pioneer groups had in common, besides their ethnic identity, was their precious heritage of a staunch faith in God, a proud capacity for hard work, and an unflagging determination to wrest an honest, decent livelihood from the good earth. And this heritage, I venture to say, was the secret of their ultimate success.

—Translated by J. S. H.

A field-stone cairn erected 1975 near Selz, N.D.,
in honor of Catholic pioneer settlers.
(Photo by Fred F. Fleck)

2. The John Felchle Story

Originally published in the McClusky Gazette (1930)

As young ambitious people, we left the old home in Teplitz, Bessarabia, and all that the word implies, and boarded the train at Wesselyi Kut on March 1, 1894. A week later we embarked on the steamer that was to take us from Bremen to New York.

While on board ship, a terrific storm rocked the boat to such an extent that we all believed we would perish in the cold waves without seeing America. Almost everybody was seasick, but I managed to stay on my feet and help to wait on some who were sick. On the ninth day we landed in New York and thanked God that we were again able to enjoy the pleasure of having solid ground under our feet.

To our sorrow we learned that two of the families in our party had not yet arrived. Karl Moser and Peter Heissler had left Bremen four days ahead of us, but nothing definite was known in New York regarding the steamer on which they crossed the ocean. One report was to the effect that the steamer had suffered irreparable damage and was drifting around at the mercy of the elements. Later we found out that the storm had driven the boat off course to the south where it finally ran into a sandbank and was grounded there. When the supply of food was virtually exhausted, and the passengers were facing death from starvation, and hopes of being rescued were at the lowest ebb, a ship was sighted, but it appears that the stranded vessel was not seen. Three shots had to be fired before the sighted steamer noticed the boat and changed course to come to its aid. When the steamer drew close the joy of the stranded passengers knew no bounds. The distance they had drifted away from the regular course may be imagined when it is considered that their entire trip to New York took 32 days.

We had, of course, continued our journey from New York by railway and arrived hale and hearty in Eureka, S.D. on April 4, 1894, as strangers in a strange land, as we thought. But to our great surprise I met there our old friend and comrade Henry Stein, who invited us to his house at once, and of course we accepted the invitation. Our joy was somewhat dampened when we saw that Henry's wife was sick in bed but, undaunted, Henry at once got busy at the kitchen stove and brewed for us a cup of American coffee which was really delicious and a great change from the stuff that we had during the long trip.

A short while later, Wilhelm Moser appeared and wanted to greet his brother Karl, but we were obliged to convey to him the sad news about the vessel that was stranded off-course on a sandbank. Wilhelm then took us along to his farm which was located about 20 miles southwest of Eureka. Of course, we made the trip in a wagon, and it was bitter cold. The farmers had been at work seeding but the ground was again frozen solid. Well, well, I thought, that is surely a wonderful beginning in America—the seed in the ground, the ground frozen, and in April at that.

The next day a good acquaintance of mine from Russia came over from the vicinity of Bowdle, S.D. and took me along to his American-born neighbor, who hired me to work for him at $18.00 per month. This man, Frank Wendling, was sowing wheat, and when my friend talked to him in English, of which I didn't understand a word, I just stood there with eyes and mouth open, realizing that I had run up against something really strange. I wondered if they really understood each other, but I was soon to learn that they did and that the conversation had not been in vain. Our friend Knecht certainly had accomplished something, for he turned to me and said, "Well, John, the deal is made."

My new boss then stepped down from the grain drill and I was expected to go ahead with the job of seeding wheat. Yes, that was easier said than done. As a greenhorn just arrived from Russia, I hadn't the slightest idea about American farm machinery, and it was lucky for me that the horses had more sense than I had.

At that time this country had a Democratic administration and everything was cheap. After six months I was able to acquire an old wagon for $12.00, a yoke of oxen for $57.00, a cow for $23.00, and two little pigs. So I packed up and started out in our prairie schooner, which was really no schooner at all, for it had no top on it.

PRICES IN THE PIONEER DAYS (1885-1895)
In Eureka, So. Dakota

Flax	$1.25 per bushel		Hand plow		$18.00
Wheat	.45 " "		Harrow		7.00
Barley	.25 " "		Wagon		20.00
Potatoes	.25-.45 per sack				
Flour	1.50 for 100 lbs		Land, quarter	(1885)	3.75 an acre
Butter	.05 per lb.		" "	(1900)	5.00 " "
Eggs	4-5 cts a dozen		" "	(1911)	22.00 " "
Buffalo bones	$6-$8 a ton		" "	(1916)	17.50 " "
A team of oxen	$100.00		" "	(1920)	16.50 " "
Chickens	two for 25		Farm work	(1885)	6.00-13.00 a month
			Work for threshing rig		2.00 a day

270

We bade farewell to our friends at Eureka on October 8, 1894, and arrived in Fessenden, N.D. ten days later. All along the route we met good hospitable people, although they were all strangers and all Americans. David Erfle, my brother-in-law, lived 14 miles south of Fessenden and there, in a sod house, we took up our winter quarters. John J. Ahl and his family were there too; and so there were 23 persons crowded together in the one "mansion." Before going to bed, we had to put our clothes under our pillows, or we might have had a hard time finding them the next morning.

We kept the sod shack warm by burning straw, and our menu cards didn't show as many courses as they do today. Nevertheless, we had a bit of variety: bread and coffee, and coffee and bread. Oh yes, we also had meat occasionally when we managed to get a rabbit. But that did not happen very often, since the money to buy ammunition was generally lacking. Fortunately, I had a pig that weighed about 70 pounds, but then what was that for our brotherly tribe of 23 people!

I was making 50 cents a day loading wheat into railroad cars, and you can easily imagine that we had to do some pinching to get through the winter. At such wages we could not hold swell parties, but we pulled through, nevertheless.

In the spring of 1895 I filed a claim on a homestead 11 miles to the southwest of Fessenden and on it I built a sod shack. The walls of this edifice were soon built, but then came the question of the roof. That was not so easily answered, for there was no money to buy lumber and shingles. But where there's a will, there's a way. So I hitched my oxen to the wagon and drove 30 miles to the "woods" where we got some poles and brush. These were used as rafters, stringers and supports for the sod which we laid on top of the brush. Then we added a coat of asphalt, the kind that is found just beneath the black soil, and we had a roof for very little money. Of course, it took a lot of time and labor, but when we moved into that lowly sod house and surveyed our prairie domain we felt as rich as if Uncle Sam had made us king of all North Dakota. My father had filed on a homestead adjoining ours.

Each of us had a pair of oxen and with them we broke the prairie to sow flax, but it was already rather late in the season when we finished, although we had only broken 13 acres each. You see, we had to wait until the neighbor had finished his work in order to be able to borrow his breaking plow. We seeded the flax right on top of the overturned sod; and left the rest up to the Lord.

We harvested 90 bushels of flax each, and it was worth 60 cents a bushel. Wheat brought from 35 to 40 cents a bushel. A hundred-pound bag of flour cost $1.20, and shoes were $1.25 a pair. Wages were $1 a day for making hay, $1.50 a day for work in the harvest fields, and $3.00 for a man and team for threshing. Beef was dirt cheap, and butter could hardly be sold at all, but we did not have much of these products to sell.

After five years of homesteading, we made final proof on our land, received the patent deed, and sold it at $10.00 an acre on the installment plan. Then my father, my brother-in-law John Mauch, and I bought a half-section each in what was then McLean, but now Sheridan county, from the Northern Pacific Railway Company at $4.00 an acre on the ten-year payment plan at six per cent interest. The down-payment of $125.00 was a big sum of money in those days, and we had to borrow it from a bank in Fessenden at a high rate of interest.

That was in the spring of 1889, and again we had to build everything new out of the same materials as before. The following fall we packed up all our belongings and moved to our new location. This time the move was not much of a hardship, for our entire equipment consisted of five horses, seven head of cattle, and a couple of dozen chickens.

Our barns were built of sod, even the roof. One night the coyotes got busy and scratched a hole through the roof and stole almost all of our chickens. We could have cried. The women were particularly downcast, for the chickens were quite a help to them in preparing our meals. However, we finally agreed that we could be glad that they did not get us, for at that time these beasts often looked in through the windows to see if we were asleep. Up to now we had no gun, for we didn't have the money to buy one. We considered ourselves lucky when we had enough money to buy our daily bread.

Going to town was a major event in those days, for we had to go either 30 miles to Bowdon, or to Harvey which was 40 miles. But during the second year after our move to this location, the Northern Pacific Railway began to extend its line westward. That was slow work because the country was quite rough and hilly, but it finally came along.

One fall morning, I think it was in 1902, I started out with a load of flax, with Bowdon as my destination. After travelling along about seven miles straight across the prairie, I saw two men in the distance, working on the open prairie exactly at the place where the town of Goodrich now stands. Coming closer to them, I recognized one of the men as Carl Tomey, the operator of the elevator at Harvey. I certainly was surprised to see what they were doing there when they said they were putting up scales to weigh flax which they intended to buy. When I wanted to know how soon they expected to be ready for business, they replied, "In about two hours." I said, "In that case, I can help you; I'll unload my flax right here." "Sure," was the answer.

272

That suited me fine, and I unhitched my horses and went to work. I asked Mr. Tomey how he intended doing business buying flax when he had no elevator. He replied that he did have an elevator "a real big one, the whole prairie right here." Well, we soon had the scales installed and I was the first man to bring a load of flax to the new town. I drove onto the new scales and unloaded in the "great elevator" by pulling out the endgate and letting the flax run on the ground. I got my money too, and if I remember right the price was $1.50 a bushel.

I was happy and drove home, picturing a rosy future for ourselves and the territory in the light of the new event. But my wife was in a different frame of mind when she saw a team coming across the prairie about noon. Knowing well enough that I generally came home about ten o'clock in the evening from such a trip, she was naturally quite frightened. When I came closer and she was able to recognize our horses, she felt sure that something had gone wrong. Her first question was, "What has happened to you?" I said, "Calm yourself, mother, we now have a new town and its name is "Wonderful." Then I explained to her what had happened, and our stock in the future rose about 75 points.

Work on the railroad progressed steadily and soon the freight train was able to come all the way to the town I had named "Wonderful" but which is now known as Goodrich. In the meantime Mr. Tomey had bought a great deal of flax, but his elevator was never filled. One day a great wind and rainstorm struck "his elevator" and the surrounding countryside, doing great damage to the flax and causing Mr. Tomey to suffer a heavy loss. But when the freight train arrived this hazard was eliminated, as he could now load the flax into the cars.

With the arrival of the new railroad, the farmers gained new hope and courage. My brother-in-law, John Mauch, and myself had often planned to go back to Wells county, but our father always restrained us by telling us there was a good prospect of a new town being built in the vicinity. His foresight was better than ours and today we are glad that we listened to him, and stayed.

In those days our post office was a little country store on John Wittmayer's farm, about nine miles north of what is now Goodrich. At that store many things that the farmers needed could be purchased, even flour and machinery.

While that was our address we had to work real hard, for the children were still small and for many years we had to have hired help. In time we got more land under cultivation and no longer needed to hire strangers. Some years we had as much as 1000 acres in crop, to which the Lord gave his blessing. We were able to buy 12 quarter sections of land in this vicinity at from $4.00 to $34.00. On four of these farms we had all the necessary buildings and we found "gold" on every quarter section—not on the surface but six inches under it. We did not have to borrow money, and, thank God, we have no debts on the land. Yet people say there is no money in farming; but I assert that the contrary is the truth. However, I maintain that diversification is necessary; alongside of small grain, one must also raise cattle and hogs. Out of the latter branch of farming we have made from $1200.00 to $1500.00 nearly every year.

Our family is a large one; we have raised seven sons and each one of them has two sisters. Each of our sons received a farm, except one who is working on a ship out of Vancouver, British Columbia.

We have weathered many a storm and have often heard it thunder, too. In 1923 a tornado struck our farm demolishing a large new barn. We had to build a new one and do a lot of repairing on other buildings, even on the house. Fortunately, we received enough insurance to cover about one-half of the expenses.

We have paid a large sum of money for taxes in this country during those thirty years we have lived here, and even though we have no money to speak of, we're thankful that we have our home.

I am sorry to see that so many of our young people do not take to farming nowadays, but would rather go to the cities. But I can say that the best and most honest living can be made on the farm. Of course, all people cannot be on the farm; some people must also be in the cities. I lived in town for two winters, but could not stand it any longer and had to go back to the farm. However, I will soon be forced to abdicate, for the children are all grown up and naturally want to go their own way and live their own lives as they see fit. Nevertheless, when I think that I had my home there and labored there for thirty years, my heart bleeds when I think of leaving it at all. Therefore, I say to anybody who owns a farm: "Value it as you would a treasure, as a home sweet home where you can live in peace and quiet."

XV.   From the Kutschurgan to Saskatchewan

Alsatian Pioneers on the Prairie

1. The Kutschurganer Come to America

The Kutschurgan colonists were settled in 1808 in six villages that were established under Czar Alexander I in a steppeland area that lay between the Kutschurgan Liman and the Baraboi River, some 30 miles northwest of Odessa. The settlers who had emigrated from northern Alsace, the southeastern Palatinate and central Baden gave their new villages the ancestral names of Selz, Kandel, Baden, Strassburg, Mannheim and Elsass. Their inhabitants became known as Kutschurganer, since the area was designated as the Kutschurgan *volost,* district.

The land apportioned by the Russian Crown to the 440 founding families amounted to 70,587 acres. For the year 1816 when the total population of the six villages was 2,189, this meant that the land portion for each individual inhabitant (man, woman, and child), was about 25 acres, so that the average family of four at that time was able to make a fairly decent living on its 100 acres of plowland. But this was no longer possible three generations later when, in 1890, the population of the six villages had risen to 11,896—a fivefold increase—and the average family now had eight children. The land portion of the individual inhabitant now amounted to only five acres, so that the average family had only about 40 acres of plowland—hardly enough to provide a decent standard of living.

Thus the overpopulation of the villages on the one hand, and the scarcity and high cost of available land in the Odessa area on the other hand, made it necessary for large numbers of families to emigrate and look for land in more remote regions. Some families decided to move to Siberia where land was plentiful and cheap, but the large majority opted for the New World, especially the United States and Canada.

The first Kutschurganer emigrated to America in 1882 and settled near Scotland, S.D., but later moved to Ipswich. However, the massive immigration of the Catholic Black Sea Germans began in 1885 when many families

settled near Ipswich and in the town of Aberdeen. In the years 1889 and
1890, Catholic Kutschurganer established the settlements at Hague, Strassburg and places in Pierce County, North Dakota. In 1892 many colonists
from Selz, Kandel, and Mannheim gave up their original homesteads near
Eureka, S.D., and found new homes near Harvey and Selz, North Dakota. In
1898 a new Kutschurgan settlement was established around Orrin, originally
known as Kandel. Similar settlements arose in Balta, Brazil, Devil's Lake, and
Rugby. By 1900 the Catholic Black Sea Germans were the strongest ethnic
element in Pierce County and the adjoining McHenry County. By 1905 the
Kutschurganer had virtually occupied all the available homestead land in the
districts of Towner and Karlsruhe.

The homesteads of the Kutschurganer in the area of Towner and the
adjacent localities were, however, to be of short duration. Most of the land
turned out to be unsuitable for grain farming and after three or four years

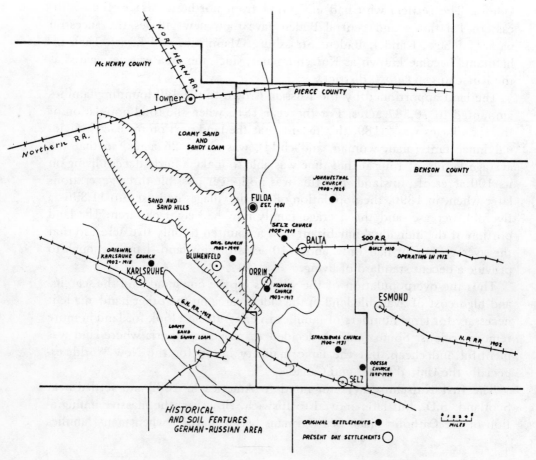

the disillusioned settlers began to look about for more fertile land. Fortunately, vast areas of excellent wheatland became available when the Canadian government opened up the western prairies to colonization. Land agents appeared in the Dakotas and in Minnesota seeking to recruit settlers for the uninhabited prairie land of Saskatchewan and Alberta.[1] The Kutschurganer in North Dakota were immediately interested and sent scouting parties to Western Saskatchewan to examine the promised land.

2. F. J. Lange, Founder of St. Joseph's Colony

The man who must be regarded as the guiding genius and chief founder of the new settlement that was to become known as St. Joseph's Colony was a German-American by the name of F. J. Lange who had come as a young boy with his father from Oldenburg in Westphalia and grew up in St. Paul, Minnesota. After completing his studies at Harvard and Kansas State University, he was active for a time as a schoolteacher in St. Paul. At that time the city was the chief thoroughfare of all the landseekers who wished to settle in the Great Northwest, but Mr. Lange noted that no efforts were made to

Mr. F. J. Lange, founder of
St. Joseph's Colony

---

[1] The two new provinces were carved out of the Northwest Territories in 1905.

settle the Catholic landseekers in Catholic districts. He, therefore, became deeply interested in this project and proposed to settle 17 Catholic families of German background in northern Minnesota in August, 1902. When he discovered that the available land was insufficient, he became aware that good farming opportunities were being offered in Saskatchewan. With initiative and determination he succeeded in settling the 17 families at Windhorst.

At the same time some Benedictine monks from Collegeville, Minnesota were interested in establishing a Catholic colony about 100 miles east of Saskatoon for a large number of families who wished to leave Stearns County for greener pastures. Mr. Lange was asked to be the general supervisor of the colonization project and in two years, 1903 and 1904, the extensive woodland area in the Humboldt district was almost completely settled and became known as St. Peter's Colony.

In his activities as a promoter of immigration and settlement, Mr. Lange also encountered many landseekers, especially German-Russians in the Dakotas, who did not want to be settled on land that was covered with bush and scrub, but preferred grassland similar to that of the steppes of South Russia. To satisfy these demands, Mr. Lange decided to establish a colony on the open prairie. On July 25, 1904, he drove with horse and buggy from Saskatoon in a southwesterly direction to Eagle Hill Creek and from there to the southern end of the elongated Tramping Lake. On the west side of the lake he continued due north until he reached the end of the lake near the Scott coulee. He then crossed over to the east side and after continuing for several miles he returned to Saskatoon. He liked the region very much. The land was treeless, quite flat; the soil was fertile and generally free of rocks and stones.

At his own expense, Mr. Lange now hired eight knowledgeable men to conduct an extensive survey and to make a precise report of the condition of each section of land within a 25-mile strip extending 50 miles on the west side of Tramping Lake, roughly from the subsequent location of Wilkie in the north to Ermine in the south. This assignment, begun August 24, 1904, was completed in two months. According to the report, the area in question was quite level and the soil that averaged six inches of humus was excellent. The prairie was not wooded; only in the ravines and gullies of Tramping Lake were some trees to be found. There was also plenty of wild life on the prairie: herds of antelope, also foxes and badgers, and thousands of wild ducks on the lakes and the sloughs.

Since Mr. Lange had no funds to promote his colonization project, he travelled to Ottawa to seek help from the government. Here he met Sir

Wilfred Laurier who favored the idea of establishing a Catholic colony in western Saskatchewan and appointed Lange as an immigration agent with headquarters in St. Paul and a salary of $100.00 a month. He was now able to advertise the colonization project in Catholic papers in the Dakotas and also in Russia. Under the name "Catholic Settlement Society," of which Mr. Lange was the president and Mr. W. Benz the secretary, there appeared articles and advertisements in the leading Catholic papers of the Dakotas and adjoining states. The response was greater than anyone had expected. Inquiries began to pour in and parties of scouts arrived in Saskatoon and Battleford to seek out and inspect the land of promise. In due course, scores of settlers were arriving in colonist trains and moving into the designated area to look for the surveyor's iron stake that would indicate to each land-seeker the quarter section that would be his homestead.

The emerging St. Joseph's Colony formed a fairly regular rectangle that extended 44 miles from north to south and 72 miles from east to west. It comprised 77 townships, each of which had an area of 36 sq. miles, so that the total area was 2,772 sq. miles. Its geological elevation was about 2000 feet above sea level. Few hills rose above the flat prairie; none higher than 150 feet. There was also a total lack of fresh-water lakes. Not only the elongated Tramping Lake, but also all the other lakes were alkali. No fish could live in the brackish water. On the other hand there were numerous sloughs, large and small, which contained run-off water from rain and snow.

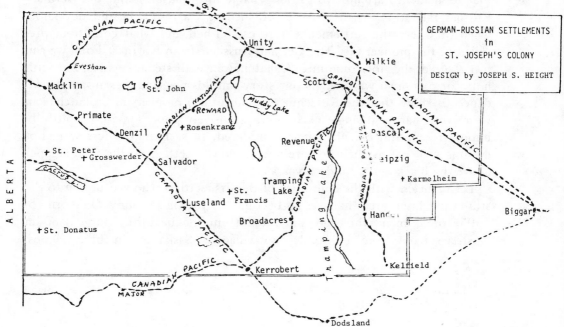

GERMAN-RUSSIAN SETTLEMENTS
in
ST. JOSEPH'S COLONY

DESIGN by JOSEPH S. HEIGHT

3. The First Settlers

In his book, *"Russian-German Settlements in the United States,"* Dr. Richard Sallet makes the astonishing statement that "the people who emigrated from the Dakotas to Canada were by no means poor people."[2] He points out that a certain German-Russian, who had sold his homestead near McClusky, N.D., purchased 1,280 acres of land near Morse, Sask., and began in the spring of 1910 to bring it under cultivation with a gangplow and a steam engine. According to another report, dated 1909, a total of 90,000 people, mostly farmers from the United States, are alleged to have brought along an average of $1,000 per person; and some farmers had brought along capital as high as $40,000.

What Dr. Sallet failed to recognize was that many of those affluent immigrants were not really homesteaders in the first place but "get-rich-quick" sod-busters who were interested in buying cheap land, at least an entire section, quickly breaking it up with tractors and large plows, and then selling it to homesteaders for a sizable profit. Many of these American farmers never settled on the land they bought, but came up to Saskatchewan every year to put in the crop and to harvest it.

While Dr. Sallet pays much attention to the sensational news items that appeared in the *Dakota Freie Presse* (Jan., Feb., March of 1910), it is obvious that he made no attempt to gather reliable information about the German-Russian migration to the prairie provinces. As a result, he did not know when or where the settlements were established and what conditions prevailed in the pioneer era. The German-Russians from North Dakota, we can rest assured, did not come into Saskatchewan with steam engines, but with horse or ox-drawn wagons. As our story unfolds we shall present ample evidence to show that the Kutschurgan (and other) pioneers in Saskatchewan were, with hardly a single exception, primitively poor, some even pitifully impoverished. Indeed, all things considered, these homesteaders were not even as well off as their remote ancestors who settled on the wild steppes above the Black Sea a hundred years earlier.

Let us begin with the epic story of the first settlers who ventured into the still uninhabited area that was to become St. Joseph's Colony. On April 15, 1905, three men who had emigrated from the beautiful Burgenland in Austria set out from the nondescript village of Saskatoon in three wagons,

---

[2] Richard Sallet, *Russian-German Settlements in the United States* (Fargo, 1974). Tr. by Lavern J. Rippley and Armand Bauer, p. 33.

doubt Jakob Mueller and Bartel Schmidt, both of them Kutschurganer who had emigrated from Mannheim a couple of years earlier and homesteaded for a short while in the Towner area of North Dakota. It is significant that a month later another party of three Kutschurganer, namely Johann Gutenberg, George Reiter and Johann Jahner came by train from Towner to Battleford, where they hired a wagon and team of horses to travel 65 miles south to explore the land on the west side of Tramping Lake. They were satisfied with what they saw and returned to the USA to prepare for the expedition to the new homestead land the following spring.

To enable the settlers to locate their homesteads on their return, Mr. Benz decided to leave behind his pitched tent as a marker on the open prairie. The men returned via Battleford to Saskatoon to organize a first expedition to the homestead area they had selected. The party consisted of five men, namely the Kutschurganer Dominik and Jakob Müller, who appear to have been brothers; Frank Perlinger from Austria; a young German named John Zimmer from Wisconsin; and a young Oblate priest named Theodor one drawn by a team of horses, the others by oxen. The men were Franz Wurzer, Melchior Schermann, and Rudolf Schmidt. It would appear that the men also brought their families with them. In all likelihood this little caravan was also accompanied by four other men, namely Anton Kellerhofer, George Kappel, Jakob Gerlinski and Vincenz Kolenovsky, but their country of origin can no longer be determined. Because of the refractory behavior of the oxen, the small caravan did not reach Battleford until April 21. Here the settlers purchased 36 head of cattle (cows and oxen) and some necessary provisions. They left Battleford on April 23 and after a two-day journey in a southwesterly direction they reached their homesteads on April 25 in the vicinity of the later hamlet of Pascal, several miles from the site of the later village of Leipzig.

After a few days the men returned to Battleford to purchase some lumber and other supplies. During their absence a sudden blizzard swept across the prairie and drove the 36 head of cattle from their homestead location. After searching in all directions, two of the settlers arrived at Sixty Mile Bush, where a halfbreed named Des Charley had his primitive abode. With the aid of his field glasses he succeeded in locating the lost cattle some twenty miles away and promised to get them back to the settlers' homestead for the price of $25.00.

On May 1, 1905, Mr. W. Benz, an agent of the Catholic Settlement Society, brought three landseekers by wagon from Battleford to the east side of Trampling Lake on a scouting expedition for homestead land. The men were J. Mueller, B. Schmidt, and John Hohnwart. The first two were no

Schweers, a German missionary who was appointed to look after the arriving immigrants.

The party left Saskatoon on May 5 and after a day's travel they were able to find a night's lodging with Tom Peet, an American who was homesteading near present-day Asquith. The second day it rained quite heavily and progress across the soggy prairie was difficult and slow. The wagons moved at a

Father Schweers and first settlers

snail's pace and often one or the other got stuck in a morass. The men had to spend their second night under the wagons on a bed of wet blankets. On the third night the party stopped at Sixty Mile Bush, where the friendly half-breed Indian Des Charley gave the Germans a lodging in his hut and set before them a meal of sun-dried pemmican, jerked beef that was as tough as leather. It rained all night and the water kept seeping through the drafty roof. In the morning Father Schweers said Mass outdoors while the small congregation stood in half a foot of water. The wagons continued to roll westward all day, but as evening approached the men were unable to find the tent which Mr. Benz had left as a marker. Again the men had to spend a rainy night in their wet blankets under the wagons.

The tent

The next day the men spotted the tent that was pitched only a few miles from the present-day Leipzig. The party reached the spot in the evening of May 11, 1905 and camped there for the night. The next morning—it was a beautiful sunny day—Father Schweers said Mass in the tent, the first Mass to be held in the area of the new colony. Dominik Mueller constructed a simple little altar from the boards of a wooden-crate and the two Austrians were the Mass servers. The occasion was later designated as marking the birth of St. Joseph's Colony.

Site of first Mass near Pascal

After Mass the men set out in various directions to find some wood that was needed for building material and for fuel. Father Schweers mounted his horse and rode in the direction of Tramping Lake which lay to the west. After riding about four miles he was still unable to see the lake. He dismounted and climbed up a bluff from where he saw a large valley with very steep banks and there he caught a first glimpse of the alkali lake. He noted that there were nice large trees and bushes in all the ravines. He returned to the camp with the good news that one of their problems was solved. The men likewise were able to report that they had located a spring with excellent water.

The next day the party started on their return trip to Saskatoon. The journey was uneventful. The most exciting thing that happened was that Father Schweers shot his first rabbit on the prairie. In Saskatoon the settlers began with the task of moving their families, their livestock, and farm and household equipment. On May 20 a large caravan set out across the prairie. The weather was pleasant but the rough jolting ride in the wagons was hard on the womenfolk and the children. Some of the women became ill. A baby died and had to be buried on the open prairie. After arriving at the site of the homesteads, the men set about the task of building sod huts. With a one-share breaking plow drawn by two horses the grassy topsoil was turned over and the foot-wide sod cut into three-foot lengths. The slabs were then hauled to the building site by means of a stone boat and they were mounted like bricks, course after course, to form the four walls of the house.

The first sod house was started by Rudolf Schmidt and he managed to complete the four walls, but instead of covering them with a roof he simply placed a makeshift layer of boards over one corner of the wall. Here his family had to find shelter for several months.

The first sod house

The distinction of erecting the first complete sod house in the St. Joseph's colony belonged to the Kutschurganer Dominik Mueller from Mannheim. While his kinsman Jakob cut the sod and brought it to the building site, Dominik quickly laid down the sod slabs, course after course. He put up the four walls in a single day and the second day was needed to put on the roof which consisted of a framework of poles over which a layer of brushwood and sod was laid. This was, obviously, not the first sod house that Dominik had built, for like most of the German-Russian settlers in North Dakota, he had built an earlier sod house on his homestead near Towner.

Shortly after the arrival of the first settlers on their homesteads, Father Joseph Laufer, an Oblate missionary who had helped to establish the earlier St. Joseph's Colony at Balgonie, east of Regina, arrived in the new colony. As the official superior of the missions, Father Laufer must be regarded, along with Father Schweers, as the religious founder of the colony. It is not without deeper significance that Father Laufer, who entertained a deep devotion to his patron saint, St. Joseph, should himself have become its founder and patron. But he not only attended to the spiritual welfare of the pioneer settlers in both colonies; he also spent much time and zeal in collecting and distributing articles of clothing and food among the poorer families. He was a man of stately vigorous physique that inspired respect and awe, as

Father Joseph Laufer, OMI

well as a man of gentle and generous disposition that made him loved by all who knew him. He was a native of Alsace, having been born in Strassburg/Neudorf, and hence proficient in both German and French, and we should add, also in his Alsatian dialect. He was ordained a priest in 1886 and was sent by his Oblate superior to work as a missionary in Saskatchewan. It must have been for him a most surprising coincidence when he discovered that his parishioners in Balgonie as well as in the Tramping Lake district were for the most part of Alsatian ethnic origin and spoke a dialect that was remarkably similar to his own.

At the request of Father Laufer, the new homesteaders in the vicinity of the later railway station of Pascal began work on the construction of a wood-frame building that was intended to serve both as a parish church and a rectory. The house was completed by mid-October, and a 43-foot well was also dug to provide water. Father Schweers was put in charge of the small pioneer community and also had the task of visiting the new communities that were being established on the west side of the lake. Since the house soon became too small to accommodate the growing number of settlers, Father Schweers was able to buy a larger woodframe house which had been built by

The first church and rectory

285

The Mounties arrive with provisions

Frank Zimmer and Adam Knobel, but who had now taken up new homesteads near Carmelheim. With a bit of remodelling the house was easily converted into a church, complete with steeple and sacristy. The humble little
church was dedicated to S⁺ Pascal Baylon in honor of the diocesan Bishop
Pascal, O.M.l.

Pioneer wood-frame
church near Pascal

Father Laufer, like a veritable "Sankt Nikolaus" from Strassburg, returned
to the colony at Christmastime 1905 and brought with him a whole wagonload of clothing, shoes, underwear, and eatables, which were distributed
among all the families in the community.

4. The Westsiders Arrive

While the new settlers on the east side of Tramping Lake were getting established, other groups of landseekers continued to come to central and
western Saskatchewan. In mid-June of 1905 a contingent of German-Russian
settlers from the area of Towner, N.D., arrived by train in Saskatoon. There
were seven men, for the most part Kutschurganer, namely Barthel (fr.
Bartholomeus) Schmidt and Martin Weber from Mannheim, Andreas Schan
and Johannes Volk from Baden, Valentin Brossart from Selz, and Rafael Ell
with his son Benedict from the Beresan colony of Rastadt.

In the village of Saskatoon—its population in 1905 was only 300—they
were met by Father Schweers who made a point of meeting all the immigrant
trains that passed through. After attending Mass the party continued on its

286

way to Battleford and were lodged in the Immigration House which had been provided for them in the old Army Barracks. Since the clearance papers of the immigrants were delayed, the party had to remain in Battleford for another eight days. However, the men took the opportunity to travel 65 miles south by wagon in order to examine and select suitable homestead land on the west side of the lake. After returning to Battleford, they filed their claims and purchased the necessary supplies to get established on the prairie.

On June 27, Father Laufer conducted the small wagon train from Battleford on a 66-mile stretch of the old Indian trail that passed near the Tramping Lake coulee. The homesteads of the new settlers lay in the so-called East Prospect district in the general vicinity of what was later to become the village of Revenue. For the people, especially the women and children, it was a long and wearisome journey. The younger men and teenage children had to take turns in helping to herd the cattle behind or alongside the wagon train. This was no easy job, for again and again the obstinate oxen would run headlong into a nearby slough and it was a struggle to get them out again on dry land. The halfway mark between Battleford and the homesteads was Teepee Hill which presented such a steep incline that six or eight horses had to be hitched in tandem teams to get the wagon to the top. During the night the women and children had remained in the wagons while the men slept on the ground. But several men had to stay awake to look after the horses and cattle.

The Kutschurgan contingent arrived at Bartel Schmidt's homestead land which was located on the northeast quarter of section 13, in township 38, range 21, west of the third meridian. Since it was already getting dark, the others could not locate their homesteads until the following day. The party stayed together and said a common prayer of thanks for having been brought safely to their new home. For the first time they slept under their own open sky. However, since there had been a recent rain, the ground was still muddy and the people had to spread their bedding under the wagons and cover themselves with skins and horse-blankets. But there was such a heavy frost during the night that the blankets were white with hoarfrost in the morning. Barthel had to use an axe to knock the frozen mud off the wagon wheels.

After a frugal breakfast the other families set out across the prairie to locate the iron stake that stood at the northeast corner of each quarter and indicated the number of the section, the township, and the range. The pioneer homesteader had to make sure the numbers corresponded with those he had on his receipt. The settlers were also informed that only the sections with even numbers, except sections 8 and 26, were available for homesteads.

All odd-number sections belonged to the Canadian Pacific Railway, except numbers 11 and 29, which were reserved as School Land.

The Canadian government offered each male immigrant of 18 years or over a homestead of 160 acres, that is, a quarter section. This land was free; the $10.00 that the homesteader paid was simply for the registration and filing fee. However, to obtain title to the land, the settler was required to live on his homestead for at least six months a year for a period of three years. He was also required to "prove up" on his homestead, that is, he had to put at least 30 acres under cultivation and was required to erect a permanent dwelling on the property. After three years, the government granted him the title in fee simple.

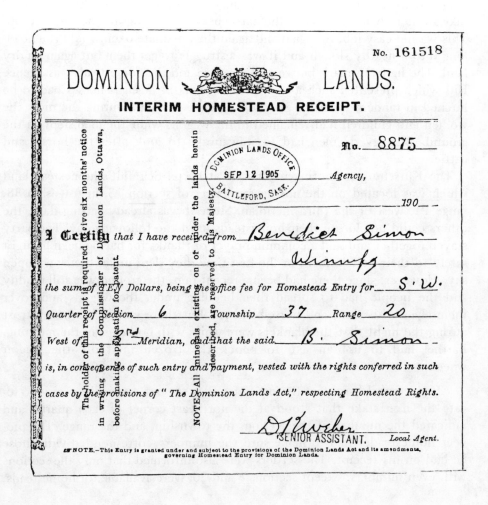

No. 161518

DOMINION LANDS.
INTERIM HOMESTEAD RECEIPT.

Ɉo. **8875**

DOMINION LANDS OFFICE
SEP 12 1905
BATTLEFORD, SASK.

Agency,

_____190__

I Certify *that I have received from* Benedict Simon

Winnipeg

the sum of TEN *Dollars, being the office fee for Homestead Entry for* S.W.

Quarter of Section **6** *Township* **37** *Range* **20**

West of 3rd *Meridian, and that the said* B. Simon

is, in consequence of such entry and payment, vested with the rights conferred in such cases by the provisions of "The Dominion Lands Act," respecting Homestead Rights.

D T Kircher

SENIOR ASSISTANT. *Local Agent.*

NOTE.—This Entry is granted under and subject to the provisions of the Dominion Lands Act and its amendments, governing Homestead Entry for Dominion Lands.

(left margin text, vertical) To receive six months' notice required of Dominion Lands, Ottawa, the holder of this receipt the Commissioner of before making application for patent in writing

NOTE All minerals existing on or reserved to His Majesty, under the lands herein described, are

Father Laufer had also filed on a quarter section (NE¼, Sec. 32, Rge. 21, W. 3rd Meridian) and his nearest neighbors were Andreas Schan and Rafael Ell. The first Mass to be held on the west side was celebrated by Father Laufer on his own homestead on June 29 in a tent. He returned to Battleford on July 1, but came back to his homestead on Sunday, July 9. After Mass the settlers agreed to carry out Father Laufer's proposal to get some lumber from Battleford to build a 21 by 16 foot shanty to provide both a small chapel and living quarters for the priest. The building was completed by the end of July.

Fr. Laufer's shanty chapel and residence

Besides the seven pioneer families who arrived in the East Prospect district, there was another family, namely that of Franz Zerr, who apparently travelled alone from Saskatoon and arrived at his homestead on June 29, 1905. Since Mr. Zerr wrote an interesting account of his migration from Towner to the homestead west of Tramping Lake, it is of historical import that his narrative be preserved in this pioneer history.

Franz Zerr, the second eldest son of Peter Zerr, was born Dec. 12, 1879 on the village of Yeremyevka, a daughter colony of Franzfeld/Odessa where his father and mother were born. The Zerr kinship of Franzfeld was by all odds the largest of any in all the German colonies of Russia. Franz Zerr was a nephew of Bishop Antonius Zerr and it was in a copy of the bishop's history of the Zerr kinship that Franz wrote his account (in German) of his experiences in North Dakota and in Saskatchewan. Franz Zerr's father died in 1898 and Franz, a young bachelor of 21, left his native village on Nov. 10, 1900 and emigrated to America. He arrived in Towner, N.D., on Christmas Eve and remained with close acquaintances during the winter.

5. The Zerr Report

Of his experiences as a homesteader in North Dakota, Franz Zerr wrote as follows: "In March of 1901 I went out to my farm which was 10 miles south of Towner. I began to break up the land and decided I would sow flax, for this was the only grain that seemed to thrive well on newbreak, but the crop

I harvested was rather poor. Fortunately, I received some money from my brother to whom I had sold my land in Russia. So on November 4th I married Elisabeth Weber, the daughter of Casimir Weber and Gertrude Volk.

I continued to farm for four years, but without success. The land was simply no good for grain farming, since the soil was too sandy. At that time various Canadian land agents appeared in our area and told us farmers about the good land that was available in western Canada. We therefore sent a delegation to Saskatchewan to determine if the land provided good prospects for grain farming. The men returned with the most favorable reports. We now spared no effort to sell our homestead quarter but all we were able to obtain for the 160 acres was the ridiculous sum of 300 dollars. We then got ready to travel by train from Towner to Saskatoon, Saskatchewan. We also owned three horses and four cows, a single-share walking plow and some household furniture and utensils. All our livestock and household goods were loaded into a freight car for which we paid freight charges amounting to $160.00.

The immigration train entered Canada at Portal and then moved through Weyburn and Regina, where we had the opportunity of conversing with some of our German-Russian people. At Saskatoon we unloaded our livestock and equipment from the train and loaded our belongings into the wagon to which we hitched our three horses, while the cows were attached to the rear.

We started out across the open prairie in the direction of Tramping Lake which lay about 125 miles to the west. The sun was our compass, and since the lake ran in a north-south direction, we could hardly miss it if we kept travelling due west. After a six-day journey we reached the east side of the lake, but our homestead was located on the west side. After having fed our horses in the afternoon, we continued on our journey in a northwesterly direction until we came to a coulee where we were able to cross over to the west side. It was now almost dark and we had to spend another night under the open sky.

The next day—it was June 29, about eleven o'clock in the morning—we arrived on our homestead quarter section. We were overwhelmed with joy. We unhitched the horses and began to unload our things right onto the open prairie. I had to think of economizing, for upon our arrival on my own land all the money I possessed amounted only to $80.00. We also had about ten

cured hams and a bag of flour. We had plenty of milk, butter, and eggs. But any other kind of food was simply out of the question.

We had also brought along a tent, and that was indeed a stroke of good luck. Actually the tent belonged to Mr. Benz who had lent it to us for ten days. So we were able to have a good shelter until we were able to construct a more permanent dwelling. First of all we broke up sufficient sod to build a barn for the horses and cows. But as soon as the barn was finished we used it as a temporary family dwelling while the house was under construction. Instead of using sod, we made sun-dried bricks of clay. When the four walls

Adobe house of Franz Zee

were completed we drove down to one of the ravines of Tramping Lake to get some poles and brushwood for the substructure of the roof. This was then also covered with a double-thick layer of sod slabs. After the house was plastered with clay inside and out, we moved in, although we had to use horse-blankets to cover the door and window openings. We then drove to Battleford to purchase the windows and doors. The round trip took all of three days. We had to take along provisions of food, for we generally had to stay overnight on the open prairie. There was a farmer's place where we could have stopped overnight but, only the well-to-do could afford his prices.

Since we were now seven families to be settled in this area, we always agreed to get together at one of the homesteads on Sundays. On those occasions we always prayed the Rosary together. On one Sunday a stranger drove up in a buggy and stopped in front of our sod house. When we asked who he was, he replied that he was Father Schweers, an Oblate missionary. Ah, who can describe the joy that filled our hearts! We were no longer alone and forsaken. We almost carried him on our hands. He celebrated a Mass in our humble abode the following morning. Everyone went to Confession and re-

Father Schweers, with his horse
Charley and buggy

ceived Communion. How ardent were the prayers of that little pioneer group on the endless prairie! We all felt redeemed.

With my three horses and my single-share hand plow it was a slow and hard job to break up the prairie sod, but with God's help I succeeded in plowing up 25 acres during the summer and fall. My brother-in-law Casimir Weber had a disk with which I was able to work up the sod to some extent. However, since I had no seed drill to put in the grain the following spring, I had to sow 20 acres in wheat and five acres in oats by the most primitive method known to man, namely scattering the seed grain by hand. When this was done I tied together several poles to form a drag with which the scattered grain could be covered with some soil."

Mr. Zerr's description gives us a first-hand account of the way in which the pioneer homesteader got established. Since it is most unlikely that any of the settlers owned a tent, the family had to use their wagon for a

A Sod Barn

temporary makeshift shelter until they had constructed a small sod hut that would ultimately serve as a barn, but was used as a family shelter until a regular sod house or an adobe house could be constructed. Of course, there were variations in the use of the wagon as a temporary shelter. For instance, Bartel Schmidt and his son Bernhard built a three-foot high enclosure of sod on top of which they placed the overturned hayrack. They lived here for a month while they were busy building the sod barn and making hay for the winter. They then moved into the sod barn and began building an adobe house of sun-dried clay bricks. During the summer while the men were making hay and breaking the prairie sod, Mrs. Schmidt and her 18-year-old daughter Margaret were busy with the task of filling wooden molds with clay and letting them dry in the sun. They then laid the clay bricks, course by course, until the four walls of the house were completed. This kind of work was nothing unusual for women in the pioneer years. In fact, it appears that the women frequently constructed the walls of the sod houses, while the men undertook the more difficult task of constructing the roof.

Adobe house with attached barn built by Barthel Schmidt.
Children: John Volk and sister Margaret.

Not all prairie soil was suitable for the making of a sod house. In sandy areas the sod tended to fall apart when it was handled. A good building sod had to have abundant roots and fibers. The clay was mixed with water and worked up with the aid of horses which tramped around in the clay pit until the loam had a certain viscous consistency. It was formed into bricks by the use of wooden molds and set out to harden in the sun. This type of adobe construction had already been used by the colonists who were settled on the steppes of South Russia a hundred years earlier. It continued to be used by poor people in later decades, for the adobe house could easily endure for

Clay blocks drying in the sun.
(Background: Stacked slabs of manure fuel)

Clay block house in colony of Speier/Od.
(In use for 100 years)

293

Sod house and attached barn of pioneer Valentin Brossart

two or three generations. By contrast, the sod house was much more fragile, since it tended to sag and crumble after a few years.

Another task that confronted the homesteader was to locate good water for man and beast. In the first years some of the settlers near Tramping Lake were able to find some springs that provided excellent water. But there was now the formidable task of getting the water to the homestead. Farmers often had to haul the water two or three miles every day, winter and summer, both for the household and for the livestock. Some homesteaders succeeded in digging wells that produced an ample supply of good water.

The making of hay was a task that had to be undertaken the first summer if the homesteader wanted to have a supply of fodder for his livestock during the winter months. Most of the settlers had a hay mower and a rake that enabled them to set up two or three stacks of hay. In some instances where other fuel was lacking, hay was used to stoke the stoves. In the summer the womenfolk and the children gathered the dry buffalo or cow chips they found on the prairie. Firewood was also obtainable, but the settler had to haul it either from the ravines of Tramping Lake or from the more distant bush area north of Unity.

As we have already mentioned, colonist Franz Zerr was able to break 25 acres of prairie sod with his handplow and three horses. Not all settlers were able to do as well, for some had only oxen which could not match the productivity of horses. But some homesteaders, like Barthel Schmidt, preferred to spare the horses from such hard work and used oxen to break up the land.

In the fall of the year it was also necessary that the homesteader made a special trip to Battleford to buy essential supplies of food and clothes for the coming winter. In many instances, the first settlers hardly had enough money to do much shopping of any kind. To be sure, almost every settler had one or two cows that would provide some milk, butter and cheese. Many also had a small clutch of chickens that provided some eggs. But generally speaking, meat was scarce, for none of the first settlers had any extra cattle.

The prairie might provide some wild game, for there were ducks and prairie chickens and rabbits, but we seldom hear that any of the settlers were successful hunters. In the entire area of St. Joseph's colony, no fish of any kind were available, for all the lakes, large and small, were alkali. On the other hand, there was a great abundance of wild fruit that grew in the sheltered coulees of Tramping Lake. There were the so-called Saskatoon berries that resembled blueberries in color, size and taste, but they grew in clusters on trees. There were also black currants and gooseberries, and lots of wild strawberries and chokecherries. The last mentioned were small and not much for eating, but they made excellent wine.

6. The First Winter

The Provincial Government, in its concern for the well-being of the colonists, commissioned the Northwest Mounted Police to make regular visits to the settlements throughout the winter in order to attend to any critical need among the people for food, fuel, or clothing. In such cases the destitute homesteaders were to be supplied with cured bacon, flour, sugar, coffee and tea. Fortunately, the winter of 1905/1906 was quite mild and there was only moderate snowfall. But there were days when it got cold enough so that a traveller could easily freeze his feet while on a journey. Since the settlers had no overshoes, they wrapped their feet in heavy gunny sacks.

For the seven families on the west side it was a long, lonesome winter. To be sure, the families visited each other often enough and enjoyed a good *"Maastub."* However, they were virtually cut off from the outside world.

Father Schweers, who had his residence at Pascal on the east side would visit the small community every other week and hold a religious service in one of the homes. Franz Zerr or one of the other settlers would have to get him by sleigh along a 16-mile detour around the north end of the lake. In the summer they sometimes brought him across the lake by boat. The first baptism in the new settlement was that of John Volk's daughter Margaret who was christened in the home of Barthel Schmidt in September of 1905. On November 23, Franz Zerr's second daughter Gertrude was also baptized in the Schmidt home. In both instances, Barthel's 18-year-old daughter Margaret was chosen as the godmother.

For the small community of pioneers the winter was beset with considerable hardship and sacrifice. The unvarying diet of "Riwwelsupp," noodles and pancakes caused one settler to describe the winter of 1905 as "a continuous period of fast and abstinence." But the warm-hearted Father Laufer had not forgotten his little flock in the East Prospect district, for in the late fall of the year he arrived with a big wagonload of potatoes! And shortly before Christmas the big Alsatian with the flowing beard surprised the isolated settlers by bringing complete outfits of clothing for the children of the seven families.

But there were also times when grief and tragedy befell the settlers. The first death in the small community was that of John Volk's child which Father Laufer buried on his own homestead. The first adult to die was Mrs. Barbara Degenstein. She had worked too hard making adobe bricks for the new church and died soon after the church was dedicated in July of 1907.

The flow of immigrant settlers into the new homestead area west of Tramping Lake continued throughout 1906 as wave upon wave of wagon trains rolled from Battleford to the homestead lands in the south. The first settlers to arrive were the recently married couple Anton (Tony) Reis and wife, who reached East Prospect on March 26. Anton had emigrated as a bachelor in 1900 from Selz/Odessa and had been farming near Towner for five years. In that time he had acquired 4 horses, a cow, a pig, some chickens, a few pieces of farm machinery and, last but not least, a beautiful young wife. In the spring of 1906 he loaded his earthly goods into a freight car that brought him to Battleford. Before leaving for his homestead he bought enough lumber to build a 12-by-12 foot shack. The weather was still quite mild for several days after their arrival in the East Prospect district, so that he and his wife could sleep under the wagon until the shack was constructed. However, the weather suddenly turned so stormy and cold in mid-April that they feared for the life of their only cow. Since there was no shelter available for her, they brought her into the shack and tethered her to the foot of the bed. While the shack was liveable enough in summer but not in the winter, they built a sod house in which they and their four young children lived for six years.

Like all the pioneer settlers, Mr. and Mrs. Reis experienced hard times in the early years of settlement. For three or four months they didn't have a nickel, and their daily diet consisted of white turnips, bread, and milk. On one occasion Tony was fortunate in being able to earn $35.00 for transporting a newly-arrived settler 85 miles to his homestead. Since the Reis farm lay on the Battleford-Tramping Lake trail, many migrating settlers stayed there overnight on their way further south to Denzil or Salvador. Thus Mrs. Reis was kept busy baking bread for the wayfaring guests.

7. The Kutschurganer Are Coming!

While the settlement of the first founding families was under way in the summer of 1905, several scouting parties from North Dakota were travelling through townships 36 and 37 to find suitable land for German-Russian immigrants. Early in June, Mr. Bernhard Hoffart with two or three companions travelled by wagon from Saskatoon to the west side of Tramping Lake. Another party under the leadership of Anton Gutenberg had likewise made a tour of inspection in the same region. A third party consisting of Thaddeus Usselmann, Johannes Lang, and Johannes Eckert likewise visited the Revenue-Tramping area in the summer of 1905. They liked what they saw, took options on land for themselves and their immediate relatives and friends, and returned to N. Dakota. The reports of the three parties were so favorable that scores of German-Russian settlers in the area of Towner, Karlsruhe and Harvey put up their homestead quarters for sale and began to prepare for a mass exodus from the land on which they should never have settled.

In the spring of 1906, the Kutschurganer loaded their livestock, their farm equipment and their household goods into twenty freight cars of a special pioneer settlers' train that was to take them to the promised land in western Saskatchewan. While the women and children travelled in the two coaches, the men had to ride in the freight cars to take care of the livestock that needed to be fed and watered. The colonist train entered Saskatchewan at Portal and rolled in a northwesterly direction through Weyburn, Regina, and Saskatoon, until it reached its destination in North Battleford. The newly built C.N.R. crossed the North Saskatchewan River between the present-day Langham and Plenty and continued in a westerly direction along the north bank of the river and past North Battleford to a junction located seven miles west of South Battleford. At this junction the immigrant settlers removed their belongings from the freight cars. The livestock was driven across the river where the water was quite shallow. The wagons could also ford the river with the equipment. The people, however, were taken across on a ferry. They then drove with their wagons to South Battleford where they were given lodging in the Immigration Houses.

We have here a most remarkable and fascinating parallel to the earlier migration which the ancestors had made a hundred years ago when they travelled from the Rhineland valley plains to the steppes of the Black Sea. The tremendous desire for land had impelled our Alsatian and Palatinate ancestors to travel almost two thousand miles by river routes and overland roads to what was then known as New Russia. A hundred years later the same innate desire for land impelled their descendants in Russia to travel

297

several thousand miles by water and by land from the Kutschurgan to Saskatchewan.

Czar Alexander I granted each German settler 60 dessiatines (= 162 acres) of Crown land. Similarly, the Canadian government, following the example of the American Homestead Act, provided each homesteader with a quarter section of free land. He was permitted to take up the homesteader quarter by paying a fee of $10.00. After "proving up" on this quarter, he was permitted to file a so-called "pre-emption claim" for another quarter section at three dollars an acre, payable in five installments beginning three years after taking possession of the land. In their inimitable Alsatian dialect, "unser Leit" invariably spoke of a *"Scheckse Land,"*—a section of land, or a *"Vartel,"*—a quarter, a *"Klemm,"*—a claim, and of course of the *"Brie- emsch,"*—the pre-emption.

Mr. Anton Gutenberg and wife Teresa
Pioneers of 1906

After the impatient guests of the Immigration Houses had loaded their wagons and rounded up their cattle for the four-day trek to the south, the Gutenberg caravan of 45 wagons rolled along the Tramping Lake trail in a southwesterly direction. Some of the Kutschurganer were travelling in ox-drawn wagons, but most of them had horses. Young boys had the job of keeping the cattle on the move behind or beside the wagon train. Travelling was slow and sometimes there were delays, especially when some oxen or cows decided to run off into a nearby slough to drink water or cool off. In the evening the wagon train came to a halt for the night. The horses were watered and fed. The women started camp fires to brew some tea and cook a kettle of soup. After the frugal repast, horse-blankets were spread under the wagons and the weary wayfarers lay down to sleep. This was not always a simple matter, for in the humid weather they were often tormented by swarms of mosquitoes. It became necessary to build a smudge to keep them away.

At seven in the evening of Saturday, May 12, 1906, the Kutschurgan cara- van arrived at its destination on the Gutenberg homestead which was located on the S.E. quarter of section 32, township 36, range 21. Everybody, young and old, became excitedly happy and after a fervent prayer of thanksgiving for the safe journey, the weary wayfarers went to sleep on their new home-land while the moon shone down brightly upon them in peaceful benediction. This would be the last time that this immigrant party would be together, for in the morning each family would be impatient to set out in a certain direction to locate the quarter section of land that would be their homestead and livelihood. As far as it has been possible to ascertain, there were 34 families in this Kutschurgan caravan, namely:

Andreas ADAMS	Philip HUMMEL	Peter SCHNEIDER
Michael ADAMS	Johannes JAHNER	Wendelin SCHWAB
Peter BERTSCH	Philip KRAFT	Philip SENGER
Joseph FROEHLICH	Anton LANG	Cyrillus SIMON
Stanes FROEHLICH	Mary LATURNUS	Adam VOLK
Karl Ludwig FROEHLICH	Anton LAUINGER	Peter VOLK
Anton GUTENBERG	Lorenz MAIER	Kasimir WEBER
Anton HALTER	Mrs. Joh. MAIER	Rochus WELTER
Engelbert HALTER	Georg REITER	Andreas WELTER
Lambert HEIDT	Jakob SAHLI	Stephan WERAN
Ignatz HEIDT	Georg SANDER	
Philip HEIDT	Michael SANDER	

A contingent of some 50 families arrived during the summer and were for the most part settled in the Tramping Lake district. As far as can be determined, the names of the heads of households were:

Georg BLEILE	John FRISON	Rochus KRAFT
Joseph BLEILE	Sebastian FRISON	Konrad KOBLE
Sebastian BOHN	Alfons FROEHLICH	Johannes LANG
Amand BROTZEL	Joseph GANJE	Felix LANG
Andreas BURGART	Johannes GANJE	Josef LASCHILIER
Karl DUCHSCHERER	Jakob GEREIN*	Kaspar LATURNUS
Johannes ECKERT	Andreas HEIDT	Joseph MITZEL
Johann EICHENLAUB	Jordan HERLE*	Jakob REITER
Ignatz ELDER*	Bernhard HOFFART	Christian REITER
Kaspar ELDER*	Georg JOCHIM	Bernhard REITER
Michael FETSCH	Kaspar JOCHIM	Jo ·ph REITER

---

*Names with an asterisk indicate that these homesteaders were settled in the Revenue district.

Henry REITER	Benedict SIMON	Louis WEBER
Rochus RISSLING*	Michael SITTER	Philip WEBER
Johannes SANDER	Anton USSELMANN*	John WELTER
Stephan SANDER	Joseph USSELMANN*	Franz WELTER
Andreas SCHAAN	John USSELMANN*	Paul ZAHN
Kasper SCHELL	Thadeus USSELMANN*	Johannes ZAHN
Joseph SCHELL	Andr.-Peter VOLK	
Andreas SCHWAB	Joseph WAGNER	

8. Getting Settled

The next day, even though it was a Sunday, the various families moved out to the quarter section for which they had filed. The first thing that needed to be done was to select a good site for the new homestead. Most often the site chosen was at one of the corners of the quarter section, or near it. Many settlers chose a somewhat elevated place—a knoll or a ridge. Some sites were close to a slough which would provide water for the livestock and the poultry. After determining the site for the sod house, the homesteader would break enough sod to provide the building material for the walls and the roof. After being cut into 3-foot lengths, the slabs of sod were hauled to the building site by means of a stone boat.

However, even before the Kutschurganer homesteaders were able to start building a shelter, the sky clouded over and the rains came that were to last for the next eight days. The families had to seek shelter under the overturned wagon boxes and hayracks. Most of the food was saved, but much of the clothing was rain-soaked. The horses and cows, hobbled or tethered to the wagons, were left without shelter under the open sky. The poor people, cramped together in the confined space of the wagon box, with no opportunity to cook a warm meal or to dry their wet clothes on a line, became depressed and morose, for it seemed to them that the rain would never end.

After a week of rain the sun again shone brightly over the vast expanse of the green prairie. The settlers now lost no time in constructing some kind of abode. Most of them started building a small barn, for this did not require much time or labor. The family could then use it as a fairly comfortable shelter until the sod house or the adobe house was completed. A goodly portion of the construction work was done by the women, as we have indicated earlier. The typical sod or adobe house of the first settlers measured only

---

*Names with an asterisk indicate that these homesteaders were settled in the Revenue district.

GERMAN-RUSSIAN PIONEER SETTLERS
in
TRAMPING LAKE DISTRICT MAY 1906

I. GROUP	II. GROUP
Andreas ADAMS	Andreas BURGART
Michael ADAMS	Sebastian BOHN
Peter BERTSCH	Karl DUCHSCHERER
Joseph FRÖHLICH	Magd. DUCHSCHERER
Stanes FRÖHLICH	Johannes ECKERT
Karl L. FRÖHLICH	Jch. EICHENLAUB
Anton GUTENBERG	Michael FETSCH
Anton HALTER	Alfons FRÖHLICH
Engelbert HALTER	Sebastian FRISON
Lambert HEIDT	Johannes FRISON
Ignatz HEIDT	Joseph GANJE
Philip HEIDT	Johannes GANJE
Philip HUMMEL	Andreas HEIDT
Johannes JAHNER	Georg JOCHIM
Philip KRAFT	Rochus KRAFT
Anton LANG	Felix LANG
Kaspar LATURNUS	John LANG
Anton LAUINGER	Joseph LASCHILIER
Lorenz MAIER	Joseph MITZEL
Mrs. John MAIER	Jakob REITER
George REITER	Bernhard REITER
Jakob SAHLI	Joseph REITER
Georg SANDER	Paul REITER
Michael SANDER	Andreas SCHAAN
Peter SCHNEIDER	Andreas SCHWAB
Wendlin SCHWAB	Benedict SIMON
Philip SENGER	Michael SITTER
Cyrillus SIMON	Joseph WAGNER
Joseph SIMON	Louis WEBER
Adam VOLK	Joseph MOSER
Andreas VOLK	Heinrich REITER
Rochus WELTER	Philip WEBER
Andreas WELTER	Paul ZAHN
Stephan WERAN	Johannes ZAHN

Design by Sr. Louise V. Heit

Add:
John Vetter, sec 22, NE¼
Nick Veller, sec 28, NE¼
Gottl. Sander, " 28 NW¼
Nick Scherr, sec 33, NE¼
Alex Dreser, sec 34, NW¼

Township 38

Township 37

Range 22   Range 21   Range 20

Legend

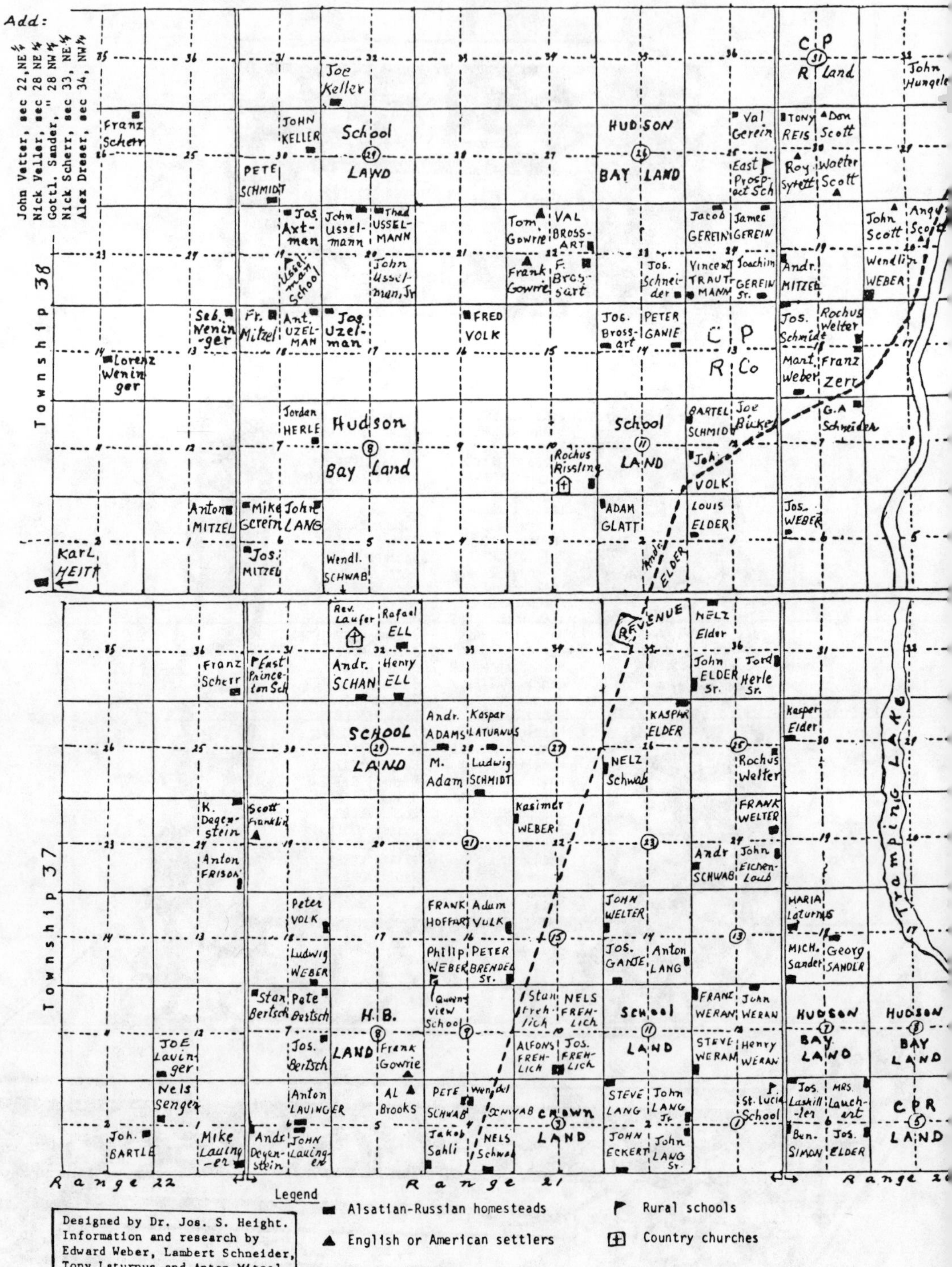

Designed by Dr. Jos. S. Height.
Information and research by
Edward Weber, Lambert Schneider,
Tony Laturnus and Anton Mitzel.

■ Alsatian-Russian homesteads   ▶ Rural schools

▲ English or American settlers   ⊞ Country churches

302

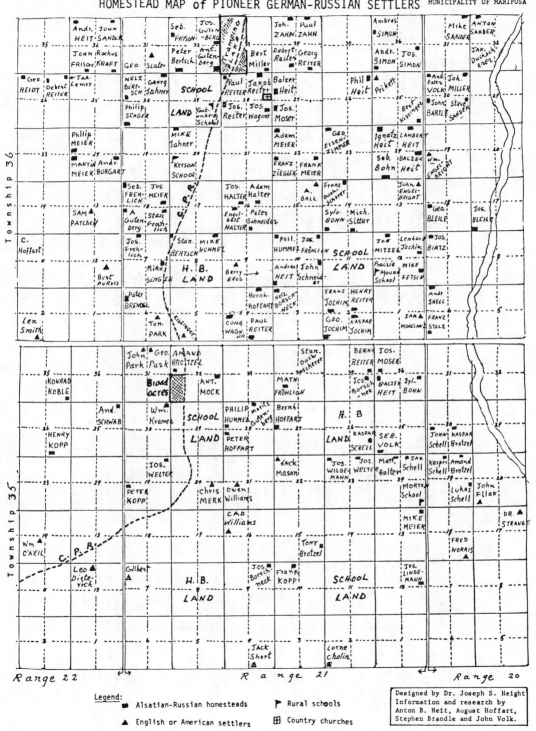

HOMESTEAD MAP of PIONEER GERMAN-RUSSIAN SETTLERS   MUNICIPALITY OF MARIPOSA

Legend:
■ Alsatian-Russian homesteads   ⚑ Rural schools
▲ English or American settlers   ⊞ Country churches

Designed by Dr. Joseph S. Height
Information and research by
Anton B. Heit, August Hoffart,
Stephen Brandle and John Volk.

303

Name of Settler	Location	Emigrated from..	Ancestral home	
Adams, Andreas	Tr. Lake	Elsass/Od.	Lauterburg/Weissenburg	Als
Bartle, Johannes	Tr. Lake	Selz/Od.	Bergzabern	Pf
Baumstark, Ignatz	Tr. Lake	Selz/Od.	Oberlauterbach/Wssnbg.	Als
Bertsch, Peter, Natz.	Tr. Lake	Selz/Od.	Mothern/Wssnbg.	Als
Bertsch, Jos., Stanisl.	Tr. Lake	Selz/Od.	Mothern/Wssnbg.	Als
Bitz, Kaspar	Revenue	Kandel/Od	Roppenheim/Bischweiler	Als
Bleile, Georg & Josef	Tr. Lake	Selz/Od.	Seltz am Rhein	Als
Bohn, Sebastian, Syl.	Tr. Lake	Baden/Od.	Steinmauern/Rastatt	Ba
Borschneck, Natz & Jos.	Tr. Lake	Kandel/Od.	Rohrweiler/Bischweiler	Als
Brendel, Peter	Tr. Lake	Selz/Od.	Nehweiler/Wssnbg.	Als
Brotzel, Amand & Kasp.	Broadacres	Elsass/Od	Oberbrüden/Backnang	WU
Deibert,	Tr. Lake	Selz/Od.	Sessenheim/Bischweiler	Als
Degenstein, Andreas	Revenue	Mannheim/Od	Weinheim/Mannheim	Ba
Duchscherer, Andreas	Tr. Lake	Mannheim/Od.	Beinheim/Wssnbg.	Als
" Franz, Natz	Tr. Lake	Mannheim/Od.	Beinheim/Wssnbg.	Als
Eckert, Johann	Tr. Lake	Josephstal/Od	Schleithal/Wssnbg.	Als
Eichenlaub, Joh.	Tr. Lake	Selz/Od.	Nehweiler/Wssnbg.	Als
Eisenzimmer, Georg	Tr. Lake	Selz/Od.	Nehweiler/Wssng.	Als
Elder, Kaspar	Revenue	Mannheim/Od	Beinheim/Wssnbg.	Als
Ell, Rafael, Benedict	Revenue	Rastadt/Od	Durmersheim/Rastatt	Ba
Fehler, Nick	Revenue	Elsass/Od	Seltz/Wssnbg.	Als
Fetsch, Michael	Tr. Lake	Selz/Od.	Niederlauterbach/Wssnbg.	Als
Frison, Sebastian, Joh. & Anton	Tr. Lake	Selz/Od.	Oberseebach/Wssnbg.	Als
Frehlich, Alfons, Natz, Stanes, Joe, Seb.	Tr. Lake	Mannheim/Od.	Landau (?)	Pf
Ganie, Josef	Tr. Lake	Mannheim/Od	Beinheim/Wssnbg.	Als
Ganie, Peter	Revenue	Mannheim/Od	Beinheim/Wssnbg.	Als
Gerein, Joachim, Jak.	Revenue	Mannheim/Od	?	
Glatt, Adam	Revenue	Kandel/Od	Plittersdorf/Rastatt	Ba
Gutenberg, Anton, Josef, & Moritz	Tr. Lake	Strassburg/Od.	Winzenbach/Wssnbg.	Als
Halter, Engelbert, Adam, Josef & Matt.	Tr. Lake	Baden/Od	Steinmauern/Rastatt	Ba
Heilmann,	Tr. Lake	Elsass/Od	Kandel/Germersheim	Pf
Heit, Lambert, Philip. Natz & Balzer	Tr. Lake	Mannheim/Od.	Kaidenburg/Wssnbg.	Als
Heit, Andreas, Georg	Tr. Lake	Mannheim/Od.	Kaidenburg/Wssng.	Als
Heit, Karl	Revenue	Selz/Od	Kandel/Germersheim	Pf
Herle, Jordan	Revenue	Mannheim/Od	Hunspach/Wssnbg.	Als
Hoffart, Bernh., Franz	Tr. Lake	Kandel/Od.	Hayna/Germerseim	Pf
Hummel, Philip	Tr. Lake	Kandel?/Od.	Bellheim/Germersheim	Pf
Jahner, Georg & Mich.	Tr. Lake	Kandel/Od	Jockgrim/Germersheim	Pf
Jochim, Kaspar, Franz	Tr. Lake	Selz/Od.	?	
Keller, John	Revenue	Kandel/Od.		
Koble, Gabriel, Konrad	Broadacres	Elsass/Od		
Kraft, Rochus	Tr. Lake	Baden/Od.	Steinmauern/Rastatt	Ba
Lang, Anton, Steve, John	Tr. Lake	Mariental/Od	Hornberg?/Calw	WU
Laturnus, Maria, Anton	Revenue	Mannheim/Od.	Oberseebach/Weissenburg	Als
Lauinger, Anton, Mike	Tr. Lake	Strassburg/Od.	Riedeelz/Wssnbg.	Als
Laschiller, Josef	Tr. Lake	Mariental/Od.	Büchelberg/Germersheim	Pf
Lemere,	Tr. Lake	Kandel/Od.	Riedeelz/Wssnbg.	Als
Lindemann, Joseph	Broadacres	Selz/Od.	Oberlauterbach/Wssng.	Als
Meier, Martin, Philip	Tr. Lake	Mannheim/Od.	Sufflenheim/Bischweiler	Als
Meier, Franz, Adam	Tr. Lake	Mannheim/Od.	Sufflenheim/Bischwlr.	Als
Miller, Johannes	Tr. Lake	Mannheim/Od.	Reichenbach/Karlsruhe	Ba
Mitzel, Josef, Andreas	Revenue	Strassburg/Od.	Plittersdorf/Rastatt	Ba
Moser, Joseph	Tr. Lake	Mannheim/Od.	Königstein/Oberpfalz	Pf
Platz, Joseph	Tr. Lake	Selz/Od.	Brühl/Mannheim	Ba
Reis, Anton	Revenue	Selz/Od.	Nehweiler/Wssnbg.	Als
Reiter, Bernhard, Debert, Georg, Jakob, Jos., Paul	Tr. Lake	Kandel/Od	Sulzbach/Rastatt	Ba
Rissling, Rochus	Revenue	Selz/Od	?	
Sander, Stefan, John	Tr. Lake	Selz/Od.	Bischweiler	Als
Sander, Georg, Michael	Revenue	Selz/Od.	Bischweiler	Als
Sahli, Johannes	Tr. Lake	Kandel/Od.	Waldprechtsweiler/Rast.	Ba
Schan, Andreas	Revenue	Baden/Od.	Oos/Rastatt	Ba
Schell, Josef, Kaspar	Broadacres	Elsass/Od.	Kandel/Germersheim	Pf
Scherr, Franz, Domenik	Revenue	Selz/Od	Jockgrim/Germersheim	Pf
Schiele, Ignatz	Revenue	Mannheim/Od.	Ubstadt/Bruchsal	Ba
Schmidt, Bartel	Revenue	Mannheim?/Od.	Schwedelbach/Kaisersl.	Pf
Schneider, Peter	Tr. Lake	Mannheim/Od.	Sufflenheim/Bischwlr.	Als
Schwab, Andreas, Ignatz, Wendelin, Peter	Tr. Lake	Mannheim/Od.	Busenbach/Karlsruhe	Ba
Senger, Philip	Tr. Lake	Strassburg/Od.	Riedeelz/Wssnbg.	Als
Simon, Andr., Jos., Ambros	Tr. Lake	Selz/Od.	Rotenfels/Rastatt	Ba
Sitter, Michael	Tr. Lake	Kandel/Od.	Würth/Grmsheim	Pf
Stolz, Franz	Broadacres	Selz/Od	Winzenbach/Wssnbg.	Als
Trautmann, Vincent	Revenue	Elsass/Od	Beinheim/Wssnbg.	Als
Usselmann, Thaddeus, Anton, Joseph, Johann	Tr. Lake	Selz/Od.	Niederseebach/Wssnbg	Als
Volk, Andres, Andr-Peter	Tr. Lake	Elsass/Od.	Jöhlingen/Karlsruhe	Ba
Volk, Johannes, Friedr.	Revenue	Baden/Od.	Steinmauern/Rastatt	Ba
Wagner, Joseph	Tr. Lake	Selz/Od.	Winzenbach/Rastatt	Ba
Weber, Wendelin, Philip	Tr. Lake	Mannheim/Od.	Beinheim/Wssnbg.	Als
Welter, Franz, Rochus, Joh.	T.L. Rev.	Elsass/Od.	Plittersdorf/Rastatt	Ba
Weninger, Sebastian	Revenue	Selz/Od.	Obergrombach/Bruchsal	Ba
Weran, Stefan	Tr. Lake			
Zann, Paul, John	Tr. Lake	Selz/Od.	Rheinzabern/Grmsheim	Pf
Ziegler, Franz	Tr. Lake	Elsass/Od.	Jöhlingen/Karlsruhe	Ba
Zerr, Franz	Revenue	Franzfeld/Od	Nehweiler/Wssnbg.	Als

Katie	Mrs Teresa	Regina	Teresa	Katie	Tony	Joe	Mrs Eva	Lawrence
Lauinger	Gutenberg	Zahn	Zahn	Gutenberg	Zahn	Lauinger	Lauinger	Lauinger

Anton Gutenberg Sod House & Barn (1907)

14 by 16 feet, and was divided into only two rooms. Both the inside and the outside of the house were plastered with a clay mixture and calsomined in white or in pastel colors. Instead of a wooden floor, the sod house simply had a layer of clay which was levelled off and tightly packed. It was sometimes sprinkled with green grass clippings to settle the dust and to make it easier to sweep when necessary. Because of the thick walls both the sod as well as the adobe house were warm and cosy in the winter, and pleasantly cool in the summer. However, under the impact of a heavy rainfall, some water would often seep through the sod-covered roof and drip into the room below, creating a number of puddles on the floor and on the furniture. The harassed housewife would attempt to place pots and kettles under the drip-

Franz Ziegler's
pioneer adobe house

305

ping spots in order to catch the water. Mrs. Joseph Bertsch recalls that the first building she and her husband put up was a sod barn in which the entire family slept with the horses and cows. One night a mighty rainstorm tore a big hole in the roof and her father called out to the frightened family "Cover yourselves as well as you can. The sky is now our roof." But everyone had to lie there in the water until morning.

Most of the settlers brought along a cast-iron cookstove and cooking utensils. Those families who had no stove and could not afford to buy one at Battleford had to build their own stove in the Russian manner, namely out of sun-baked clay bricks. Since such a stove took up a lot of room it was mounted into one of the outer walls of the kitchen, so that the large oven extended outside. In this type of oven 10 to 12 loaves of the finest bread could be baked at one time. No batch of bread ever tasted better.

The story is told that one of the pioneer homesteaders, Bernhard Hoffart, tried to buy an iron stove from the Hudson Bay Company store in Battleford, but the manager would not give him credit for the $10.00 stove. This meant that his poor wife had to cook all summer over an open fire in the yard. In the fall, after he had earned some money, he went back to the store with the necessary cash and got the stove. When he came home with the proud possession he discovered that the merchant had given him too much change. A few days later he made the long trip back to the store and returned the surplus money to the merchant who was too astonished to utter a word. However, like other businessmen, he quickly realized that these "Russian furriners" were "honest to goodness" people who deserved to be given credit whenever they wanted it.

As for other household furniture, most of the settlers brought with them at least a bed, a table, and some chairs. After they were fairly well established, some of the homesteaders who had skills as cabinetmakers produced large wooden kneading troughs, butter churns, kitchen cabinets, chairs, cradles, and coffins. All in solid, sturdy construction and attractively painted.

To illuminate the little sod house, they used coal-oil lamps or candles. But the lamps were used only in winter, for in summer when people worked hard all day, they went to bed when it got dark.

An urgent and important task for the homesteader was to find water for the home and the livestock. Usually the men from two or three families would collaborate in digging a well. Since the water in shallow wells was generally only surface water, it was necessary to dig to a depth of 20 to 30 feet in order to get good drinking water. The first well to be dug was on the Anton Gutenberg homestead. It took four men four days to dig a 17-foot shaft that produced an ample supply of good water for eight neighboring families. The well remained in regular use for over 50 years.

In the early pioneer years, women who were with child were invariably confronted with a worrisome situation, for there was not a single doctor in the entire region, and sometimes not even a mid-wife. Mrs. Anton Gutenberg had the distinction of giving birth to the first baby in the new pioneer community of Tramping Lake. The event occurred on July 23, 1906, ten weeks after the settlement was established. In recalling the event, she said, "Our one-room sod house was finished, but it still had no windows and doors. My husband therefore hung up horse-blankets for curtains to cover up the windows. Mrs. Joe Reiter, who was our nearest neighbor, had just come to our well to get water when I felt the first labor pains. My husband went out and told her of my condition. She came in at once and stayed and helped until it was all over. Both the baby girl, whom we named Anna, and I were fine. We women always helped each in any emergency."

"But not every pregnant mother was as lucky as I happened to be. One day Mr. Joseph Ganje drove into our yard with a pair of oxen hitched to a stone boat. His young wife was about to go into labor and he had come to fetch Grandmother Zahn who was a good mid-wife. My husband offered to drive Grandmother in his wagon, since it was a trip of five miles, but Mr. Ganje thought there would be enough time. He was mistaken, and both the mother and her first child died. It was so sad. It also happened to be the first funeral in the pioneer community."

While the Kutschurganer were getting established, the small East Prospect community, which had broken about 200 acres of land the previous summer, seeded their wheat and flax crop in the spring of 1906. At harvest time the crops were cut by two binders that were available. However, since there was no threshing machine, the sheaves were strewn evenly on a hard, dry threshing floor of clay and threshed out by running a wagon and horses over the layer until the kernels were knocked out of the husks. This was called "threshing with the horses." The straw was then removed with large pitch forks and the grain was swept together on a pile and run through a sieve, and finally winnowed in the wind. The wheat was kept for seeding the next crop, but some was also sold to the newly-arrived settlers.

In his eyewitness account, Franz Zerr stated: "After the nice warm winter, we had a beautiful summer (1906), for the sun shone in the daytime and at night we had soft, gentle rains. But not all the sown grain fell into the ground, and the birds devoured most of it, and we were afraid that we might not harvest enough for seed. But the Lord was good to us. After the wheat was ripe it was cut by a binder and threshed out by the use of horses. The wheat yielded 12 bushels per acre and the oats yielded 20 bu. per acre. Thus we were able to survive for another year."

It should be remarked that only those settlers who had been homesteading in North Dakota for a few years and managed to acquire three or four horses, a couple of cows, and a bit of farm machinery, were in a position to break up about 25 acres of virgin prairie during the summer and autumn after their arrival. But there were some homesteaders who had just migrated

Breaking sod with oxen (Courtesy of Otto Lutz)

from Russia to North Dakota at the time when many of their countrymen were getting ready to settle in Saskatchewan. These recently immigrated landseekers had, of course, no opportunity to acquire livestock or machinery. For instance, Vincent Tratumann, who had emigrated from Mannheim/Odessa in the fall of 1905, spent the winter with some friends or relatives near Towner. In the spring he came with the Gereins to the Revenue district. However, since he had no livestock and farm implements, he had to hire out as a farm laborer for three years at a wage of only $25.00 a month. Then, in

Breaking the sod
with a hand plow

1909, he took out a loan, bought 3 horses, a plow and a wagon, and started farming. One summer he also worked for an Englishman named Gordon Fowley, a sod-buster who owned a herd of oxen and decided to break up the prairie in a big way. He therefore bought a section of school land and began operations with five large three-bottom plows, each of which was drawn by six oxen. After he finished plowing up the 640 acres, he sold the entire section to pioneer settler John Volk for about $5.00 an acre.

Plowing with three teams in tandem

Another pioneer, Peter Ganje, farmed with oxen for the first three years, then took out a loan to buy horses and better farm equipment. He had first built a small sod house, then constructed a larger two-room house of sun-dried "Lehmstaan," clay stone, with a small *"Vorheisel,"* closed-in porch. The adobe house was used until 1916.

Another homesteader, Jakob Gerein, who had left Georgental, near Mannheim in 1902 with his sons Jim and Jakob, settled near Towner, N.D., where they tried to farm for a few years, but without success. They arrived in Battleford in May and each of them filed on a homestead. They had brought

The self-binder

their belongings with them in two freight cars, with the livestock in one and the household and farm equipment in the other. They also had a tent in which they lived until they had constructed a log house, which was no doubt a unique sight on the treeless prairie.

Jim Gerein's work horses   (Courtesy of Norman McKenzie)

Ignatz Heit barn with windmill and farm horses. (Courtesy of Jack Heit)

Many of the settlers who arrived in 1906 were better equipped than those of 1905. Thus Kasimir Weber brought with him 4 horses, 3 cows, a few pigs, a walking plow, a two-bottom gang plow, a harrow, a disk, a shoe-drill, and a binder. He plowed up 30 acres during the first summer, seeded it in oats the following spring in order to provide feed for his livestock. In the same summer he was able to make 45 loads of hay from a slough. He must have had a grass mower and a large hay rake.

The summer and fall of 1906 was a very busy time for the 65 Kutschurganer families who had settled on the west side of Tramping Lake. Not only the men but also the women worked at the job of building a sod house or an adobe house for the family. The women also helped with the haying; indeed, they had the arduous job of "setting" the haystack, a job which required a good deal of skill. Everywhere one could see the man walking behind the breaking plow, with a shoulder harness to help him hold the plow to a proper depth, while a second man, usually one of his sons, would guide the team of horses. If the weather was favorable and the horses remained strong, a good plowman could get from 25 to 30 acres of new break ready for the next year's crop.

After the plowing was done, the homesteader had to think of getting the necessary provisions, clothing and fuel for the coming winter. In the first years of settlement, shopping was a major expedition. For their food staples and farm supplies, the settlers had to make a trip of 50 or 60 miles to the nearest store, namely the Hudson Bay Store at Battleford. Fortunately, in those days, you were still able to get something for your money, for everything had a reasonable price. (No fancy packaging, no phoney advertising, no rip-offs!). A hundred pounds of fine flour (not enriched!) cost $2.00 if it came in white cotton bags, and $1.80 if it was in brown bags. The frugal Kutschurgan women preferred the white bags, for they could eventually be used to make dish cloths or children's undershirts. A yard of good flannel cost 5 cents a yard. An iron stove could be bought for only $10.00. A pair of men's sturdy Oxford shoes cost only $1.50.

In the fall of 1906 Mr. Anton Lang went on a shopping expedition with $60.00 and returned home with a three-deck wagonload full of food and clothing to supply the needs of his family for an entire year. But very few homesteaders had that much cash. One of them, Peter Bertsch, had to sell one of his two precious cows, in order to be able to purchase essential provisions for the winter. Although there were seven children in the family, he could only afford to buy two pairs of shoes. One pair was for the father, while the other pair was large enough to fit the mother and any one of the four elder daughters. When one was wearing the shoes, the others had to wrap their feet in gunny sacking if they had to go outdoors.

Sometimes it was the wife who had to undertake the shopping expedition. Mrs. George Jahner, who made such a trip, has related the following account: "The winter of 1906/1907 was frightfully cold and the worst we have ever experienced while we lived on the prairie. I drove by sleigh to Battleford, a distance of almost 60 miles, to buy some things for our family and also for all of our neighbors. The snowdrifts were so deep that my sleigh upset and when I got to Battleford I heard that it was 53 degrees below zero. I did not have sufficient money to sleep in the hotel, and the livery stable where the teamsters usually stayed with their horses was completely filled up. So I camped out beside some bushes with my sleigh and horses. Since it was too cold to think of sleeping, I sat up all night and kept my little camp fire going."

On November 3, 1906, the settlers in the Tramping Lake district had their first prairie fire. It lasted one day and one night. The smoke was so dense that it blotted out the sun. The cattle in the stalls moaned and bellowed, and tried to break loose from the halters by which they were tethered. The men hitched up their plows and drew fire-guard furrows around the buildings and the haystacks. The women helped the men to fight the fire by dipping sacks into water and attaching them to end of a fork to douse the flames that were encroaching on the homestead yard. Everybody, especially the children, were very frightened until the advancing line of fire had swept past their homestead.

Since the winter of 1905/1906 was remarkably mild, the settlers were quite shocked at the rigorous winter of 1906/1907. Not only was that winter very long and cold, it was also characterized by very heavy snowfall and frequent snowstorms. Old-timers recall it was the worst winter they had ever experienced on the prairie. The blizzard created such large snowdrifts that the sod houses and sod barns virtually disappeared from view. Whenever there was a blizzard the settlers had to stretch a rope between the house and the barn, so that they would not lose their way, coming or going. In the spring there were still big piles of snow on the shady side of the buildings as late as the end of June. In the winter it was hazardous to drive in a sleigh across the prairie. People who went to visit their relatives or friends for an evening would arrive before sundown and before supper. They not only stayed until late in the evening but until the next morning, since the absence of regular roads and landmarks made it virtually impossible for them to find their way back home during the night.

After every blizzard or heavy snowstorm the Mounties made their rounds among the homesteaders, in spite of the fifty-below weather. On one such

A sod house in wintertime

occasion, in 1906, two Mounties came to Father Schweer's shack only to find it almost completely enveloped in snow. They shovelled their way in and found the priest hungry and half-frozen. The appearance of the red-coated riders of the prairie was always a welcome sight to the lonely settlers. "They were good to us," said one pioneer with sincere feeling, "without their aid we would never have lived through that terrible winter."

In their large toboggan sleighs the Mounties succeeded in transporting large quantities of food staples, such as flour, sugar, lard, cured pork, tea and coffee over the snow-covered prairie. These staples provided a very monotonous diet, but it was a means of survival. Father Schweers was speaking for all the settlers when he claimed, "I never ate so many pancakes in all my life as I ate that winter." Among the colonists it became known as the *"Pancake Winter."*

Because of the large amount of snow, spring in 1907 came very slowly. As late as mid-May the snow banks were still so big that Mr. Wendel Weber broke the shafts on his buggy. Seeding started in the latter part of the month. In the Tramping Lake area about 70 homesteaders were able to seed approximately 1,700 acres. But the great expectations of a good crop failed to materialize. Because of the late seeding, a severe frost in early August damaged the unripened wheat. The yield was only 6 or 7 bushels an acre, and the price at Battleford was about 35 cents a bushel. The harvesting was mostly done with binders, but some settlers used grass mowers and field rakes. However, the grain was threshed by machines. In the Revenue area an Englishman named Clyde Smith of Scott did the threshing for the German settlers with a steamer and threshing machine. The following year, a German settler, Frank Dietrich, operated a similar outfit. Mr. Wm. Englebright and his son were the first homesteaders to operate a threshing rig in the Tramping Lake area.

Because of the poor crop, many of the younger settlers left their homesteads to find a job that would provide them with a bit of sorely needed money. Some found work doing grading for the railroad beds that were being constructed for both the Canadian Pacific and the Grand Trunk Pacific railways that were running northwest from Saskatoon to Wilkie and Scott respectively. A settler who had a pair of horses could do grading work and earn $30.00 a month plus lodging and board.

Otherwise there were not many job opportunities in the pioneer years except as farm hands. For instance, Jordan Herle of Revenue was able to work with a threshing crew at Asquith, near Saskatoon, and earned $20.00 a month, of which he saved every penny. He also scrounged around and managed to obtain four sacks of potatoes.

In the summer and fall of 1907, the homesteaders were able to plow up some more prairie, with the prospect of putting in a larger crop the following spring. The crop turned out better that year, although it also suffered some frost damage and received an inferior grade. In the Revenue area a certain Mr. Adler who had a threshing rig did most of the threshing;

The year 1908 showed an improvement in several respects. The crop turned out fairly well and people were able to stook the sheaves in the field and get them threshed by local farmers who had a threshing outfit. Adam Herle of Revenue threshed about 500 bushels of wheat and hauled them to the grain elevator in Scott.

The year 1909 proved to be very good. There was a fine crop and the wheat yielded about 30 bushels to the acre, while the price was a respectable 56 cents per bushel. However, as in all the preceding years, the grain suffered some damage from frost, which depreciated its market value. This was also the year when the government allowed new settlers to take up homesteads or pre-emptions in the odd-number sections, excepting the school sections 11 and 29, and the Hudson Bay Company sections 8 and 26.

In 1911 there was a severe frost with a stand of almost 50 bushels to the acre. In this year the land was assessed for taxes for the first time at four cents an acre, which meant that settlers had to pay $6.40 taxes on their homestead quarter.

9. Pastoral Pioneering

With the formidable influx of Catholic Kutschurganer into the westside of Tramping Lake in 1906, Father Schweers found it necessary to take up residence in Father Laufer's homestead shanty. In the course of the summer a sizable number of families were added to the original group of seven, whereas the southern group numbered at least 70 immigrant families by the end of the summer. It appears that Father Laufer first visited this group on the Feast of Pentecost and held the first Mass for them in a tent on the Anton Halter homestead. After the services some of the people expressed the desire to build a small church on the prairie, and one of the settlers, Jakob Reiter, promptly offered to donate five acres of land to the Church on the S.E. corner of the N.E. quarter of Sec. 28, Twp. 36. Father Laufer gladly granted permission, and work on the church was begun in July but not completed until September. It was, of course, a homely little sod church only 14 by 15 feet, but nonetheless it stood as an appropriate symbol of the faith and courage of the pioneers. The church was blessed on September 29, St. Michael's Day, and dedicated to the militant archangel by Fathers Schweers and Brabender.

Tramping Lake:
Sod church of the pioneers (1906)

On August 15, 1906, the Feast of the Assumption, Father Schweers made his first appearance in the Tramping Lake district. After saying Mass at the home of Anton Halter, he announced that he would hold a Corpus Christi procession the next day. For this event he requested that a group of young men come in the early afternoon to rehearse some hymns for the occasion. However, after the midday lunch, a group of young men and girls gathered in the Halter granary where Pete Schwab and a couple of associates picked up their musical instruments and everybody began dancing. In the meantime Father Schweers began to wonder why nobody was turning up for the rehearsal, when some kind soul told him, "Oh, they're all dancing over in the granary." Without further ado Father Schweers marched over to the place, while someone sounded the alarm: "Father Schweers is coming!" The girls all got scared, but Pete Schwab told them to go on dancing; he would settle the matter. He put down his accordian and went out to meet Father Schweers. Nobody heard what was said, but he got a resounding box on the ears as the priest announced that he would not hold a Mass on Corpus Christi Day. However, many people indicated that the entire community should not be punished because of the behavior of a few young fellows. The priest relented, and the procession was held after all.

Father Schweers stayed in the community for several more days to prepare a group of eight children—5 girls and 3 boys—for their First Holy Communion. To make the occasion a little more festive for the children, he asked Mrs. Theresa Gutenberg to prepare a post-communion breakfast for the group. When she asked him what she should prepare, he replied that any-

315

thing would do. So she prepared some potato salad, hamburgers, and pie.

Father Schweer's pastoral activities grew more arduous and wide-spread month after month. Not only did he have to look after the settlers in three townships along the west side of Tramping Lake, but he also had to travel with horse and buggy to visit a number of smaller communities of pioneers that had recently sprung up in the west and southwest, namely the Leibel community, the Ulrich community, and the Schachtel community.

In 1906 and 1907, a sizable group of Kutschurganer and Liebentaler were settled in an area that lay about half way between Kerrobert and Macklin. Among the first settlers were Peter Leibel and his five adult sons: Joseph, George, John, Philip and Peter who had emigrated from the colony of Josephstal which was one of the four Catholic villages in the Grossliebental district near Odessa. Three Schäfer families namely Joseph, Peter, and Ferdinand were from the same colony. Since there was no village in the

Peter Leibel, pioneer settler near Salvador

entire region by which one might have identified the new settlement, it became known simply as the *"Leibel Gemeinde"*—the Leibel community, particularly since the visiting priests usually held Mass in Peter Leibel's house. However, the majority of settlers in this group were Kutschurganer and had close ties with the homesteaders in the Revenue and Tramping Lake areas. Among the known names of the other settlers in the Leibel community were: Michael Hopfinger, Georg Herle, Michael Deibert, Jakob Klein, Anton Usselman—all from Selz; Adrian Meier and Artus Ivanov from Mannheim; Peter Bartsch and Jakob Heilmann from Elsass, and A. Feldmann from Strassburg.

The pioneer church, measuring 30 by 30 feet, was built in 1909 of wood, not of sod, about six miles from the subsequent village of Salvador, on the S.W. ¼ of Sec. 5, Twp. 38, Rge, 25. A beautiful rectory was built in 1912. The church, which was beautifully furnished in subsequent years, was dedicated to St. Henry. With the coming of the railway and the development of villages, the little church of St. Henry was soon too small to contain the increasing number of families, many of whom were living too far away to the north and northwest. One group of parishioners decided to build a new church at Salvador, while the other larger group built a large 50' by 28' church in the village of Denzil in 1915. The family names of some of the early settlers were: Deck, Leibel, Vetter, Klotz, Rissling and Wildemann from the Liebental colonies; Hauck, Leier, Vetter, and Volk from Elsass; Buechler, Klötzel and Meier from Mannheim; Urlacher and Lantz from Karlsruhe, and some 8 or 9 families from the Volga and the Crimea. In 1923 the parish of Denzil had 80 families; in 1930 there were 120 families.

A large influx of Catholic immigrants from the Volga and the Crimea took place in 1909 and 1910. New settlements arose at Grosswerder, and in the parishes of St. Donatus and St. Peter, ten miles south of Macklin.

Another settlement of Kutschurganer was established in 1904 at Allan, 40 miles southeast of Saskatoon. Most of the family names of the pioneer settlers are also to be found in the Tramping Lake and neighboring districts. Among the first settlers were:

Balzer Bitz	N. Kary	Joseph Senger
Rudolph Boehm	Johannes Klotz	Kaspar Selzler
Joseph Brossart	Andreas Kraft	Johannes Boechler
Jakob Brossart	Jakob Kraft	Franz Boechler
M. Deibert	Martin Leier	Johannes Schan
Ignatz Germann	M. Loran	A. Schatz
N. Hauk	A. Marbach	H. Scherr
Joseph Hegele	Anton Pflieger	L. Schnurr
T. Hulm	Andreas Senger	Karl Silbernagel

Joseph Weninger	Joseph Volk
Wendel Weninger	Joseph Zacher
Paul Wald	Zeiler
N. Weisbeck	Zerr
Usselmann	Berger
Dukart	
Engel	
Martian	

Allen, Pastor and Church

317

Since Father Laufer was now devoting himself to the new parishes on the east side of the lake, his shanty on the west side now became Father Schweer's more or less permanent residence. But the rectory-chapel had long ago become too small to accommodate the increasing number of settlers in the Revenue area. In the spring of 1907, it was therefore decided to erect a church, not of wood, since that would be too expensive, but of *Lehmstaan,* namely of sun-dried clay blocks similar to the adobe houses that many of the settlers had constructed on their homesteads. While this type of structure was not the "invention" of Father Schweers, as his confrère Father Schulte was pleased to maintain in his book, it may well be conceded that he proposed that each family in the community should pledge to manufacture a certain number of *Lehmsteine.* With this kind of community enterprise the church could literally be constructed "dirt-cheap," for there were not even any labor costs involved. It appears that the task of manufacturing the clay bricks was largely carried out by the women, just as was the case in the building of the sod or adobe houses. In any event, Mrs. Barbara née Fröhlich Degenstein became ill while working on the clay bricks, and subsequently died.

Revenue adobe church and
parishioners (Photo 1916)

The site chosen for the new church was on the homestead of Rochus Rissling (S.E. quarter of Sec. 10, Twp. 39), which was located about a mile north of the later village of Revenue. Work on the church began in July and the building was completed in September of 1907. Some time later the walls of the building were plastered with clay and calsomined.

In the summer of 1908 the little settlement had the honor of being visited by Bishop Pascal of Prince Albert. For this memorable occasion a long cavalcade of riders rode out to meet the distinguished visitor. The new church was consecrated and dedicated to St. Charles Borromeo.

It seems that Father Schweers, no longer venturing to spend another winter in Father Laufer's drafty shack, became the resident parish priest of St. Michael's Church in the fall of 1908. Although December was already a cold winter month and snow covered the ground, he decided to hold a Midnight Mass on Christmas Eve in the little sod church on the prairie. Every homesteader brought a barn lantern along to guide him on the way to the church and these lanterns were also used to illuminate the church. Before the service was over a blizzard swept across the prairie and the people could not venture to drive home but had to stay in the crowded church until daybreak. They stayed awake by singing hymns, and Father Schweers consoled them with the thought that the only shelter the Holy Family was able to find on the first Christmas Eve was a sheep barn located in a cave.

In the spring of 1910 Father Schweers was appointed parish priest of Scott where a small church and a rectory had already been built. Though the parish had only about twenty families, it was expected that the railway town would expand by leaps and bounds. The community of St. Charles now became a mission of the Scott parish. In 1913 Father Schweers was transferred to Allan to take charge of the large German-Russian community there, and Father Forner, O.M.I. was posted to Scott.

Father Forner in his cutter

Catholic church in Scott. Fr. Forner, OMI and abbot Ott

Since the population of the Revenue district was steadily growing, the adobe church that had been built in 1907 was becoming too small to accommodate the faithful. Accordingly, Father Forner began a campaign in 1917

Father Forner in his buffalo coat

319

to raise the necessary money for the construction of a new church. The people responded so generously in the following three years that their pastor succeeded in collecting the sum of $11,000. A German architect, Franz Schroffel from Edmonton, drew up the plan for a wood-frame church measuring 96 by 100 feet, and construction began on June 17, 1918. On August 19 the church was solemnly dedicated amid the jubilation of the eighty families who belonged to the parish.

Revenue: Rectory and church (1918)

The parish hall

Father Nelz, O.M.I., who replaced Father Forner as parish priest in 1921 completed the interior of the church in succeeding years. In 1926, St. Charles Church obtained a resident priest in the person of Father Rosenthal, who built a large beautiful rectory in January 1927 and, a year later, erected a parish hall, the largest of its kind in the entire St. Joseph's Colony.

St. Charles Church and rectory

In the spring of 1910 a new Oblate missionary, Father Joseph Guth, O.M.I., arrived in the Tramping Lake district and was appointed parish priest of St. Michael's Church. Like Father Laufer, he was a native Alsatian, having been born in the village of Wasselone in Upper Alsace in 1885. He was ordained in Strassburg in 1909. Father Guth was a tall handsome man of dignified bearing, with an affable and humorous disposition. He must have been quite surprised and perhaps pleased to note that his parishioners were also of Alsatian ancestry, as was obvious from the dialect which they spoke.

At the time of Father Guth's arrival the parish had increased to 62 families and 28 self-supporting single men. Since the old sod church could not accommodate such a large congregation, Father Guth and the people quickly agreed that a new church had to be built without delay. Construction of the wood-frame church began in June and the 30-by-50 foot structure was completed in the fall of the same year. The Ulrich community, later named the St. Francis parish, now became a mission which was taken care of by Father Guth for the next four years. The parish continued to grow in the next few years, especially after the C.P.R. railway was laid through the district in 1913 and the village of Tramping Lake was established one and a half miles northwest of the country church.

Father Joseph Guth, OMI, first parish priest of St. Michael's

Father Guth was a man of many talents. He had a large garden in which he raised a variety of vegetables, including cucumbers and pumpkins. Near the parish house he had a grove of trees and shrubs. In the first few years, he owned two beautiful lively sorrel ponies which he hitched to bis buggy whenever he visited his mission or his fellow priests. In 1917 he bought an Overland car, one of the first autos to be seen in the district. He was also the only resident in the entire St. Joseph's colony to install a Delco electric plant in his parish house as early as 1917.

One of his chief hobbies was photography. Equipped with both large and small cameras, he loved to take pictures at every opportunity, particularly on the festive occasions of children's First Communion, baptisms, and weddings. In 1917 he also organized the first church picnic on such a grand scale that it astonished everyone. The women served two full meals on long tables that were set up alongside the church. In the afternoon there were various contests and races for the children, and an exciting baseball game in the nearby

321

Author J.S.H.

Catholic-Church

Tramping Lake, Sask.

cow pasture. There were also various games of chance, raffles, and wheels of fortune at which the lucky participants could win all kinds of novelties. Children and adults enjoyed the novel refreshments known as Coca-Cola and Orange Crush, and many got acquainted with a confection called chewing gum.

In the evening after it got dark, Father Guth showed the first movie ever seen in the entire St. Joseph's Colony. In the tightly packed church, an incredulous audience watched in amazement as the silly antics of Charlie Chaplin flickered on the linen screen. After the show the people were treated to an exhibition of fireworks under the star-lit prairie sky.

In November of 1918 the so-called Spanish Influenza spread rapidly throughout the world, claiming more victims than were killed in the World War. In the parishes of Tramping Lake and Revenue, the majority of families came down with the flu, and many people, both young and old, died. Father Guth was also stricken, but recovered. Throughout the epidemic there was no doctor or nurse available in the entire district.

In the fall of 1919, Father Guth became seriously ill and travelled by train to Edmonton, Alberta, where he was admitted to the Misericordia Hospital. His case was diagnosed as terminal cancer and he died a couple of weeks later at the youthful age of thirty-seven years. For his parishioners, his passing was a grievous loss, for he was loved and admired by all. He had been pastor of the community for only ten years, and it would take another two years before a successor could be found in the person of Father Theodor Christ, O.M.I.

Oblate Pioneers in St. Joseph's Colony
Sitting: P. Palm, P. Krist, P. Schweers
Standing: P. Schwebius, P. Guth

The name of the Oblates of Mary Immaculate is inseparably linked with the history of German settlements in St. Joseph's Colony. Father Laufer, the energetic spiritual founder of the colony, and Father Schweeres, the intrepid missionary of the pioneer communities, were soon followed by their dedicated colleagues Fathers Guth, Forner, Palm, Schwebius, Brabender, Christ, Nelz, Bieler, and Schulz. All honor to those zealous apostles of the prairie who served the German-Russian pioneers in the years of poverty and struggle. They braved the rumbling rain and the blinding blizzard on their hazardous trips to outlying mission settlements. They knew the pangs of hunger and thirst, the depths of loneliness, and the crunch of hardship and affliction. They sowed the seed and others came to reap the harvest. If you would see their monuments, you need only view the stately churches that rise everywhere above the rolling plain as visible testimonials of their achievement.

10. The Coming of the Railway

In the summer of 1908 the Grand Trunk Pacific[3] succeeded in laying its new railway line as far as Scott, and on August 7 the first train came puffing into the village carrying a small shack on a flat-car which was to serve as a railway station. For the German settlers in the Revenue and Tramping Lake districts, the coming of the railway was a godsend. They no longer needed to travel to Battleford for their supplies and they now had an excellent opportunity to sell their grain at a railway center that was within a reasonable distance from their homesteads. With the coming of the railway Scott quickly became a boom town. Within two years the population increased from 50 to 850 souls. Business buildings were springing up everywhere like so many mushrooms. The small village suddenly became a town of trade and commerce, a bustling farmers' market in a radius of 40 and more miles. By 1910 the town boasted of having 4 general stores, 2 hotels, 2 hardware stores, 3 lumber yards, 3 livery stables, 3 real estate offices, a bank, a drugstore, various offices, 3 churches and 3 grain elevators. The following year the Canadian Government established an Experimental Farm near Scott for the development of a wide variety of trees, shrubs, cereal grains, and flowers.

In 1911 the CPR applied for a charter to build a railway branch line from Wilkie to Kerrobert, a distance of 45 miles. The Board of Trade at Scott op-

---

[3]The name of the Grand Trunk Pacific was changed to the Canadian National Railway (CNR) in 1912.

posed this plan unless the charter compelled the CPR to route the railway through Scott. Judge Robert Ney appeared before the Railway Committee in the House of Commons at Ottawa on behalf of the Scott Board of Trade. When the CPR officials refused to route the proposed railway line through Scott, the charter was not granted. Instead, the company received a charter that permitted it to build a railway to Kerrobert from a point on the newly built CPR line from Wilkie to Kelfield, immediately south of the Reford railway station. This decision was to mark the beginning of the end of Scott's exuberant hopes of developing into an important agrarian city. As soon as the Wilkie-Kerrobert railway line was in operation in 1913, Scott was no longer of any importance to the farmers in the Revenue-Tramping Lake district and the town steadily dwindled and declined until it was nothing more than a ghost town while its erstwhile rival continued to flourish and grow from year to year.

While the town of Scott was in its heyday in 1909, it became the Canadian headquarters of the Luse Land Development Company, a Minnesota firm which operated out of St. Paul. On the first and third weeks of the summer months, the company ran a special train for landseekers from St. Paul via North Dakota and Winnipeg to Scott in western Saskatchewan where, according to the company's advertisement, they could see "the most beautiful prairie farmland ever found anywhere on God's green earth."

One of these trains leaving St. Paul on July 7, 1909, transported 58 farmers from Minnesota, Iowa, Nebraska and the Dakotas in two palatial private coaches to Scott in western Saskatchewan where the company had thousands of acres of excellent land for sale. There the landseekers would be given the best opportunity "to inspect, with a view to investment, the farming lands of this most wonderful country." After a breakfast at 6:30 in the dining car, farmers were piled into a dozen horse-drawn democrats (2-seater buggies) and six Reo automobiles which the company had brought along from St. Paul. On later excursions they switched to Cadillacs. Since this was to be a two-day excursion trip, a wagon with provisions and a cook were brought along and a second wagon was sent ahead with tents and blankets to provide the guests with lodgings for the night.

The caravan of autos and democrats travelled across the roadless prairie in a southwesterly direction to an area which was later to become known as the district of Luseland. After the landseekers had viewed and inspected the land for almost two days, the caravan returned to Scott where the train was waiting to take them back to the USA. In subsequent excursions the Luse Land Company brought as many as 300 people to Scott. Its method of promotion and advertising must have been successful, for within a short time the district of Luseland was settled by many German-American farmers.

The coming of the railroad was an event of the greatest significance to the people who were settled along the west side of Tramping Lake, for those ribbons of steel represented vital links of communication and commerce with the outside world. The homesteader was now no longer isolated, forsaken, forgotten; he was a vital part of the world. He could now send the fruit of his agrarian labor to far-off cities and countries. In turn, he could obtain the goods and services he needed for continuing growth and development.

The advent of the railroad set in motion the beginnings of the town of Tramping Lake. Two men, Mr. Joseph Schill and Mr. Ivans, made a start when they decided to establish a grocery store in a makeshift shack. With lumber hauled from Scott, they later built a combined store and post office. It was the first building in the new town and, with the exception of an annex at the rear, it is still Schill's Store today. The second building erected the same year was the Hardware Store operated by the Tompsett Brothers. This store was taken over by two German-Russian businessmen, Abel and Volk, in 1916.

In 1914 the town continued to grow with the addition of Bowman's Implement Shop, the Security Lumber Yard operated by Walter Richardson, and a grain elevator erected by the Searle Grain Company—the first of the six elevators that were to become the imposing landmarks of the town and the district.

In the following three or four years the town was enhanced with the addition of the Bank of Commerce, managed by Mr. Kennedy from Kerrobert. A second lumber yard was opened by the Beaver Lumber Company. F. Welter opened the first blacksmith shop; Frank Gillen operated a butcher shop. In 1918 Wahl and Volk opened a General Store which became the Wahl, Hoffart, and Eckert Store in 1920. In 1933 Wahl and Hoffart each started his own general store.

Only five years after the Grand Trunk railway came to Scott, the Canadian Pacific completed its railway line from Wilkie to Kerrobert and began operation in June of 1913. Railway stations were subsequently opened on the townsites of Revenue, Tramping Lake, and Broadacres. Soon there was regular train service twice a week, Tuesdays and Thursdays, from Wilkie to Kerrobert in the forenoon, and from Kerrobert to Wilkie in the afternoon.

While the boom in the village of Scott created an optimistic euphoria of impending growth and greatness, the town of Saskatoon, some 150 miles to the east, was likewise having fantastic visions of becoming a prosperous metropolis in the very near future. In 1905 and 1906 when the German-

Russian immigrant trains were rolling through Saskatoon on the way to Battleford, Saskatoon was still only a nondescript town of seven or eight hundred families. However, by 1908 it could boast of three transcontinental railways that passed through the city, namely the Canadian Pacific, the Canadian Northern, and the Grand Trunk Pacific. When the boom came in 1908 the population of the city rose to about 10,000 souls, and the exuberant mayor flatly predicted that it would increase to 100,000 "in a few years." The city councilors lost no time in acquiring 15,000 acres or more than 23 sections of prairie land, which in those days could be bought for $5.00 an acre. This land which lay adjacent to the city limits was then subdivided into city lots which were intended to provide room for sufficient individual homes to house a half a million people! Thus the future city would have had a diameter of at least six miles.

The result of this grandiose plan for the expansion of Saskatoon was that a horde of real estate speculators appeared on the scene, all eager to transform the fantastic dream of the mayor and his aldermen into a most lucrative reality. Where there had been only 18 real estate businesses in the city in 1908, there were 257 of them four years later when the boom reached its peak. By curious contrast, in 1974, after 60 years of development, Saskatoon had only 59 realtors.

Another grandiose scheme envisioned by the city fathers was the creation of a huge industrial center. Accordingly, 450 acres were acquired north of the city where the new Eldorado of industry, named "Factoria," was to arise from the lowly prairie sod. Scarcely realizing that the future growth and prosperity would be almost entirely dependent on the development of prairie agriculture, the planners of "Factoria" indicated that the prairie could provide unlimited amounts of clay, sand, and gravel from which the principal industries would produce concrete, glassware, and crockery. The manpower, it was seriously pointed out, would be furnished "by cheap Slav labor." Maybe the fantastical planners were thinking of using the German-Russian and Ukrainian immigrants who were flocking into the province in those days!

But alas, the big boom bubble was fated to be short-lived; it burst silently and ignobly in the summer of 1913 and with it the megalomania of the city planners and the greedy land speculators. All that survived as a curious historical by-product are the small, narrow lots which the city planners had deliberately designed to enable the real estate speculators to make fantastic profits from those small parcels of land, as though there were a shortage of that commodity on the vast and thinly populated prairie.

11. The Little White Schoolhouse

In the early years of pioneer struggle, there was neither enough money nor enough time available to build and operate the public schools that were needed to provide an elementary education for the children of the immigrant settlers. Not until 1911-1912—at least a half dozen years after settlement— did it become possible to build a few small wood-frame schoolhouses in the rural districts of the municipalities of Tramping Lake and Mariposa.[4] The one-classroom building ordinarily measured about 20-26 feet, with two or three windows on the east and the west walls. Its construction of shiplap siding, which was invariably painted white, whereas the shingled roof was green, had the one great drawback that it was not insulated against the rigors of the Canadian winter. The building stood in lonely isolation on the prairie, except for the two little white backhouses behind the school. The school-room furniture was of the simplest kind. Besides the desk and chair for the teacher, there were several rows of homemade two-seater desks for the pupils, and a large blackboard on the front wall.

The first school in the Revenue area was the Elderton School, which was built in 1910 on the N.W. quarter of section 35, Twp. 37, Rge. 21. The first teacher was Miss Maxwell who was succeeded by Charles Irwine. In 1923 the original name of the school was changed to the Revenue School, which at that time had 60 pupils distributed in Grades I to VI.

In the Tramping Lake area, the first schoolhouse measuring about 20 by 26 feet was built in 1912 on the S.E. quarter of section 14, Twp. 36, Rge. 21. It was originally called the Kerson School, after the province of Kherson (Cherson) in South Russia, from where all of the Catholic immigrants had come. A few years later it was renamed the Gutenberg School, in honor of Anton Gutenberg, the leader of the first transport of immigrant settlers. The first class comprised 30 children, and the first teacher was a certain Mr. Huwald. Since the rural schools had no teacherages until the early twenties, the first teachers had to obtain room and board in one of the nearby farm-houses.

In the early years, the attendance at the country schools was irregular and beset with insuperable difficulties. The schools were closed throughout the

---

[4]There were 8 rural schools in the districts of Revenue and Tramping Lake. Five of these were in townships 37 and 38, namely Elderton, East Prospect, Usselman, Queensview and St. Lucia. Three schools were in the townships 35 and 36 (Mariposa municipality), namely Kerson (Gutenberg), Prairie Mound, and Morton. The eight schools lay in an area that extended 24 miles from north to south and 10 miles from east to west, a total area of 240 sq. miles. This means that the average attendance area for each school was approximately 35 sq. miles.

winter months. Not only were the distances to the schools too great, the weather was frequently too inclement to expose the children to the hazards of blistering cold and blinding blizzards. Moreover, among the pioneer settlers, horses were still too scarce and precious to use them for regular transportation in winter. But one of the greatest obstacles were the schoolhouses themselves, for they could not be properly heated.

The country schools were, therefore, open only for about 40 days during the summer months. But even during that time, attendance was often poor and irregular, for in those days of pioneering, the able-bodied teenagers, both boys and girls, were frequently needed to help with the work in field, garden, and the household. It is understandable that many young people did not get much schooling in those years. Indeed, one might say that a whole generation of children who were of grade-school age between 1900 and 1912 (i.e. the period of pioneering in N. Dakota and Sask.), grew up more or less illiterate. There were, however, some exceptions, for with the development of the village schools, it became possible for young unmarried men, who had missed out in school, to attend evening classes in the winter months, in order to learn how to speak, read, and write English.

In the early twenties, the facilities and the organization of the rural school were considerably improved. Near the schoolhouse a small two-room dwelling was erected where the teacher—usually a bachelor—could live at least during the warmer months of the school year. A large potbellied stove was

East Prospect School (1955)
- Courtesy of Norman McKenzie

installed at the rear of the school, and usually a half-dozen boys would be charged with the task of keeping it well-stoked with wood or coal. Behind the little white schoolhouse, a small red barn was built wherein the horses that brought the children to school in winter could be stabled. Under these improved conditions, it became possible as early as 1921 to make school attendance compulsory. Children were now equipped to drive to school even in cold weather, except when there were snow storms. In the spring and fall, they were also able to participate in organized games, such as soccer football, baseball, and softball.

With the growth of the village of Tramping Lake, a new school was needed to replace the overcrowded Gutenberg School. In 1918 the Tramping Lake School District was established and the front section of the recently-built Slater Cafe was converted into a temporary classroom for the primary grades. In 1920 the so-called Cottage School was built at the south end of Main Street. In 1929 a two-room brick school was constructed in the same area to accommodate the Junior High School.

An event of auspicious significance was the coming of the Ursuline Sisters of Prelate in 1924 to take over the operation of the Tramping Lake Schools from Grades I to XII. Until 1972—a period of 48 years—an impressive roster of highly qualified teaching nuns dedicated themselves to the noble task of providing an excellent education for the pupils and students of the entire district. In that period twenty-four young women from the parish found their vocation in a religious order: 16 with the Ursulines of Prelate, and 8 with the Sisters of Notre Dame at Leipzig.

In 1927 two Sisters of Notre Dame came to the Revenue parish to teach in the Junior and Senior rooms. They remained until 1938 when they were replaced by Ursuline Sisters from Prelate who introduced High School courses. In subsequent years modern school buildings were constructed and all grades from one to twelve were taught until 1950 when the Sisters discontinued teaching in Revenue. In the 23 years that they served in this parish, the following Ursulines held teaching positions: Sisters Veronica, Rose, Michaela, Beatrice, Perpetua, Margareta, Aquina, Frances, Clara, Anastasia, Valeria, Nicolet, Bernarda, Josephine, and Benedicta. Nine young women from the Revenue parish chose a vocation in a religious order, and sixteen graduates of the Wilkie School became teachers.

With the coming of the railway, the pioneer settlers envisioned the promising opportunity for progress and development. The early years had been fraught with hardships and setbacks of various kinds, but with their unflagging dedication to hard work and their unwavering confidence in God's blessing, the German-Russian immigrants were able to make good progress in turning the barren prairie into fertile fields of grain. They quickly emerged from the lowly estate of homesteaders living in dingy sod huts and spending weeks of back-breaking toil plodding behind the single-bottomed breaking plow.

Hardly ten years after his arrival on the naked prairie, the humble homesteader was able to build himself a two-story wood-frame house which was large enough to accommodate his expanding family. The typical German-Russian farmhouse on the prairie provided two large rooms on the first floor, one for the kitchen which also served as the family room, and the other the "Verderstub"—the front room or parlor. Two smaller rooms at the rear provided the parent's bedroom and stairways leading to the cellar and the upper floor. On the second floor were two large bedrooms, one for the girls and the other for the boys. On either side there were small rectangular rooms which provided storage space. Below the house in a spacious cellar, vegetables and fuel supplies were stored.

As in the case of the German-Russian homes in the Black Sea colonies, the houses on the prairie invariably had the long axis oriented east and west,

Balthasar Heit farmhouse (1923)

while the entrance to the house was on the south side of the house. As in Russia, the doorway was enclosed by a vestibule or small anteroom called the *"Vorheisel."* Many of the prairie settlers adopted the American feature of the open porch on the front side of the house. As was the custom in Russia, they also built a *"Summerkich"*—a summer kitchen near the house, which was used for cooking, baking, and weekday eating during the summer work season. Near the house also stood the low-roofed ice house which provided the German housewife with convenient refrigeration throughout the summer months. And in an inconspicuous spot not too far behind, stood a little white shed known as the backhouse.

John Scott farm (1915). Note car in background (Courtsey of Norman McKenzie)

In the rear portion of the farmyard stood the barn, a large elongated building that could accommodate from 12 to 16 horses, half a dozen cows, and as many pigs. The huge hip-roof made it possible to store large amounts of hay and oat sheaves. The commonest color for these barns was a bright red, with roofs of vivid green. Every farmer also had two or three large granaries on the rear yard to store the surplus wheat and necessary seed grain. A chicken coop was usually attached to the barn or one of the granaries. Also in the backyard and usually fairly close to the barn, was the well that supplied the water for the livestock as well as for the household.

While the first settlers had only a few of the needed farm implements, namely a single-share walking plow, a disk, a shoe drill, a hay mower, a field rake, and a wagon, it was not long before he was able to afford a two-bottom gang plow, a self-binder, a disk-type seed drill, a winnowing mill, a second wagon, a buggy or a democrat, a bob sleigh, and a cutter. With this kind of equipment and sufficient horse power, he was soon able to afford the purchase of another section or two of land and carry on his farming operations with two or three teams at the same time.

Thaddeus Usselmann farm, near Revenue

The Adam Glatt farm near Revenue

Much of this rapid progress in prairie farming, it should be borne in mind, was made possible through the appearance of modern farm machinery which had been created by American inventive ingenuity. Indeed, it has justly been remarked that the unprecedented development of modern farming on the prairies of the United States and Canada was primarily due to three apparently simple inventions, namely barbed wire, the iron windmill, and the two-by-four. The barbed wire, for instance, eliminated the need of herdsmen to keep the horses and cattle on the pasture land and out of the grain fields. The windmill eliminated the burdensome and time-consuming chore of drawing water for the livestock. The handy two-by-four served a hundred and one

334

uses on the farm. With it you could construct joists, rafters, stringers, and studs in building a house, a barn, or a shed; with this versatile piece of lumber you could manufacture tables, benches, chairs, and bedsteads; or window and door frames; or the cribbing of a well, a water tank; or a coal bin; a scaffolding or a corral; stalls or stanchions; a railing or a stairway, a skid or a stone boat, and so forth. All in all, it is extremely difficult to imagine how the American and Canadian farmers could have managed without the use of these three basic items.

13. The Roaring Twenties

As we have already indicated, the German-Russian farming on the prairie really made impressive headway after the C.P. Railway began operation in 1913. In 1915 the farmers of Tramping and Revenue had their first bumper crop. Big threshing machines appeared on the scene, most of them powered by I.H.C. gas entines, but Herle and Elder of Revenue and Andrew and Joe Simon of Tramping Lake also operated steam outfits as early as 1915. Joseph Elder drove the first car in Revenue as early as 1913, and Febr. Bauman of Tramping Lake operated a chain-drive Maxwell the same year. The number of cars increased during the First World War and were a common sight in succeeding years.

IHC Mogul Boacking tractor on Scott farm in 1911   (Courtsey of Norman McKenzie)

The twenties saw a great increase in wheat production. Many farmers now owned two or three quarters of land, and very good crops were produced in 1925, 1927, and 1929. Although the farmers were generally using horses for practically all the farm work, a few began using small tractors for plowing in the mid-twenties.

An Aultman Taylor tractor of 1916

A Small IHC separator

As the size of the wheat crops continued to increase from year to year, additional grain elevators were constructed. By the end of the twenties, Tramping Lake had six of them dominating the skyline at the north end of town, namely a Searle, a Federal, a McLaughlin, a United Grain Growers, and two Pool elevators. However, in years of bountiful crops the big six were unable to handle all the incoming grain. At threshing time, long lines of wagons laden with wheat were awaiting their turn to get unloaded. Oftentimes farmers were unable to haul all their wheat directly from the threshing machines to the elevators, but had to leave it in large piles on the wheatfields.

When the wheat stood tall

Freight trains that commuted between Wilkie and Kerrobert six days a week were needed to haul the accumulated grain to eastern terminals.

A field of stooked grain

In those halcyon days, threshing was an exciting affair, for it required a crew of many men, and sometimes a few women, to work efficiently all day in order to get the job done while the weather remained favorable. For this reason many a farmer decided to buy his own threshing outfit—usually a small 20-inch separator and a 15-30 McCormick gas tractor—which he could operate with his adult sons and, if need be, his daughters, with perhaps some additional help from a relative or neighbor.

Harvesting on the Scott farm (1915)   (Courtesy of Norman McKinzie)

But there were much larger outfits, some powered by steam engines, others by gas tractors. One of the biggest tractors was the 50-75 OIL PULL combined with a mighty 42-inch CASE separator, which required an operating crew of 20 to 24 men. The wide feeder with a divider board at the center could handle all the bundles that two men (the teamster and a spike pitcher) on either side could pitch into it. A third spike pitcher was on the ground to clean up the sheaves that accidentally slipped off the feeder. In five minutes the rack was empty and the teamsters were off at full speed across the field where a free-roaming spike pitcher was waiting to help them reload the rack as quickly as possible.

Threshing with an I.H.C. Aultman-Taylor in 1915

Actually, the big outfit was able to keep a dozen or more teams busy hauling bundles in order to keep the mill running to full capacity. Besides the bundle-haulers, there were the engineer, the separator man, and the water tank hauler. Finally, with such a big outfit, the farmer needed to provide half a dozen wagons with teamsters to haul the threshed grain to the granary or the elevator.

The working day for the threshing crew was a very long one. The teamsters had to get up at 4:30 a.m. to feed the horses and harness them. Call for breakfast was sounded at 5:30. The men gathered in the cook car where the two cooks, generally women, had already prepared a substantial meal of porridge, flap-jacks, bacon and eggs, beans and fried potatoes, a stack of toast, and gallons of coffee.

Promptly at 6 o'clock, the OIL PULL began to cough and chuff, the long drive-belt started to turn and the separator wheels whirred noisily, as two loads left over from the night before pulled up, one to each side of the feeder. A luncheon was brought into the field at mid-morning and again in mid-afternoon. At twelve o'clock the teamsters unhitched where they were, and the horses were watered and fed. The men crowded into the cook car for a hearty meal, relaxed for a brief half-hour, and hurried back to the job that kept them busy until the sun sank in the West. The horses were unhitched on the set and brought into the farmer's barn where they were unharnessed and fed. After supper the weary men lost no time in finding their bunk or if there was no bunk car, they literally "hit the hay" that was stored in the top level of the barn. Usually the threshing crew got along very well together. There was a fine spirit of comradeship, a lot of prankish fun, competition and a sense of achievement. They had done a good job, for which the bundle-haulers received $5 a day, which in those days was considered good pay.

For the farmers the roaring twenties were years of productivity and affluence. Their new-found prosperity could be observed in their spacious new homes and huge barns gleaming with bright paint and lightning rods glistening in the sun. It could also be observed in the virtually self-sufficient way of life. The prairie farmers raised their own supplies of meat, processed it, and produced a variety of traditional sausage and headcheese. They were well-provided with eggs and dairy products, and made their own cream, butter, and cheese. In their spacious gardens, they raised large quantities of vegetables of various kinds, from potatoes to sunflower seeds. In the fall they put up sauerkraut and cucumbers in barrels. In many instances, their bread and pastries were made from the flour that was milled from the farmer's own wheat. Thus the housewife's shopping list for groceries was limited to items like sugar, tea, and coffee; salt and spices; some kinds of dried legumes and fruit. In those days, the German-Russian farmers could celebrate a three-day wedding without laying out any significant amount of cash for the food that appeared on the festive tables.

In the twenties, clothing and household furnishings were also easily available. Every housewife owned a sewing machine and was able to make most of the everyday clothes for the entire family, such as infant wear, skirts, blouses, and undergarments for the womenfolk, and shirts and trousers for the men and the boys. Suits, overcoats, winter underwear, shoes, and stockings were generally obtained from the large mail-order houses of Eaton's and Simpson's, which also supplied the farmers with all kinds of household furnishings and farming equipment, including wagons and windmills. The old catalogues generally provided an ample supply of cheap toilet paper for the outhouse.

In the twenty-five years during which the pioneer settlers of St. Joseph's colony had become efficient and well-to-do farmers who contributed millions of bushels of grain to the gross national product, practically no improvements had been made in the construction of provincial and municipal highways. To be sure, the pioneer wagon trails that crisscrossed the colony had been replaced with dirt roads that ran between the sections in a regular checkerboard pattern. The construction of these roads was a simple matter

Anton Gutenberg house.
Going to church in a closed-in sleigh

of plowing up a wide strip on the road allowance and levelling it off with a harrow. But many years passed before these roads were covered with a layer of gravel. In the rainy seasons, they were even worse than the earlier wagon trails. Indeed, even as late as the mid-fifties, the gravelled roads were among the worst roads on the North American continent. Anyone venturing to drive on these roads during wet weather could expect to sink down to the axles in the mud or to slither into a ditch. When the weather was dry, the traveller was exposed to the hazard of being stifled by clouds of dust.

Model T Ford in 1911

From left to right: Father Guth, Joe Elder
Mrs. J. Elder: her sister: Miss Mary Gutenberg   —Courtsey of Mrs. Katie Hoffart

In the late twenties, the Provincial government began building a hard-surface road west of Saskatoon through the almost uninhabited region that stretched in the direction of Biggar. But the road extended only some 50 miles to the nondescript hamlet of Perdue, where it became a "rue perdue," a road lost and forgotten in the semi-arid hills of the Biggar district. The road was not completed until the late sixties when it finally reached Kerrobert.

On the other hand, in the well-populated German-Russian triangle of St. Joseph's Colony, where the provincial government had collected generous amounts of land taxes for almost half a century, not a single hard-surface road could be found. When, in 1952, the Revenue Board of Trade submitted a petition to the Minister of Transport, T. C. Douglas, to provide an all-weather road that would link No. 14 three miles north of Scott via Revenue, Tramping Lake, and Broadacres with No. 51 that was running west to Kerrobert, Douglas replied evasively that he "would file the petition for future reference, since considerable work still had to be done on the main highways." It was only in the seventies that a hard-top road was constructed, but that road did not link Kerrobert with Scott and Wilkie, but ran from Kerrobert to Unity. Thus the road leading from Kerrobert via Tramping Lake to Wilkie remained what it had always been—hazardous second-rate gravel road that needed constant maintenance.

THE PRAIRIE IS MY GARDEN —Harvey Dunn

14. Religious and Cultural Development

After the death of Father Guth the parish of St. Michael's was without a resident priest for two years, during which Father Forner made occasional trips to Tramping Lake to hold services for the congregation. On July 1, 1921, P. Theodore Christ, one of the older missionaries in Saskatchewan, became the new parish priest of a community which now comprised more than a hundred families. Since the woodframe church, about two miles southeast of the village, had become much too small to accommodate such a large congregation, it was decided to build a much larger church in the town. Construction began on June 15, 1922, and on Christmas Eve, Father Christ was able to celebrate the first Mass in the new House of God. The building,

St. Michael's church and rectory (1932)

St. Michael's Church interior

342

measuring 135 by 50 feet, was constructed in Romanesque style and had a full-size concrete basement. It was constructed of brick and tile throughout at a cost of $40,000, not counting all the free labor that was donated by the men of the parish. It was the largest church in the entire St. Joseph's Colony and the first and only one to be constructed of brick. The building evoked the admiration of all people far and wide. A Protestant railwayman who was travelling through Tramping Lake in January of 1923 freely remarked: "The entire district is very proud of this edifice, and justly so, for the building of such a church attests to the solid foundation of this farming community and to its remarkable religious spirit."

In January of 1924, Tramping Lake made a new advance, when Father Christ invited the Ursulines of Prelate to teach in the village school. They labored with unstinting dedication for almost five decades in the field of primary and secondary education with remarkable and widely recognized success.

Aerial view of church and school area (1955)

Background: St. Joseph's Convent; Rectory; Church   -Courtesy of Sister Veronica Heit
Foreground: Composite High & Elementary; High School
      & Elementary; Tramping Lake Public School

On July 1, 1026, Father Ludwig Hermandung, OMI, a native of Westphalia, Germany, and a former missionary in German Southwest Africa, became parish priest of St. Michael's. Under his tenure, religious organizations began to flourish. Many of the men joined the VDCK, the *"Volksverein Deutsch-Canadischer Katholiken,"* which had already been established in Winnipeg in 1909. Among the objectives of this Society were: to provide aid to the poor, especially the victims of the War; to establish German libraries in the parish, to foster the development of German choirs and folk theater. For the women

Aerial View of Tramping Lake (1955) Courtesy of Balthasar S. Heit

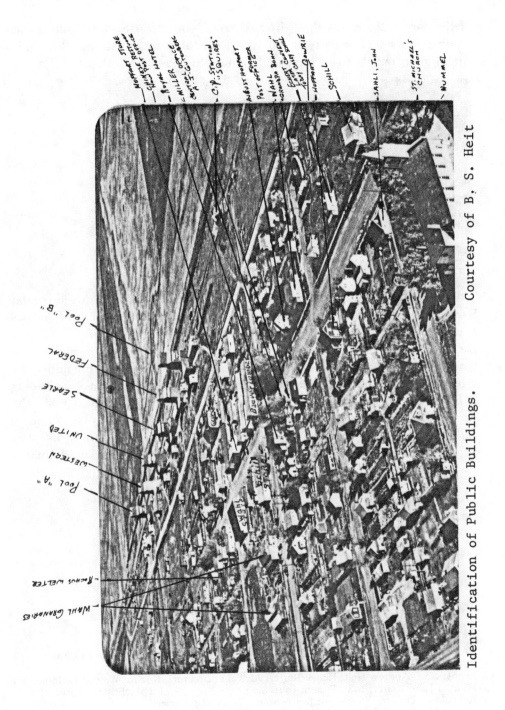

Identification of Public Buildings. Courtesy of B. S. Heit

of the parish, there was the *"Altar Verein,"*—the Altar Society—and in succeeding years this well-organized group was able to donate an altar and a communion rail—both of imported Carrara marble—to St. Michael's Church.

```
PASTORS OF ST. MICHAEL'S PARISH
1906-        P. Joseph Laufer
1906-1909...P. Theodor Schweers
1910-1920...P. Joseph Guth
1920-1921...P. A. L. Forner
1921-1926...P. Theodor Krist
1926-1937...P. Ludwig Hermandung
1938-1940...P. Emil Twardochleb
1940-1953...P. Thomas Schnerch
1962-1967...P. John Fetsch
1967-1968...P. F. Lenz
1968-.......P. K. Klein
```

Fr. Ludwig Hermandung, OMI

Father Hermandung created a novel sensation when he introduced regular Sunday-night movies in the basement hall of the church. Since the movies featured the big-name films that were shown in the cities of Regina and Saskatoon, they attracted not only the local parishioners, but also people from as far away as Wilkie and Kerrobert. A male church choir under the direction of Mr. A. E. Wahl also achieved distinction as an outstanding *"Sängerchor"* in competition with other German choirs throughout the province. A German Folk Theater performed many fine plays, mostly rollicking comedies in dialect, but occasionally also serious plays, like *Das Vierte Gebot*—"The Fourth Commandment," by the Austrian dramatist Anzengruber.

Tramping Lake Men's Choir

Front; —?—; Andrew Heit; Henry Reiter; Al Wahl (director); Rochus Welter; J. Ganje; J. Welter
Middle: John Welter, John Frison, John Sander; —?—; —?—; Ed Machtmes; Balth. Heit
Rear: Mike Fetsch; —?—; —?—; Joe Frison; —?—; Philip Weber

In general, the use of the Alsatian mother tongue and the cultivation of folksong and ancestral traditions remained fairly strong until the mid-forties. However, with the advent of the powerful media of radio and television, the influence of tradition began to wane, and the younger generation looked upon their distinctive ethnic heritage as something old-fashioned and felt that Anglo-Saxon conformity was something modern and exciting. Though all of the younger set still understood their ancestral vernacular, they generally preferred to speak English. Hardly any of them could read High German, for this foreign language was never offered in Elementary or in High School.

In the matter of acculturation, it is interesting to note that some married couples began, in the fifties, to ignore the traditional baptismal names derived from the Church calendar, and proceeded to endow their offspring with novel secular names derived from the stars of screen and television. Instead of time-honored names such as Mary, Barbara, Elizabeth, Magdalena, we now hear names like Shirley, Peggy, Brenda, Cynthia, Collette, Colleen, Roxanne, and the like. Similarly, instead of Biblical names like John, Peter, Philip, Joseph, Anton, Balthasar, etc., we are now confronted with strange-sounding Celtic or Irish names, like Douglas, Bradley, Daryl, Duane, Craig, Bruce, Randolph, Blaine, Bryce, and the like. Since the Germanic surnames are retained, it is obvious that combinations like Bradley Ostermeier, Bryce Schaumleffel, and Roxanne Weissenburger sound curiously like exotic hybrids.

Through these and similar activities, such as the celebration of weddings, christenings, namesdays, and holydays of the Church calendar, the spiritual and cultural life of the people was continually enhanced. People were leading a good happy life in peace, freedom, and security.

These carefree days, however, were to become rudely disrupted in 1927-1930 when the notorious Ku Klux Klan conducted a vicious campaign of bigotry in Saskatchewan against their three arch-enemies: the Negroes, the Catholics, and the Jews. Late in 1926, the knights of the white bedsheet, Hugh Emmons and Lewis A. Scott, experienced Klan organizers from Indiana, appeared in the province with the avowed plan of "getting dollars out of the people by feeding them 'antis.' "

The hooded preachers of hate were particularly active in Regina, Moosemin, Fort Qu'appelle, Indian Head, Grenfell, Kipling, Ceylon, and Radville. But they also appeared in the Kindersley and Kerrobert districts where they set up their fiery crosses at night. The Orange Lodge, representing the fanatical wing of the ultra-Protestants, contributed most to the Klan's success in organizing the K.K.K. in Saskatchewan. Indeed, the Grand Organizer of the Orange Lodge, a certain W.H.G. Armstrong, initiated over 10,000 Orange-

347

men into the hooded society. Twenty-six ministers of several Protestant denominations, particularly of the United Church of Canada, became bona fide members of the Klan. The response of these WASP converts to the Kluxers was enthusiastic, and they began to protest vociferously against the influence of the Catholic Church which, they charged, had turned Saskatchewan into "a papal state." They also inveighed against the foreign influence of the French Catholics in their schools, where they taught religion and the French language.

Fortunately, there were plenty of level-headed, fair-minded Protestants who would have nothing to do with the hooded fanatics and their campaign of hatred and vilification. Several United Church ministers from Biggar, Saskatoon, and Moose Jaw vigorously denounced the entire campaign, and the Hon. G. Gardiner, the Liberal Premier of Saskatchewan, attacked the Klan in the Leigslature. Prominent Catholic laymen and clergy who had borne the brunt of the Klan attacks reproached the Klan and its new-found supporters for undermining the goodwill and understanding that had existed among the various religious denominations in the province. By 1930 the influence of the Klan had waned to the vanishing point.

BUFFALO BONES ARE PLOWED UNDER — Harvey Dunn

15. The Dirty Thirties

The Great Depression began in the early thirties and lasted almost to the end of the decade. On the Great Plains of the USA and Canada, the depression was also aggravated by the occurrence of the terrible dust storms that caused widespread devastation to the grain crops year after year.

These devastating storms which began in the early thirties increased in intensity from year to year. High winds were quite common on the prairie, particularly in the late spring and oftentimes also in mid-winter when they gave rise to blizzards. Dust storms, however, were something new, and were made possible by two converging factors, namely the occurrence of a period of drought and the fact that the topsoil had become pulverized by the frequent use of the moldboard plow, along with the disk and the harrow, year after year since the prairie sod was broken. The storms often raged for days on end, whirling the fine dust miles into the air and blotting out the sun. Just like fine powdery snow was piled in snowdrifts by a raging blizzard, so did the drifting dust cover the highways and pile up around the farm buildings and the implements. The sown grain in the shot blade was cut off or choked by the driving dust. Livestock had to be kept in the barns during the storm. No one could venture into the open without some kind of mask or filter over

A southern Saskatchewan highway in the thirties

his mouth and nose. The dust even seeped into the house covering everything with a fine almost invisible layer. In some districts the havoc was so dreadful, that farmers packed their belongings into wagons, moved their families and the remaining livestock to the bush country in the north, and again became pioneer homesteaders.

In 1931 the price of wheat went down to 19 cents a bushel, and oats sold for seven cents. A milch cow was worth only two cents a pound, and eggs were five cents a dozen. Hides did not bring enough to pay for the cost of shipping them. Hay became so scarce that it had to be shipped in from distant parts. Coal was not available at all. Most of the cattle had to be sold because not enough fodder grew on the parched fields. Farmers were reduced to the expedient of feeding the proliferating Russian thistle to the cattle.

Money was scarce, and many families were suffering from shortages of food. By 1936 there were 286 families on relief out of a total of 298 who lived in the municipality of Tramping Lake, namely in the districts of Revenue and Scott. Generally speaking, the German-Russian people, no matter how poor they had become, were too proud to accept any kind of hand-out from the government. Very often the reeve of the municipality had to talk needy people into accepting relief, however paltry the amount.

During the years of bountiful crops, the provincial government had garnered a sizable amount of land taxes from the hardworking pioneers of the prairie, and should have been able to afford to grant a decent quota of relief to the farmers on whose shoulders lay the future welfare of every village, town, and city, including the provincial capital. But the government allowed the municipalities to distribute only the niggardly pittance of $6.00 per needy family per month. That was only 20 cents a day for families who often had as many as eight or ten children. However, if a really desperate family required more relief, the reeve had no alternative but to take a portion away from another family. Fortunately, the people were not completely at the mercy of the government which, at that time, was ironically still known as the Liberal Party. Farmers who were somewhat better off, ungrudgingly helped out their less fortunate neighbors. In the end, the people survived, and even outlived the Liberal regime.

Oftentimes the municipalities did not have the necessary funds to help the farmers in their economic plight. Accordingly, when a farmer with ten cows applied to the relief office for some fodder for his hungry cattle, he was told to sell the livestock if he could not find any feed for them. In these desperate straits, he had no alternative but to sell five of his cows for 48 dollars. That was less than one cent a pound. In 1936, the young farmer, Melford Schille, sold six cows for $56.00.

The son of a pioneer settler, J. P. Senger, was born in 1908 a couple of miles southwest of Tramping Lake. He married in 1930 and began farming in that area, but moved to a farm near Scott in 1933. He tells us about some of his experiences during the depression in the following brief report: "In 1932 there were poor crops and a sudden drop in the price of grain. I sold 1,100 bushels of wheat at 23 cents a bushel. Since there was not enough feed for the livestock through the winter months, I applied to the government for fodder, but the Municipality made me sell over half of my cattle, for which I received one cent per pound. In 1935 I received relief in the amount of $3.00 a month for groceries to feed my family. It was tough to make ends meet. During the winter months I set a trap-line for weasels. Every day I walked through the snow on a 12-mile round trip, with gunny sacks wrapped around my boots, since I could not afford to buy a pair of overshoes. I trapped from 50 to 60 weasels during the winter and managed to sell the pelts for 50 cents each. The depression continued until 1939, and the crops produced barely enough to provide feed and seed. I was able to ship two cans of fresh cream a week, each containing 5 gallons, but I could obtain only two or three dollars a can, or about six cents a pint. However, we got along. Everybody seemed to be happier than people are nowadays. Certainly, everybody was more content and more sociable."

WOMAN AT THE PUMP — Harvey Dunn

351

16. Forlorn Farmsteads and Vanishing Villages

Revolutionary changes in the traditional methods of farming were already taking place in the mid-fifties. After the critical experience of the dust-bowl catastrophe, the farmers began to realize that the time-honored moldboard plow that had been a great boon for many years had now become a terrible bane that spelled the ruin of agriculture. The old plow was therefore replaced by the one-way disk and seeder. Tractor power now came into general use, and machines of enormous size and astonishing efficiency appeared on the scene. The old self-binder was replaced by the mammoth self-propelled

The coming of the combine (Courtesy Jack Heit)

combine. Two men could now handle a reaping-threshing operation that formerly required at least 12 or 15 men. With the development of anti-freeze, it now became possible to drive cars all year round. Most communities now also obtained the benefit of rural electrification.

In the realm of education, the little white schoolhouse on the prarie was now replaced by the consolidated, multiple-roomed school in the village. This meant that the children had to be bussed from the country into the town.

These changes also brought about the demise of the time-honored farmstead. In due course, most of the farmers took up residence in the village where they were close to the church, the school, and the stores. In some instances, the old farm house was moved into town, but the barns were left on the farm and used as machine sheds. Thus the old farmsteads were destined to become deserted and forlorn derelicts of the past. In an area where there used to be four or five beautiful farms, only one or two farms are still in operation. Many of the names of the pioneer settlers are no longer represented by a descendant heir. The entire countryside formerly alive with people and their farming activities, is now almost uninhabited and unfrequented. The numerous sons and daughters who grew up on these large farms have long since been scattered to all points of the compass. While a few are still living in the district, most of them have found a livelihood in the larger towns and the cities of western Canada.

The fate of the villages on the prairie of western Saskatchewan has also been one of decline and demise. While a few villages, like Tramping Lake, had a period of continuing growth because of the farmers who decided to retire here, smaller villages, like Revenue, have practically become extinct.

Most of the farmers in the Revenue district preferred to seek retirement in Wilkie, Unity, or in the city of Saskatoon. Eventually the parish became so small that the church was closed and subsequently dismantled. The remaining parishioners were incorporated into the St. Michael's Parish at Tramping Lake.

A revolutionary change has also occurred in the Catholic Church after Vatican II. From the very beginning of the parishes in the St. Joseph's Colony, the use of the German language played an important part in all the religious services. Though the Mass was said or sung in Latin, German hymns were generally sung during the so-called *Volksmesse,* and all the sermons were of course delivered in German. Popular devotions on the various feasts of the Virgin Mary and during religious processions were invariably held in German. However, when the use of Latin was discontinued in the liturgy, no effort was made by the German or the German-Russian clergy to opt for the use of German in the celebration of the Mass. Instead, English was introduced, probably on the assumption that the younger generation was more familiar with that language than with their mother tongue. That sounded the death knell of a culture that had survived for 150 years under Russian autocracy.

With the passing of the old-timers, an entire folk culture, with its ancient Alsatian vernacular and its rich tradition of folklore and folksong was fated to die out, leaving no more than a faded memory among the descendants. The culture that our forefathers had proudly preserved during their long sojourn on the steppes of Russia was destined to disappear in less than sixty years of Anglophone domination in Canada. While the emperors of Russia had been interested in helping the non-Russian minorities to preserve their language and ethnic traditions, the British-dominated government of Canada was determined from the beginning to amalgamate all foreign ethnic groups in the big "melting pot." In this enterprise, the chauvinist establishment which controlled the media of education and communication had little difficulty in "acculturizing" the smaller ethnic groups. It discovered, however, that the strong-willed and well-organized ethnic group known as the French-Canadians adamantly refused to be liquidated in the Anglo-Saxon melting pot.

The passing of the present generation of old-timers marks the end of an ethnic culture and way of life that had characterized and ennobled the German-Russian settlers whose roots go back to Alsace, Baden, and the Palatinate on the river-valley plains of the Upper Rhine. Ironically, the identity of this ethnic group, despite its 75-year existence in Saskatchewan, has hardly been recognized by the Anglo-Saxon establishment. No memorial or historical marker rises from the agrarian plain to attest to the contribution which this pioneering people made to the opening up of the West, and their achievements will probably never be fully appreciated.

If by chance, in some not too distant future, a stranger should lose his way while travelling through the deserted Tramping Lake countryside between Wilkie and Kerrobert, he may be startled by the many mounds of field stones that had been removed from the plowland by the industrious bare hands of the pioneers. The lone traveller may also come across an isolated clump of scraggly trees near the rickety skeleton of an old windmill or a weather-beaten ramshackle barn; and if he looked around a bit, he might discover the relic of a battered self-binder or a rusty moldboard plow. Further up the road, he would perhaps catch sight of an old rural cemetery where rows of wrought-iron crosses rise staunchly above an undergrowth of weeds and grasses. Though most of them are quite illegible, the name plates give sufficient indication that their bearers were German. But the piles of field stones, the windmill, the moldboard, and the binder convince the inquisitive stranger that those forgotten pioneering peasants had conquered the semi-arid expanse of prairie with their horse-drawn plows and transformed it into a veritable sea of golden grain.

Above the lonely and lost wayfarer, high in the big blue prairie sky, a squadron of Canada geese on its smooth flight to the south fills the air with its repetitive honking that sounds like an alien refrain: "Roosaki . . . Roosaki . . . Roosaki. . . ."

Song of Remembrance

Where are the old-timers gone,
That robust race of pioneers?
Where are their memories flown
Of joy and grief in by-gone years?

Where are the tales they used to tell
Of life and love when they were young?
Where are the songs they sang so well,
The hearty sounds of the mother-tongue?

Where are the sayings wise and true
From tradition's ample store?
Where are the customs old and new
That grace the lives of rich and poor?

Shall their history turn to dust,
Windswept from the short-lived memory?
Will it be saved in sacred trust
As a living heirloom for posterity?

XVI.   Personal Reflections by the Author

Dr. Joseph S. Height

Professor, linguist, historian

It is understandable that the readers who have become interested in this history of their ancestors might also like to know something about the author and his background, as well as the reasons that induced him to produce the book. Within the brief limits of space available, I shall attempt to give merely a thumbnail sketch of my life and my activities as an ethnic historian.

Both of my parents came to America in 1900 from the Kutschurgan district near the Black Sea—my father from Mannheim and my mother from Baden. They had originally homesteaded with their parents near Towner, N.D., but the land was so poor that both families migrated to western Saskatchewan in 1906 and settled on the west side of Tramping Lake, 150 miles due west of Saskatoon. There, in a little sod-house on the prairie, I was born on December 21, 1909. I received my primary education in the pioneer country schools of the district and chose to get my secondary education at St. John's College, Edmonton, where I specialized in foreign languages, viz. Latin, Greek, French and German. Subsequently, I was able to pursue the study of history and philosophy for three years in Germany.

After my return to Canada, I taught German and Latin for a couple of years at St. Paul's College and edited a bilingual family monthly at Regina. During the Second World War I taught in private schools in Victoria and Vancouver, and obtained my B.A. and M.A. degrees in Philosophy and German from U. B. C. After earning my Ph. D. at the University of California in 1948, I taught German at Northwestern for four years, and several years at Wabash College in Indiana. From 1959 until my retirement I taught German and Linguistics at Franklin College.

Aside from teaching, I have also been active in research and publication. As a sequel to my doctoral thesis, *"Goethe's lyric poetry in English translation,"* I published a collection of my translations in the book, *"The Gold of Goethe,"* in 1964. I also provided the English text for the American edition of Dr. Stumpp's book, *"Die Russlanddeutschen."*

Since St. Michael's parish where I grew up was almost entirely composed of families who had come from the Kutschurgan colonies, the Alsatian-Franconian dialect remained in dominant use for several decades. The rich heritage of traditions was cherished and cultivated by young and old. I loved to hear the convivial German folksongs that were often sung at the *Maastub* and various festive occasions, and I used to listen with rapt attention to the lively stories of the old folks and their reminiscences of the *"Haamet"* in Russia. Though my curiosity about their life over there continued to increase, I was never able to gain a clear conception of the origin and growth of the colonies on the steppe.

As the years went by and the old-timers were passing from the earthly scene, I began to realize that not only our beloved mother tongue and all the familiar traditions were gradually ebbing away, but also the oral history of our people was doomed to be utterly forgotten, unless an effort was made to preserve it from ultimate extinction. Deep within me I felt that our hardy pioneering forebears did not deserve to vanish in the limbo of total oblivion, and I made the firm resolve to undertake the task of researching and preserving the complete history of our people.

In the years that followed I lost no opportunity to search for information, oral and written, about the history and ethnic culture of our ancestors. I kept my eyes open for significant books and articles, pictures and illustrations. At every opportunity I studied the history of our people in Alsace, Baden, and the Palatinate, so as to become familiar with their cultural background, their ancestral dialects and folklore. I corresponded with scholars in Germany and France regarding the emigration records of the colonists and the villages from which they came. In later years I visited the emigration regions of the Upper Rhine and gave a series of lectures on the history of the colonies in several villages of Lower Alsace.

In 1970 I began to analyze and organize the material I had accumulated over the years and to transform it into a manuscript for the 28-chapter book that was to contain a comprehensive history of the 17 Catholic mother colonies in the Odessa area. In 1972—more than 25 years after I started my research—I was able to publish the long-awaited book under the title, *"Paradise on the Steppe."* Three years later I put out a companion volume, *"Homesteaders on the Steppe,"* which contained the history of the 17 Lutheran colonies in the same area.

The promotion and distribution of these books was no easy task, for the people for whom they were written were no longer confined to the pioneer settlements in the Dakotas and Saskatchewan, but were now scattered far and wide from Texas to Alaska and from the Mississippi to the Pacific. I needed to contact a large number of localities, in order to awaken the interest of our people in the new publications. After a slow start, the books began to attract attention and arouse astonishment. As I had hoped, the best of "unsere Leit" were proud to acquire and preserve the history of their ancestors as a precious heirloom for their childen and grandchildren.

2. Ancestral Alsace Revisited

It had been five years ago when I first visited Alsace, the land from which my remote ancestor and hundreds of his fellow countrymen had emigrated in 1808, in order to settle on the wild steppes between the Dniester and the Boug above the Black Sea. During my weeklong visit in the Lauterecke I was not only able to become well acquainted with the villages and its people, but I also had the opportunity of presenting a series of lectures, in several places, on the topic of Alsatian emigration to Russia. These lectures, which were illustrated with numerous slides, created something of a sensation, and I soon became known as "the German-Russian Alsatian from America."

My return to the land of my forefathers in 1968 was therefore a kind of home-coming for me. I arrived in Strasbourg two days after Easter and had the pleasure of making the personal acquaintance of Professor Jean Schweitzer, with whom I had been in correspondence for almost five years.

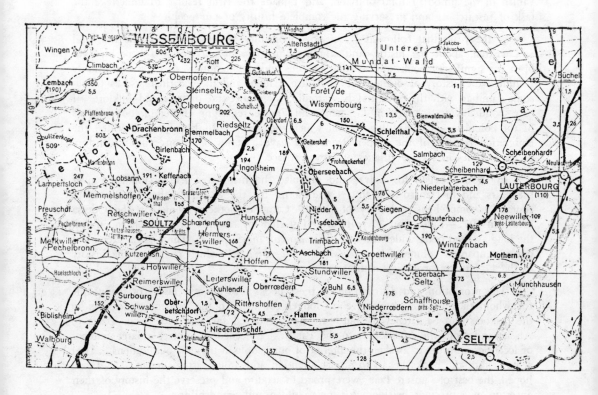

Being a native of Niederlauterbach (only a few kilometers from my ancestral village of Kaidenburg), Professor Schweitzer is not only a distinguished "Heimatforscher" of Lower Alsace, but also a devoted scholar of Alsatian emigration to Russia. Indeed, it is largely through his intensive research that we have been able to determine the local origins of hundreds of pioneer settlers in Russia. During my stay in his hospitable home we had the opportunity of discussing many things of mutual interest. A couple of days later Professor Schweitzer drove me in his car to the Lauterecke, some 40 miles to the north, where we visited the thousand-year old town of Weissenburg and several equally old villages in the area, including Trimbach, where we called on its congenial pastor, Father Heinrich. I then came to nearby Kaidenburg, where my former hosts, Mr. and Mrs. Bogner, were already awaiting me. I intended to remain in the Lauterecke for a few days, to visit former acquaintances and to stroll through the countryside. Unfortunately, the weather turned rainy and cold, so that I did not get around as much as I had hoped. On Whitsunday, however, I was invited to a First Communion party at Lauterburg, where a large gathering of family, relatives, and friends was celebrating the occasion with much feasting on delicious Alsatian food and drink. Of course, everyone spoke Alsatian, and I had the opportunity of using my own Kutschurgan dialect, which was virtually identical with their

Author visits ancestral village of Kaidenburg
(hidden in the valley) in 1964

own. I could not help feeling at home with this hospitable people, whose gaiety and sense of humor was as enjoyable as their cuisine.

Since the weather continued to be pretty nasty, I decided to leave Alsace again, with the idea of returning later in the summer. I therefore took a train to Kaiserslautern in the Rheinpfalz, where I wished to become acquainted with Dr. Fritz Braun, the director of the Heimatmuseum and a noted ethnnologist of the Palatinate people. I passed through many villages in the area of Bergzabern and Landau, from which a great many of our German-Russian pioneer settlers, especially those of the Beresan district, originally came. I spent about two days with Dr. Braun, exchanging ideas and materials, and enjoying the hospitality of his home.

On my second visit to Alsace, my good friend Professor Schweitzer again took me by car to the Lauterecke. We first stopped in Seltz to call on maire Schneider and the pastor, Father Criqui, both of whom I had met five years earlier. We then drove on to Oberseebach, where I encountered the Bogners, who brought me back to Kaidenburg.

The weather was wonderful, and the farmers were already busy with the harvest. The very next day I decided to take a walk through some of the villages nearby, to do some sightseeing, and take a few pictures. It was a very hot day, and after I had walked a few miles I came to the village of Schleital, which consists of a single street about 2½ miles long and has the reputation of being the "longest village in France." After walking about a mile and taking some pictures of street scenes, I was getting both tired and thirsty.

Road signs in Lower Alsace

Suddenly I noticed a tavern in front of me and went in. Several men were sitting around tables drinking Alsatian wine and beer. I took off my hat and sat down at one of the tables, where 3 heavy-set Alsatians were sitting. After saying "Bon jour" (Alsatians never say: "Guten Tag"), I ordered a glass of beer, and began to make some casual remark about the weather (in Alsatian), and then added: "Ja, warum schaffen'er heit nit uff'm Feld?" One of the men replied: "M'r henn halt nix zu due." So I said: "Jo, awwer uff'm Weg vun Salmbach bis uff Schlaadl haw ich g'sehne, as d'Weibsleit en der Riewe schaffe, un ihr huckt do im Schatte, trinkt Wei un macht Maastub." To which the other Alsatian replied with a grin: "Jajo, die selle nar schaffe!" We kept on talking for about twenty minutes about the crops and the weather, when one of men asked me, from what village I was. When I told him that I was from no Alsatian village, but was an American tourist, the men at this table (and at the others) were utterly astonished and wanted to know, how come that I could speak their Alsatian like a native. Of course, I had to tell them about my ancestor from Kaidenburg and the hundreds of other families that had emigrated from the Alsatian villages in the Lauterecke (over 45 families from Schleital alone) and settled in the pioneer steppe-villages of Selz, Strassburg, Elsass, Sulz, Mannheim, etc.

The following day I revisited Selz and took the occasion to look up a family by the name of Welter who was living in a large beautiful "Fachwerk" house that was built over 200 years ago. While we were sitting at the table enjoying a glass of Riesling, Mr. Welter showed me a picture of a Welter family that once lived in Selz, Russia. The man in the picture had been mayor of Selz and had made a visit to his ancestral home before the first World War. Soon after his return to Russia he emigrated to Canada. I took a second look at the picture and recognized the man as Johannes Welter, a pioneer settler in my own home town!

My third trip to Alsace was made about two weeks later, when I returned to deliver four illustrated lectures in four of the villages. In one village, Salmbach, about 100 people were in attendance, and it was long after mid-night when we parted. But I was asked by the friendly mayor to join him and some friends for a glass of wine, and it was after three o'clock before the "Maastub" was over.

In the course of the next day a school teacher drove me in his car through a number of villages, to enable me to take pictures. One of the villages was Neeweiler, from where the ancestor of Bishop Zerr originally came. Indeed, five Zerr families (father and four married sons) emigrated from this village to Franzfeld in 1807. I was surprised to find that not only the local tavern keeper, but also a large number of other families in this village were named

Zerr, just as I had found many Frison families in Oberseebach, the ancestral village of Bishop Frison. Indeed, most of the family names of the Kutschurgan and Liebental colonists are still to be found in the Lauterecke.

The ancestral homeland of Alsace has many scenic beauties. The landscape is that of a gently rolling countryside, partly wooded, but for the most part laid out in a giant patch-quilt of small, narrow fields of only two or three acres each. Fine wheat is grown here; in fact, this area has been under cultivation for more than a thousand years. However, the farming is diversified. A good deal of tobacco is grown and many kinds of vegetables. There are also large fields of beets which are used for cattle fodder, for there are no pastures in the entire area. All the cattle, including dairy cows, are kept in the barns all year round. In recent years many farmers have bought small tractors, but others still use traditional horsepower. Everywhere I saw women and children working in the fields. At harvest time everyone works from early morning until late at night. However, many Alsatians, especially younger men, have found work in German factories across the Rhine and the Lauter. They are picked up every morning by big busses and brought home in the evening. Certainly, farming in Lower Alsace is not a very profitable business, but the people live fairly well and their houses are neat and attractive. Many people drive cars and are generally well dressed.

The Alsatians, like our German-Russian forbears, are a very religious people. Their churches, though old, are beautiful, and services are held in Latin, German, and French. Although all the people can speak French, they generally speak Alsatian and have, in general, stubbornly retained their Alsatian customs and way of life. "Des isch's Elsass, nit Frankreich," is the proud motto of the typical Alsatian. In character, spirit, and social manners, they are remarkably like our own German-Russian Kutschurganer, Liebentaler, and Beresaner. Ethnologically and culturally, they are our next-of-kin.

3. The Interest in Ethnic History

The following testimonials are indicative of the remarkable and quite unexpected outburst of interest among families of German-Russian background in the ethnic history of their forefathers in Russia. As the author of the two related books *"Paradise on the Steppe"* and *"Homesteaders on the Steppe,"* I am of course deeply appreciative of the warm and even enthusiastic reception that has been extended to them, and I am especially grateful to the thousands of families who, by acquiring copies of the books, have helped to preserve the epic story of our people for future generations.

To be sure, not everyone who read the book and liked it went to the trouble of expressing their appreciation in writing. However, in gratitude to those who took the time to write, I feel it is befitting that their comments should be preserved within the pages of this book of *"Memories of the Black Sea Germans."*

"By your tireless research you have brought a new dimension into the lives of the descendants of our German ancestors from the steppes of Russia. Let me express my eternal gratitude. All the descendants of those brave and good pioneering ancestors owe you a vote of gratitude for enabling them to preserve the history of our people."

—Joseph C. REICHERT, Austin, Texas.

"Your book, *"Paradise on the Steppe,"* arrived yesterday, and my husband and I have had difficulty putting it down. It is beautifully written, historical, and factual, and yet it has the warmth of a love story. I am proud to be raising five descendants of those courageous pioneers."

—Mrs. Robert D. ZARR, Bay Minette, Alabama.

"I have read your book and will continue to study it. It's a wonderful book. I count it among my great treasures."

—Mrs. Wm. HEDLIND, Lake Oswego, Oregon.

"Your book, *"Paradise on the Steppe,"* is excellent. I rejoiced and mourned while reading the history of these courageous, industrious good people. You deserve great credit."

—Mrs. A. R. M., Hartford, Conn.

"Words cannot express the enjoyment that my dear *"Paradise on the Steppe"* has brought me. I love the book; it's indeed a treasure."

—Mrs. Martha Gress-MEMMER, Reno, Nevada.

"Thank you for making this fine work available to us who know so very little about our ancestors. This wonderful book is bound to become 'the Bible of our people.' "

—August SCHALL, Bismarck, N. Dak.

"This beautiful book deserves to be in the home of every Catholic family whose forefathers came from the region of Odessa."

—Miss Elizabeth RISSLING, Toronto, Canada.

"A beautiful book, beyond all expectations. A literary masterpiece, rich in years of research. It holds the reader spellbound to the very end. As I read the very moving account of the tragic fate that befell our people in the Soviet Union, I could not restrain my tears. Thousands of readers will have the same experience."

—Sister Louise HEIT, Prelate, Sask., Canada.

"I received your book, *"Paradise on the Steppe,"* and almost died of nostalgia when I read it and saw the pictures of the many scenes and objects my parents used to mention."

—Ann BACH, Rutland, B.C., Canada.

"I've always wanted to know more of my German-Russian ancestry. Little did I dream there would ever be a publication like *"Paradise on the Steppe."* I want you to know that I and my family really appreciate your fine book."

—Arthur A. SCHERR, Omaha, Nebraska.

"I cannot praise your book too highly. It is a great treasure to me, and I and my relatives will be forever grateful to you for having undertaken the great task of recording the history of our people."

—Joseph A. GANJE, Tucson, Ariz.

"In this day of growing ethnic awareness, the book, *"Paradise on the Steppe,"* certainly fulfills my desire to know more about my ancestors. My link with the past now seems *real,* and not merely historical."

—Richard E. OTT, Harborside, Maine.

"Our German-Russian people should be most thankful to you for publishing this marvellous history of their ancestors—their struggles during the colonization of the Ukraine, along with the traditions and culture they preserved for generations."

—Larry LEIER, Williston, N.D.

364

"I just finished reading your book, *"Paradise on the Steppe."* What an impressive account of the experiences of those poor people! My family's ancestors were among them. Thank you for writing this wonderful book."

—Anna BERGER HELDERMAN, Eureka, Calif.

"All of us (I and my three daughters) thoroughly enjoyed your book and are sincerely grateful to you for your dedication in publishing such a fine historical work. Thanks to your efforts, my ancestors have become alive to the point where I feel I actually knew them."

—Florence CHRISTOFFERSON, San Bernardino, CA.

"I have read your book, *"Paradise on the Steppe,"* with great interest and deep gratitude. No finer book has ever been written about our forefathers in Russia."

—Johannes ABEL, Boise, Idaho.

"I have read your book from cover to cover twice, and it is my greatest source of reference in researching my family history in Russia. Many thanks for your wonderful book. It has made me feel proud, sad, and angry, but most of all I am thankful that someone who was capable took the time to give us our history."

—Delores SCHAN IGGULDEN, Milwaukie, ORE.

"Many, many thanks for your wonderful book. It is most revealing, most enlightening, all beautiful. Once I began reading, I couldn't stop.

—Lewis R. MARGUARDT, Phoenix, Ariz.

"I am very fascinated with your new book. You have made it possible for the third generation to appreciate their ethnic background."

—Connie LACHER, Ogema, Minn.

"Thank you for all the work you have done to bring us this wonderful book."

—Betty WANNER, Seattle, Wash.

"A magnificent work of cultural and historical art."

—Timothy KLOBERDANZ, Sterling, Colo.

"I read your book, *"Paradise on the Steppe,"* with interest, for I was born in Russia. I read it with pride, with thankfulness, with wrath and fury, with grief and sympathy, with sorrow. I hope you will continue to have the strength, the time, and the means to continue writing this amazing story on which you have spent so much work and study. Some aspects of the book would make a fantastic movie."

—Rev. A. SIMON, OMI, Parshall, N.D.

"I congratulate you on the very fine book you have published, and thank you for the tremendous amount of work and research you have put into it. I found it both fascinating and solid in its historical portrayal of our people. It made so many things that my parents and friends have recounted over the years so very real to me. Thank you for recording these facts in a permanent book."

—Msgr. Frank GEREIN, Vic. General of the Regina diocese.

"The author recreates an entire culture, and succeeds in breathing into the dry bones of history the revivifying breath of life, so that the descendants of those pioneers on the steppe may know from what great stock they have sprung, and knowing, may not forget."

—Rev. P. NOVEKOWSKY, Munster, Sask.

"I have found your book most interesting, enlightening, and heart-warming. It provides ample material to give one a feel for the time and conditions under which our ancestors lived."

—Rev. Jos. S. AXTMANN, Drake, N.D.

"A wonderful historical documentary! Our people owe you a debt of gratitude. Thank you in the name of the untold thousands of our industrious and honest German settlers in Russia who were brutally persecuted and murdered in the USSR."

—Dr. Konstantin FRANK, Hammondsport, N.Y.

"We received your splendid book. What a heart-breaker! And yet what delightful accounts of the traditions, folksongs, and folk festivals. And the chapters on the Communist persecution indeed bring tears. We congratulate and praise you for this greatest monument to our beloved colonists who suffered so much, and must surely be remembered in generations to come. We proudly join those who desire to save their story for posterity."

—Lawrence and Gloria ZERR, Salt Lake City, Utah.

"I am pleased and impressed with the book, *"Paradise on the Steppe."* It is a great tribute to those brave and God-fearing pioneers. I am truly thankful that God led you to write of them, so that their remarkable story is not lost to mankind."

—Jennel WILLIAMS, Norman, Okla.

"Paradise on the Steppe" is a precious, fascinating book. Besides containing a detailed account of the migration of the German people from Germany to Russia, it contains a wealth of interesting articles on the customs, habits, and folklore of our people. I particularly enjoyed the accounts of the festivals,

celebrations, and the folk songs written in the German-Russian dialect. What a chance to learn and to appreciate how our forefathers lived!"

—Edward WEBER, principal, Wilkie, Sask.

"I congratulate you on your great achievement. It must have been a difficult task to gather all the necessary information for such a book. I have to admit that I shed many tears when I read about the fate of our poor persecuted people."

—D. ZENTNER, Toronto, Ontario.

"I thank you with all my heart for your efforts in writing this historical book about our people. I found it most fascinating and informative. It was very touching to find the family names of my ancestors in the book and to become familiar with the dear old *Heimat* of my parents."

—Mrs. S. H. Leibham-Vaughan, Saskatoon.

"I want to commend you on your wonderful book. It is well written and easy to understand. What a wonderful way to enlighten the younger generation about their ancestors' courage and fortitude! How grateful we should be! Thank you!"

—Mrs. A. G. Wildemann-THORDASON, Vancouver, B.C.

"Our family is the proud owner of your book and we shall always be grateful to you for writing the story of our forefathers. The detailed account of their immigration to Russia and of the persecution under the Soviet regime is interesting, educational, and truly heart-rending! The accounts of the customs of our people, their dialect and folklore are for us a never-ending source of delight."

—Mike and Kay KARY, Vibank, Sask., Canada.

"It's a monumental work for history and posterity. In his research the author has exemplified the spirit of the Biblical injunction: "Collegite fragmenta ne pereant." (Collect the fragments so that they won't perish.)
                                        —Rev. Thomas SCHNERCH, OMI, Prelate, Sask.

"For me the book is an indescribably precious possession, an unforgettable book that was created by dint of much labor, dedication—and love."
                                        —Mrs. Leo FELLER, Kankakee, Illinois.

"The Germans-from-Russia ethnic group for whom this fascinating book was written should be most proud and pleased to possess such an excellent portrayal of the history and the heritage of their ancestors."
                                        —Otto H. HIEB, Oakland, California.

"This very beautiful book has given me the greatest joy. The comprehensive work is superbly illustrated, nicely readable, and attractively printed. The author has masterfully demonstrated his ability to give a faithful portrayal of the life of the German colonists in its many-sided aspects of folk culture. We have here a standard work that will be absolutely indispensable for every German-Russian in America and also for every "Heimatforscher."
                                        —Prof. Jean SCHWEITZER, Strasbourg, France.

"An outstanding work hitherto lacking in this field. A lucid, factual book that not only give ample evidence of the author's great knowledge but also of his love of the subject. A monumental work that belongs into the best libraries and into the humblest homes."
                                        —N. LAYBOURN, AP journalist, Strasbourg, Fr.

"I read with the greatest interest your superbly illustrated documentary history of the origin, development, and demise of the German colonies near Odessa. I was deeply moved by the final chapters which told of the persecution suffered by these people and their steadfast adherence to their faith and ethnic culture."
                                        —Dr. Werner MONTAG, German consul, Detroit.

"Paradise on the Steppe" is a remarkable achievement. The story of the Bolshevist terror, the war years, the repatriation of the German refugees and their dispersion is indeed terrifying and heart-rending.
                                        —Ward SCHORI, publisher, Evanston, Illinois.

"Your books on the German-Russian people are a great source of inspiration to those of us who are wandering in the wilderness."

—Paul J. Polansky, Turre/Aleria, Spain.

"I am very proud to own your book *PARADISE ON THE STEPPE*. I have read it from cover to cover, some parts three or four times. The book is for me a precious memento of the old homeland. No one could have described the meaning of "Heimat" more beautifully than you did in the last paragraph of your book."

—Rochus WEICHEL, Portland, Oregon.

"I think this book is just about the most wonderful book I've ever come across. The author certainly did a wonderful job and I am sure he made many people happy."

—Sr. Rosa DECK, IBMV, Toronto, Canada.

"I thank you heartily for your magnificent book, *"Homesteaders on the Steppe."* Again and again I turn the pages of this outstanding work, which for the first time incorporates, in truly prolific fashion, all the essential things that can be said on the subject and presents them to the reader in a most engaging manner. For me it is, of course, of particular interest that my native community of Hoffnungstal is treated in such great detail."

—Friedrich FIECHTNER, Stuttgart, Germany.

"With your two books, *PARADISE ON THE STEPPE* and *HOMESTEAD-ERS ON THE STEPPE,* you have performed a great service to the German-Russian people from the Black Sea area and have bequeathed books of enduring value to the descendant young generation in the USA and Canada."

—Johann LUTZ, Murrhardt/Wü, Germany.

"Your invaluable book on our people and their heritage is truly something that has never been equalled in the past, nor will it be so in the foreseeable future. You deserve the highest of accolades for your work on behalf of the Black Sea Germans, both Catholic and Evangelical-Lutheran."

—Paul E. REEB, St. Francis, Kansas.

"This new book and your *"Paradise on the Steppe"* make a beautiful pair and certainly "cover the waterfront" as far as the history of the German colonies in the Odessa area is concerned."

—Col. Theodore WENZLAFF, Sutton, Nebr.

369

"Dr. Height has again demonstrated his ability to give a faithful portrayal of the life of an ethnic group in its many-sided aspects of culture. The carefully composed work gives evidence of his literary talent and his familiarity with all facets of German-Russian history and culture. On every page one senses how deeply the author was dedicated to the task of raising an enduring monument to the Evangelical colonies of the Black Sea region."
—Prof. Jean SCHWEITZER, Strasbourg, France.

"You have produced a most wonderful book in *"HOMESTEADERS ON THE STEPPE."* It is nothing short of a miracle that you were able to put together so much information and history into a single volume."
—George A. DEWEY, Eaton, Colorado.

"This book is one of the most interesting pieces of social history I have ever read. Anyone even remotely interested in the role which this important pioneering people played in both Russian and American history will find in this volume a treasure trove of living history."
—Rev. Paul DOUGLAS, Apena, S. Dak.

EPILOGUE

A Humorous Eulogy

by Dr. Rodney Hood
on the occasion of the retirement of
Dr. Joseph Height in 1975

It is customary, in English, to begin a fairy tale or any story with the time-honored words: "Once upon a time." In German the rough equivalent of this is: "Es war einmal." So that is where I shall begin. *"Es war einmal ein Professor!* By nationality, *ein amerikanischer Professor,* and by residence, *ein indianisch-amerikanischer Professor.* But he was not always so, for his native country lay to the north of ours, and thus we should call him *ein kanadisch-indianisch-amerikanischer Professor.* Indeed, to be more specific, *ein saskatchewanisch-kanadisch-indianisch-amerikanischer Professor.*

This professor's family, however, did not originate in Saskatchewan. It had migrated over the border some time before his birth, and by virtue of

370

this he was *ein amerikanisch-saskatchewanisch-kanadisch-indianisch-ameri-kanischer Professor,"* in fact, *"ein norddakotsich-amerikanisch-saskatche-wanisch-kanadisch-indianisch-amerikanischer Professor."*

But, as he himself could tell you in great detail, the family had reached North Dakota after an emigration and voyage of many thousands of miles from its European homeland in the Kutschurgan district near the Black Sea of South Russia. So he really should be called *ein kutschurganisch-südrussisch-norddakotisch-amerikanisch-saskatchewanisch-kanadisch-indian-isch-amerikanischer Professor.*

But even this is not a complete description of his ethnic identity. For his family, about the time of Napoleon, had migrated to South Russia from their native village of Kaidenburg in the vicinity of Weissenburg in Lower Alsace, which at that time was a part of France. Thus, by rights and in truth, he was *ein kaidenburgisch-elsässisch-französisch-kutschurganisch-sudrussisch-norddakotisch-amerikanisch–saskatchewanisch–kanadisch–indian-isch-amerikanischer Professor.* Thus in a single word do we observe the mellifluous grace and beauty of the German tongue!

Now this personage came in the course of time to Franklin College, where for the past fifteen years he has been active in his discipline, introducing linguistic studies to this campus, and embodying the liberal arts. He has published a book of his own poetry. It was Goethe's poetry, to be sure, but he rendered it into English in a remarkable achievement, preserving the rhythms of the original in his translation—a most difficult thing to do. He has made for himself beyond all this a specialty, the study of the history of the German Russians, to which people he belongs, as translator, author, and lecturer on many aspects of this specialization. Doubtless his greatest achieve-ment in this field is the publication of three books that present a compre-hensive cultural history of the Catholic and the Lutheran mother colonies in the region of Odessa.

And now that he has reached this height in his career as a teacher and a scholar, we wish to recognize Herr Professor Doktor Height in grateful appre-ciation for all he has contributed, and wish him liberty *(Freiheit),* the pursuit of *Glückseligkeit,* and *Gesundheit* in the years to come!

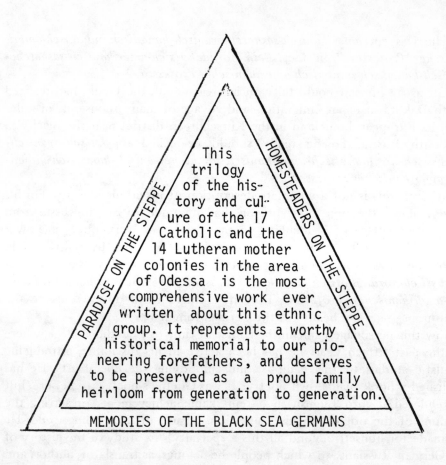

PARADISE ON THE STEPPE

HOMESTEADERS ON THE STEPPE

This trilogy of the history and culture of the 17 Catholic and the 14 Lutheran mother colonies in the area of Odessa is the most comprehensive work ever written about this ethnic group. It represents a worthy historical memorial to our pioneering forefathers, and deserves to be preserved as a proud family heirloom from generation to generation.

MEMORIES OF THE BLACK SEA GERMANS

PIONEERING

We shall not travel by the road we make.
Ere day by day the sound of many feet
Is heard upon the stones that now we break,
We shall come to where the crossroads meet.

For us, the heat by day, the cold by night,
The inch-slow progress and the heavy load,
And death at last to close the long grim fight
With man and beast and stone; for them the road.

—Anon.